Outstanding Dissertations in Linguistics

Edited by

Laurence Horn
Yale University

A Routledge Series

Outstanding Dissertations in Linguistics

Laurence Horn, *General Editor*

Layers in the Determiner Phase
Rob Zamparelli

Phonological Relations between Words
Laura Benua

Consonant Strength
Phonological Patterns and Phonetic Manifestations
Lisa M. Lavoie

Patterns of Reduplication in Lushootseed
Suzanne Urbanczyk

The Serial Verb Construction Parameter
Osamuyimen Stewart Thompson

Long-Distance Dependencies
Mihoko Zushi

The Morphosyntax of the Algonquian Conjunct Verb
A Minimalist Approach
Julie Brittain

Turn-Taking in English and Japanese
Projectability in Grammar, Intonation and Semantics
Hiroko Furo

Morphologically Governed Accent in Optimality Theory
John Alderete

Minimal Indirect Reference
A Theory of the Syntax-Phonology Interface
Amanda Seidl

Distinctiveness, Coercion and Sonority
A Unified Theory of Weight
Bruce Morén

Phonetic and Phonological Aspects of Geminate Timing
William H. Ham

Vowel Reduction in Optimality Theory
Katherine Crosswhite

An Effort Based Approach to Consonant Lenition
Robert Kirchner

The Synchronic and Diachronic Phonology of Ejectives
Paul D. Fallon

Grammatical Features and the Acquisition of Reference
A Comparative Study of Dutch and Spanish
Sergio Baauw

Auditory representations in Phonology
Edward S. Flemming

The Typology of Parts of Speech Systems
The Markedness of Adjectives
David Beck

The Effects of Prosody on Articulation in English
Taehong Cho

Parallelism and Prosody in the Processing of Ellipis Sentences
Katy Carlson

Production, Perception, and Emergent Phonotactic patterns
A Case of Contrastive Palatalization
Alexei Kochetov

Raddoppiamento Sintattico in Italian
A Synchronic and Diachronic Cross-Dialectical Study
Doris Borrelli

Presupposition and Discourse Functions of the Japanese Particle *Mo*
Sachiko Shudo

The Syntax of Possession in Japanese
Takae Tsujioka

Compensatory lengthening
Phonetics, Phonology, Diachrony
Darya Kavitskaya

The Effects of Duration and Sonority on Contour Tone Distribution

A Typological Survey and Formal Analysis

Jie Zhang

LONDON AND NEW YORK

First published in 2002 by
Routledge

Published 2013 by Routledge
2 Park Square, Milton Park, Abingdon, Oxfordshire OX14 4RN
711 Third Avenue, New York, NY 10017, USA

First issued in paperback 2016

Routledge is an imprint of the Taylor and Francis Group, an informa business

Library of Congress Cataloging-in-Publication Data for this book is available from the Library of Congress

ISBN 13: 978-1-138-96846-2 (pbk)
ISBN 13: 978-0-415-94156-3 (hbk)

For my family

Table of Contents

Acknowledgments

For someone who had not the slightly idea what a fricative was a few years back, this has been quite a journey...

There are many people who have helped me throughout this journey and made my years of going through the process the most fulfilling years of my life. But first and foremost, my thanks go to my teacher Donca Steriade.

Donca is the kind of advisor that every student dreams to have. The ideas in this work were formed from many many hours of discussion in her office, with her clarifying or challenging every one of my arguments (or lack thereof). I thank her for her unparalleled intelligence, which has guided me through empirical and theoretical puzzles; her motherly concern for every one of my career moves, be it a conference presentation, a written-up paper, or a job interview; her contagious love of linguistics, which I have fortunately contracted. And I thank her for never losing faith in me, even after drafts after drafts of writing that are 'simply abhorrent'. Donca Steriade is far beyond just a great linguist and a great teacher. She is a real *mensch* in every sense of the word. It is a great honor to be her student.

My deepest gratitude also goes to Bruce Hayes, who enthralled me with the beauty of phonology as a scientific pursuit in my first ever phonology class. He has remained supportive throughout my graduate career. His influence on me, not only as a phonologist, but also as a scientist, is profound. I will forever remember the trepidation every time I go into his office for an appointment, anticipating all the hard questions he will ask. There are still many of his questions for which I have no answers. These questions will not be forgotten. They will guide me throughout my career.

Special thanks also go to Sun-Ah Jun, Ian Maddieson, Donka Minkova, and Moira Yip: Sun-Ah for teaching me phonetics; Ian for being an encyclopedia of data and always demanding my best work; Donka for her extremely careful reading of this work and detailed feedback; and Moira for many helpful discussions on issues related to this work.

I thank all the speakers that participated in my phonetic experiments: Alhaji Gimba, Virgie Kee, Haiyong Liu, Elton Naswood, Yiem Sunbhanich, and

Viphavee Vongpumivitch. I am also grateful to Russ Schuh and Aaron Shryock for answering my questions about Chadic languages.

To all my teachers at UCLA, thank you for all you have taught me, linguistics and otherwise. In particular: Susie Curtis, Pat Keating, Ed Keenan, Hilda Koopman, Peter and Jenny Ladefoged, Pam Munro, and Colin Wilson.

To my friends and colleagues, thank you for your support: Victoria Anderson, Heriberto Avelino, Marco Baroni, Roger Billerey-Mosier, Rebecca Brown, Leston Buell, Elena Suet-Ying Chiu, Melissa Epstein, Christina Foreman, John Foreman, Daniel Hole, Chai-Shune Hsu, Amanda Jones, Jongho Jun, Sahyang Kim, Natasha Levy, Ying Lin, Haiyong Liu, Patrick Manalastas, Amy Schafer, Wendy Swartz, Siri Tuttle, Motoko Ueyama, Yihua Wang, Richard Wright, Kie Zuraw…

Special thanks to Matt Gordon, for many long discussions on tone and stress, and for setting a high standard for me to follow; and to Taehong Cho, for your inspirational diligence, for keeping me company during late-night lab sessions, and for feeding me delicious Korean food.

Very special thanks to Adam Albright, Ivano Caponigro, and Harold Torrence, for the wonderful dinner parties, tea times, and movie outings. Without you, my years at UCLA would have been much less happy.

To Umberto Ansaldo, a very special friend: Thank you for your emails and phone calls. It is amazing how much one can benefit from the emotional support of a friend so far away.

To Dan Silverman: Thank you for your patience, your trust, your humor, and your encouragement.

To Judson (aka Suān Suān): What you have done for me over the years is too much to be thanked for, so I won't. Instead, now I am ready to tell you what this work is all about.

Finally, I thank my family—Shen Shi-Guang, Shen Huan, Zhang Ze-Quan, Zhang Yang, Lü Hong, Zhang Chao-Min, and my departed grandmother Chen Jing-Ding—for respecting my choice of switching from EE, in which I could have had a lucrative career, to linguistics, in which I might starve to death. In particular, I thank my aunt Shen Shi-Guang, for being there for me every single minute of my life and never asking for pay-backs. This work is dedicated to all of you.

The Effects of Duration and Sonority on Contour Tone Distribution

CHAPTER 1

Background

1.1 TWO EXAMPLES OF CONTOUR TONE DISTRIBUTION

The term "tone language" usually refers to languages in which the pitch of a syllable serves lexical or grammatical functions. In some tone languages, the contrastive functions of pitch are sometimes played by pitch *changes* within a syllable. Pitch changes of this kind are called contour tones. The distribution of contour tones in a language, i.e., under what phonological contexts contour tones are more readily realized, has been of much theoretical interest, as it sheds light on both the representation of tone (Woo 1969, Leben 1973, Goldsmith 1976, Bao 1990, Duanmu 1990, 1994a, Yip 1989, 1995) and the relation between phonetics and phonology (Duanmu 1994b, Gordon 1998, Zhang 1998). This work is an in-depth investigation of the distribution of contour tones.

1.1.1 Contour Tones on Long Vowels Only

By way of an example, let us consider languages which have both contrastive vowel length and contour tones. In these languages, it is often the case that contour tones are restricted to phonemic long vowels; e.g., Somali (Saeed 1982, 1993), Navajo (Hoijer 1974, Kari 1976, Young and Morgan 1987, 1992), and Ju|'hoasi (Snyman 1975, Dickens 1994, Miller-Ockhuizen 1998) all display this pattern.

The ubiquity of this type of contour-tone restriction prompts analysts to posit the following principles regarding tonal representation: first, the mora is both the contrastive segmental length unit and the tone-bearing unit (TBU); second, a contour tone is structurally composed of two level tones; and third, each mora can only be associated with one tone (Trubetzkoy 1939, McCawley 1968, Newman 1972, Hyman 1985, McCarthy and Prince 1986, Zec 1988, Hayes 1989, Duanmu 1990, 1994a, Odden 1995, among others). Working together, these principles ensure that a contour tone can occur on a phonemic long vowel, which has two moras, but not on a phonemic short vowel, which has only one mora.

In the Optimality-theoretic framework (Prince and Smolensky 1993), the above principles can be translated into the markedness constraint in (1), which bans many-to-one mappings between tones and moras. Here, we assume that a "tone" means a "pitch target".

(1) $*\begin{matrix} T_1 \ T_2 \\ \diagdown\!\diagup \\ \mu \end{matrix}$: two tones cannot be mapped onto one mora.

If we assume that the relevant tonal faithfulness constraint here is MAX(tone), as defined in (2), then by ranking the markedness constraint in (1) over the faithfulness constraint in (2), as shown in (3), we can capture the restriction of contour tones to phonemic long vowels. The tableaux in (4) show that, under this ranking, when two tones are associated with a short vowel underlyingly, only one tone will survive on the surface—(4a); but when they are associated with a long vowel, both tones can survive—(4b).

(2) MAX(tone): if tone T is in the input, then it must also be in the output.

(3) $*\begin{matrix} T_1 \ T_2 \\ \diagdown\!\diagup \\ \mu \end{matrix}$ » MAX(tone)

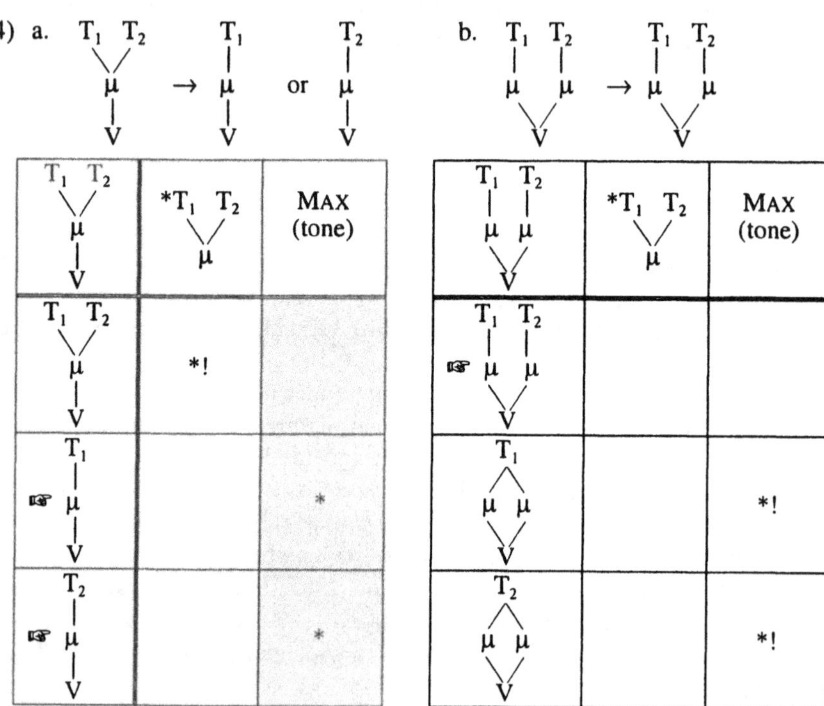

Instead of explaining this contour tone restriction representationally as shown above, we may opt to provide a positional markedness (Alderete et al. 1996, Zoll 1998, Steriade 1999) account in Optimality Theory.[1] Generally speaking, this approach singles out markedness constraints specific to prosodically weak positions from the context-free markedness constraints and ranks positional markedness over context-free markedness. Then when the relevant faithfulness constraint is ranked in between, the marked structure will be banned in weak positions targeted by the positional markedness constraints, but allowed elsewhere.

To show the working of this approach schematically, let us posit the constraints in (5) (McCarthy and Prince 1995, Beckman 1997).

(5) a. IDENT(F): let α be a segment in the input, and β be any correspondent of α in the output; if α is [γF], then β is [γF].
b. *[+F]: no [+F] is allowed in the output.
c. *[+F]-P: no [+F] is allowed in position P in the output.

Constraint (5a) requires the faithful realization of F from the input to the output; constraint (5b) bans [+F] in the output; and crucially, constraint (5c) bans [+F] in the prosodically weak position P in the output. Then with the constraint ranking in (6), we generate the pattern in which the marked value [+F] is banned in the weak position P, but allowed elsewhere. Illustrative tableaux are given in (7): when [+F] occurs in position P in the input, it will be realized as [-F], since the faithful candidate violates the most highly ranked positional markedness constraint *[+F]-P (7a); when [+F] occurs elsewhere however, it will be faithfully realized, since this candidate only violates *[+F], while its unfaithful rival violates the higher ranked IDENT[F] (7b). Of course, [-F] in the input will always be realized as [-F], since there is no markedness constraint against [-F]. Therefore, we generate the pattern in which F is neutralized in the weak position P, but contrastive elsewhere.

(6) Positional markedness ranking: *[+F]-P » IDENT(F) » *[+F]

[1] Another option in Optimality Theory for this type of positional restrictions is positional faithfulness (Steriade 1995, Alderete 1995, Beckman 1997). Given that the choice between positional faithfulness and positional markedness does not bear on the discussion here, to streamline the discussion, I delay the argument for positional markedness until Chapter 7.

(7) a. [+F] is realized as [-F] in P:

[+F]-P	*[+F]-P	IDENT(F)	*[+F]
[+F]	*!		*
☞ [-F]		*	

b. [+F] is faithfully realized elsewhere:

[+F]-(¬P)	*[+F]-P	IDENT(F)	*[+F]
☞ [+F]			*
[-F]		*!	

There are three different ways in which the positional markedness schema could be applied to the contour tone case in question, and the different modes of application reflect different levels of phonetic details that the phonological system is claimed to incorporate. Let me spell them out in detail.

The first is what I will call the "general-purpose positional markedness approach." It acknowledges that a phonemic short vowel, being short on duration, is at a disadvantage for the realization of *any* phonologically marked structures, and a contour tone is such a structure. The positional markedness constraint is then *CONTOUR-(-long), as defined in (8a). The context-free markedness constraint *CONTOUR and the relevant faithfulness constraint IDENT[tone] are defined in (8b) and (8c) respectively. In these definitions, a contour tone is not considered a concatenation of level tones, but a tonal unit whose pitch changes during its time course.

(8) a. *CONTOUR-(-long): no contour tone is allowed on a syllable with a short vowel.
b. *CONTOUR: no contour tone is allowed on a syllable.
c. IDENT(tone): let α be a syllable in the input, and β be any correspondent of α in the output; if α is has tone T, then β has tone T.

To account for the restriction of contour tones to long vowels, we employ the ranking in (9): the first ranking pair ensures that no contour tone will surface on a short vowel; the second ranking pair ensures that a contour tone on a long vowel will be faithfully realized in the output.

(9) *CONTOUR-(-long) » IDENT(tone) » *CONTOUR

This approach differs from the moraic approach in the following respects. First, the licensing condition of contour tones does not exclusively rely on the contrastive mora count of the vowel; any prosodically strong position that facilitates the realization of phonological contrasts can be a preferred contour tone licenser. Second, it does not rely on the representation of contour tone as a concatenation of level tones and the tonal targets and moras do not have to stand in a one-to-one relationship.

The second approach within positional markedness has exactly the same execution as the first one for this particular contour tone restriction in question. But it differs in one crucial conceptual respect: instead of targeting positions that are at a disadvantage for *any* phonological contrasts, it *selectively* targets positions that are at a disadvantage for the *particular* contrast in question, and I will term this approach the "contrast-specific positional markedness approach." As I will show in Chapter 2, the realization of contour tones crucially relies on the sonorous duration of the syllable rime. Short vowels are targeted positions for contour tone neutralization for this very reason. But given that they also happen to be perceptually and articulatorily weak for many other phonological contrasts, they cannot tease apart the tradition and contrast-specific approaches. Other positions however, with their different phonetic characteristics, may be able to. E.g., in Chapter 4, we will see that prosodic-final position, though a weak position for many contrasts, is a preferred position for contour tones due to its prolonged duration resulted from final lengthening.

The third possibility within positional markedness is to refer to the phonetic properties of long vowels directly, and I will term this the "direct approach." Like the contrast-specific approach, it also recognizes that phonemic long vowels are better contour tone bearers because they have a long sonorous duration, which is the crucial phonetic dimension on which the realization of contour tones rely. But unlike the other two positional markedness approaches, which only refer to the phonological feature that distinguishes a phonemic long vowel from a phonemic short vowel, namely, [+long], it directly refers to the phonetic properties that are crucial to contour tone realization—duration and sonority. Let us assume for now that the contour tone bearing ability of a syllable is proportional to an index C_{CONTOUR}, which is a weighted sum of duration and sonority.[2] Then the positional markedness constraint under this approach is *CONTOUR-C_{CONTOUR}(-long), as defined in (10).

(10) *CONTOUR-C_{CONTOUR}(-long): no contour tone is allowed on a syllable with a C_{CONTOUR} value that is equal to or smaller than C_{CONTOUR}(-long).

With the same constraints IDENT(tone) and *CONTOUR as in (8b) and (8c) and the ranking as in (11), this approach also accounts for the restriction of contour tones to long vowels, as the previous two positional markedness approaches.

---

[2] The index C_{CONTOUR} is discussed in detail in §3.2.

(11) *CONTOUR-$C_{CONTOUR}$(-long) » IDENT(tone) » *CONTOUR

1.1.2 Contour Tones on Stressed Syllables Only

Another commonly attested restriction on contour tone distribution is that they are only allowed on stressed syllables. For instance, in the penultimate-stress language Xhosa (Lanham 1958, 1963, Jordan 1966, Claughton 1983), contour tones are generally restricted to the penultimate syllable of a word. In Jemez (Bell 1993), the initial syllable carries the word stress, and it is the only position in which a contour tone is allowed.

This contour tone restriction can again be captured in different ways.

First, we may assume that stressed syllables are bimoraic while unstressed syllables are monomoraic under the Stress-to-Weight principle. Further assuming that contour tones are concatenations of level tones and each level tone needs a mora to be realized, we can see that the restriction of contour tones to stressed syllables is explained just as the restriction of contour tones to phonemic long vowels.

Second, in both the general-purpose and contrast-specific positional markedness approaches, 'no contour on unstressed' can be justifiably singled out from the context-free markedness constraint, as an unstressed position, being shorter in duration and lower in amplitude, is not only at a disadvantage for the realization of contour tone contrasts, but other phonological contrasts as well. Therefore, the positional markedness constraint is *CONTOUR-(-stress), which is defined in (12). The constraint ranking that captures this contour tone restriction is shown in (13).

(12) *CONTOUR-(-stress): no contour tone is allowed on an unstressed syllable.

(13) *CONTOUR-(-stress) » IDENT(tone) » *CONTOUR

Third, we can also appeal to the 'direct approach' and refer to the index $C_{CONTOUR}$ for stressed and unstressed syllables in the account. The positional markedness constraint is *CONTOUR-$C_{CONTOUR}$(-stress) as defined in (14). With this constraint outranking IDENT(tone), which in turn outranks the context-free *CONTOUR, as shown in (15), the restriction of contour tones to stressed syllables can likewise be captured.

(14) *CONTOUR-$C_{CONTOUR}$(-stress): no contour tone is allowed on a syllable with a $C_{CONTOUR}$ value that is equal to or smaller than $C_{CONTOUR}$(-stress).

(15) *CONTOUR-$C_{CONTOUR}$(-stress) » IDENT(tone) » *CONTOUR

1.2 QUESTIONS RAISED BY THE EXAMPLES

So far, we have seen two distinct distributional properties of contour tones—attraction to long vowels and attraction to stressed syllables, each of which can be accounted for in four different ways: representationally by mora counts; or positional markedness, which encompasses three possibilities: general-purpose, contrast-specific, or directly phonetic. Given these possibilities, one of our tasks is to determine which one is a better account for the data.

To address this question, let me first briefly evaluate the characteristics of these analyses and see what different predictions they make.

The representational account crucially relies on the mora as both the unit of length and weight and the unit of tone bearing. It acknowledges that duration and sonority play crucial roles in contour tone distribution since it acknowledges the following two implicational hierarchies: (a) If a phonemic short vowel has *x* moras, then a phonemic long vowel has at least *x* moras (Trubetzkoy 1939, Hyman 1985, McCarthy and Prince 1986, Hayes 1989, among others). (b) If segment *s* is moraic and segment *t* has a higher sonority than segment *s*, then segment *t* is moraic (Zec 1988). But the role of duration and sonority in the account can only be said to be conditional. For example, it is possible that a phonemic short vowel in some environment is phonetically longer than a phonemic long vowel in some other environment. This account will still consider the former to have fewer moras than the latter. This account also restricts the role that duration and sonority can play to a binary, at most ternary one, as contrastive length is usually binary (short and long) and maximally ternary (short, long, and extra-long), and languages only distinguish up to three degrees of syllable weight (light, heavy, and superheavy). This account therefore predicts that we can only in principle distinguish three kinds of tonal distribution—tones allowed in only trimoraic syllables, in at least bimoraic syllables, and all syllables. Moreover, under the assumption that contour tones are concatenations of level tone targets and each level tone needs a mora for its realization, the number of tonal targets in a contour tone must be identical to the number of moras in the syllable that carries it.

The general-purpose positional markedness account, however, does not necessarily single out duration and sonority as the crucial factor for contour-bearing. It only requires that the positions referred to in positional markedness constraints be at some articulatory or perceptual disadvantage for any phonological contrast. E.g., when all else is equal, non-initial positions are predicted to be worse contour tone licensers than the initial position, as the initial position has been widely shown to be a privileged licenser for many other phonological contrasts (Trubetzkoy 1939, Haiman 1972, Goldsmith 1985, Hulst and Weijer 1995, Steriade 1995, among others). The moraic account does not make this prediction. Moreover, when there are two prominent positions P_1 and P_2 in a language, there is no principle in the general-purpose positional markedness approach that determines which one will be *more* privileged for contour-tone bearing, since the theory does not mandate any a priori ranking between *CONTOUR-(-P_1) and *CONTOUR-(-P_2) due to the fact that P_1 and P_2 are distinct positions that do not have a common phonetic ground on which they can be compared.

The contrast-specific positional markedness approach specifically identifies positions that are rich in the sonorous rime duration as preferred positions for contour tones. Therefore, its predictions differ from the general-purpose approach in that the initial position, which is generally documented to have no or very little lengthening effect (e.g., Oller 1973 for English; Fougeron 1999 for French; Cho and Keating, to appear, for Korean), should not be privileged for contour tones; and that prosodic-final positions, though they do not have the phonetic advantages such as less variable articulation (Ohala and Kawasaki 1984, Kohler 1990, Browman and Goldstein 1995) and processing advantage (Marslen-Wilson 1989) that initial position enjoys (and consequently not a privileged position for many other phonological contrasts), should nonetheless be privileged contour tone bearers because of final lengthening (Oller 1973, Klatt 1975, Beckman and Edwards 1990, Edwards et al. 1991, Wightman et al. 1992, among others). But given that the contrast-specific approach still refers to independent phonological features such as [long] and [stress], it is similar to the general-purpose approach in that it still does not differentiate two prominent positions P_1 and P_2 in any principled way.

Finally, the direct approach makes the following predictions. First, like the contrast-specific approach, the distribution of contour tones directly depends on duration and sonority. Therefore, a position can be privileged for contour tones if and only if it has advantages in these phonetic dimensions. Second, since the approach encodes phonetic properties such as $C_{CONTOUR}$, which is defined on the basis of duration and sonority, two different prominent positions in a language can be directly compared with regard to their contour tone bearing abilities, since their $C_{CONTOUR}$ values can be directly compared. The position with a greater $C_{CONTOUR}$ is predicted by this approach to be a better contour tone licenser. Third, given that the categories needed here to characterize contour tone distribution are phonetic categories of duration and sonority rather than phonological categories of vowel length or weight contrasts, the number of the possible levels of distinction is considerably less limited than what is allowed in an approach that only refers to structural entities.

The different predictions of the four different approaches are summarized as in (16).

(16)

	Crucial phonetic dimensions	Levels of distinction	Comparability of privileged positions
Moraic representation	Duration, sonority (conditional)	Two, at most three	Yes (by mora count)
General-purpose PM	Prominent position for any contrast	Not restricted	No
Contrast-specific PM	Duration, sonority	Not restricted	No
Direct PM	Duration, sonority	Not restricted	Yes

The following section briefly summarizes the kinds of data that I have looked at to evaluate these predictions.

1.3 HOW THIS WORK EVALUATES THE DIFFERENT PREDICTIONS

1.3.1 A Survey of Contour Tone Distribution

To determine what phonetic dimensions are crucial to contour tone distribution and how many levels of distinctions are necessary to characterize the distribution, we need to investigate what patterns of contour tone distribution are attested across languages. Therefore, one task that this work undertakes is to conduct a cross-linguistic survey of contour tone distribution. Specially, I examine cross-linguistically the contexts in which contour tones are more likely to occur. The survey aims to be both representative of contour-tone languages and genetically balanced. It includes 187 genetically diverse contour tone languages and more heavily weighs towards language phyla in which contour tones are common, e.g., Sino-Tibetan languages. The result of the survey will point to the direction of the correct theory for contour tone distribution.

To preview the results, the survey shows that only positions with phonetic advantages in duration and/or sonority are privileged contour tone carriers, and that more than three levels of distinction in contour tone bearing ability sometimes need to be made; i.e., the survey supports the direct approach.

1.3.2 Instrumental Case Studies

The other dimension on which the three approaches can be differentiated is the comparability of different privileged positions. For one particular language, it is possible that there are multiple positions that provide better docking sites for contour tones. Which position surfaces as a better position, and on what account, can shed light on our choice of the correct approach.

If we find that languages strictly respect the mora count in determining contour tone bearing ability, such that a structurally trimoraic syllable is always a better contour tone bearer than a bimoraic syllable, which is in turn better than a monomoraic syllable, then we must conclude that the representational account is superior. If we find that the best position for contour tones in a language is always the one that induces the greatest advantage in duration and sonority (i.e., $C_{CONTOUR}$) regardless the structural properties of syllable, then we conclude that the direct approach is superior, since it makes exactly this prediction. Lastly, if we find languages in which a better position for contour-bearing is P_1 despite the fact that position P_2 possesses a greater value for $C_{CONTOUR}$, and the privilege of P_1 cannot be structurally attributed, then the general-purpose or the contrast-approach is the best, and the decision between the two will be made according to the survey discussed in 1.3.1.

I conducted instrumental studies of duration in languages where two different factors influencing the crucial durational interval for contour tone bearing can be singled out. E.g., in a penultimate-stress language, both the penult and the ultima may enjoy durational advantages—the former from lengthening under stress, the latter from final lengthening; in languages with both vowel length and coda sonorancy contrast, the rime of CVVO (O=obstruent) enjoys the durational advantage of having a [+long] vowel, while the rime of CVR (R=sonorant) enjoys having a sonorant coda. The question is that in the language in question, whether the phonological pattern of contour tone distribution is in synchrony with the language's specific structural properties of syllables, or specific phonetic pattern of duration, or neither. The languages under study are: Xhosa, Beijing Mandarin, Standard Thai, Cantonese, Navajo, and Somali.

To preview the results, I show that in all the languages under phonetic investigation, the position that is the most accommodating of contour tones in the language is always the one that is demonstrably the best for contour tone realization phonetically, i.e., with the optimal combination of duration and sonority. The durational comparison of the same two positions in different languages may yield different results, and the contour tone licensing behavior in these different languages differ accordingly to the language-specific phonetics. Therefore, the phonetic results also support the direct approach to contour tone licensing.

1.4 PUTTING CONTOUR TONE DISTRIBUTION IN A BIGGER PICTURE

1.4.1 Phonetically-Driven Phonology

Regardless of which approach for contour tone distribution turns out to be the best, one must acknowledge that all four approaches being entertained here are phonetically based to some extent. Even the representational approach partially bases the moraic assignment on phonetic dimensions. The fact that many phonological patterns are phonetically natural has long been noticed by phonologists (Stampe 1972, Ohala 1974, 1975, 1979, 1983, Lindblom 1975, 1986, Hooper 1976, Donegan and Stampe 1979, among others). E.g., Stampe (1972) gives four arguments for the phonetic motivation for phonological processes: the need for feature classes organized according to articulatory and acoustic properties to describe phonological substitutions; the assimilative nature of context-dependent substitutions; the optionality of substitutions corresponding to how much 'attention' is given to the utterances; and the correspondence between the degree of generality in substitution and the degree of physical difficulty involved in the articulation.

But as a theory of phonology, the incorporation of phonetic rationale encountered insurmountable difficulties in the rule-based theoretical framework. Given that the phonetic properties of linguistic units are only observable through the output of an utterance, the phonetic natural processes mentioned above are necessarily output-oriented. But in a rule-based framework, since the phonetic naturalness of the output cannot be directly referred to in the analysis, it can only be achieved through indirect 'fixes' provided by the system. Therefore, when different fixes are carried out in one language to arrive at a single phonetically natural output, the theory must refer to these fixes individually. The mysterious functional unity of individual rules has been termed 'conspiracy' by Kisseberth (1970). As a consequence, it is difficult in a rule-based framework to make statements on the phonetic naturalness of phonological systems that are general and rigorous enough to serve as the guideline for a serious scientific theory.

With the advent of Optimality Theory (Prince and Smolensky 1993) in phonology, the issue of phonetic naturalness has been revisited in many recent works (Steriade 1995, 1999, 2000, 2001a, b, Flemming 1995, Jun 1995, Kaun 1995, Boersma 1998, Kirchner 1998, Gordon 1999a, Hayes 1999, Zhang 2000). Optimality Theory is a particularly suitable tool to address this issue since now phonological generalizations can be expressed through output-oriented markedness constraints. On the one hand, it provides an explicit way of addressing the conspiracy problem in rule-based phonology mentioned above; on the other hand, it invites encoding phonetic rationale directly in the analysis of phonological patterning, since with the notion of faithfulness to underlying representation, general statements on the phonetic markedness of phonological forms can finally be made within the theory proper without reducing phonology to [tatatatata]. More generally, constraint conflict yields a more sophisticated functionalism in that it can capture not only exceptionless markedness laws, but also markedness tendencies, since different markedness constraints can be ranked with respected to each other. These premises provide an environment for the question 'to what extent is phonology phonetically-driven' to be answered in a scientifically more rigorous way.

Precisely due to these reasons, Optimality Theory also provides an environment in which phonological research can be conducted deductively (Hayes and Steriade, to appear). Based on articulatory and perceptual considerations, the deductive strategy provides us with a clear expectation on what patterns we are expected to find when we look at the phonological behavior cross-linguistically. As we will see throughout the book, it is preferable to the traditional inductive strategy in discovering linguistic universals in two respects. Where it succeeds, it provides a unified account for phenomena that are conceived as unrelated in traditional phonology. Where it fails, we know we must on the one hand further our knowledge in the articulation, perception, and processing of linguistic materials, on the other hand provide more comprehensive and factually precise descriptions of linguistic patterns, and these will potentially lead to a better understanding of the issues at hand. If we had proceeded inductively, we would not have noticed that something worth attending to has escaped our attention. In sum, Optimality Theory is explicit and falsifiable functionalism.

1.4.2 Positional Prominence

The behavior of contour tone licensing belongs to a class of phonological patterning that has received a great deal of attention as the testing ground for phonetically-driven phonology—positional prominence. It refers to patterns in which a greater number of phonological contrasts is attested in certain positions, such as stressed syllable, long vowel, root-initial position, syllable onset, etc. E.g., in Western Catalan, there are seven contrasting vowel qualities in stressed syllables, but only five in unstressed syllables (Hualde 1992, Prieto 1992) (17a). In Shona, there are five contrasting vowel qualities in root-initial syllables; but in non-initial syllables, the mid vowels /e/ and /o/ do not occur contrastively—they can only surface as a result of harmony with root-initial mid vowels (Fortune 1955) (17b). In Fuzhou Chinese, syllable onset accommodates a wide array of contrasts, while syllable coda can only be /ʔ/ or /ŋ/ (Liang and Feng 1996) (17c). The contour tone restrictions fit snugly in this characterization. E.g., as we have seen, in Xhosa, there are three contrasting tones in stressed syllables—High, Low, and Fall, but the contour tone Fall cannot occur in unstressed syllables (Lanham 1958, 1963, Jordan 1966) (17d).

(17) a. Western Catalan (Hualde 1992, Prieto 1992):

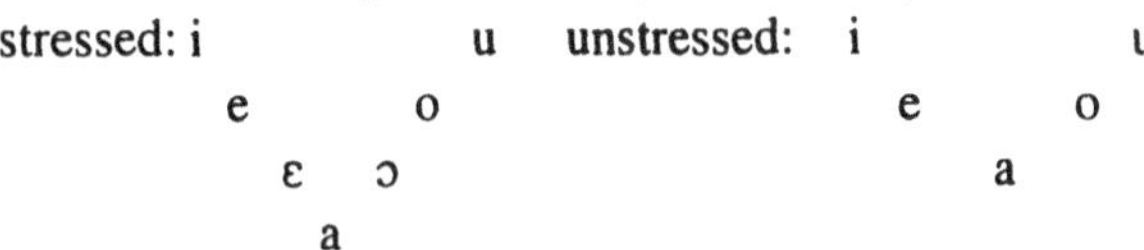

b. Shona (Fortune 1955):

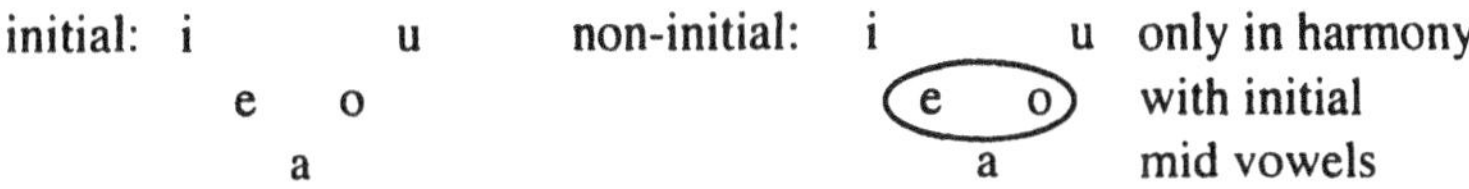

c. Fuzhou Chinese (Liang and Feng 1996):

onset:	p, p^h	t, t^h	k, k^h	coda:	ʔ, ŋ
		ts, ts^h			
		s	x		
	m	n	ŋ		

d. Xhosa (Lanham 1958, 1963, Jordan 1966):

stressed: H, L, $\widehat{HL}$ unstressed: H, L

Positional prominence is arguably phonetically motivated. From the perceptual point of view, some positions provide better acoustic cues to certain features, which lead to better perception of these features; e.g., various psycholinguistic studies on word recognition, phoneme monitoring, and mispronunciation detection have shown that stress makes vowel quality (Small and Squibb 1989, McAllister 1991) and consonantal properties such as VOT and place of articulation (Cutler and Foss 1977, Cole and Jakimik 1978, Connine et al. 1987) more saliently perceptible. From the production point of view, certain features are more easily articulated in some positions; e.g., as I will discuss in greater detail in Chapter 2, pitch contours require a certain amount of duration to be implemented (Arnold 1961, Hirano et al. 1969, Lindqvist 1972, Ohala 1978) and are thus more easily articulated in positions that are inherently rich in duration. From the processing point of view, the word-initial position has been shown to be particularly important in lexical access and word recognition by numerous psycholinguistic studies (Brown and McNeill 1966, Horowitz et al. 1968, 1969, Marslen-Wilson and Welsh 1978, Marslen-Wilson and Tyler 1980, Marslen-Wilson and Zwitserlood 1989, among others, summarized in Marslen-Wilson 1989).

1.4.3 Competing Approaches to Positional Prominence

In §1.2, I laid out four different approaches to the positional prominence effects regarding contour tones. Let me put these approaches in the context of positional prominence in general and see what the theoretical implications are for these approaches.

Beyond the patterns of contour tone distribution, which is the focus of this work, the overarching question that is being explored is how close the correlation is between phonological patterning regarding positional prominence and phonetic differences in perception and production induced by different positions. In particular, I aim to use the contour tone data to explore two distinct aspects of this question.

1.4.3.1 Contrast-Specific vs. General-Purpose Positional Prominence

The first aspect of the question is whether the correlation is contrast-specific or general-purpose. We know that different phonological features require the support of different phonetic properties. E.g., to distinguish coronal consonants from consonants of other places of articulation, the presence of C-V formant transitions is crucial. This is because the shape of the C-V formant transitions clearly distinguishes coronals from non-coronals (Ohala 1990). But for the anteriority contrast within coronal consonants, i.e., whether the coronal is retroflexed or not, the crucial formant transitions are from the vowel to the consonant (Steriade 1995, 2001a, Hamilton 1996). For obstruent VOT contrasts, they are better perceived in a position that has processing advantages (Shields et al. 1974, Cole and Jakimik 1978, Marslen-Wilson and Welsh 1978). For contour tones, as I will show in Chapter 2, the most crucial factors for their realization are duration and sonority (production: Arnold 1961, Hirano et al. 1969, Lindqvist 1972, Ohala 1978; perception: Black 1970, Greenberg and Zee 1979).

Apparently, different positions provide different phonetic properties. Consequently, some positions provide phonetic properties that are crucial for some contrasts, but not others. We should therefore expect the phonological effect of positional prominence to be contrast-specific. E.g., prevocalic position provides a consonant with C-V, but not V-C formant transitions, thus it should be a preferable position for the [±coronal], but not the [±anterior] contrast; for postvocalic consonant however, the situation is the reverse. Word-initial position provides processing advantage, but not extra duration, thus it should be a good licenser for VOT contrasts, but not for contour tones. Prosodic-final positions, on the other hand, have extra duration due to final lengthening, but do not have any independent processing advantage, thus they should be preferable positions for contour tones, but not for VOT contrasts.

The behavior of some phonological patterning has corroborated this hypothesis. For example, Steriade (1995, 2001a) shows that although most consonant place contrasts are more likely to be licensed in prevocalic position, retroflexion is usually only contrastive in postvocalic position. But for most phonological patterning regarding positional prominence, the contrast-specificity of the effect remains a hypothesis. In (18), I lay out the two competing hypotheses regarding positional prominence, the first of which being the one I will lend support to in this work.

(18) a. *Contrast-specificity hypothesis*: for a featural contrast [±F], the positions within the word in which the contrast is selectively preserved are the ones that provide better cues for the contrast [±F]; speakers pay attention to phonetic properties that specifically benefit the contrast in question, and construct phonology accordingly.

b. *General-purpose hypothesis*: there exist positions within the word which are better licensers for any type of contrast; phonology is insensitive to phonetic properties, and positional prominence is due to a notion of generic prominence.

For contour tone licensing, the moraic approach and apparently the general-purpose positional markedness approach can both be deemed as espousing the general-purpose hypothesis. The role of the mora in phonology is multi-faceted; e.g., it has been used as both a weight unit and a tone bearing unit. This presupposes that contour tone licensing will behave identically to other kinds of phonological licensing that also rely on the mora in the language.

The contrast-specific and the direct approaches in positional markedness, however, do link the contrast in question with the phonetic properties that are important for the realization of this contrast, since the positional markedness constraints either recognize the positions that are identified according to these phonetic properties or refer to these properties directly.

1.4.3.2 The Relevance of Language-Specific Phonetics

The second aspect of the question on the correlation between positional prominence and phonetics is on the relevance of language-specific phonetics to positional prominence. It originates from the observation that for different positions that induce one type of phonetic advantage, there might be magnitude differences among these positions. Of course, this is only a meaningful question if positional prominence is contrast-specific, since the magnitude of 'generic' prominence cannot be compared without referring to specific phonetic properties. Let us take the sonorous duration of the rime as an example. Both stress and being in prosodic-final position can induce lengthening of duration;

which one has a greater effect? Or compare a CVR (R=sonorant) syllable and a CV:O (O=obstruent) syllable, the former benefiting from having a sonorant coda, the latter benefiting from having a long vowel; which one has a longer sonorous rime duration? Moreover, these magnitude differences may be language-specific. It is possible that in language A, a stressed non-final syllable has a longer sonorous rime duration than an unstressed final syllable when all else is equal, while in language B the durational pattern is the opposite. It is also possible that in language X, CVR has a longer sonorous rime duration than CV:O when all else is equal, while in language Y the durational pattern is the opposite. Therefore the question is: 'is phonology tuned to such language-specific phonetic differences?' Given that the sonorous duration of the rime is the primary tone carrier, as I will show in Chapter 2, we can turn this into more concrete research questions such as 'do language-specific durational differences between stressed and ultima, or CVR and CV:O, translate into corresponding phonological difference on contour tone licensing?' Again, I lay out two competing hypotheses for this question, as in (19), the first of which being the one I will lend support to in this work.

(19) a. *Direct hypothesis*:
- Language-specific phonetic differences affect the distribution of phonological contrasts.
- As a consequence, speakers not only have to identify privileged positions, but also have to keep track of the relative magnitude of the phonetic advantage induced by different positions in their language.
- The influence of phonetics must be directly encoded in phonology.

b. *Structure-only hypothesis*:
- Language-specific phonetic differences do not affect phonological contrast distribution.
- As a consequence, speakers only have to identify certain positions in which certain contrasts are more saliently perceived or easily produced.
- Beyond that phonology is autonomous.

The direct hypothesis clearly corresponds to the direct approach discussed in §1.1 and §1.2, since by referring to the phonetic properties of the positions instead of just the positions in the constraints, the grammar keeps track of the relative magnitude of the phonetic advantage induced by the position, if there is any. The general-purpose and contrast-specific positional markedness approaches, however, are inherently structure-only by referring to phonological positions.

To summarize, three possible phonetic interpretations of positional prominence have emerged. They are schematically shown in (20). The first hypothesis is that positional prominence is general-purpose. Then within the notion that positional prominence is contrast-specific, there are two specific hypotheses: whether it is tuned to language-specific phonetic magnitude differences, or not.

(20) Possible interpretations of positional prominence

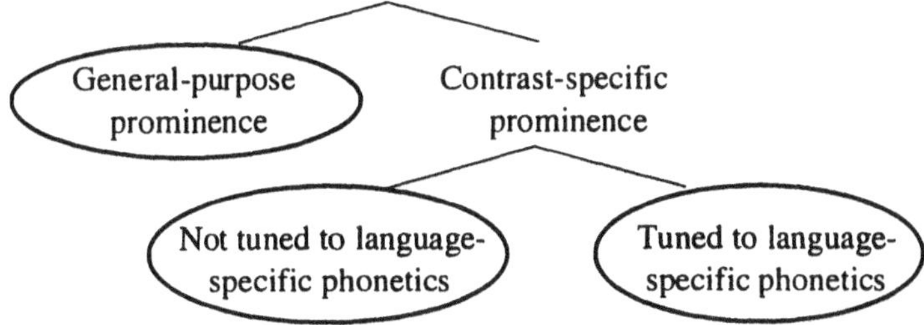

I hope it is clear now that the goal of this work does not stop at providing a comprehensive analysis to contour tone licensing. The contour tone behavior is also a test case for studying the properties of positional prominence in general. Specifically, the behavior of contour tone licensing is used to show that positional prominence effects are contrast-specific and tuned to language-specific phonetics. Upon demonstrating that the duration of the sonorous portion of the rime is the crucial phonetic parameter for the production and perception of contour tones, I examine the positions where languages license the appearance of contour tones and see how they relate to the sonorous duration of the rime in these positions. By showing in a large-scale survey that only positions with higher $C_{CONTOUR}$ values are privileged contour tone licensers, I argue that positional prominence is contrast-specific; by showing in phonetic studies of individual languages that language-specific durational differences between different positions directly affect the distribution of contour tones, I argue that positional prominence is tuned to language-specific phonetics.

Another goal of the dissertation is to provide an Optimality-theoretic model to capture the interaction between phonetic factors such as duration and sonority and phonological patterns of contour tone realization. As I have mentioned, statements on the phonetic naturalness of phonology can only be considered a scientific theory if they are made formal, rigorous, and falsifiable, and Optimality Theory provides us with a tool to do exactly this. We have also seen that if positional prominence is contrast-specific and tuned to language-specific phonetics, current accounts in the Optimality-theoretic framework are inadequate. Therefore this work also proposes an approach that overcomes these inadequacies. The most significant move is to formally encode phonetic categories in phonology. As for the distribution of contour tones, the relevant phonetic categories are the $C_{CONTOUR}$ categories.

In the following section, I outline the organization of this work.

1.5 OUTLINE

In Chapter 2, I discuss the phonetics of contour tones, the main objective of which is to establish the importance of the sonorous portion of the rime in the production and perception of contour tones.

Informed with the knowledge of contour tone phonetics, Chapter 3 defines the *Tonal Complexity* scale, discusses the details of the phonetic index $C_{CONTOUR}$, and identifies the phonological factors that may influence the $C_{CONTOUR}$ value of a syllable. Furthermore, empirical predictions of the direct approach to contour tone distribution are also laid out in this chapter, and they are compared with the predictions of the other approaches.

Chapter 4 documents the typological survey on the positional prominence effect of contour tones. The survey found that four properties of a syllable make it more privileged for contour-bearing: having a phonemic long vowel or a sonorant coda, being stressed, being in the final position of a prosodic domain, and belonging to a short word. The contour-bearing privilege is expressed through implicational hierarchies, such as 'if syllable *x* can carry contour tones, then syllable *y* can carry contour tones with equal or greater complexity,' which establishes syllable *y* as a more privileged contour bearer. All these factors are among the factors that increase the $C_{CONTOUR}$ value of a syllable in Chapter 3, and more than three levels of distinction in contour tone bearing ability are sometimes needed. These findings provide evidence that positional prominence is contrast-specific, and are consistent with both the contrast-specific and the direct approaches to contour tone licensing. Explanations are also provided for why certain factors that increase the $C_{CONTOUR}$ value do not affect the behavior of contour tone licensing.

Chapter 5 documents the series of phonetic studies that provides support for the direct approach to contour tone licensing. The languages under study are those in which two different factors influencing sonorous rime duration directly conflict. The moraic approach and the two other positional markedness approaches, given that they do not refer to phonetic facts of duration and sonority in the language in question, predict unattested patterns. This is also evidence for the relevance of language-specific phonetics for positional prominence.

In Chapter 6, I summarize the arguments against the moraic approach to contour tone distribution. I also discuss the possibility of using tonal melody to capture the advantages of prosodic-final syllables and syllables in shorter words for contour-bearing. The question originates from the observation that ALIGN constraints envisioned by McCarthy and Prince (1993) may generate some of these effects without having to refer to the durational advantages of these syllables directly in the analysis. I discuss two types of tonal association—

lexical association and tonal melody mapping—and show that the alignment approach is inadequate for either type of languages.

In Chapter 7, I propose a formal Optimality-theoretic approach to the positional prominence phenomena regarding contour tones. I propose three families of constraints: markedness constraints against certain contour tones on certain syllable types, markedness constraints against extra duration on the syllable, and faithfulness constraints on tonal realization. The constraints in each family are intrinsically ranked according to scales of phonetic difficulties or the number of categories away from the canonical realization. Interleaving these three families of constraints, we predict that in contexts with shorter duration, one of three things may occur: the contour is flattened; the syllable is lengthened; or both contour-flattening and syllable-lengthening are employed. These predictions match the contour distribution patterns attested in the survey.

Chapter 8 provides analyses for the contour tone distribution in five representative languages—Pingyao Chinese, Xhosa, Mitla Zapotec, Gã, and Hausa—in the proposed theoretical apparatus.

Chapter 9 summarizes the findings and outlines the contribution of this work to our understanding of phonological patterning.

CHAPTER 2

The Phonetics of Contour Tones

2.1 OVERVIEW

The question of concern in this chapter is 'what are the phonetic properties that determine a syllable's ability to bear contour tones?' I show that the most crucial phonetic parameters for contour tone bearing are the duration and sonority of the rime portion of the syllable. I show this in three steps: the importance of sonority, the importance of duration, and the irrelevance of syllable onsets.

2.2 THE IMPORTANCE OF SONORITY FOR CONTOUR TONE BEARING

The main perceptual correlate of tone is the fundamental frequency (f_0). Therefore the perception of tone crucially depends on the perception of f_0. Given that the spectral region containing the second, third and fourth harmonics is crucial in the perception of fundamental frequencies in the range of speech sounds, as shown by Plomp (1967) and Ritsma (1967), we infer that tonal perception crucially depends on the presence of second to fourth harmonics (see also House 1990 and Moore 1995 for review of psychoacoustic literature). Since we also know that sonorous segments possess richer harmonic structures than obstruents—the crucial second to fourth harmonics are usually present in sonorants, but not in obstruents—we are led to conclude that sonorants are better tone bearers than obstruents. Moreover, vowels typically have greater energy, and thus stronger acoustic manifestation of harmonics, in the high-frequency region than sonorant consonants. Therefore they are better tone bearers than sonorant consonants. But given that the crucial harmonics for tonal perception are still present in sonorant consonants, we expect this distinction to be less effective than the one between sonorants and obstruents.

The above points are clearly illustrated in the narrow-band spectrogram in (1) (adapted from Gordon 1998). The vowel [a] has a rich harmonic structure across the frequency range; the sonorant nasal [m] has a clear f_0 and the first, second, and third harmonics; the obstruent [z], on the other hand, does not have a clear harmonic structure, even though its f_0 is present.

(1) Harmonics of vowel, sonorant consonant, and obstruent consonant:

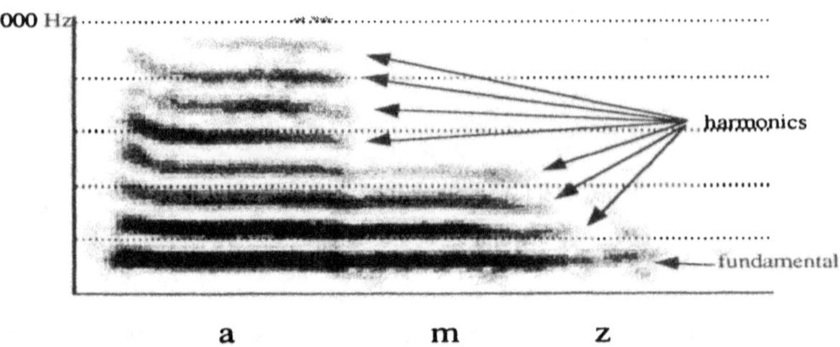

The tone bearing abilities of vowels, sonorant consonants, and obstruent consonants are summarized in (2).

(2) Tone bearing abilities of vowels, sonorant consonants, and obstruent consonants:

Vowel	→	Rich harmonics in h_2—h_4	→	Best tone carrier
Sonorant C	→	Weaker harmonics in h_2—h_4	→	Good tone carrier
Obstruent C	→	No harmonics in h_2—h_4	→	Worst tone carrier

2.3 THE IMPORTANCE OF DURATION FOR CONTOUR TONE BEARING

High sonority is not the only necessary phonetic dimension for a segment to carry tones. Tone bearing ability, especially contour tone bearing ability, is also crucially dependent on duration. This is determined by both the production and perception of contour tones.

The production of contour tones is crucially different from that of other complex segments that require more than one oral constrictions (e.g., [k͡p] in Yoruba or clicks in Khoisan and Bantu) in that for contour tones, the acoustic change results from the state change of one single articulator—the vocal folds. Therefore the laryngeal muscle contraction and relaxation, which determine the vocal fold tension (Arnold 1961, Hirano et al. 1969, Lindqvist 1972, Ohala 1978), must be sequenced to produce the pitch variation in a contour tone. This determines that, unlike a complex segment whose different oral constrictions can be separately planned and overlapped, a contour tone requires sufficient duration to be implemented. More specifically, a complicated contour tone, which involves more pitch targets, would involve more complicated muscle state change, and thus prefer a longer duration to facilitate implementation; a contour tone with farther-apart pitch targets would require the muscles to contract or relax to a greater degree, and thus also prefer a greater duration of its carrier (Sundberg 1973, 1979). Moreover, Sundberg (1973, 1979) reports that it takes longer to implement a pitch rise than a pitch fall with the same pitch excursion.[1] The correlation between duration and contour tone bearing that we can conclude from contour tone production is summarized in (3).

(3) The correlation between duration and contour-bearing ability:

a. The greater the number of pitch targets, the longer duration it requires.

e.g.

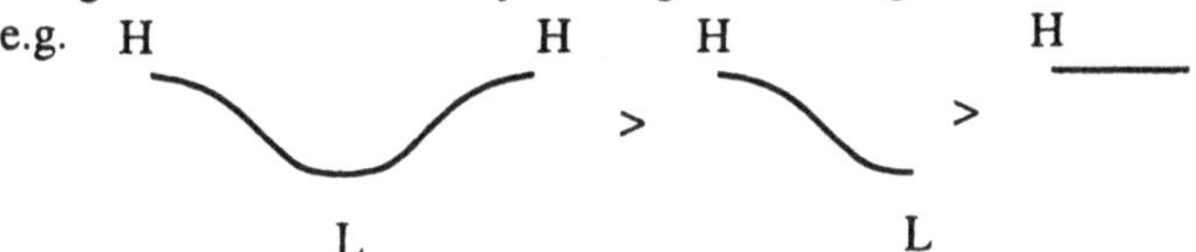

b. The greater the pitch excursion, the longer duration it requires.

e.g.

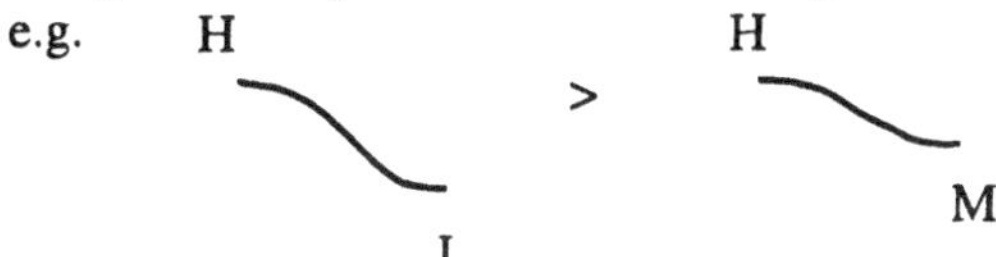

---

[1] One account is that while pitch rise is primarily the result of the contraction of cricothyroid muscles, which leads to an increased longitudinal tension of the vocal folds, pitch fall is the combined result of the contraction of the external thyroarytenoid muscles, the vertical movement of the larynx as well as the relaxation of the cricothyroid muscles (Lindqvist 1972, Kakita and Hiki 1976, Ohala 1978, Sundberg 1973, 1979, Erickson, Baer and Harris 1983). Thus all else being equal, a pitch fall, whose implementation is aided by more muscle groups, takes a shorter time than a pitch rise. Sundberg (1973, 1979) gives another possible account: the external thyroarytenoid muscles not only shorten and lax the vocal folds, but also constrict the larynx tube. Therefore, they can be said to have the function of protecting the larynx and the lungs. Protecting muscles can be assumed to be well developed and quick in operation because of their importance to vital functions. The cricothyroid muscles, on the other hand, do not have any protective function, and hence their being not as quick in operation becomes understandable (paraphrase of Sundberg 1979: 76-77).

c. A rise requires a longer duration than a fall of equal pitch excursion.
e.g.

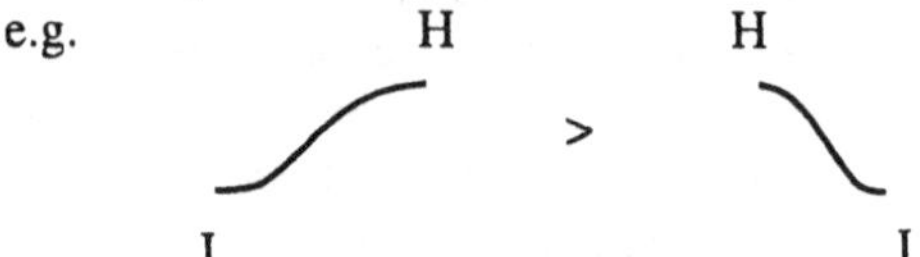

Auditorily, contour tones are different from other contour segments such as prenasalised stops and affricates. Although the production of the latter group of sounds also requires one articulator to go from one position to another, the acoustic consequence of such change is sudden; e.g., the frication noise is formed the moment the oral occlusion is loosened, and the transition between the two states has no perceptual consequence. But for contour tones, the gradual stretch or relaxation of the vocal folds has a continuous acoustic effect, and the transition from the beginning state to the end state carries a significant perceptual weight in the identification of the tonal contour (Gandour 1978, 1983, Gandour and Harshman 1978). This determines that a longer duration is preferred for contour tones, since studies have shown that the perception of such gradual pitch change is enhanced when the duration on which the change is realised is longer. E.g., Black (1970) and Greenberg and Zee (1979) document that given the same pitch excursion, the longer the duration of the vowel, the more 'contour-like' the tone is perceived by the listener. Moreover, Greenberg and Zee (1979) show that listeners cannot perceived pitch changes reliably when the duration is below 90ms.

2.4 THE IRRELEVANCE OF ONSETS TO CONTOUR TONE BEARING

Lastly, it must be acknowledged that there is no correlation between syllable onset duration and tone-bearing ability, even when the onset is a sonorant.[2] Kratochvil (1970) points out that syllable onsets in Mandarin show erratic pitch patterns. Howie (1970, 1974) shows that the pitch carried by sonorant onsets is simply the transition between the tone of the preceding syllable and the tone carried by the rime of the current syllable, and his results are replicated by a

---

[2] The influence of the onset consonant on the pitch of the following vowel, such as the depressor effect in Southern Bantu (Beach 1924, Doke 1926, Lanham 1958, Cope 1959, among others), the correlation between consonant type and synchronic tone rules in Chadic (Hyman 1973, Hyman and Schuh 1974, among others), and tonogenesis in Sino-Tibetan (Maspéro 1912, Karlgren 1926, Haudricourt 1954, Maran 1973, Matisoff 1973b, Hombert 1975, Li 1977, Hombert et al. 1979, among others), are not instances of onset carrying *contrastive* tone, since the pitch in question here is usually *determined* by the voicing property of the onset.

series of studies by Xu (1994, 1997, 1998, 1999). The reason for this is probably perceptual. House (1990), through a series of psychoacoustic experiments, shows that rapid spectral changes, especially rapid increases in spectral energy, significantly decrease the hearer's sensitivity to pitch movement. Therefore, the hearer is less sensitive to pitch information during the transition from the onset consonant to the vowel. Moreover, studies have shown that coda sonorants often have vowel-like qualities; therefore, the transition between a vowel and a coda sonorant is smoother. For example, coda laterals often vocalize, as in English (Lehiste 1964, Bladon and Al-Bamerni 1976, Sproat and Fujimura 1993), Polish (Teslar and Teslar 1962, Stieber 1973, Rubach 1984), Catalan (Recasens et al. 1995, Recasens 1996), and Portuguese (Hall 1943, Feldman 1967, 1972). Coda nasals are sometimes realized as nasal glides, as in Mandarin Chinese (Wang 1997). Bladon (1986) explains this as follows: since vowel-to-sonorant transitions predominantly consist of spectral offsets, and spectral offsets are perceptually less salient than spectral onsets, vowel-to-sonorant transitions are more vulnerable to assimilation than sonorant-to-vowel transitions. Consequently, this does not only give an extra boost in sonority for the coda sonorant to enhance its tone-bearing ability, it also determines that the spectral change between a vowel and a following sonorant is less drastic, which means that the hearer's sensitivity to pitch during this transition is less affected than during the transition between an onset sonorant and the vowel. A possible consequence of these perceptual effects on the linguistic system is that, during the transition between the onset and the vowel, which is a location where the hearer's sensitivity to pitch movement is limited, no significant pitch information is encoded.

2.5 LOCAL CONCLUSION

From the above discussion, we are led to conclude that tone bearing ability is directly related to the sonorous portion of the rime of a syllable: the longer the sonorous rime, the higher the tone bearing ability. Also, a vowel is a better tone bearer than a sonorant consonant. Just from the phonetics itself, it is not entirely clear how duration interacts with sonority in terms of tone bearing ability. But it is safe to say that when two syllable types have the same sonorous rime duration, the one with a longer vocalic duration has a higher tone bearing ability.

CHAPTER 3

Empirical Predictions of Different Approaches

3.1 OVERVIEW

This chapter lays out empirical predictions of the most phonetically-informed approach to contour tone distribution—the direct approach—and compares them with predictions of the other approaches. I start by defining a $C_{CONTOUR}$ scale, which indicates a syllable's contour-bearing ability, and a *Tonal Complexity* scale, which indicates a the phonetic 'complexity' of a contour tone. I then identify the phonological factors that may influence the $C_{CONTOUR}$ value of a syllable. Predictions regarding contour tone distribution of the different approaches are made against the backdrop of these two phonetic scales.

3.2 DEFINING $C_{CONTOUR}$ AND TONAL COMPLEXITY

The preceding chapter establishes that the realization of contour tones relies on two aspects of the rime: duration and sonority. Therefore, we may hypothesize that it is the weighted sum of these two factors that is proportional to the contour tone bearing ability of the syllable. I term this weighted sum $C_{CONTOUR}$. Suppose that Dur(V) and Dur(R) represent the duration of the vowel and the sonorant consonant in the rime respectively. One possible way of constructing $C_{CONTOUR}$ is shown in (1).

(1) $C_{CONTOUR} = a \cdot Dur(V) + Dur(R)$

The following heuristics can be used to determine the value of the coefficient *a*.

First, we know that the longer the sonorous rime duration, the greater the contour tone bearing ability. Therefore, if $Dur(V_i)$ and $Dur(R_i)$ represent the vocalic and sonorant coda duration for position P_i, and $Dur(V_1)+Dur(R_1)$ >

$\mathrm{Dur(V_2)+Dur(R_2)}$, then $C_{\text{CONTOUR}}(P_1) > C_{\text{CONTOUR}}(P_2)$; i.e., $a\cdot\mathrm{Dur(V_1)+Dur(R_1)} > a\cdot\mathrm{Dur(V_2)+Dur(R_2)}$. From this, we derive the range of a as in (2).

(2) Range of a as determined by Heuristic 1:

- if $\mathrm{Dur(V_1)>Dur(V_2)}$, then $a>\dfrac{\mathrm{Dur(R_2)-Dur(R_1)}}{\mathrm{Dur(V_1)-Dur(V_2)}}$;
- if $\mathrm{Dur(V_1)<Dur(V_2)}$, then $a<\dfrac{\mathrm{Dur(R_1)-Dur(R_2)}}{\mathrm{Dur(V_2)-Dur(V_1)}}$.

Second, we know that when two rimes have comparable sonorous duration, and one is a VV rime while the other is a VR rime, the VV rime has a greater contour tone bearing ability. Therefore, if $\mathrm{Dur(V_1)} = \mathrm{Dur(V_2)+Dur(R_2)}$, then $C_{\text{CONTOUR}}(P_1) > C_{\text{CONTOUR}}(P_2)$; i.e., $a\cdot\mathrm{Dur(V_1)} > a\cdot\mathrm{Dur(V_2)+Dur(R_2)}$. Substituting $\mathrm{Dur(V_1)}$ with $\mathrm{Dur(V_2)+Dur(R_2)}$, we get $a>1$, as given in (3).

(3) Range of a as determined by Heuristic 2: $a>1$.

The choice of a should satisfy both heuristics, and it should be independent from whether $\mathrm{Dur(V_1)>Dur(V_2)}$ or $\mathrm{Dur(V_1)<Dur(V_2)}$.

Let us first consider the situation $\mathrm{Dur(V_1)>Dur(V_2)}$. The range of a as determined by Heuristic 1 is $a>\dfrac{\mathrm{Dur(R_2)-Dur(R_1)}}{\mathrm{Dur(V_1)-Dur(V_2)}}$. Since this heuristic is relevant when $\mathrm{Dur(V_1)+Dur(R_1)} > \mathrm{Dur(V_2)+Dur(R_2)}$, we know that $\dfrac{\mathrm{Dur(R_2)-Dur(R_1)}}{\mathrm{Dur(V_1)-Dur(V_2)}}<1$. Therefore, the range of a from Heuristic 1 is not as stringent as the range $a>1$ from Heuristic 2. Hence, when $\mathrm{Dur(V_1)>Dur(V_2)}$, the required range for a is simply $a>1$.

Now consider the situation $\mathrm{Dur(V_1)<Dur(V_2)}$. The range of a as determined by Heuristic 1 is $a<\dfrac{\mathrm{Dur(R_2)-Dur(R_1)}}{\mathrm{Dur(V_1)-Dur(V_2)}}$. The condition for this heuristic tells us that $\dfrac{\mathrm{Dur(R_2)-Dur(R_1)}}{\mathrm{Dur(V_1)-Dur(V_2)}}>1$. Taking into account Heuristic 2, which requires $a>1$, we derive the following range for a: $1<a<\dfrac{\mathrm{Dur(R_1)-Dur(R_2)}}{\mathrm{Dur(V_2)-Dur(V_1)}}$.

Taking the intersection of the a ranges in both conditions $\mathrm{Dur(V_1)>Dur(V_2)}$ and $\mathrm{Dur(V_1)<Dur(V_2)}$, we derive the final range for the coefficient a, as shown in (4).

(4) $1<a<\dfrac{\mathrm{Dur(R_1)-Dur(R_2)}}{\mathrm{Dur(V_2)-Dur(V_1)}}$

Further determination of the upper limit for *a* is an empirical question. It would rely on languages in which Heuristics 1 is relevant (i.e., $Dur(V_1)+Dur(R_1) > Dur(V_2)+Dur(R_2)$) under the condition $Dur(V_1)<Dur(V_2)$. Standard Thai and Cantonese turn out to be languages of this sort. Discussion of this point is further taken up in §5.2.3 and §5.2.4.

Given the definition of $C_{CONTOUR}$, we can now construct a *Tonal Complexity* scale, which is a scale measured by phonetics. With our limited understanding of the exact mapping between pitches and pitch carriers, we are only in a position to define the scale relationally as in (5). But this will not vitiate our ability to make predictions based on the scale, as we will see later in this chapter.

(5) *Tonal Complexity*:
For any two tones T_1 and T_2, let C_1 and C_2 be the minimum $C_{CONTOUR}$ values required for the production and perception of T_1 and T_2 respectively. T_1 is of higher *Tonal Complexity* than T_2 iff $C_1>C_2$.

Therefore, the correlation between $C_{CONTOUR}$, which is determined by the duration and sonority of the rime, and its ability to carry complex contour tones can be schematized as in (6).

(6)

$C_{CONTOUR}$		Tonal complexity
greater	——>	higher
V		V
V	——>	V
V		V
smaller	——>	lower

From the discussion of contour tone phonetics, we already know that the following three parameters of a tone influence its position in the *Tonal Complexity* scale: the number of pitch targets, the pitch excursion between two targets, and the direction of the slope. In a more rigorous fashion, the influence of these three parameters can be summarized as in (7).

(7) For any two tones T_1 and T_2, suppose T_1 has *m* pitch targets and T_2 has *n* pitch targets; the cumulative falling excursions for T_1 and T_2 are Δf_{F_1} and Δf_{F_2} respectively, and the cumulative rising excursions for T_1 and T_2 are Δf_{R_1} and Δf_{R_2} respectively. T_1 has a higher *Tonal Complexity* than T_2 iff:

a. $m>n$, $\Delta f_{F_1} \geq \Delta f_{F_2}$, and $\Delta f_{R_1} \geq \Delta f_{R_2}$;
b. $m=n$, $\Delta f_{F_1} \geq \Delta f_{F_2}$, and $\Delta f_{R_1} \geq \Delta f_{R_2}$ ('=' holds for at most one of the comparisons);
c. $m=n$, $\Delta f_{F_1}+\Delta f_{R_1}=\Delta f_{F_2}+\Delta f_{R_2}$, and $\Delta f_{R_1} \geq \Delta f_{R_2}$.

Condition (7a) states that if T_1 has more pitch targets and T_1's cumulative falling excursion and rising excursion are both no smaller than those of T_2's, then T_1 is of higher tonal complexity than T_2. This is true in virtue of (3a) and (3b) in Chapter 2, according to which T_1 requires a longer minimum duration in the sonorous portion of the rime than T_2. If we use the Chao letters (Chao 1948, 1968) to denote tones, with '5' and '1' indicating the highest and lowest pitches in a speaker's regular pitch range respectively, then the contour tone 534 has a higher tonal complexity than 53.

Condition (7b) states that if T_1 and T_2 have the same number of pitch targets, and at least one of T_1's cumulative falling excursion and rising excursion is greater than that of T_2's, and the other one is no smaller than that of T_2's, then T_1 is of higher tonal complexity than T_2. This is true in virtue of (3b) in Chapter 2. As an example, 535 has a higher tonal complexity than 545, 534, or 435.

Condition (7c) states that if T_1 and T_2 have the same number of pitch targets and the same overall pitch excursion, but the cumulative rising excursion in T_1 is greater than that in T_2, then T_1 is of higher tonal complexity than T_2. This is true in virtue of the fact that the percentage of rising excursion in T_1 is greater than that in T_2, and according to (3c) in Chapter 2, T_1 requires a longer minimum duration in the sonorous portion of the rime than T_2. As an example, 435 has a higher tonal complexity than 534, since $m=n=3$, $\Delta f_{F_1}+\Delta f_{R_1}=\Delta f_{F_2}+\Delta f_{R_2}=3$, and $\Delta f_{R_1}=2>\Delta f_{R_2}=1$.

These comparisons must be made under the same speaking rate and style of speech, because the pitch excursion of a tone might change under different speaking rates and styles of speech. I assume that the consistent phonological behavior of speakers under different speaking rates and styles is due to their ability to normalize duration and pitch across speaking rates and styles (see Kirchner 1998, Steriade 1999 for similar views). This is discussed in more details in §6.2.

Tones are represented phonetically by f_0 in Hz throughout the book. This is because that the main perceptual correlate of tone is f_0, as I have mentioned, and the relation between the physical and auditory dimensions of f_0 (in Hz and Bark respectively) is fairly linear for the sounds of interest in this work (Stevens and Volkman 1940).[1]

3.3 PHONOLOGICAL FACTORS THAT INFLUENCE DURATION AND SONORITY OF THE RIME

Given that $C_{CONTOUR}$ is the crucial indicator of a syllable's tone bearing ability, and that $C_{CONTOUR}$ is determined by the duration and sonority of the rime, it is

[1] Stevens and Volkman (1940) show that the auditory scale for pure tones is fairly linear under 1000Hz. Linguistically relevant tones are well within this range.

important for us to discuss the factors that influence these properties of the rime. I identify four such factors here: segmental composition, stress property, whether the rime is prosodic-final, and the number of syllables in the word to which the rime belongs.

The segmental composition factor includes the long vs. short distinction on the vocalic nucleus and the sonorant vs. obstruent distinction on the coda. All else being equal, a VV rime has a longer sonorous duration than a V rime, and a VR (R=sonorant) rime has a longer sonorous duration than a VO (O=obstruent) rime. Moreover, a VV rime has a higher sonority than a VR rime. As shown in §2.2, when they have comparable duration, this difference alone may affect their tone bearing ability. Two other effects also fall under the rubric of segmental composition: the height of the vowel and the voicing specification of an obstruent coda. Lower vowels involve a greater jaw movement and thus require a longer duration to be implemented than higher vowels (Lindblom 1967, Jensen and Menon 1972). A voiced obstruent coda induces lengthening of the preceding vocalic nucleus, while a voiceless obstruent does not have such an effect (House and Fairbanks 1953, Peterson and Lehiste 1960, Chen 1970, Klatt 1973, 1976). Therefore, all else being equal, $V_{[-high]}$ has a longer sonorous rime duration than $V_{[+high]}$, and Vd (d=voiced obstruent) has a longer sonorous rime duration than Vt.

Together with pitch and amplitude, duration is usually taken as one of the key phonetic correlates of stress. This has been shown in numerous phonetic studies in various languages (e.g., for English: Fry 1955, Lieberman 1960, Morton and Jassem 1965, Adams and Munro 1978; for Polish: Jassem 1959; for Spanish: Simoes 1996; for Arabic: de Jong and Zawaydeh 1999). Therefore it is reasonable to assume that all else being equal, a stressed syllable has a longer sonorous rime duration than an unstressed syllable.

A rich body of phonetic literature has shown that the final syllable of a prosodic unit is subject to lengthening (Oller 1973, Klatt 1975, Cooper and Paccia-Cooper 1980, Beckman and Edwards 1990, Edwards et al. 1991, Wightman et al. 1992). We thus expect that all else being equal, a final syllable in a prosodic unit has a longer sonorous rime duration than a non-final syllable in the same prosodic unit.

Lastly, a syllable in a shorter word has a longer duration than the same syllable in a longer word. This is clearly established for English and Swedish by a series of phonetic studies (Lehiste 1972, Klatt 1973b, Lindblom and Rapp 1973, Lindblom et al. 1981, Lyberg 1977, Strangert 1985). From this we deduce that the sonorous rime duration for a syllable in a shorter word is longer that for the same syllable in a longer word. The studies also indicate that the greatest difference is induced by the monosyllabic vs. disyllabic distinction.

The parameters that influence the $C_{CONTOUR}$ value of the rime are summarized in (8).

(8) a. *Segmental composition*: VV>V, VR>VO, VV>VR, $V_{[\text{-high}]}>V_{[\text{+high}]}$, Vd>Vt.
b. *Stress*: $\sigma_{[\text{+stress}]}>\sigma_{[\text{-stress}]}$.
c. *Final position in a prosodic domain*: $\sigma_{\text{final}}>\sigma_{\text{non-final}}$.
d. *Syllable count in word*: σ in *m*-syllable word > σ in *n*-syllable word (*m*<*n*).

Again, since under different speaking rates and styles, the duration of the same syllable can vary, these comparisons are made under the assumption that the syllables involved are uttered in the same speech condition, and that speakers are able to normalize duration across speaking rates and styles. Speakers' normalization ability is supported by perceptual studies that show that speaking rate of the stimuli influences listeners' perceptual boundary between two segments if this boundary is dependent on duration (e.g., Port 1979, Miller and Liberman 1979, Miller and Grosjean 1981, Pols 1986). We may further assume that the C_{CONTOUR} values used throughout the book are calculated under the canonical speaking rate and style and can be appropriately referred to as "Canonical C_{CONTOUR}."

Given that there are multiple factors that can systematically influence the C_{CONTOUR} value of a syllable, it is the combined effect of all these factors that determines the ultimate C_{CONTOUR} value of a syllable. E.g., if maybe the case that an unstressed word-final CVO in a monosyllabic word has a systematically different C_{CONTOUR} value from a stressed non-final CVV in a disyllabic word.

3.4 PREDICTIONS OF CONTOUR TONE DISTRIBUTION BY DIFFERENT APPROACHES

3.4.1 The Direct Approach

So far, I have explicitly laid out two phonetic scales that share an intimate relation—C_{CONTOUR} and *Tonal Complexity*. Now we are in a position to make specific empirical predictions concerning contour tone distribution in the different approaches under consideration here.

The predictions of the most phonetically-informed theory of contour tone licensing—the direct approach—are as follows:

(9) Predictions of the direct approach for contour tone distribution:
a. Contour tones only preferentially occur in positions in which there are factors that induce a greater C_{CONTOUR} value, i.e., longer sonorous duration or a higher vocalic component in the rime, and these positions are: long-vowelled, sonorant-closed, stressed, prosodic-final syllables, syllables

that occur in shorter words, with a lower vowel, or closed by a voiced obstruent.

b. Within a language, when there are multiple factors that induce greater $C_{CONTOUR}$ values, their contour tone licensing ability corresponds to the degree of enhancement of $C_{CONTOUR}$: the greater the $C_{CONTOUR}$ value, the greater the contour tone licensing ability.

The predictions in (9) can be translated into implicational hierarchy in the line of(10).

(10) Implicational hierarchy predicted by the direct approach:
In language *L*, for any two syllable types σ_1 and σ_2 with $C_{CONTOUR}$ values $C_{CONTOUR}(\sigma_1)$ and $C_{CONTOUR}(\sigma_2)$, if $C_{CONTOUR}(\sigma_1)>C_{CONTOUR}(\sigma_2)$, and σ_1 can carry a contour tone T, then σ_2 can carry contour tones with complexity equal to or greater than T.

The first prediction in (9) emerges from the relevance of contrast-specific phonetics in the direct approach to contour tone distribution (§1.4.3). With its constraints directly referring to phonetic properties that are important for the realization of contour tones, i.e., duration and sonority of the rime, the approach can single out positions that are poor in these phonetic properties and ban contour tones on these positions by higher ranked positional markedness constraints.

The second prediction in (9) emerges from the fact that the direct approach is sensitive to language-specific phonetics (§1.4.3). To see this more clearly, let us consider a language L in which two distinct properties of a syllable—P_1 and P_2—can both induce a greater $C_{CONTOUR}$ value for the syllable. Assume that there exist syllables with property P_1 but not P_2 and syllables with property P_2 but not P_1, and that L has contour tones with distributional restrictions related to P_1 and P_2. Now consider two types of syllables which are exactly the same except that one has the property P_1, and the other has the property P_2. Further assume that $C_{CONTOUR}(P_1) > C_{CONTOUR}(P_2)$, and that the effect of the $C_{CONTOUR}$ value increase is additive—i.e., if a syllable has both properties P_1 and P_2, then its $C_{CONTOUR}$ value is even greater.[2] Therefore, we arrive at the following phonetic scale: $C_{CONTOUR}(P_1\&P_2) > C_{CONTOUR}(P_1) > C_{CONTOUR}(P_2)$. We may then consider the following positional markedness constraints, as in (11).

[2] This kind of additive lengthening effect has been documented for English in Klatt (1973), which shows that a stressed syllable in prosodic-final position is longer than a stressless final syllable or a stressed non-final syllable. In §5.2.2, this effect is also documented for Beijing Chinese.

(11) Positional markedness constraints in a direct approach:

a. *CONTOUR(¬$C_{CONTOUR}(P_1\&P_2)$): no contour tone is allowed on syllables whose $C_{CONTOUR}$ value is less than $C_{CONTOUR}(P_1\&P_2)$.

b. *CONTOUR(¬$C_{CONTOUR}(P_1)$): no contour tone is allowed on syllables whose $C_{CONTOUR}$ value is less than $C_{CONTOUR}(P_1)$.

c. *CONTOUR(¬$C_{CONTOUR}(P_2)$): no contour tone is allowed on syllables whose $C_{CONTOUR}$ value is less than $C_{CONTOUR}(P_2)$.

Since these constraints refer to a unified phonetic scale—$C_{CONTOUR}$, and we know that $C_{CONTOUR}(P_1\&P_2) > C_{CONTOUR}(P_1) > C_{CONTOUR}(P_2)$, if we acknowledge that universal constraint rankings can be projected from phonetic scales (Prince and Smolensky 1993: p.67), a universal ranking is imposed upon the three constraints in (11), as shown in (12).

(12) *CONTOUR(¬$C_{CONTOUR}(P_2)$) » *CONTOUR(¬$C_{CONTOUR}(P_1)$) » *CONTOUR(¬$C_{CONTOUR}(P_1\&P_2)$)

We also need two general constraints, as defined in (13).

(13) General constraints:

a. *CONTOUR: no contour tone is allowed on a syllable.

b. IDENT(tone): let α be a syllable in the input, and β be any syllable corresponding to α in the output; if α is has tone T, then β has tone T.

With the ranking in (12) and the general constraints in (13), the factorial typology of the direct approach makes the predictions in (14). When IDENT(tone) is ranked at the bottom of the hierarchy as in (14a), no contour is allowed to surface on any syllable. When IDENT(tone) is ranked between the positional markedness and general markedness constraints as in (14b), contours are only allowed on syllables with $P_1\&P_2$ simultaneously, since all other P_1~P_2 combinations ($\neg P_1\&P_2$, $P_1\&\neg P_2$, $\neg P_1\&\neg P_2$) will have $C_{CONTOUR}$ values smaller than $C_{CONTOUR}(P_1\&P_2)$, and thus violate *CONTOUR(¬$C_{CONTOUR}(P_1\&P_2)$). When IDENT(tone) is ranked between *CONTOUR(¬$C_{CONTOUR}(P_2)$), *CONTOUR(¬$C_{CONTOUR}(P_1)$) and *CONTOUR(¬$C_{CONTOUR}(P_1\&P_2)$) as in (14c), contours will be allowed on any syllables with property P_1, but not on syllables only with P_2. But when IDENT(tone) is ranked between *CONTOUR(¬$C_{CONTOUR}(P_2)$) and *CONTOUR(¬$C_{CONTOUR}(P_1)$) as in (14d), contours will not only be allowed on syllables with P_2, but also on syllables with P_1. This is because $C_{CONTOUR}(P_1) > C_{CONTOUR}(P_2)$, which determines that having contours on syllables with P_1 will not violate the highly ranked *CONTOUR(($C_{CONTOUR}(P_2)$)). And finally, when IDENT(tone) is ranked on top, contours are allowed on all syllable types.

(14) Factorial typology (the direct approach):

	Constraint ranking	Contour tone restriction predicted
a.	*CONTOUR(¬$C_{CONTOUR}(P_2)$), *CONTOUR(¬$C_{CONTOUR}(P_1)$), *CONTOUR(¬$C_{CONTOUR}(P_1\&P_2)$), *CONTOUR ⇓ **IDENT(tone)**	No contour tone on any syllable
b.	*CONTOUR(¬$C_{CONTOUR}(P_2)$), *CONTOUR(¬$C_{CONTOUR}(P_1)$), *CONTOUR(¬$C_{CONTOUR}(P_1\&P_2)$) ⇓ **IDENT(tone)** ⇓ *CONTOUR	Contour tone only on syllables with $P_1\&P_2$ simultaneously
c.	*CONTOUR(¬$C_{CONTOUR}(P_2)$), *CONTOUR(¬$C_{CONTOUR}(P_1)$) ⇓ **IDENT(tone)** ⇓ *CONTOUR(¬$C_{CONTOUR}(P_1\&P_2)$), *CONTOUR	Contour tone only on syllables with P_1
d.	*CONTOUR(¬$C_{CONTOUR}(P_2)$) ⇓ **IDENT(tone)** ⇓ *CONTOUR(¬$C_{CONTOUR}(P_1)$), *CONTOUR(¬$C_{CONTOUR}(P_1\&P_2)$), *CONTOUR	Contour tone only on syllables with P_1 or syllables with P_2
e.	**IDENT(tone)** ⇓ *CONTOUR(¬$C_{CONTOUR}(P_2)$), *CONTOUR(¬$C_{CONTOUR}(P_1)$), *CONTOUR(¬$C_{CONTOUR}(P_1\&P_2)$), *CONTOUR	Contour tone on all syllable types

Therefore, the factorial typology shows that under the direct approach, the pattern of contour tone licensing is tied to the language-specific phonetics of P_1 and P_2 in that the licensing pattern always observes an implicational hierarchy: if a contour tone can surface on syllables with the smaller $C_{CONTOUR}$ value, then it can surface on syllables with the greater $C_{CONTOUR}$ value (cf. (10)). If in another language L', the $C_{CONTOUR}$ values of P_1 and P_2 are reversed, such that $C_{CONTOUR}(P_1) < C_{CONTOUR}(P_2)$, then the prediction of this approach for L' is that if a contour tone can surface on syllables with P_1, then it can surface on syllables with P_2.

Let us compare these predictions with those made by the competing approaches.

3.4.2 Contrast-Specific Positional Markedness

The contrast-specific positional markedness approach does acknowledge that contour tones selectively gravitate to positions that have phonetic advantages for contour tone bearing. Therefore it makes the same prediction (9a) as the direct approach. But given that it refers only to positions, not the phonetic properties of the positions in the markedness constraints, it does not make the prediction in (9b); i.e., when there are multiple factors that induce greater $C_{CONTOUR}$ at play, it does not predict which one is a better contour tone licenser. Let me spell out the argument in detail with language L that we considered in the previous section.

Since P_1 and P_2 are properties that increase the syllable's contour tone bearing ability, under this approach, we may justifiably single out two positional markedness constraints that penalize the realization of contour tones on syllables without these properties, as defined in (15).

(15) Positional markedness constraints in the contrast-specific approach:

a. *CONTOUR($\neg P_1$): no contour tone is allowed on syllables without property P_1.

b. *CONTOUR($\neg P_2$): no contour tone is allowed on syllables without property P_2.

Crucially, given that P_1 and P_2 are distinct properties of the syllable, there are two possible scenarios for the ranking between the two positional markedness constraints: first, there is no universal ranking between them, since there is no phonetic dimension, such as $C_{CONTOUR}$, on which the effectiveness of these constraints can be directly compared; second, there is a universal ranking between them handed to the speaker by UG, but there is no a priori reason to believe that the ranking accords to the $C_{CONTOUR}$ comparison between P_1 and P_2. In either case, we cannot rule out the ranking *CONTOUR($\neg P_2$) » *CONTOUR($\neg P_1$) in a principled way.

To complete the analysis, we also need the two general constraints *CONTOUR and IDENT(tone) as defined in (13).

The factorial typology of these four constraints again predicts five distinct patterns of contour tone realization, as shown in (16). When IDENT(tone) is ranked at the bottom, no contour is allowed on any syllable; when IDENT(tone) is ranked between the positional markedness and general markedness constraints, contours are only allowed on syllables with P_1&P_2 simultaneously, since all other combinations ($\neg P_1\&P_2$, $P_1\&\neg P_2$, $\neg P_1\&\neg P_2$) violate at least one of the highly ranked *CONTOUR($\neg P_1$) and *CONTOUR($\neg P_2$); when IDENT(tone) is ranked between the two positional markedness constraints, contours are only allowed on syllables with P_1 (if *CONTOUR($\neg P_1$) » IDENT(tone) » *CONTOUR($\neg P_2$)) or on syllables with P_2 (if *CONTOUR($\neg P_2$) » IDENT(tone) » *CONTOUR($\neg P_1$)); and finally, when IDENT(tone) is ranked on top, contours are allowed on all syllable types.

(16) Factorial typology (the contrast-specific positional markedness approach):

	Constraint ranking	Contour tone restriction predicted
a.	*CONTOUR($\neg P_1$), *CONTOUR($\neg P_2$), *CONTOUR ⇓ **IDENT(tone)**	No contour tone on any syllable
b.	*CONTOUR($\neg P_1$), *CONTOUR($\neg P_2$) ⇓ **IDENT(tone)** ⇓ *CONTOUR	Contour tone only on syllables with $P_1\&P_2$ simultaneously
c.	*CONTOUR($\neg P_1$) ⇓ **IDENT(tone)** ⇓ *CONTOUR($\neg P_2$), *CONTOUR	Contour tone only on syllables with P_1
d.	*CONTOUR($\neg P_2$) ⇓ **IDENT(tone)** ⇓ *CONTOUR($\neg P_1$), *CONTOUR	Contour tone only on syllables with P_2
e.	**IDENT(tone)** ⇓ *CONTOUR($\neg P_1$), *CONTOUR($\neg P_2$), *CONTOUR	Contour tone on all syllable types

From the factorial typology, we can see that the contrast-specific approach make two different predictions from the direct approach. First, it predicts that it is possible to have contour tones only on syllables with P_2, despite the fact that syllables with P_1 have a greater contour tone bearing ability; the direct approach, however, predicts an implicational relation which allows contour tones on P_2

provided that contour tones on P_1 are allowed. Second, the direct approach predicts the scenario in which either P_1 or P_2 can license contour tones; this falls out directly from the implicational relation 'if P_2, then P_1' in this approach. But the structure-only approach formally cannot predict disjunctive licensing, as the factorial typology shows.

The second discrepancy in the predictions seems to disappear if we allow constraint disjunction (Smolensky 1995, Kirchner 1996, Crowhurst and Hewitt 1997) for the contrast-specific positional markedness approach. I.e., if we define a disjoined constraint *CONTOUR($\neg P_1$)$\cup$*CONTOUR($\neg P_2$), which is only violated when both *CONTOUR($\neg P_1$) and *CONTOUR($\neg P_2$) are violated as shown in (17), then the ranking in (18) will give us the disjunctive licensing pattern, since having either P_1 or P_2 will suffice to satisfy the disjoined constraint, which is the only constraint that outranks IDENT(tone).

(17) Evaluation of *CONTOUR($\neg P_1$)$\cup$*CONTOUR($\neg P_2$)

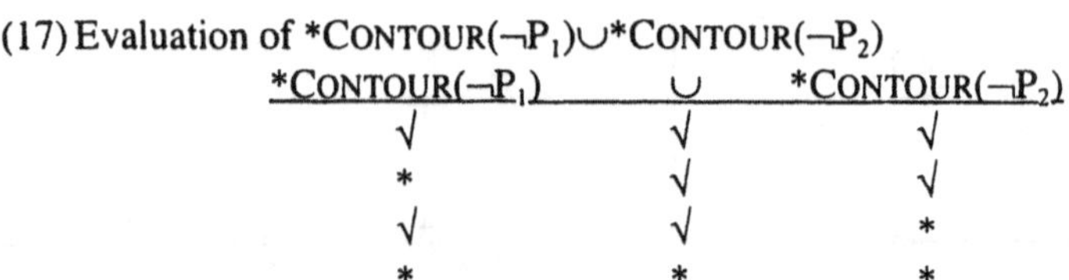

*CONTOUR($\neg P_1$)	$\cup$	*CONTOUR($\neg P_2$)
√	√	√
*	√	√
√	√	*
*	*	*

(18) *CONTOUR($\neg P_1$)$\cup$*CONTOUR($\neg P_2$) » IDENT(tone) » *CONTOUR($\neg P_1$), *CONTOUR($\neg P_2$), *CONTOUR

One immediate disadvantage of this move is that it has to stipulate an extra mechanism, i.e., constraint disjunction, to make a prediction that falls out naturally in the direct approach. And in fact, even with constraint disjunction, the difference in prediction still does not completely disappear. Consider a language with three distinct properties P_1, P_2, and P_3 that may induce higher $C_{CONTOUR}$ values, and the magnitudes of their effects are such that $P_1>P_2>P_3$. Let us also assume that the magnitudes of the additive effects are such that $P_1\&P_2> P_1\&P_3>P_2\&P_3$. The direct approach predicts the following implicational hierarchies: if $P_2\&P_3$, then $P_1\&P_3$, $P_1\&P_2$; if $P_1\&P_3$, then $P_1\&P_2$. But the contrast-specific approach, given its structure-only characteristic, does not predict such implicational hierarchies, since nothing in the disjunctive mechanism prevents *CONTOUR($\neg P_2$)$\cup$*CONTOUR($\neg P_3$) to be ranked higher than *CONTOUR($\neg P_1$)$\cup$*CONTOUR($\neg P_3$) and *CONTOUR($\neg P_1$)$\cup$*CONTOUR($\neg P_2$).

Given that constraint disjunction does not reconcile the differences between the direct and the contrast-specific approaches, I opt to disregard it for now to keep the predictions clear. In later discussions of contour tone distribution patterns, I will discuss its insufficiency in more detail.

I summarize the crucial predictions of the contrast-specific positional markedness approach in (19).

(19) Predictions of the contrast-specific positional markedness approach for contour tone distribution:

a. Contour tones only preferentially occur in positions in which there are factors that induce a greater $C_{CONTOUR}$ value, i.e., longer sonorous duration or a higher vocalic component in the rime, and these positions are: long-vowelled, sonorant-closed, stressed, prosodic-final syllables, syllables that occur in shorter words, with a lower vowel, or closed by a voiced obstruent.

b. Within a language, when there are multiple factors that benefit the crucial phonetic properties for contour tones, any one of the factors may turn out to be the best contour tone licensor, regardless of the degree of phonetic advantage the factor induces as compared to the other factors.

c. Disjunctive licensing is not allowed.

3.4.3 General-Purpose Positional Markedness

For the general-purpose positional markedness approach, given that the phonetics of contour tones per se plays no role in determining their distribution, there is no a priori reason for them to preferentially target positions with abundant sonorous rime duration; thus their distribution should not be significantly different from that of other phonological features, such as vowel quality or consonant place. This is determined by the general-purpose nature of this approach. Beckman (1997), in a comprehensive study of positional prominence effects, identifies the following inventory of privileged linguistic positions: root-initial syllables, stressed syllables, syllable onsets, roots, and long vowels. Among these positions, root-initial syllables, stressed syllables, and long vowels are syllable-based and can be considered as proper carriers for lexical tones. Therefore, this approach should predict these positions to be advantageous contour carriers. Compare this list with the list in (8), we do not expect to find effects of prosodic final position or the number of syllables in the word on contour tone licensing; but we expect to find the word-initial position to be a favored position for contours, even though it is not durationally privileged.

Similarly to the contrast-specific approach, general-purpose positional markedness also does not make the prediction in (9b); i.e., when there are multiple factors that foster the crucial phonetic properties for contour tones, it does not predict which one is a better contour tone licenser. This is again due to the fact that it does not specifically refer to the relevant phonetic properties for contour tone realization in the constraints. Moreover, as in the contrast-specific approach, disjunctive licensing is not allowed without constraint disjunction. The crucial predictions of the general-purpose positional markedness approach is summarized in (20).

(20) Predictions of the general-purpose positional markedness approach for contour tone distribution:

a. Root-initial syllables, stressed syllables, and long vowels are privileged contour tone carriers; final syllable in a prosodic domain and syllables in shorter words are not privileged contour tone carriers.

b. Within a language, when there are multiple factors that benefit the crucial phonetic properties for contour tones, any one of the factors may turn out to be the best contour tone licensor, regardless of the degree of phonetic advantage the factor induces as compared to the other factors.

c. Disjunctive licensing is not allowed.

3.4.4 The Moraic Approach

The representationally-based moraic approach crucially relies on the mora as both the unit of length and weight and the unit of tone bearing. Among the competing approaches, it has the least phonetic flavor. The extent to which phonetics is relevant in this approach is that a more sonorous segment is more likely to be moraic than a less sonorous segment. This can be seen from the following implicational hierarchies regarding moraicity: if a consonant is moraic, then a vowel is moraic; if an obstruent consonant is moraic, then a sonorant consonant is moraic (Hyman 1985, Zec 1988, Hayes 1989). But as I have mentioned, the role of duration and sonority in the moraic theory can only be said to be conditional. E.g., it is possible that a phonemic short vowel in some environment is phonetically longer than a phonemic long vowel in some other environment.[3] The theory will still consider the former to have fewer moras than the latter. Moreover, the usually non-structural lengthening such as final lengthening is predicted not to have an effect on the tone-bearing ability of the syllable, since its non-structural nature determines that it does not change the moraic structure of the syllable. For the same reason, the durational advantage of syllables in words with fewer syllables should not have an effect on contour tone distribution either.

The moraic approach also restricts the role that duration and sonority can play to a binary, at most ternary one. This is because contrastive length is usually binary (short and long) and maximally ternary (short, long, and extra-long), and languages only distinguish up to three degrees of syllable weight (light, heavy, and superheavy). It therefore predicts that we can only in principle distinguish three kinds of tonal distribution—tones allowed only in trimoraic syllables, in at least bimoraic syllables, and everywhere. Moreover, under the assumption that contour tones are concatenations of level tone targets and each

[3] Such is the case for Standard Thai and Cantonese, as we will see in Chapter 5.

level tone needs a mora for its realization, the number of tonal targets in a contour tone must be identical to the number of moras in the syllable that carries it.

Therefore, the prediction of the moraic approach for contour tone distribution can be summarized as in (21).

(21) Predictions of the moraic approach for contour tone distribution:

a. The contour tone bearing ability of a syllable depends on the moraic structure of the syllable. Syllables with higher mora counts, such as long-vowelled, sonorant-closed, stressed syllables, are privileged contour tone carriers. Syllables that do not have higher mora counts than ceretis paribus syllables, such as prosodic-final, root-initial syllables and syllables in shorter words, are not privileged contour tone carriers.

b. The contour tone bearing ability of different syllables can be directly compared by their mora counts. But only up to three levels of distinctions can be made.

3.5 LOCAL CONCLUSION

The discussion on the phonetics of contour tones in Chapter 2 has enabled us to lay out empirical predictions of the competing approaches to contour tone distribution. The following two chapters of the book aim to evaluate the predictions of the competing approaches in the face both typological and phonetic data. Chapter 4 documents a survey of contour tone distribution in 187 languages, which serves as a test for which positions are privileged contour tone carriers. Chapter 5 documents phonetic studies of duration in languages with multiple lengthening factors, which serve as a test for the implicational relation between the stronger and weaker lengthening factors in their contour tone licensing ability. To preview the results, I show that contour tone distribution is indeed sensitive to the duration and sonority of the rime (i.e. C_{CONTOUR}), and in languages that have competing durational factors, the one that induces a greater C_{CONTOUR} increase is always the one that licenses contour tones more readily. This illustrates the necessity for a theory of phonology in line with the direct approach which incorporates contrast-specific and language-specific phonetics, as it makes more restrictive, yet more accurate predictions.

CHAPTER 4

The Role of Contrast-Specific Phonetics in Contour Tone Distribution: A Survey

4.1 OVERVIEW OF THE SURVEY

This chapter documents the results of a typological survey of the positional prominence effects regarding contour tones. Specially, I examine the contexts in which contour tones are more likely to occur cross-linguistically, and through this examination, I aim to test the hypothesis that the distribution of contour tones reflects the phonetic correlation between the duration and sonority of the rime on the one hand, and the contour tones the syllable is able to carry on the other, and see whether the direct approach to contour tone distribution is superior to the other approaches. As I have mentioned in §1.4.3, this is also a test case for the contrast-specificity hypothesis of positional prominence in general, since the phonetic properties that are crucial for contour tones might not be crucial for other phonological contrasts. Then if the occurrence of contour tones is sensitive to these phonetic properties per se, we know that positional prominence is not a generic phenomenon that applies in the same fashion to all contrasts, in other words, it is contrast-specific. The data will also bear on the relevance of the phonetically-based, fine-grained concept $C_{CONTOUR}$ in phonological patterning, since only through such a concept can the distribution of contour tones be captured in a uniform fashion and at the same time be distinguished from the distribution of other phonological features in a principled way.

The survey is composed of 187 genetically diverse tone languages with contour tones. The *Ethnologue* (Grimes 1996) was used as the basis for the language classification. The data sources for the typology include grammars, dictionaries, and articles published in linguistic journals. Two considerations underlie the choice of languages—genetic balance and representation of contour tones. To ensure the genetic balance of the languages surveyed, two factors were controlled. For every language phylum that has tone languages, at least one language from that phylum was included. Also, more languages were included for language phyla that have a richer internal structure according to Grimes

(1996). To ensure that the typology is representative of contour tone languages, the selection was skewed towards language phyla in which contour tones are common, e.g., Sino-Tibetan languages. The pie-chart in (1) outlines the genetic composition of the survey. The languages included in the survey, grouped according to their genetic classification, are given in the table in (2). Aliases to a language are given in parentheses following the language. For Chinese languages in the Sino-Tibetan phylum, Grimes (1996) only lists the dialect groups as the smallest unit. In the survey, I include multiple dialects for most of the dialect groups. In this case, the names of the dialect groups are given in italics, followed by the names of the dialects. The sources consulted for each language are listed in Appendix.

(1) Genetic composition of the survey (187 languages):

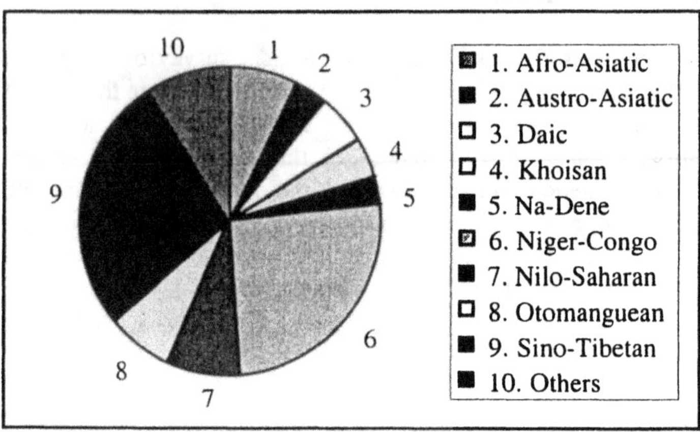

(2) Genetic classification of languages included in the typology:

Language phylum	No. of languages	Languages
Afro-Asiatic	14	Agaw (Awiya), Beja (Bedawi), Bolanci (Bole), Elmolo, Galla (Booran Oromo), Hausa, Kanakuru, Margi, Moča (Shakicho), Musey, Ngizim, Rendille, Sayanci, Somali
Austro-Asiatic	6	Brao, Bugan, Muong, So (Thavung), Sre, Vietnamese
Caddoan	2	Caddo, Kitsai
Creole	1	Nubi
Daic	10	Southern Dong, Gelao, Khamti, Lao, Maonan, Saek, Ron Phibun Thai, Songkhla Thai, Southern Thai, Yong

Indo-European	1	Lithuanian
Iroquoian	1	Oklahoma Cherokee
Keres	1	Acoma (Western Keres)
Khoisan	8	!Xóõ, !Xũ (Kung-Ekoka), Ju|'hoasi (Kung-Tsumkwe), Korana, Nama, Naro, ǂKhomani Ng'huki, Sandawe
Kiowa Tanoan	2	Jemez (Towa), Kiowa
Miao-Yao	4	Tananshan Hmong, Lakkja, Mjen, Punu
Mura	1	Pirahã (Mura-Pirahã)
Na-Dene	5	Western Apache, Chilcotin, Navajo, Sarcee, Sekani
Niger-Congo	48	Abidji, Aghem, Babungo (Vengo), Bamileke, Bandi, Kivunjo Chaga, Chicewa, Ciyao, Etung, Gã, Haya, Igbo, Kambari, Kenyang, Kikuyu, Kimbundu, Kinande, Kinyarwanda, Kisi, Kɔnni, Kpele, Nana Kru, Wobe Kru, Kukuya (Southern Teke), Lama, Lamba, Lokele, Luganda, Machame Chaga, Chimahuta Makonde, Chimaraba Makonde, Mbum, Mende, Zing Mumuye, Ngamambo, Ngazija, Ngie, Ngumbi (Kombe), Nupe, Ólusamia, Runyankore, Sechuana, Shi, Tiv, Venda, Xhosa, Yoruba, Zulu
Nilo-Saharan	15	Bari, Camus, Datooga, Dholuo, Didinga, Lango, Logo, Lulubo, Maasai, Meidob, Nandi (Kalenjin), Päkot, Chamus Samburu, Toposa, Turkana
Oto-Manguean	13	Comaltepec Chinantec, Lalama Chinantec, Lealao Chinantec, Quiotepec Chinantec, Chiquihuitlan Mazatec, Jicaltepec Mixtec, Tlacoyalco Popoloca, San Andrés Chichahuaxtla Trique, San Juan Copala Trique, Isthmus Zapotec, Macuitianguis Zapotec, Mitla Zapotec, Sierra Juarez Zapotec

Sino-Tibetan	51	*Gan*: Nanchang; *Hakka*: Yudu;,*Huizhou*: Shexian, Tunxi; *Jin*: Changzhi, Pingyao, Shuozhou, Xinzhou, Yangqu; *Mandarin*: Beijing, Chengdu, Guiyang, Hefei, Huojia, Kunming, Lanzhou, Nanjing, Wuhan, Xi'an, Xining, Yanggu, Yinchuan, Zhenjiang; *Min Dong*: Fuzhou;,*Min Nan*: Chaoyang, Haikou, Shantou, Zhangping; *Wu*: Changzhou, Chongming, Lüsi, Ningbo, Pingyang, Shanghai, Suzhou, Wenling, Wuyi; *Xiang*: Anren, Xiangtan; *Yue*: Cantonese, Taishan, Zengcheng; Apatani, Tiddim Chin, Lahu, Lisu, Lushai, Chang Naga, Rongmei Naga, Lhasa Tibetan, Rgyalthang Tibetan
Siouan	1	Crow
Trans-New Guinea	2	Mianmin, Siane
Witotoan	1	Ocaina (Huitoto)

To briefly preview the results of the typology, it clearly demonstrates that only factors that increase the $C_{CONTOUR}$ value of a syllable as identified in §3.3—segmental composition, stress, proximity to prosodic boundaries, and the number of syllables in the word—influence the distribution of contour tones in principled ways. The greater the $C_{CONTOUR}$ value a syllable type has, the more likely it can carry tones with higher tonal complexity. Being in the prosodic final position and being in shorter words do contribute positively to contour bearing, while being in root-initial position does not. There are also languages with more than one contour licensing factor, i.e., disjunctive licensing. In other words, the predictions of the direct approach are borne out. In the 187 languages, 159 languages only have contour tone restrictions that observe the implicational hierarchies predicted by the direct approach, as discussed in §3.4.1); five languages have both restrictions that observe and restrictions that do not observe the implicational hierarchies; and 22 languages have no restrictions on contour tone distribution.

In the following sections, I discuss the influence of these factors on the distribution of contour tones one by one and illustrate with examples.

4.2 SEGMENTAL COMPOSITION

4.2.1 General Observations

Among the four segmental composition factors that affect the sonorous rime duration, i.e., length of the vocalic nucleus, sonority of the coda consonant, height of the vocalic nucleus and the voicing specification of the coda obstruent, only the first two are attested to have an effect on the distribution of contour tones in the typology. The effects can be stated as the implicational hierarchies in (3).

(3) All else being equal,
  a. if CV can carry contours, then CVV can carry contours with equal or greater tonal complexity;
  b. if CVC can carry contours, then CVVC can carry contours with equal or greater tonal complexity;
  c. if CVO can carry contours, then CVR and CVV(C) can carry contours with equal or greater tonal complexity;
  d. if CVR can carry contours then CVV can carry contours with equal or greater tonal complexity.

These implicational hierarchies are established through the observations in (4). 'Occurs more freely' includes the following scenarios: (a) contour tones can occur in the former contexts but not the latter; (b) the contour tones that can occur in the former contexts are a superset of the contours that can occur in the latter contexts; and (c) the pitch excursion of a contour tone is greater in the former contexts than the latter. The percentages in (4) indicate the ratio of languages in the survey that observe the given contour distribution.

(4) Contour tones occur more freely:
  a. on CVV(C) than CV(C) in 38 languages (20.3%);
  b. on CVV(C) and CVR than CVO and CV in 66 languages (35.3%);
  c. on CVV(C), CVR and CVO than CV in four languages (2.1%).

The languages that observe the contour tone distribution patterns in (4) are listed in (5).

(5) a. Contour tones occur more freely on CVV(C) (38 languages):

Language phylum	No. of languages	Languages
Afro-Asiatic	3	*Beja (Bedawi), Kanakuru, Somali*
Caddoan	1	*Kitsai*
Iroquoian	1	Oklahoma Cherokee
Khoisan	2	*Ju|'hoasi (Kung-Tsumkwe), Sandawe*
Mura	1	Pirahã (Mura-Pirahã)
Na-Dene	4	*Western Apache, Navajo, Sarcee, Sekani*

Niger-Congo	12	*Aghem*, Chicewa, Ciyao, *Gã*, *Kenyang*, Kikuyu, Kinyarwanda, Lamba, Lokele, *Zing Mumuye*, Shi, Zulu
Nilo-Saharan	7	*Datooga*, *Dholuo*, *Didinga*, Logo, *Meidob*, *Nandi (Kalenjin)*, Päkot
Oto-Manguean	2	Jicaltepec Mixtec, Tlacoyalco Popoloca
Sino-Tibetan	3	*Tiddim Chin*, *Fuzhou*, *Lushai*
Siouan	1	Crow
Witotoan	1	Ocaina

b. Contours occur more freely on CVV(C) and CVR (66 languages):

Language phylum	No. of languages	Languages
Austro-Asiatic	6	Brao, Bugan, Muong, So (Thavung), Sre, Vietnamese
Caddoan	1	Caddo
Daic	9	Southern Dong, Khamti, Lao, Maonan, Saek, Ron Phibun Thai, Standard Thai, Songkhla Thai, Yong
Indo-European	1	Lithuanian
Keres	1	Acoma
Khoisan	4	Korana, Kɔnni, Nama, Naro
Kiowa Tanoan	1	Kiowa
Miao-Yao	3	Lakkja, Mjen, Punu
Niger-Congo	3	Kisi, Kɔnni, Tiv, Yoruba
Nilo-Saharan	1	Turkana
Oto-Manguean	2	San Andrés Chichahuaxtla Trique, San Juan Copala Trique
Sino-Tibetan	33	Cantonese, Changzhi, Changhou, Chaoyang, Tiddim Chin, Chongming, Fuzhou, Haikou, Hefei, Huojia, Lahu, Lisu, Lüsi, Chang Naga, Nanchang, Nanjing, Ningbo, Pingyao, Shanghai, Shantou, Shexian, Shuozhou, Suzhou, Lhasa Tibetan, Tunxi, Wenling, Wuyi, Xinzhou, Yangqu, Yudu, Zhangping, Zengcheng, Zhenjiang

c. Contours occur more freely on CVV, CVR and CVO (4 languages):

Language phylum	No. of languages	Languages
Afro-Asiatic	3	Hausa, Musey, Ngizim
Niger-Congo	1	Luganda

Among the 38 languages in (5a), 22 languages have CVR in their syllable inventory. These languages were in italics. Of these, 21 exhibit the pattern in which a long-vowelled syllable always has a greater contour-bearing ability than CVR, regardless of whether it is closed by a coda, or whether the coda is a sonorant or an obstruent. These 21 languages illustrate not only that a long vowel is a better tone carrier than a short vowel, but also that a vowel is a better tone carrier than a sonorant consonant. The other language—Fuzhou—has the pattern CVVR>CVR>CVVO>CVO (Jiang-King 1996, Liang and Feng 1996), and therefore illustrates the difference between VV and V and between coda sonorant and coda obstruent in contour-bearing. That CVR has a greater contour-bearing ability than CVVO is a surprising pattern, and this pattern is also attested in languages like Standard Thai and Cantonese. §5.2.3 and §5.2.4 discuss phonetic data from Standard Thai and Cantonese. The finding is that the phonological long vowel or diphthong in CVVO is in fact very short phonetically. In the rest 16 languages in (5a), syllables are either all open or can only be closed by an obstruent. These languages only illustrate the VV/V distinction in contour tone bearing.

For (5b), all 66 languages have CVO; it includes 27 Chinese languages which do not contrast vowel length in open syllables, but the vowel in open syllables is either phonetically long or a diphthong; it also includes languages from the Austro-Asiatic, Daic, Miao-Yao, and Sino-Tibetan phyla that have similar data pattern to Fuzhou mentioned above; namely, CVR is more tolerant of contour tones than CVVO, where VV here indicates phonological long vowel or diphthong. The fact that the number of languages in this category (66 languages) is overwhelmingly greater than the the number of languages that exhibit the pattern CVV>CVR (21 languages) corroborates the prediction that the sonorant/obstruent distinction is more crucial than the vowel/sonorant distinction in the distribution of contour tones. This is also consistent with the typological results in Gordon (1999a).

In the following section, I discuss representative examples that establish the implicational hierarchies regarding the effects of segmental composition on contour tone distribution.

4.2.2 Example Languages

4.2.2.1 Contour Tones Occur More Freely on CVV(C)

As I have mentioned, Ju|'hoasi (Snyman 1975, Dickens 1994, Miller-Ockhuizen 1998) and Navajo (Wall and Morgan 1958, Sapir and Hoijer 1967, Hoijer 1974, Kari 1976, Young and Morgan 1987, 1992) are languages in which contours tones occur more freely on long vowels than elsewhere.

Let us first look at Navajo. There are four contrastive tones in Navajo: High, Low, Fall, and Rise. Syllables can be closed by a sonorant or an obstruent, and syllable nuclei can be a short vowel, a long vowel, or a diphthong. Therefore, the syllable types in Navajo are CV, CVO, CVR, CVV, CVVO, and CVVR. There are no restrictions for the distribution of level tones High (H) and Low (L), but the contour tones Fall (H͡L) and Rise (L͡H) can only occur on long vowels and diphthongs. This is illustrated by the examples in (6) (from Wall and Morgan 1958 and Young and Morgan 1987).

(6) Navajo examples:

	H	L	H͡L	L͡H
CV	sá**ní** 'old one'	**ǹ̩tʃà** 'you're crying'	—	—
CVO	tì**níʃ**ʔį̀į̀ʔ[1] 'I'm looking'	pì**tìɬ** 'his blood'	—	—
CVR	háá**ʔál**t'èʔ 'exhumation'	pì**kʰin** 'his house'	—	—
CVV	**tíí** 'this'	**ɦìkàì** 'white'	**sáà**nìì 'old woman'	há**kòó**nèèʔ 'let's go'
CVVO	**ɬóóʔ** 'fish'	pì**nììʔ** 'his face'	**tʰáàʔ**tì 'three times'	**tèíʒ**nííɬton 'they shot at him'
CVVR	à**stsáán** 'woman'	pì**jììn** 'his song'	tàtí**nîîlʔ**į̀į̀ɬ 'we'll look at him'	**tèíl**ʔá 'they extend'

For Ju|'hoasi, there are four tone levels: Super High (a̋), High (á), Low (à) and Super Low (ȁ). There are also two tonal contours: SL͡L and L͡H. The words only come in four types—CV, CVV, CVm and CVCV. The full range of possible tonal patterns attested in each word type is given in (7) (from Miller-Ockhuizen 1998).

---

[1] The hooks under the vowel /ii/ indicate nasalization on the vowel.

(7) Ju|'hoasi examples:

CV:	bá	'father'	tzi̋	'outside'
	cà	'sweet potato'	bő̤	'porcupine burrow'
CVm:	cóm	'genital organ'	ŋ!a̋m	'inside'
	g|àm	'cheek'	ŋ!ȍm	'medicine'
CVV:	gúí	'salt'	|ʔʰa̋ű	'tree branch'
	n‡òè	'vulture'	n!ȁ̤ȍ̤	'bow'
	bȁ̤à̤	'stick game'	dshàú	'wife, woman'
CVCV:	g!árú	'drum'	zànì	'the last-born'
	zȁhȁ	'saw'	g!ȁnì	'root'
	kàqé	'marula'	córà	'smoke'

The following observations emerge from the data in (7): contour tones SL-L and L-H can occur on CVV syllables, but cannot occur on CV or CVm syllables. On CV and CVm, only the four level tones can occur.

4.2.2.2 Contour Tones Occur More Freely on CVV(C) and CVR

The languages in which contour tones occur more freely on CVV and CVR include two types: (a) languages in which vowel length is contrastive and (b) languages in which vowel length is not contrastive, but vowels in open syllables are either phonetically long or diphthongs. The former type includes languages such as Kiowa (Watkins 1984), Lithuanian (Kenstowicz 1972, Young 1991), and Nama (Beach 1938, Davey 1977, Hagman 1977), and the latter type includes many Sino-Tibetan, especially Chinese languages, e.g., Fuzhou (Liang and Feng 1996), Pingyao (Hou 1980, 1982a, b), and Wenling (Li 1979).

For the former type, let us take Nama, a central Khoisan language, as an example. Hagman (1977) claims that in Nama, there are three tone levels—High (á), Mid (ā), and Low (à), and moras are the tone-bearing units. The moraic segments are vowels and coda nasals [m] or [n], and these nasals are the only sonorant codas in the language. On CVV and CVN stems, the following tonal patterns are attested: H, M, H͡M, M͡H, L͡H, L͡M, as shown in the first two columns in (8). On CV stems, only level tones H, M, and L are attested, as shown in the third column in (8). CVO syllables also occur as the result of suffixing the masculine singular marker *-p* or feminine singular marker *-s* to CV morphemes. These obstruent suffixes do not introduce tones to the CV stem, as shown in the last column in (8).[2] It is not clear to me how the gap in L tone on CVV and CVN came about. It is possible that whatever mechanism that generated contour tones on CVV and CVN historically were at play on CV and CVO as well, but the lack of sufficient duration on these syllable types did not

---

[2] All data given here are from Hagman (1977).

allow the contour tones to surface, and L tone occurred instead. Synchronically, present-day speakers simply regard the lack of L tone as a gap in the lexical pattern and learn it as such.

(8) Nama examples:

	CVV	CVN	CV	CVO
H	ʔúú 'along, following'	ǂ'áń 'know'	tí direct quotation particle	kòmáp 'the bull'
M	nēē 'this'	kxáókūn̄ 'suspect'	hē vocative particle	ʔáokàrāp 'the enormous man'
L	—	—	kà indefinite tense particle	káísìp 'bigness, greatness'
H͡M	ǀxáā 'with'	ǀám̄ 'two'	—	—
M͡H	xūú 'from, away from'	xām̄ḿ 'lion'	—	—
L͡H	!nòó 'quiet down'	tàń 'conquer'	—	—
L͡M	hàā 'come'	ǀ'òn̄ 'name'	—	—

The latter type of languages that favor CVV and CVR for contour tones can be illustrated by two Chinese dialects—Pingyao, and Wenling. In these Chinese dialects, syllables are in the shape of CV, CVN (N=m, n, or ŋ), or CVO (O=p, t, k, or ʔ). The vowel in CV is either a diphthong or phonetically long. It is usually more than twice as long as the vowel in CVO (see Zhang 1998 for duration data on Pingyao). The attested tones on these syllable types in these languages are summarized in (9). The tones are represented in Chao letters. '1' indicates the lowest pitch and '5' indicates the highest pitch in the speaker's regular pitch range.

The facts in Wenling are very simple: contour tones can only occur on CV and CVN syllables. On CVO, only level tones are attested. In Pingyao, the observation is slightly more complicated. A wide range of contour tones can occur on CV and CVN. On CVO, contour tones can also occur. But compared to contours attested on CV and CVN, these contours are of lower tonal complexity (see (5)-(7) in Chapter 3): the two contour tones on CVO—23 and 54—are lower on the *Tonal Complexity* scale than 13 and 53, which occur on CV and CVN.

(9) Tones in Pingyao and Wenling:

	CV or CVN	CVO
Pingyao	13, 53, 35	23, 54
Wenling	55, 33, 42, 31, 13	5, 1

Let us notice that the data in (9) may pose two problems for a representational analysis which only considers contrastive length units to be relevant to contour tone distribution.

First, since there is no vowel length contrast in these languages, there is no structural pressure to posit the vowel in CV to be bimoraic. Then the advantage of CV syllables as contour carriers is not explained. The problem maybe solved by positing a minimal-word requirement of two moras: a CV syllable must be lengthened to bimoraic in the phonology. But then problems arise for CVO syllables: if the obstruent coda is non-moraic, we cannot explain why there is no lengthening for the vowel in CVO in order to satisfy the minimal-word requirement; if the obstruent coda is moraic, we cannot explain why it is, at least sometimes, not tone-bearing.

Second, since the distinction between CV(N) and CVO on their tone-bearing ability is reflected not only in the presence or absence of contours, but also in the degree of pitch excursion, it is not clear how the latter distinction can be captured by moraic representations. We will come back to this point in §6.1.

4.2.2.3 Contour Tones Occur More Freely on CVV, CVR, and CVO

Only four languages in the survey display the pattern in which contour tones occur more freely on CVV, CVR, and CVO than CV. They are Hausa (Newman 1986, 1990), Luganda (Ashton et al. 1954, Tucker 1962, Snoxall 1967, Stevick 1969, Hyman and Katamba 1990, 1993), Musey (Shryock 1993a, 1996), and Ngizim (Schuh 1971, 1981). In fact, all four languages, contour tones can only occur on CVV, CVR, and CVO. The fact that there are languages that display this pattern is slightly surprising, as we have shown that obstruents lack the crucial harmonics for tonal perception, and thus should not act as tone bearers (see §2.2). But a closer look at these languages suggests that they are less surprising than they first appeared to be.

There are three lexical tones in Hausa—High (H), Low (L), and Fall (H͡L). H and L tones can occur on all syllable types—CVV, CVR, CVO, and CV, while H͡L can only occur on CVV, CVR, and CVO. In a brief phonetic study of Hausa, Gordon (1998) found that the vowel in CVO is significantly longer when it carries a falling tone than when it carries a level tone (112ms for High-toned vowel, 105ms for Low-toned vowel, 133ms for Fall-toned vowel). His study included only three CVO words—one with H, one with L, and one with H͡L, each with eight repetitions. To corroborate the validity of the above claim about vowel duration, I conducted a similar phonetic study which included 17 CVO words—seven with H, six with L, and four with H͡L. All words in the word list are disyllabic, with the first syllable being the target CVO syllable. The vowel nucleus of the target syllable is always /a/. The complete word list is given in (10). Target syllables are in bold; H=á, L=à, and H͡L=â.

(10) Hausa CVO word list:

H	L	H͡L
máskíí 'greasiness'	**gàs**kéé 'indeed'	**kjâs**sáá 'old grass mats'
ʃákkà 'doubting'	**hàt**táá 'even *x*.'	**kâg**gá 'round houses'
táfkì 'large pond'	**kàf**tân 'caftan'	**tâb**báà 'scars'
ʃáddá 'hole of latrine'	**ƙàt**tíí 'huge'	**gâɓ**ɓáá 'joints'
tábkà 'did much of sth.'	**àd**dá 'matchet'	
ɓázgè 'became severed'	**càz**bíí 'praying beads'	
dábbà 'any animal'		

The same native speaker of Hausa as in Gordon's experiment participated in the study here. He read the word list, each word with five repetitions. The data were digitized with a sampling rate of 20kHz onto Kay Elemetrics Computerized Speech Laboratory (CSL) and the duration of the vowel in the target syllables was measured from the spectrogram window. The result of the duration measurements is plotted in (11). The error bars incidate one standard deviation. As we can see, the average duration of the vowel in CVO is longer when it carries H͡L than when it carries H or L. A one-way ANOVA with vowel duration as the dependent variable and tone as the independent variable shows a significant effect: $F(2, 82)=17.865$, $p<.0001$. Fisher's PLSD post-hoc tests show that the difference between H and H͡L is significant at $p<.005$ level, and the difference between L and H͡L is significant at $p<.0001$ level. This pattern is consistent with Gordon (1998)'s results.

(11) Hausa vowel duration in CVO (ms):

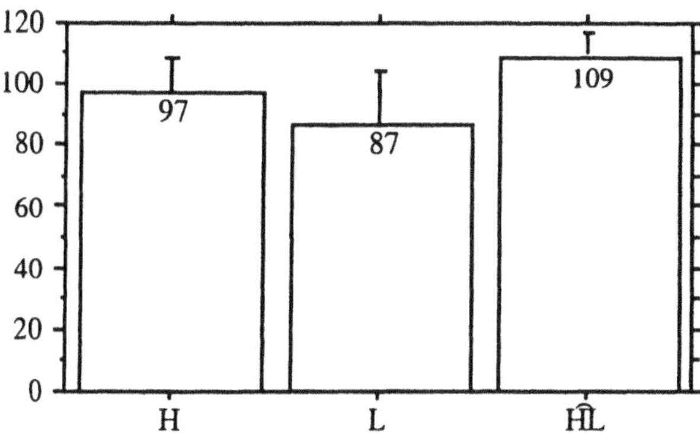

For CVO syllables that carry HL̂, the pitch excursion of the falling contour was also investigated and it was compared to the falling excursion of HL̂ on CVV syllables. Three words with each syllable type were included in the investigation. The word list is given in (12).

(12) Hausa HL̂ word list:

CVV		CVO	
láàlá	'indolence'	**kâg**gá	'round houses'
jáàráá	'children'	**gâɓ**ɓáá	'joints'
máàráí	'a kind of bird'	**râg**gá	'rags'

Pitch tracks of the tokens were made using *PitchWorks*, a software system for pitch tracking developed by SCICON R&D. The pitch values (in Hz) at the beginning and end of the vowel in the first syllable of each word were measured. Results show that the average pitch fall for the CVO syllables is only around 50% of that for CVV syllables (20Hz for CVO, 41Hz for CVV). Relatedly, for the words in (12), the vowels in Fall-toned CVV and CVO have an average duration of 247ms and 107ms respectively.

Therefore a more accurate description on the contour distribution in Hausa is: HL̂ can freely occur on CVV and CVR; it can also occur on CVO upon lengthening of the vowel and reduction of the pitch excursion; it cannot occur on CV syllables. Therefore, to some extent, Hausa is similar to the Chinese dialects described in (9)—the contour restriction on CVO is manifested not by the absence of the contour, but by the pitch excursion of the contour.

One remaining question for Hausa is why CV syllables do not lengthen to carry the falling contour as CVO syllables do. A brief phonetic investigation of duration of the words in (13) (same speaker, same methods as the duration study above) shows that the vowel in CV has an average of duration of 94ms when it has a H tone and 89ms when it has a L tone. These values are apparently not much different from the vowel duration in CVO (97ms in CV́O, 87ms in CV̀O). Gordon (1998) provides some insight into this question: since there is vowel length contrast in open syllables while there is no such contrast in closed syllables, CVO has more freedom in subphonemic lengthening than CV because such lengthening does not jeopardize any contrast in CVO, but could potentially do so in CV. I adopt his view here.

(13) Hausa CV word list:

H		L	
másù	'to them'	**ƙà**hóó	'horn'
dásà	'transplanted'	**à**kúl	'stop it'
káfì	'became embedded in mud'	**à**kúú	'parrot'
káɗè	'shook dust from garment'	**fà**sú	'burst out'
káfà	'small hole'	**dà**báŋ	'different *x*'
támá	'ore'	**hà**râm	'an unlawful act by the Muslim code'

From the sources I have consulted (Ashton et al. 1954, Tucker 1962, Snoxall 1967, Stevick 1969, Hyman and Katamba 1990,1993), the contour tone restrictions in Luganda are very similar to those of Hausa. It also has tones H, L, and H͡L, and the syllable types CVV, CVR, CVO, and CV. Except for its word-final CV syllable being able to carry the falling contour (to which we will turn in §4.4.2.2), the contour restrictions are exactly the same as in Hausa: High and Low can occur on all syllables; Fall can occur on CVV, CVR, and CVO. Although none of the sources documents the phonetic details of the realization of tones on different syllable types, one source—Snoxall (1967)—mentions that the low portion of the falling contour on CVO is merely a 'psychological low tone' (p.xx). Its effect is primarily observed from the downstep it induces on the following syllable.

To corroborate this description, I located a Luganda tape in the UCLA Language Archive (made by Laura Collins in 1972). The hypotheses I set out to test were the following: first, a CVO syllable that carries a lexical H͡L would not have a significant falling pitch excursion, while a CVV syllable would; second, a H tone that follows a H͡L-toned CVO would have a lower pitch than word-initial H tone or a H tone that follows another H-toned syllable. To test these hypotheses, I found four instances of CV́Ò.CV́, two instances of CV́V̀.CV, and two instances of CV́Ŕ.CV́ on the tape. These words were read in isolation during the original recording. The limited number of tokens does not allow any statistical tests, but impressionistically, both of the hypotheses seem to be supported. First, the pitch on the CVO syllables, which supposedly carry a H͡L, does not show any significant falling excursion; but the H͡L on CVV does show a significant falling excursion. Second, the H tone on the second syllable of CV̂O.CV́ has a considerably lower pitch than both the average pitch of the first syllable and the pitch of the second syllable in CV́Ŕ.CV́. These observations can be checked against three representative tokens [kúɗdá] 'to return', [mjáàká] 'years', and [`nfúḿbá] 'I cook' in (14). The 'H͡L' tone on the first syllable of [kúɗdá] does not have any phonetic pitch fall; while the H͡L on the first syllable of [mjáàká] has a significant falling excursion. Moreover, the H tone on the second syllable of [kúɗdá] has a lower pitch than both the first syllable of [kúɗdá] and the second syllable of [`nfúḿbá]. These data indicate that the description in Snoxall (1967) is accurate: the major cue for the H͡L tone on CVO is the downstepping of the following H, not the pitch excursion on CVO itself.

(14) a. [kúɗdá] 'to return'

b. [mjáàká] 'years'

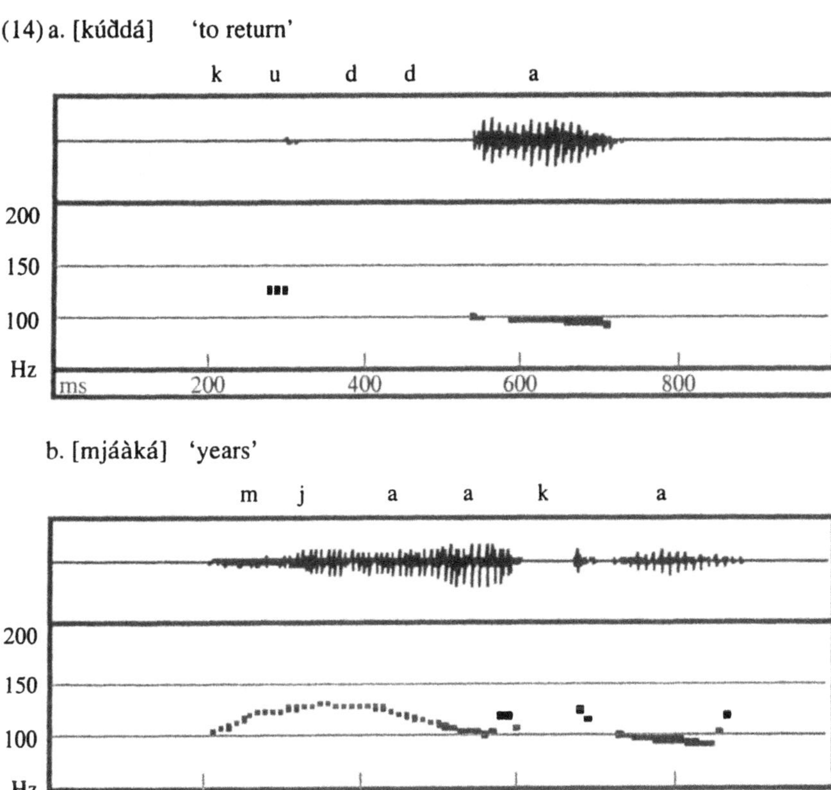

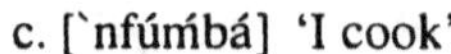
c. [`nfúḿbá] 'I cook'

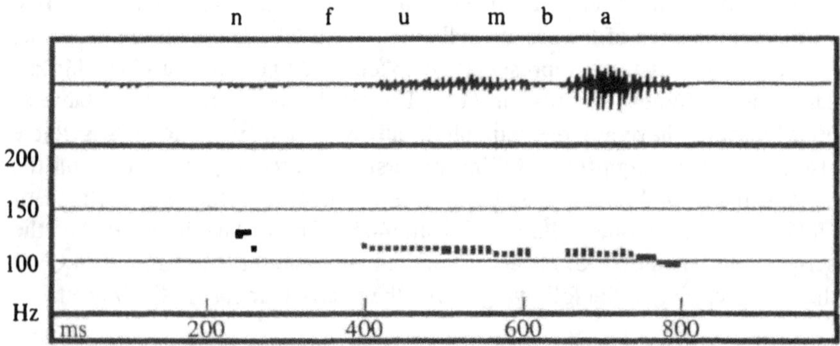

Therefore, Luganda does not seem to be an example of *surface* contour tones occurring more freely on CVV, CVR, and CVO. Rather, the phonological category H͡L on CVO is realized as a H tone followed by the downstepping of the following H. I do not have phonetic data on any CV́Ò.CV̀ sequences. Therefore it is not clear to me at this point how the falling tone in this context is realized.

In Musey, the syllable types are also CVV, CVR, CVO, and CV (Shryock 1993a, 1996). Shryock states that the tone-bearing segments in Musey are vowels and consonant codas. There are three level tones H, M, and L, and the inventory of contour tones is H͡L, M͡H, M͡L, L͡H, and L͡M. Examples of Musey tones, drawn from Shryock 1993a, are given in (15).

(15) Musey examples:

	CV	CVO	CVR	CVV
H	tʃó 'hair'	vót 'road'	jám 'head'	véé 'granary'
M	sī 'ocher'	łēk 'chicken'	mbūl 'oil'	sūū 'people'
L	tʃà 'woman'	kūlùf 'fish'	vùn 'mouth'	ŋgàà 'giraffe'
H͡L	—	—	káŋ̀ga 'down'	kúùzí 'cucumber'
M͡H	—	—	—	ʔōó 'grace'
M͡L	—	ɓa᷆k 'speech'	sūm̀ 'bear'	wāì 'argument'
L͡H	—	ʤǎt 'hat'	ɦ̀ŋ́ 'fish trap'	lùú 'frog'
L͡M	—	—	ndàī 'neighbor'	mbàī 'aunt'

Clearly, CV syllables can only carry level tones. But let us notice that CVO, which is supposedly bimoraic, can only carry two out of the five possible contour tones—M͡L and L͡H. Shryock does not give any other types of contours on CVO in either of his works. It is plausible that the missing contour pattern M͡H in CVR is accidental, but it is unlikely that three contour patterns can be accidentally missing. Therefore, the most plausible explanation is that CVO is in fact restricted for contour tone bearing. The restriction is manifested neither by the absence of contours, nor by lesser degrees of pitch excursion, but by a smaller contour tone inventory. Hence in Musey, CVV and CVR are better contour bearers than CVO, which is in turn a better contour bearer than CV.

One more complication in Musey stems from the observation that Shryock transcribes the contour tone on CVO solely on the vowel (e.g., ɮăt), while the contour tone on CVR across the entire rime (e.g., sūm̀). This indicates that he in fact does not consider the obstruent coda to be phonetically tone-bearing—the burden of the phonological contour tone falls solely on the vowel. Lacking phonetic data on this language, no definitive conclusion can be made regarding the duration and pitch excursion of the contour tones on CVO. But from personal communication, Shryock states that the CVO syllables are impressionistically longer when they carry a contour tone.

According to Schuh (1971), in Ngizim, there is a synchronic process in which a Low tone deletes obligatorily when it occurs together with a H tone on a CV syllable, but only optionally so on CVV, CVR, or CVO. Schuh (1971)'s formulation of the rule is given in (16).

(16) Complex Tone Levelling
[-H] → Ø / [+H] when both tones are on the same syllable
Conditions: Optional if [+H][-H] occurs on a long syllable (CVV or CVC)
Obligatory on a short σ or when the sequence is [-H][+H]

Therefore, it seems that a CVC syllable (CVR or CVO) in Ngizim is as good a contour carrier as a CVV syllable. Again, lacking phonetic data, it is not clear how a contour tone is realized on a CVO syllable. But from personal communication, Schuh has also expressed that CVO syllables are impressionistically longer when they carry a contour tone.

4.2.3 Local Conclusion: Segmental Effects

This concludes the discussion on the influence of segmental composition on the positional prominence behavior of contour tones. The following implicational hierarchies have been established: all else being equal, if CV(C) can carry contours, then CVV(C) can carry contours with equal or greater tonal complexity; if CVO can carry contours, then CVR and CVV can carry contours with equal or greater tonal complexity; and if CVR can carry contours then CVV can carry contours with equal or greater tonal complexity. All of these conform to the prediction of the direct approach made in §3.4.1), as we can safely conclude the following relations regarding the $C_{CONTOUR}$ values of CV, CVO, CVR, and CVV, as in (17).

(17) a. $C_{CONTOUR}(CVV(C)) > C_{CONTOUR}(CV(C))$;
b. $C_{CONTOUR}(CVV) > C_{CONTOUR}(CVR) > C_{CONTOUR}(CVO)$.

Moreover, these relations on $C_{CONTOUR}$ are the only ones that we can conclude from what we know about the phonetics of these syllable types. We observe no implicational relation between CV and CVO in their contour bearing ability. For example, in Fuzhou Chinese, CV syllables are better contour carriers than CVO; but in Hausa, CVO syllables are better contour carriers than CV. As we have seen, the contour-bearing behavior of CV and CVO is dependent on the phonetic duration of the vowel in the language in question: in Fuzhou Chinese, the vowel in CV is significantly longer than the vowel in CVO; in Hausa, the vowel in CVO is lengthened when it carries a contour tone. Therefore, the contour distribution patterns in these languages are also consistent with the prediction of the direct approach of positional prominence.

We may have noticed that long vowels being privileged contour tone carriers is also consistent with the other approaches to contour tone distribution. But as pointed out by Gordon (1998, 1999a), the fact that CVO is seldom counted as a privileged contour tone carrier indicates the contrast-specificity of weight criteria, since CVO is commonly counted as heavy for stress placement. This contrast-specificity is also governed by the phonetic peculiarity of contour tones, since as I have discussed, sonority is a necessity for tonal perception, while only preferable, but not necessary for stress attraction.

Finally, recall that in §3.3 (see especially (8) in Chapter 3), I identified four factors within segmental composition that may influence sonorous rime duration: besides VV>V and VR>VO, there are also the relations $V_{[-high]} > V_{[+high]}$ and Vd > Vt (d=voiced obstruent, t=voiceless obstruent). In the survey, I did not find any languages in which these durational differences have an effect on contour tone distribution. I will come back to this point in §4.6 where exceptions of the survey are discussed.

4.3 STRESS

4.3.1 General Observations

In 22 languages in the survey (11.8%), shown in (18), contour tones occur more freely on stressed syllables than unstressed syllables. There is no language that displays the opposite pattern in which contour tones occur more freely on unstressed than stressed syllables, when all else is equal.

(18) Contour tones occur more freely on stressed syllables (22 languages):

Language phylum	No. of languages	Languages
Afro-Asiatic	1	Sayanci
Creole	1	Nubi
Kiowa Tanoan	1	Jemez
Niger-Congo	11	Ciyao, Haya, Kinyarwanda, Chimahuta Makonde, Chimaraba Makonde, Ngazia, Ngumbi (Kombe), Runyankore, Sechuana, Venda, Xhosa
Nilo-Saharan	2	Camus, Lango
Oto-Manguean	4	Lealao Chinantec, Isthmus Zapotec, Macuiltianguis Zapotec, Sierra Juarez Zapotec
Sino-Tibetan	2	Beijing, Rgyalthang Tibetan

These observations lead to the implicational hierarchy in (19).

(19) All else being equal, if an unstressed syllable can carry contours, then a stressed syllable can carry contours of equal or greater tonal complexity.

In the 22 languages listed in (18), 11 of them are from the Niger-Congo language phylum, and all these 11 languages are Central Bantu languages. Many Central Bantu languages, especially those that have lost the vowel length contrast of Proto-Bantu, have penultimate stress. This stress has been consistently reported to have a drastic lengthening effect on the penultimate syllable. This is in fact the case for 7 out of the 11 languages here: Chimahuta Makone, Chimaraba Makonde, Ngazia, Runyankore, Sechuana, Venda, and Xhosa. In these languages, contour tones are generally restricted to the penultimate position of a word. My data source of Ngumbi (Kombe)—Elimelech (1976)—does not mention where the stress falls in this language. But from its lack of vowel length contrast and its restriction of the only contour tone—$\widehat{\text{HL}}$—to the penult,[3] we may reasonably assume that it also has penultimate stress. In Haya, there is vowel length contrast, but the sources I consulted—Byarushengo et al. (1976) and Hyman and Byarushengo (1984)—mention that there is still penultimate accent in this language. The only contour tone—$\widehat{\text{HL}}$—is also restricted to the penult in Haya. In Ciyao and Kinyarwanda, there is vowel length contrast, and the sources I consulted—Sanderson (1954), Whiteley (1966), Mtenje (1993), and Hyman and Ngunga (1994) for Ciyao; Kimenyi (1976, 1979) for Kinyarwanda—do not

[3] According to Elimelech (1976), the $\widehat{\text{HL}}$ tone may also occur word-finally. But such examples are extremely rare.

mention penultimate stress for these languages. But the penult is a more privileged position for contour tones in both languages. I will come back to them in §4.3.2.4 and §4.5.2.2 respectively.

In most northern Chinese dialects (Mandarin dialects according to Grime's classification), syllables are equally stressed. But some functional or reduplicative suffixes can be stressless. Usually, only regularly stressed syllables can carry contour tones. Stressless syllables only have level tones. Among the 14 Mandarin dialects I surveyed, only Beijing has a clear description to this effect (Chao 1948, 1968, Dow 1972, 1974). Therefore I only included Beijing in the language count here.

In the next section, I provide examples from Jemez, Xhosa, Beijing Chinese, and Ciyao to illustrate the possible effects of stress on contour tone distribution.

4.3.2 Example Languages

4.3.2.1 Jemez

Jemez, a Kiowa Tanoan language, presents a typical case in which contour tones are restricted to stressed syllables. All syllables are open in Jemez. There is vowel length contrast on the initial syllable of the word, which is also the position for word stress. Phonetic data in Bell (1993) show that stressed short vowels are longer than unstressed short vowels. There are four tones in Jemez—H, M, L and $\widehat{\text{HL}}$. The only distributional restriction is that $\widehat{\text{HL}}$ can only occur on the initial syllable of the word. Examples of Jemez are given in (20).

(20) Jemez examples:

cê	'stick'		
côtē	'antlers'	*cōtê	*hypothetical*
hõ̂:mũ̀tē	'shovel'	*hȭ:mũ̂tē	*hypothetical*

4.3.2.2 Xhosa

As I have mentioned, Xhosa (Lanham 1958, 1963, Jordan 1966, Claughton 1983) is a Central Bantu language with penultimate stress. There is no contrastive vowel length in Xhosa, and the major phonetic correlate of stress is the prolonged duration of the vocoid. All syllables are open.[4] There are three tones in Xhosa—H, L, and $\widehat{\text{HL}}$. On verb, noun, and qualificative stems, there are

---

[4] A nasal /m/ seems to occur in the coda position sometimes. But in this case, the /m/ is syllabic (Jordan 1966: p. 15).

generally no restrictions on the occurrence of level tones, except that a H cannot occur after a H͡L. But H͡L can only occur in the penultimate position, which is the stressed position. Examples of falling tones are given in (21).

(21) Xhosa examples:

úkù'ɓônà	'to see'	*ûkù'ɓònà	*hypothetical*
ísì'ɓâjà	'sheep fold'	*úkû'ɓònà	*hypothetical*
ísì'p^{h}ôxò	'fool'	*úkù'ɓònâ	*hypothetical*
áɓà'k^{h}ûlù	'big'		

Lanham (1958) reports that in penultimate word stress is only potential, but not necessary in connected speech. When the word is not in utterance-final position, the penultimate stress and lengthening are often not realized. In this case, when the last two syllables in the word have a H͡L-L tonal sequence, it is realized as H-H. This is illustrated by an example in (22): when the penultimate word stress for ísìɓâyà is lost in the utterance, it is realized as ísìɓáyá. No H͡L-H sequence is attested on two adjacent syllables in Xhosa.

(22) Xhosa tonal alternation:

ísì'ɓâyà	'sheep fold'
ísìɓáyá ésì'k^{h}ûlù	'big sheep fold'

One complication in Xhosa is that H͡L can also occur in the following grammatical morphemes: short perfect tense suffix /-ê/; indicative remote past tense prefixes /ndâ-/, /wâ-/, etc.; first syllable of the locative demonstrative copulative /nâsí/; noun class 1a plural prefix /ô-/; short 2nd positional demonstrative /lô/; and noun class 10 prefixes /ìm-, ìn-, ìɲ-, ìŋ-/. The falling tone in these morphemes does not necessarily occur in the penultimate position of the word or the utterance. But Lanham (1958, 1963) states that the vowels that carry H͡L in these morphemes are lengthened. This lengthening is also reflected in the practical orthography of Xhosa, which transcribes these vowels as long.

4.3.2.3 Beijing Chinese

As mentioned in §4.3.1, under this category falls also Beijing, a Northern Chinese dialect in which regular syllables are equally stressed, but a stressless functional or reduplicative morpheme can sometimes occur word-finally.[5] The

---

[5] As a native Chinese speaker who grew up in northern China, I believe that Beijing is just one example of many Northern Chinese dialects that have this property. But in dialect descriptions, this is not always documented. Therefore I only included

difference between Beijing and the rest of the languages mentioned in this section is that in Beijing, we identify the stressless syllable instead of the stressed syllable in a word. There are four possible tones on regular syllables in Beijing: 55, 35, 21[6], and 51. But on a final stressless syllable, only level tones can be realized. These syllables are usually described as having the 'neutral tone'. Chao (1948, 1968) gives the following description of its realization under different tonal environments:

(23) Half-Low after 55:	tʰa˥ tə.|	'his'
Mid after 35:	ʂei˧˥ tə·|	'whose'
Half-High after 21:	ni˨˩ tə˙|	'yours'
Low after 51:	ta˥˩tə.|	'big one(s)'

The fact that these stressless syllables are not specified for tone and their pitch realization is perceived as level indicates that their lack of stress has an important effect on their tone-bearing ability. These stressless syllables are extremely short. A phonetic experiment I conducted (details discussed in §5.2.2) indicates that the average duration of the sonorous phase in the rime is only about 110ms (compared to over 200ms for stressed syllables). Therefore, given that the direct approach and contrast-specific approach both acknowledge the importance of duration in contour tone bearing, either directly or indirectly, the facts of Beijing Chinese are consistently with these two approaches.

4.3.2.4 Ciyao

Ciyao (Sanderson 1954, Whiteley 1966, Mtenje 1993, Hyman and Ngunga 1994) is also a Bantu language. Unlike in Xhosa, vowel length is contrastive in Ciyao. In present-day Bantu languages, penultimate stress and lengthening are usually only attested in languages that have lost the vowel length contrast. Therefore, there is no clear mention of penultimate stress in Ciyao in the literature. In fact, Sanderson (1954) states that 'In most Bantu languages the penultimate syllable is always stressed but this is not the case for Ciyao.' (p. 2) But the following two facts indicate that we ought to be more cautious in claiming that Ciyao completely lacks penultimate stress. First, Sanderson (1954) himself hints that penultimate stress is actually often attested. He states that 'The accent never falls on the last syllable of a word, but the addition of a monosyllabic demonstrative or locative suffix shifts it so that it falls, often strongly, on the penultimate of the resulting complete word.' (p. 3) He also

---

Beijing Chinese in this category of contour tone distribution. This does not exclude the possibility that other Northern Chinese dialects in the survey also have this property.

6 This tone is realized as 213 in utterance-final position.

states that 'In words of three syllables the second tends to be more (or less) accented.' (p. 3) Second, phonetic work by Hubbard (1994) reveals that the lengthening of penultimate syllables is also present in less dramatic form in languages such as Runyambo, which has preserved the vowel length contrast in Proto-Bantu. She concludes that penultimate prominence "is a postlexical, intonational prosodic feature typical of the Bantu family" (p. 11). Therefore, we may reasonably infer that the less dramatic penultimate lengthening is also present in Ciyao, even though it is not a penultimate-stress Bantu language in the traditional sense.[7]

There are four surface tones in Ciyao: High (H), Low (L), Fall (H͡L) and Rise (L͡H). Hyman and Ngunga (1994) assume that only H is represented in the underlying representation and L is inserted as the default tone. The tonal realization rules they posit are given in (24). They assume moraic extrametricality in Ciyao: the word-final mora is extrametrical and is marked as <μ>. A circled μ represents a toneless mora in the metrical representation, and is therefore non-final. The final syllable is subject to a final shortening rule and is therefore always monomoraic.

The High Tone Spreading rule in (24a) spreads a High tone to the following mora. The Long Spread Right rule in (24b) states that in a bimoraic (=long-

---

[7] A brief phonetic study was carried out to test the hypothesis that the duration of the vowel in a penultimate syllable is longer than the same vowel elsewhere. From the discussion later in this section, the particularly relevant comparison is between a long vowel in the penultimate position and the same long vowel in the antepenultimate position. In an audio tape of Mozambique Ciyao recorded by Kathleen Hubbard in 1992, I found 12 instances of /uu/ in penultimate position and 6 instances of /uu/ in antepenultimate position. The relevant words are given below. All vowels have level tones. Hubbard (1994) does not provide English translation for the trisyllabic words.

/uu/ in penult			/uu/ in antepenult	
guuma	(3 reps)	'scream'	kuunava	'1sg object, nava'
puuga	(2 reps)	'get fresh air'	kuumenda	'1sg object, menda'
puuta	(4 reps)	'hit, beat up'	kuunona	'1sg object, nona'
suuga	(3 reps)	'swim'	kuunuma	'1sg object, numa'

These words were digitized at a sampling rate of 20kHz using the Computerized Speech Laboratory (CSL) by Key Elemetrics. Spectrograms of these words were made and the duration of the /uu/ vowel in these words was measured in the spectrogram window. Results show that the average duration for the /uu/ vowel is 128ms when it is in the penult, and is 109ms when it is in the antepenult. Given the limited number of tokens available, the comparison does not show a significant difference (one-way ANOVA, $F(1, 16)=2.24$, $p=0.15$). But this difference may well turn out to be significant when a more carefully designed study with more speakers and more tokens is carried out.

voweled) syllable, if a H tone is associated with the first mora, then it spreads to the second mora of the syllable, provided that there is a toneless mora following this syllable. Since the toneless mora is non-final, this rule serves the purpose of eliminating the possibility of having a $\widehat{HL}$ contour on a pre-penultimate long vowel. The Long Penult Delinking rule in (24c) delinks a H that is linked to the second mora of the penult if the H is also linked to the first mora of the syllable. The H Pullback rule in (24d) delinks the word-final H and spreads it to the second mora of the penult if the penult has a long vowel. The Long Spread Left rule in (24e) changes a $\widehat{LH}$ contour to H on a long vowel that is pre-penultimate.

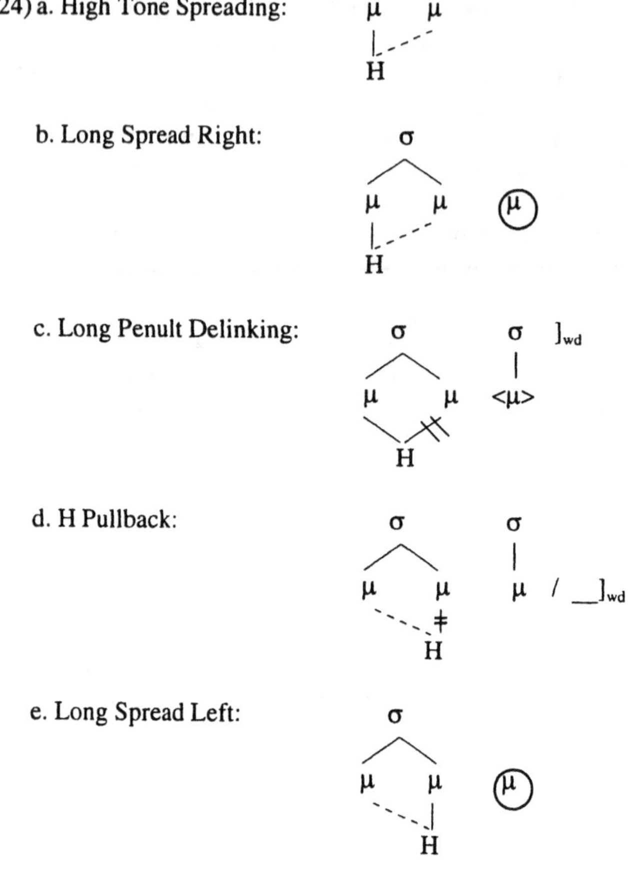

High Tone Spreading feeds Long Spread Right, which has the following consequence: a falling tone can occur on the long vowel of a penultimate syllable, but not elsewhere. This is illustrated by the derivations in (25). High Tone Spreading also feeds Long Penult Delinking. Therefore, in the penultimate position, if a H is assigned to the first mora of a long vowel, a $\widehat{HL}$ fall results.

Thus the overall consequence of rules (24a)—(24c) is that the falling contour is restricted to the long vowel of the penultimate syllable of an utterance.

(25) /ku-sevees-a/	/ku-manyiidil-a/	UR
|	|	
H	H	
ku-sévées-a	ku-mányíidil-a	High Tone Spreading
——	ku-mányíídil-a	Long Spread Right
[ku-sévées-a]	[ku-mányíídil-a]	SR
'to work'	'to know'	

When a H is associated with the final mora of the utterance, the High Pullback rule in (24d) creates a rising contour on the long vowel in the penultimate position. The Long Spread Left rule in (24e) ensures that in pre-penultimate positions, no rising tone surfaces. Therefore the overall consequence of rules (24d) and (24e) is that the rising contour is also restricted to the long vowel of the penultimate syllable of an utterance.

The conspiracy of the rules posited by Hyman and Ngunga can be clearly seen: contour tones gravitate to long vowels in the stressed position; or more precisely, they are eliminated in unstressed positions. Long vowels in pre-penultimate, interpreted here an unstressed position, cannot carry contours. The analysis Hyman and Ngunga propose does capture the facts, but it misses the conspiracy, and consequently misses the phonetic considerations that motivate the analysis. Given that these phonetic considerations are independently needed in phonology, it is quite plausible that they also play a role in the data patterns here.

4.3.3 Local Conclusion: Stress Effects

In the discussion of the influence of stress on contour tone distribution, I have established the following implicational hierarchy: all else being equal, if an unstressed syllable can carry contours, then a stressed syllable can carry contours of equal or greater tonal complexity. Given that stressed syllables are generally longer than unstressed syllables due to lengthening under stress (see §3.3), we can conclude the following relation between the $C_{CONTOUR}$ values based on stress, when all else is equal: $C_{CONTOUR}(\text{stressed } \sigma) > C_{CONTOUR}(\text{unstressed } \sigma)$. Then the implicational hierarchy established in the typology is consistent with the prediction of the direct approach (see §3.4.1).

The result of the survey regarding stress is also consistent with the contrast-specific and general-purpose positional markedness approaches, since stressed syllables are not only privileged carriers of contour tones due to their longer duration, but also privileged carriers of many other phonological contrasts.

Therefore, independently, the contour distribution facts in relation to stress do not necessary constitute an argument for the direct approach. But this section does serve the purpose of showing that the facts are at least consistent with the direct approach. Together with other facts that are only consistent with the direct approach (see §4.4, §4.5 and Chapter 5), the facts discussed in this section can be taken as part of the necessary argument. Moreover, if the durational hypothesis of Ciyao is correct, then we have a case in which the perception of stress is unclear, but the durational difference still leads to a positional effect on contour tone distribution. This scenario is only consistent with the direct approach, not the other approaches.

4.4 PROSODIC-FINAL POSITION

4.4.1 General Observations

The advantages of the final syllable for contour tone bearing has already been pointed out by Clark (1983). Clark was the first to attribute this effect to final lengthening. The languages that she claims to have such an effect include Oh̃uh̃u Igbo, Kikuyu, and Peki Ewe. My survey further establishes the correlation between final syllable and contour tone bearing. Let us notice that the effect of prosodic-final positions on contour tone distribution is only predicted by the direct and contrast-specific approaches, since these positions are not privileged contrast-licensing positions in a general-purpose fashion and are usually non-neutralizing with respect to length, hence the effect cannot be captured by the general-purpose positional markedness or the moraic approach.

In 47 languages in the survey (25.1%), contour tones occur more freely on the final syllable of words or utterances than non-final syllables. The languages that display this pattern are given in (26). There is no language that displays the opposite pattern.

(26) Contour tones occur more freely on prosodic-final syllables (47 languages):

Language phylum	No. of languages	Languages
Afro-Asiatic	5	Agaw (Awiya), Bolanci (Bole), Galla (Booran Oromo), Rendille, Sayanci
Daic	1	Ron Phibun Thai
Niger-Congo	19	Bandi, Kivunjo Chaga, Machame Chaga, Etung, Gã, Kenyang, Kikuyu, Kisi, Kɔnni, Nana Kru, Wobe Kru, Kukuya (Southern Teke), Lama, Luganda, Mende, Ngamambo, Ngazija, Ngie, Ngumbi, Tiv
Nilo-Saharan	2	Bari, Lulubo,
Oto-Manguean	3	San Andrés Chichahuaxtla Trique, San Juan Copala Trique, Mitla Zapotec
Sino-Tibetan	15	Beijing, Fuzhou, Kunming, Nanchang, Nanjing, Pingyang, Pingyao, Shuozhou, Suzhou, Shexian, Wuhan, Wuyi, Xining, Xinzhou, Yanggu
Trans-New Guinea	1	Mianmin

These observations lead to the implicational hierarchy in (27).

(27) All else being equal, if non-final syllables in a prosodic domain can carry contours, then the final syllable of the same prosodic domain can carry contours with equal or greater tonal complexity.

In the next section, I provide examples from Etung, Luganda, Mianmin, and a number of Chinese dialects to illustrate the effects of prosodic-final position on contour tone distribution.

4.4.2 Example Languages

4.4.2.1 Etung

Let us first look at Etung (Edmondson and Bendor-Samuel 1966), another Bantu language. There are three basic tones in Etung—High (H), Low (L), and Downstep (ꜜH). The syllable in Etung can be of the shape CV, CVO or CVR. There does not seem to be vowel length contrast. While there is no restriction on the occurrence of level tones, the falling and rising contours (H͡L, H͡ꜜH, L͡H) are restricted to the final syllable of phonological words. Edmondson and Bendor-Samuel accounts for this effect by considering tone to be a feature of the phonological word. They identify 12 patterns of tonal melody composed of the three level tones and map them from left to right to syllables in a phonological word. These patterns are shown in (28).

(28)

Patterns	σσσ	σσ	σ
1	L L L	L L	L
2a	L H H	L H	L͡H
2b	!H H H	!H H	!H
3	H L L	H L	H͡L
4	H H H	H H	H
5	L H L	L H͡L	—
6	L L H	L L͡H	—
7	H H L	H H͡L	—
8	H !H H	H !H	H͡!H
9	H L H	H L͡H	—
10	L H !H	L H͡!H	—
11	H H !H	H H͡!H	—

Let us take the proposed tonal melodies for granted for a moment. We notice two things in this analysis: first, the fact that contour tones only occur on the final syllable of the word is purely the byproduct of left-to-right mapping; second, it crucially depends on the derivationality of the association convention. It is not clear how this effect can be captured in a non-derivational framework like Optimality Theory without referring to the final syllable as a privileged position for contours. In fact, I will show in §6.2 that using ALIGN-R constraints (McCarthy and Prince 1993) alone cannot capture this effect. The analysis must refer to the lengthened duration of the final syllable and encode it as a privileged position to carry contours.

4.4.2.2 Luganda

Luganda presents another interesting example for this pattern. I have mentioned in §4.2.2.3 that Luganda can have a falling tone on non-final CVV, CVR, and CVO syllables, but it can also have a falling tone on a word-final CV syllable. What makes the CV syllable in final position special so that it can carry contour tones?

Luganda has a vowel length contrast, but it has a phonological rule that shortens the long vowel in final position to a short vowel, eliminating the vowel length contrast in this position (Stevick 1969). Without this contrast, it is possible that there is a strong final lengthening effect, as no length contrast will be jeopardized. Stevick (1969) in fact uses a raised dot to indicate phonetic lengthening of the final short vowel when it carries a falling tone. I therefore hypothesize that the word-final syllable is subject to strong final lengthening, and the extra duration facilitates the realization of contour tones.

To test this hypothesis, 20 disyllabic words were extracted from a Luganda tape made by Laura Collins in 1972 in the UCLA Language Archive and digitized using Kay Elemetrics CSL. The vowel duration of the initial syllable was measured for 12 words; the vowel duration for the final syllable was measured for 12 words as well, some overlapping with the former group.[8] To eliminate the influence of syllable type, vowel length and tone, all targeted syllables are open, contain a short vowel, and are level-toned.[9] The vowel quality was also matched between the two groups (seven [a]'s, two [u]'s, two [i]'s, one [e]). To compare the duration of short vowels with long vowels, seven trisyllabic words which contain a long vowel in the penultimate position were also included in the study. Among the seven measured vowels, there are three [a]'s, two [i]'s, one [e] and one [o]. The complete word list is given in (29).

(29) Luganda word list:

Non-final short vowel		Final short vowel		Long vowel	
ppátà	'hinge'	ppá**tà**	'hinge'	kù**wá:**bá	'to go astray'
kkázì	'fat woman'	kkâ**pà**	'cat'	kù**sá:**zà	'to sizzle'
màlá	'finish!'	kû**bbà**	'to steal'	mù**já:**jú	'wild cat'
mmálà	'I finish'	kû**ttá**	'to kill'	kù**wó:**lá	'to scoop out'
mpàkâ	'a dispute'	kû**ddà**	'to return'	kù**lǐ:**má	'to spy'
mbálá	'I count'	mà**lá**	'finish!'	kù**lǐ:**rá	'to eat well'
ndwáddé	'disease'	mmá**là**	'I finish'	kù**wé:**rá	'to rest'
kùvá	'to come from'	kì**vú**	'?'		
mmúlà	'pepper'	mùjá:**jú**	'wild cat'		
kìvú	'?'[10]	mù**wí**	'the giver'		
zzíkè	'chimpanzee'	nnâ:ná**nsì**	'pineapple'		
ngègê	'bream'	ndwá**ddé**	'disease'		

The duration results are given in the bar-plot in (30). A one-way ANOVA with vowel duration as the dependent variable and vowel type/position as the independent variable shows a significant effect: $F(2, 28)=63.337$, $p<.0001$. Fisher's PLSD post-hoc tests show that all pairs of comparison are significant at $p<.0001$ level.

---

8 Ideally, same words should be used for the measurement of both initial and final syllables. But due to the limited data on the tape, I could not find enough words whose initial and final syllables are matched for vowel quality, length, and tone.

9 The ratio of High vs. Low was not controlled, again due to limitation of the available data.

10 Collins (1972) does not give the English translation of this word.

(30) Luganda vowel duration (ms):

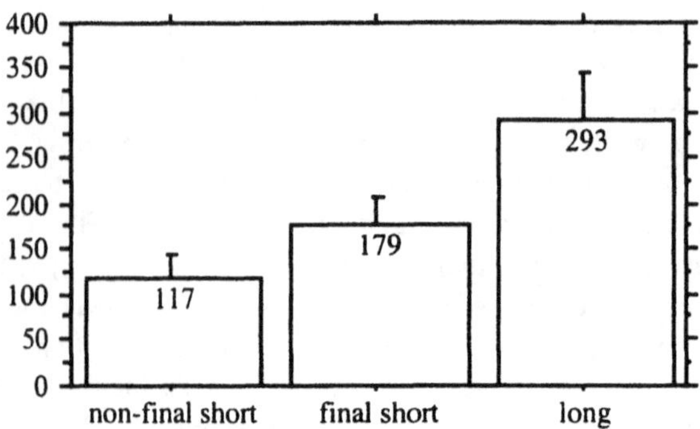

The study clearly shows that there is a significant degree of lengthening of the final short vowels. This lends strong support to the hypothesis that a lengthened duration is responsible for the privileged status of final short vowels to carry the falling contour in Luganda.

4.4.2.3 Chinese Dialects

Another group of languages that exhibits the effect of prosodic boundaries is a number of Chinese dialects; e.g., Beijing, Kunming, Nanchang, Nanjing. In these languages, there is usually one complex contour tone with three pitch targets, e.g., 214, 353. In tone sandhi behavior, this tone only surfaces in word-final position.

We can again take Beijing as an example. The third tone in Beijing is realized as 214 in isolation and word-finally, but as 21 when it precedes 55, 35 and 51, and as 35 when it precedes another 213. This is summarized in (31).

(31) a. 55-**213** → 55-**213** b. **213**-55 → **21**-55
35-**213** → 35-**213** **213**-35 → **21**-35
213-**213** → 35-**213** **213**-213 → **35**-213
51-**213** → 51-**213** **213**-51 → **21**-51

In seeking the account for the ability of final syllable to carry complex contour tones, we may again hypothesize that prosodic-final lengthening is responsible. To confirm the presence of final-lengthening in Beijing Chinese, phonetic data were collected from two male native speakers—ZJ (the author) and LHY. Each speaker was recorded reading the nonsense word *ma55-ma55* with ten repetitions in the sound booth of the UCLA Phonetics Laboratory. Both syllables in the target word were stressed equally, and the high-level tone was used for both syllables to avoid circularity. The data were subsequently digitized onto Kay Elemetrics CSL at a sampling rate of 20kHz; spectrograms were made for each token; and the duration of the vowel in the two syllables was measured from the spectrogram window. The first and last of the repetitions were not used for the analyses. The mean vowel duration for the two syllables is shown in the bar-plot in (32). The error bar indicates one standard deviation. A one-way ANOVA with vowel duration as the dependent variable and syllable type as the independent variable shows a significant effect: $F(1,30)=181.835$, $p<0.0001$.

(32) Beijing vowel duration (ms):

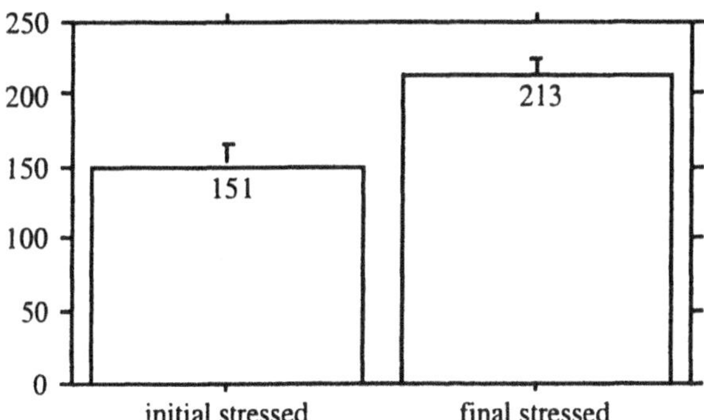

4.4.3 Local Conclusion: Prosodic-Final Effects

The following implicational hierarchy has been established in this section: all else being equal, if non-final syllables in a prosodic domain can carry contours, then the final syllable of the same prosodic domain can carry contours with equal or greater tonal complexity. Given that the prosodic-final syllable is longer than nonfinal syllables due to final-lengthening (see §3.3), we can safely conclude the following relation between the $C_{CONTOUR}$ values based on the proximity of a syllable to a prosodic boundary, when all else is equal: $C_{CONTOUR}(\sigma\text{-final}) > C_{CONTOUR}(\sigma\text{-nonfinal})$. Then the implicational hierarchy established in the typology is consistent with the predictions of the direct approach to contour tone distribution.

Moreover, the advantages of final syllables in a prosodic domain for contour bearing are only consistent with the predictions of the direct approach and contrast specific positional markedness approach. This is because, as we have seen in Chapters 2 and 3, these syllables are durationally advantageous due to final lengthening, and abundant duration is one of the most crucial factors for contour-bearing. Moreover, prosodic-final position is far from being a general-purpose prominent position. In fact, a cross-linguistic survey by Beckman (1997) shows that neutralization of contrasts is very common in non-initial syllables, which include final syllables. Consequently, we expect the segmental inventory in non-initial syllables to be typically a subset of that in root-initial syllables. The table in (33), excerpted from Beckman (1997: p.56), illustrates this point.

(33) Root-initial/non-initial inventory asymmetries:

Language	Initial σ	Non-initial σ
Tuvan (Krueger 1977)	Plain and glottalized vowels	No glottalized vowels
Turkic family (Comrie 1981, Kaun 1995)	Round and unround vowels	Round vowels only via harmony with a round initial
Dhangar-Kurux (Gordon 1976)	Oral and nasal vowels; Long and short vowels	No nasal vowels; No long vowels
Shona (Fortune 1955) (many other Bantu languages exhibit parallel facts)	High, mid, and low vowels	Mid only via harmony with a mid in the initial syllable
Malayalam (Wiltshire 1992)	Independent place of articulation in coda position	Place of articulation in coda must be shared by following onset
!Xóõ (Traill 1985)	Click and non-click consonants	No clicks
Shilluk (Gilley 1992)	Plain, palatalized, and labialized consonants	No palatalized or labialized consonants

Steriade (1995), on the other hand, shows that the word-final position is sometimes a privileged position for some vocalic contrasts, which include nasality, roundness, laxness, backness, and subtle distinctions of height. But these contrasts share the commonality that they are perceptually difficult. Apparently, contrasts in nasality, laxness, and subtle distinctions of height require perceptual differentiation of small magnitudes of spectrographic differences, and are thus perceptually difficult. Moreover, Kaun (1995) has argued that contrasts that are acoustically manifested by F2 are perceptually weaker than those that are manifested by F1 due to F2's weaker inherent intensity and higher frequency. This explains the perceptual difficulty of backness contrasts as compared to height contrasts, since the former are primarily cued by F2 and the latter primarily by F1. This is also supported by cross-linguistic studies of vowel inventories: there seems to be no vowel inventories that lack height contrasts, while a number of languages, such as Kabardian (Kuipers 1960), Higi (Mohrlang 1971), and Marshallese (Bender 1971, Choi 1992), have been reported to lack backness contrasts, as pointed out by Donegan (1985). Finally, Kaun (1995), based on the enhancement theory proposed by Stevens, Keyser, and Kawasaki (1986), argues that when the roundness opposition and the backness opposition do not stand in a mutually enhancement relationship in a language, the perceptual cues for these contrasts will be relatively weak. Steriade (1995) argues that, given that these contrasts are perceptually difficult, they will ideally seek durationally abundant positions to be realized, since 'extra duration means extra exposure to a dubious vowel quality and thus a better chance to identify it correctly' (Steriade 1995: p.20), and word-final syllables provides this extra duration due to final lengthening.

Therefore, the point is that prosodic-final positions are not general-purpose prominent positions. They specifically benefit contrasts that require a long duration, and contour tones fall under this category. These facts are only consistent with the direct approach to positional prominence.

Finally, we must address the issue whether the final syllable of a prosodic domain, or the duration advantages of these syllables, must be referred to directly in the phonology. The mora, as a phonological length unit, seems to be a viable alternative, and this is the alternative that the representational approach explores. Even though there are many languages that neutralize vowel length contrast in final position, such as Luganda (Ashton et al. 1954, Tucker 1962, Snoxall 1967, Stevick 1969, Hyman and Katamba 1990, 1993), Tagalog (Schachter and Otanes 1972), Pacific Yupik (Leer 1985), and Mutsun (Okrand 1977), final lengthening is by no means always neutralizing, and the effect of final position on contour tone distribution is not restricted to languages that have neutralizing final lengthening. Therefore, a representational approach using the mora is too restricted a theory to allow a comprehensive account of all the data patterns. Another likely alternative mentioned above is the *Generalized Alignment* schema proposed by McCarthy and Prince (1993), since intuitively, the gravitation of contour tones to the final syllable may be captured by ALIGN-R constraints. I return to this issue in §6.2, in which I show that without specifically referring to the final syllables or the durational advantage they induce, the alignment constraints themselves cannot capture all the desired effects.

4.5 NUMBER OF SYLLABLES IN THE WORD

4.5.1 General Observations

In 19 languages in the survey (10.2%), shown in (34), contour tones occur more freely on syllables in shorter words than syllables in longer words. There is no language that display the opposite pattern.

(34) Contour tones occur more freely on syllables in short words (19 languages):

Language phylum	No. of languages	Languages
Afro-Asiatic	4	Galla (Booran Oromo), Margi, Musey, Rendille
Niger-Congo	7	Abidji, Etung, Gã, Kinyarwanda, Kukuya (Southern Teke), Mende, Ngamambo
Sino-Tibetan	7	Changzhou, Chaoyang, Chengdu, Chongming, Lüsi, Ningbo, Shanghai
Trans-New Guinea	1	Siane

In the phonetic overview in Chapter 2, I have mentioned that the greatest durational difference is induced by the monosyllabic vs. disyllabic distinction. This is reflected in the typology as well. Among the 19 languages, 13 show the contour distribution difference between monosyllabic and disyllabic words, five show the difference between disyllabic and trisyllabic words, and one shows a three-way difference among mono-, di-, and trisyllabic words, as shown in (35).

(35) a. Mono- vs. disyllabic distinction (13 languages):
Margi, Rendille, Abidji, Etung, Gã, Changzhou, Chaoyang, Chengdu, Chongming, Lüsi, Mende, Ningbo, Shanghai.

b. Di- vs. trisyllabic distinction (5 languages):
Galla (Booran Oromo), Kinyarwanda, Musey, Ngamambo, Siane.

c. Mono- vs. di- vs. trisyllabic distinction (1 language):
Kukuya (Southern Teke).

These observations lead to the implicational hierarchy in (36).

(36) All else being equal, if contours can occur on syllables in an *n* syllable word, then contours with equal or greater tonal complexity can occur on syllables in an *n-1* syllable word (*n*=2, 3).

In the next section, I provide examples from a number of Chinese dialects as well as Ngamambo, Kinyarwanda, Mende, and Kukuya to illustrate the possible effects of the number of syllables in the word on contour tone distribution.

4.5.2 Example Languages

4.5.2.1 Chinese Dialects

Seven languages that exhibit effects of the number of syllables in the word are Chinese dialects. They form the bulk of the languages that have the mono- vs. disyllabic distinction. Among the seven languages, five of them—Changzhou, Chongming, Lüsi, Ningbo, and Shanghai—are from the Wu language group of Chinese. The tone sandhi of the Northern Wu dialects is typically described as 'left-dominant', while that of the Southern Wu dialects, 'right-dominant' (Yue-Hashimoto 1987). In these dialects, the tone of the 'dominant' syllable in a polysyllabic word usually determines the pitch of the whole polysyllabic domain. To encapsulate the data pattern in Shanghai, a Northern Wu dialect, Zee and Maddieson (1979) posit a series of sandhi rules that essentially achieves the following surface-true generalizations: the tones on the syllables of a polysyllabic word are determined by the tone on the initial syllable of the word; and consequently, if monosyllabic morphemes contain only simple contours with two pitch targets, then no contour tone will surface in polysyllabic compounds composed of these morphemes. For disyllabic words, the effect can be simply illustrated as in (37). For polysyllabic words, more complications are involved as to what the exact tonal realization is, but the surface generalizations stated above still hold true. For detailed description of Shanghai tone sandhi, see Zee and Maddieson (1979) and You (1994).

(37) σ_1 (T_1 T_2) σ_2 (T_3 T_4) → σ_1 | T_1 σ_2 | T_2

	σ_1		σ_2		→	σ_1	σ_2
	/	\	/	\		|	|
	T_1	T_2	T_3	T_4		T_1	T_2

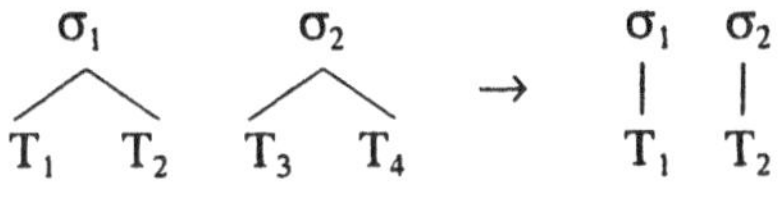

When complex contour tones with three pitch targets are present in monosyllabic morphemes, the mechanism in (37) ensures that no such complex contours will surface in disyllabic words. E.g., in Changzhou (Wang 1988), a disyllabic word with 523 followed by any tone will be realized as 5-23 tonally.

Although the mechanism in (37) captures the 'spreading' effect of tones representationally, we would like to understand why such processes take place. I argue that the reason lies in the durational difference between syllables in shorter and longer words. Duanmu (1994a) has argued that all syllables in Shanghai are monomoraic, but they are lengthened to bimoraic in the monosyllabic environment. This claim about lengthening is corroborated by comparing the phonetic data in Zee and Maddieson (1979) and Duanmu

(1994a). Zee and Maddieson (1979) have shown that the average duration for an unchecked syllable (=not closed by ʔ) that carries a level tone is 327ms. In their study, the target syllable is read in the following carrier sentence, shown in (38).

(38) ŋu doʔ ____ paʔ nõ tʰɪ
I read give you listen
'I read ____ for you to listen.'

Duanmu correctly points out that the target word in the carrier sentence lies at a major syntactic boundary and therefore constitutes a monosyllabic domain. Having carefully controlled the test material and eliminated such boundary effects, he arrives at an average duration of 162ms for Shanghai unchecked syllables. The striking difference between 327ms and 162ms clearly indicates that a Shanghai syllable is significantly longer in a monosyllabic domain than in a longer domain. This comparison lends support to the claim that the durational difference is responsible for the restriction against contour tones in disyllabic or longer domains.

In Chapter 6, when attempting to translate the generic tone spreading mechanism into OT terms, I show that the number of syllables in the word, or the durational advantage of a syllable induced by being in a short word, must be referred to in the analysis.

The two non-Wu Chinese dialects included here, Chaoyang (Zhang 1979, 1980) and Chengdu (Cui 1997), both have a complex contour as one of the lexical tones—213 in Chengdu and 313 in Chaoyang. But in both dialects, the complex contour only surfaces in monosyllabic citation form. In disyllabic forms, tone sandhi occurs and the complex tone is simplified. In Chaoyang, 313 surfaces as 33 when occurring on the first syllable of a disyllabic word, and as 11 when occurring on the second syllable of a disyllabic word. In Chengdu, 213 is realized as 13 in any disyllabic or polysyllabic utterances. We might not be able to predict from phonetics the exact shape of the sandhi tones in these dialects, but at least we are able to restrict the inventories from which the sandhi tones are drawn.

4.5.2.2 Ngamambo and Kinyarwanda

Ngamambo (Asongwed and Hyman 1976) is a typical language that makes the distinction for contour-bearing between disyllabic and trisyllabic words. In this language, the two contour tones H͡L and L͡H can only occur on monosyllabic words and the final syllable of disyllabic words. It is typical in the sense that there is usually some restriction on contour tones in disyllables. In this case, it is the final position, which we have already identified as a privileged position for contours.

In Kinyarwanda (Kimenyi 1976, 1979), a Central Bantu language, it is the initial syllable. It is slightly surprising that contour tones are restricted to the initial instead of the final syllable in disyllabic words in Kinyarwanda. But two facts in Kinyarwanda suggest that this is less mysterious than it sounds. One is the penultimate prominence in Bantu that I mentioned in §4.3.1: although Kinyarwanda has kept the Proto-Bantu vowel length contrast and does not have clear penultimate stress and lengthening, the less drastic penultimate lengthening that Hubbard (1994) has found for Runyambo might also be present in Kinyarwanda. Secondly, the final syllable in Kinyarwanda words allows a very restricted tonal repertoire: it cannot carry the H tone either. Therefore it may simply be a less prominent (e.g., unstressed) positionin Kinyarwanda. Either of these conjectures being true, the tonal distribution facts in Kinyarwanda would find a phonetically natural explanation.

Therefore, the typological findings here agree with the phonetic fact that the greatest durational difference is induced by mono- vs. disyllabic distinction. Most of the contour restrictions based on the number of syllables are based on this distinction. For the few languages that distinguish disyllables and trisyllables, there are usually additional constraints on contours in disyllables.

4.5.2.3 Mende

The best-documented language that illustrates the effect of syllable count is probably Mende (Innes 1963, 1969, Spears 1967, Leben 1971, 1973, 1978, Dwyer 1971, 1978, 1985, Conteh et al. 1983). The facts of Mende are complicated, and this effect has not be explicitly pointed out by previous researchers. Let me review the descriptions of Mende first, and then provide my own interpretation.

Leben, in an autosegmental framework, claims that there are five basic melodic patterns in Mende: H, L, HL, LH and LHL. These patterns are mapped to syllables in the word one-to-one, left-to-right. The following examples in (39) illustrate these melodic patterns in words up to three syllables (from Leben 1978):

(39) Mende examples:

	σ		σσ		σσσ	
H	kɔ́	'war'	pɛ́lɛ́	'house'	háwámá	'waistline'
L	kpà	'debt'	bɛ̀lɛ̀	'trousers'	kpàkàlî	'tripod chair'
HL	mbû	'owl'	ngílà	'dog'	félàmà	'junction'
LH	mbǎ	'rice'	fàndé	'cotton'	ndàvúlá	'sling'
LHL	mba᷈	'companion'	nyàhâ	'woman'	nìkílî	'groundnut'

Dwyer challenges Leben's tonal melody mapping view of tone in Mende. He claims that tones are associated with syllables underlyingly. His major contentions are two. First, the five tonal patterns Leben provides account for at most 90% of the Mende lexicon. Other patterns, such as HLH and HLHL are also attested, illustrated by examples in (40) (from Dwyer 1978).

(40)	a. HLH:	yámbùwú	'tree (sp)'
		lánsàná	'proper name'
		lɛ́nàá	'for now'
	b. HLHL:	náfàlê	'raphia clothed clown'
		njéngùlû	'tarantula'
		dúmbèékà	'star'

Second, the mapping analysis cannot formally capture the following contrasts: HL and HHL̂ in disyllables; HLL and HHL, LHH and LLH in trisyllables. But these contrasts exist in Mende, as shown in the examples in (41).

(41) a.	HL:	káŋ̀	'hoe'	ngílà	'dog'
	HHL̂:	kɔ́nyɔ̂	'friend'	hókpô	'navel'
b.	HLL:	félàmà	'junction'	mɔ́ŋ̀mɔ̀	'Muslim'
	HHL:	símbítì	'spider'	kɔ́kɔ́ŋ̀	'seek'
c.	LHH:	ndɛ̀ndɛ́lí	'shade'	ndàvúlá	'sling'
	LLH:	lèlèmá	'praying mantis'	kòlòbé	'none'

Dwyer hence contends that tones in Mende must be prelinked to the tone-bearing units (TBUs) in the underlying representation rather than associated to TBUs by the one-to-one, left-to-right, no-crossing *Association Conventions* (Leben 1973, Goldsmith 1976, Williams 1976, Clements and Ford 1979, Halle and Vergnaud 1982, Pulleyblank 1986, among others) during the course of the derivation.

The major criticism held toward Dwyer's prelinking ('segmental' in Dwyer's term) analysis is that it generates tonal patterns that are not attested. Conteh et al. (1983) list the following patterns in trisyllabic words that are predicted by the prelinking analysis, but not attested in Mende, as in (42).

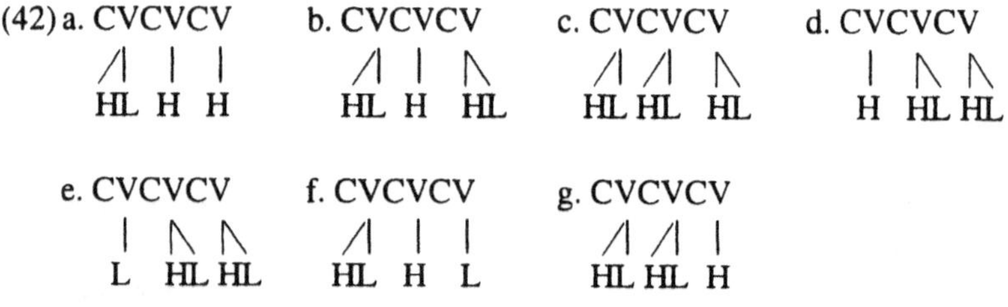

But as we can see, all patterns listed in (42) involve H͡L contours on syllables in non-final position. We have shown in §4.4 that this effect can be construed as the privilege of the final syllable in a prosodic domain to carry tonal contours as it is subject to final lengthening. Therefore, if we acknowledge the contrast-specificity of positional prominence (i.e., the direct approach or the contrast-specific positional markedness approach), we can easily eliminate the overgenerated patterns in (42). This is true for disyllabic CVCV words as well: the patterns that are conspicuously missing are the ones in which contour tones on the initial syllable.

But contour tones on non-final syllables are in fact attested in Mende. Dwyer (1978) lists a number of words with a H͡L or L͡H contour on non-final syllables, and these syllables invariably have a long vowel, as shown in (43).

(43)	L͡HH:	bèésí	'pig'
	L͡HL:	nyààpò	'mistress'
	H͡LL:	wóòmà	'back'

Leafing through Innes' *Mende-English Dictionary* (1969), not only do we find numerous examples of this sort, we also find long vowels with level tones, e.g., *sɔ̀ɔ̀* 'long' and *nɛ́ɛ́* 'boil'. Therefore vowel length does seem to be contrastive in Mende, even though Leben is not willing to commit to such a view. Dwyer also argues that the monosyllabic word for 'companion' in (39), which carries a LHL contour, should be transcribed with a long vowel—mbàâ. This argument finds support in Spears (1967) and Innes (1969), both of which transcribe the word with a long vowel.

The final complication of the Mende data is in regard to the surface realization of its rising tone L͡H. On a long vowel, a rising tone can surface as such. This is illustrated by words like *bèésí* 'pig' in (43). But on a short vowel, the rising tone usually behaves as a so-called 'polarized tone' (Innes 1963, Spears 1967, Dwyer 1978). It surfaces as a downstepped H before pause or a L tone, and as a L before a H tone which is subsequently downstepped. This is illustrated by the example in (44) (from Dwyer 1978: p.182).

(44)	UR	SR before #	SR before L	SR before H
	L͡H njǎ	nj!á	nj!á-fèlé	njɛ̀-!í
		'water'	'two rivers'	'the water'

If the above generalizations about rising tone are true without exceptions, we are inevitably led to the conclusion that the rising tone L͡H can only occur on long vowels. But Leben (1973: p.187) claims that the words for 'rice' (*mbǎ*) and 'kill' (*pǎ*) do have a rising pitch. He further asserts that the simplification of the rising tone does not apply to monosyllabic nouns and verbs. This statement is obviously in disagreement with the data in (44), which show rising simplification on a monosyllabic noun. Therefore it is plausible that the Downstepped High, or rather, Mid, is a contrastive tone in Mende. But with the scarcity of data, I cannot make any definitive statement about this. The relevant point here is the following: if a rising pitch *is to* occur on a short vowel, it can only occur on monosyllabic nouns or verbs. This statement does not contradict either of the data sources—Leben (1973) and Dwyer (1978).

We are thus led to the following picture regarding the distribution of contour tones in Mende. Long vowels can carry a complex contour with three pitch targets (L͡H͡L) in monosyllabic words; they can carry a simple contour with two pitch targets (H͡L or L͡H) in other positions. Short vowels can carry either of the simple contours H͡L and L͡H in monosyllabic words; they can carry the falling contour H͡L in the final position of di- or polysyllabic words; they cannot carry contours in other positions. These generalizations are summarized in (45).

(45) Mende contour tone restrictions:

Vowel length	No. of sylls in word	Syll position in word	L͡H͡L ok?	L͡H ok?	H͡L ok?
VV	1	final	yes	yes	yes
VV	>1	any	no	yes	yes
V	1	final	no	yes	yes
V	>1	final	no	no	yes
V	>1	non-final	no	no	no

Therefore we have shown that in Mende, a mapping analysis is not sufficient to capture all the attested tonal patterns. A non-mapping analysis aided by durational considerations makes better predictions. From the table in (45), we can clearly observe that three durational factors are relevant: vowel length, position of the syllable in the word, and the number of syllables in the word. Particularly for the effect of the number of syllables, which is the focus of this section—a monosyllabic word is a more privileged contour carrier than syllables in a longer word, since the complex contour L͡H͡L and rising contour L͡H can only occur on monosyllabic words, but not elsewhere. The fact that the rising contour has a more limited distribution than the falling contour is consistent with the prediction of the durational view of the prominence effects of contour tones, since rising tones are known to require a longer duration to implement than falling tones, as I have discussed in §2.3.

Let us also notice that, in order to capture the contour distribution facts in Mende, we need at least four durational categories for Mende: VV in monosyllabic words, which can carry L͡H͡L; VV in other positions together with V in monosyllabic words, which can carry L͡H; V in the final syllable of di- or polysyllabic words, which can carry H͡L; and V in other positions, which cannot carry contour tones. This again poses a serious problems for an analysis which only considers contrastive length units to be relevant to contour tone distribution, since no language uses a four-way contrastive length distinction. A phonetically-based account of Mende using the direct approach is discussed in §6.2.

4.5.2.4 Kukuya

The contour pattern of Kukuya is very similar to the Mende pattern as described by Leben (Paulian 1974, Hyman 1987). Paulian (1974) shows that there are also five tonal melodies in Kukuya: H, L, HL, LH, and LHL, and they are mapped one-to-one, left-to-right to syllables in the word. Examples in (46) show the mapping of tones to syllables in words with up to three syllables. The Kukuya word for 'younger brother', which is in bold in the table, has a LLH tonal pattern instead of the expected LHH pattern. Since it is not relevant to contour tones, we can simply take it as an exception to the mapping procedure. For analyses of this pattern, see Hyman (1987) and Zoll (1996).

(46) Kukuya examples:

	σ	σσ	σσσ
H	bá 'oil palms'	bágá 'show knives'	bálágá 'fence'
L	bà 'grasshopper killer'	bàlà 'to build'	bàlàgà 'to change route'
HL	kâ 'to pick'	kálà 'paralytic'	kálàgà 'to be entangled'
LH	să 'weaving knot'	sàmí 'conversation'	**m^{w}àrəgí** 'younger brother'
LHL	bvi᷈ 'he falls'	pàlî 'he goes out'	kàlə́gì 'he turns around'

Unlike Mende, no claims have been made to contradict the melody-mapping analysis of Kukuya. But let us focus on the surface tonal patterns for a moment. We can make the following generalizations: first, the complex contour L͡HL and rising contour L͡H can only occur on monosyllabic words, and second, the falling contour H͡L can only on monosyllabic words or the final syllable of disyllabic words. Therefore, Kukuya is consistent with two of the durational effects on contour tone distribution: the privilege of the final syllable in the word, and the privilege of syllables in shorter words. Moreover, it shows a three-way distinction in the effect of the number of syllables: syllables in monosyllabic words are better contour bearers (L͡HL, L͡H, H͡L) than those in disyllabic words (H͡L), which are in turn better than those in even longer words (no contours).

For a formal approach to Kukuya, see §6.2.

4.5.3 Local Conclusion: Syllable Count Effects

In this section, I have argued that the durational differences induced by the number of syllables in a word are responsible for contour tone patterning in some languages. Their relevance is illustrated by synchronic processes such as contour simplification in polysyllabic words, or distributional properties of contour tones on words of different lengths. The following implicational hierarchy has been established: all else being equal, if contours can occur on syllables in an *n* syllable word, then contours with equal or greater tonal complexity can occur on syllables in an *n-1* syllable word (*n*=2, 3). Given that the syllables in shorter words have a longer duration than the same syllables in longer words, we can establish the following relation between the $C_{CONTOUR}$ values based on the number of syllables in the word: when all else is equal, $C_{CONTOUR}$(σ-in-short-word) > $C_{CONTOUR}$(σ-in-long-word). Then the implicational hierarchy established in the typology is consistent with the prediction of the direct approach to contour tone licensing.

The fact that the number of syllables in a word is responsible for contour distribution is even more surprising than the relevance of final lengthening, as the durational difference induced by this factor very rarely, if ever, makes a difference in the number of contrasts that the syllable is able to carry. But we have shown that it indeed has an impact on where the contour tone appears. For the Chinese languages we have discussed, this durational difference constitutes the main reason why their tone sandhi involves contour simplification processes. For languages like Mende, when the melodic analysis does not stand up to close scrutiny, we must again resort to this difference to account for the lack of contours in longer words. Therefore, the advantages of syllables in shorter words for contour tone bearing in fact *only* support the direct approach and the contrast-specificity positional markedness approach.

The discussion of Mende also leads to another observation: we clearly need at least three durational categories in order to fully capture the contour distribution. We have already mentioned in §4.2.2.2 that it is not clear how to represent the different durational categories needed for contour tones with different pitch excursions by contrastive mora-counting. Mende is another clear case in which such a contrastive distinction is not sufficient to capture all the desired effects.

Finally, we must again address the issue whether the number of syllables in the word, or the duration advantages of these syllables, must be referred to directly in phonology. A likely alternative is still *Generalized Alignment*. Even though we have shown that the melody mapping analysis in Mende does not have much appeal, we cannot reject the possibility off-hand, as it might have better justifications in other languages, such as Kukuya. Then an OT translation of the *Association Conventions* might not need to refer to this particular syllable type, since intuitively, the syllables in shorter words will have a greater pressure to carry contour tones than syllables in longer words if the tonal melody on the word must be faithfully realized. I return to this issue in §6.2, in which I show that even when a melodic analysis is justified, we still need, at least some of the time, to refer to the durational advantage that syllables in shorter words have, to capture all the relevant patterns of contour tone distribution.

4.6 OTHER DISTRIBUTIONAL PROPERTIES AND EXCEPTIONS

4.6.1 Other Distributional Properties

In §4.2 to §4.5, I have discussed languages in which different $C_{CONTOUR}$ values allow contours with different tonal complexity to surface on them. But there are also languages in which contours with higher tonal complexity simply do not occur. These phenomena may also be $C_{CONTOUR}$-based. Contour tones with higher complexity are disfavored since they place a higher demand on the sonorous rime duration. This can be expressed as the implicational hierarchy in (47).

(47) For any language *L*, if tone T_1 exists, then tones that are lower on the *Tonal Complexity* scale than T_1 also exist.

This implicational hierarchy must be interpreted with caution, as this is a statement about the phonological inventory of a language. There are two reasons for such precautions. First of all, Maddieson, in *Patterns of Sounds* (1984), has pointed out that 'most of these observations and hypotheses about phonological universals necessarily concern relative rather than absolute matters. Experience has shown that few interesting things are to be said about phonological inventories that are truly universal, i.e., exceptionless.' (p.2). Many implicational hierarchies regarding the segmental inventory of a single language proposed in Maddieson (1984), e.g., '/k/ does not occur without /t/' and '/p/ does not occur without /k/', have exceptions—the first one has one and the second one has four (p.13). Therefore, the implicational hierarchy in (47) is most likely manifested as statistical tendencies rather than exceptionless generalizations. The second reason is that languages will only allow a certain number of tonal contrasts. For example, does the presence of a sharp falling tone 51 necessarily imply the presence of all of 52, 53 and 54? The answer is clearly 'no'. If a language is to employ a four-way tonal contrast, four falling tones is clearly not an ideal choice. Therefore, the implicational hierarchy in (47) is constrained by the salience of contrasts in a phonological system.

With these limitations, we only consider two likely implicational hierarchies derived from (47). They are shown in (48).

(48) a. If a language has contour tones, then it must also have level tones.
b. If a language has complex contour tones, then it must also have simple contour tones.
c. If a language has rising tones, then it must also have falling tones.

All of these statements are based on the discussion of the *Tonal Complexity* scale in Chapter 3. In that chapter, we established that tones with more pitch targets have a higher tonal complexity than tones with fewer pitch targets if the overall pitch excursion of the latter is not greater than the former, and rising tones have a higher tonal complexity than falling tones with equal pitch excursion. The second implicational hierarchy is especially of interest here, since we have only seen one case in which the difference in tonal complexity between rising and falling tones is manifested in the comparison of syllables with different $C_{CONTOUR}$ values—Mende.

All of the implicational hierarchies in (48) find strong support in the typological survey described in §4.2 to 4.5.

Of all the 187 languages in the survey, only two do not have level tones. These languages are Guiyang (Li 1997) and Pingyao (Hou 1980, 1982a, b), both of which are Chinese dialects. But languages with level tones, but no contour tones, though no included in the survey, are widely attested. The list in (49) gives some representative languages that do have contour tones.

(49) Languages with only level tones:

Language phylum	Languages
Afro-Asiatic	Shinasha (Tesfaye and Wedekind 1990)
Austro-Asiatic	Hu (Svantesson 1991), Kammu (Gandour et al. 1978, Gårding and Lindell 1977, Svantesson 1983)
Na-Dene	Carrier (Pike 1986, Story 1989), Haida (Enrico 1991), Slave (Rice 1989a, b)
Niger-Congo	Chishona (Stevick 1965, Benett 1976)
Nilo-Saharan	For (Jernudd 1983), Kunama (Thompson 1983), Majang (Bender 1983), Twampa (Thelwall 1983a)
Sino-Tibetan	Burmese (Cornyn 1964, Maran 1971, Okell 1969, Wheatley 1990), Jingpho (Maran 1971), Rawang (Morse 1963)

Of all the languages surveyed, 46 allow complex contours, all of which allow simple contours. Most of these languages belong to the Chinese or Oto-Manguean phylum. The names of the languages are given in (50).

(50) Languages with complex contour tones (46 languages):

Language phylum	No. of languages	Languages
Austro-Asiatic	2	So (Thavung), Vietnamese
Daic	4	Southern Dong, Maonan, Saek, Ron Phibun Thai
Miao-Yao	3	Lakkja, Mjen, Punu
Mura	1	Pirahã
Niger-Congo	4	Kenyang, Wobe Kru, Kukuya (Southern Teke), Mende
Oto-Manguean	6	Comaltepec Chinantec, Lalana Chinantec, Quiotepec Chinantec, Chiquihuitlan Mazatec, San Andrés Chichahuaxtla Trique, San Juan Copala Trique
Sino-Tibetan	26	Anren, Beijing, Changzhi, Changzhou, Chaoyang, Chengdu, Chongming, Fuzhou, Guiyang, Kunming, Lüsi, Nanchang, Nanjing, Ningbo, Pingyang, Pingyao, Shexian, Shuozhou, Suzhou, Taishan, Rgyalthang Tibetan, Wuyi, Xining, Xinzhou, Yanggu, Yangqu

In the survey, the number of languages that only allow surface falling tones far exceeds the number of languages that only allow surface rising tones. Thirty-seven languages belong to the former category and only three belong to the latter, as shown in (51).

(51) a. Languages with only surface falling tones (37 languages):

Language phylum	No. of languages	Languages
Afro-Asiatic	8	Agaw (Awiya), Bolanci (Bole), Elmolo, Galla (Booran Oromo), Hausa, Kanakuru, Ngizim, Somali
Caddoan	2	Caddo, Kitsai
Creole	1	Nubi
Keres	1	Acoma (Western Keres)
Khoisan	1	!Xóõ
Kiowa Tanoan	2	Jemez, Kiowa
Na-Dene	1	Chilcotin
Niger-Congo	15	Bamileke, Bandi, Ciyao, Haya, Kambari, Kinande, Kpele, Lama, Ngumbi (Kombe), Nupe, Ólusamia, Runyankore,Shi, Venda, Zulu
Nilo-Saharan	5	Bari, Camus, Datooga, Maasai, Mbum
Siouan	1	Crow

b. Languages with only surface rising tones (3 languages):

Language phylum	No. of languages	Languages
Afro-Asiatic	1	Margi
Oto-Manguean	1	Lealao Chinantec
Sino-Tibetan	1	Zencheng

For languages in the former category, many exhibit synchronic simplification of the rising tone when it is created by morphological concatenation and phonological contraction. For example, in Kanakuru, it is simplified to L (Newman 1974); in Ngizim, it is simplified to H (Schuh 1971).

We have also seen in §4.5.2.3 and §4.5.2.4 that, in Mende and Kukuya, even though a rising tone does surface, it is on the one hand more restricted in distribution than the falling tone, on the other hand prone to simplification to a downstepped H. Similar behavior of the rising tone is also attested in Gã, Kɔnni, and Tiv. In Gã, there is vowel length contrast. The falling tone H͡L can occur on a phrase-final short vowel without lengthening the vowel, but when the rising tone L͡H occurs on a phrase-final short vowel, it lengthens the vowel to long (Paster 1999). In Kɔnni, contour tones are restricted to word-final position; the rising tone L͡H is further restricted to CVN or CVVN syllables, while the falling tone H͡L can occur on word-final CV (Cahill 1999). In Tiv, contour tones are restricted to word-final position as well; the rising tone L͡H is further restricted to CVR, while the falling tone H͡L can occur on CV (Pulleyblank 1986).

The distributional asymmetries observed in phonological inventories have often been explained by positing different markedness values to the phonological entities in question. For example, we can simply attribute the relative rarity of complex contours or rising tones to the fact they are more 'marked' than simple contours and falling tones respectively. Without any independent motivation for why certain features or segments are marked, this line of reasoning could easily be circular: are they rare because they are marked, or are they marked because they are rare? Recognizing the durational requirements of different contour tones in the theory provides the basis for the markedness of more complex tones. Now the argument could go as follows: phonetics tells us that a more complex tone is more difficult to produce and perceive than a less complex one, therefore we may consider the former to be more 'marked' than the latter, and we expect the former to occur more rarely than the latter.

4.6.2 Durational Factors Not Reflected in the Contour Tone Survey

In the discussion of the influence of the segmental composition of a syllable on its sonorous rime duration in Chapter 3, we identified four such factors: vowel length, sonority of the coda, height of the vowel and the voicing quality of the coda if it is an obstruent. The influences of these factors are repeated in (52).

(52) VV>V, VR>VO, $V_{[-high]}>V_{[+high]}$, Vd>Vt.

Although numerous languages show effects of the first two factors on contour tone distribution (see §4.2), the last two factors—vowel height and voicing of the coda obstruent—do not affect the contour distribution in any languages in the typology. I would like to offer two possible explanations as to why these two factors are not reflected in the typology.

The first reason lies in the magnitude of the durational differences that these factors induce. Let us first look at the vowel height distinction. From the graph reported in Lindblom (1967), we estimate the duration of [i:], [a:], [ɪ] and [a] in Swedish to be as in (53a). The target vowels are in the medial position of a trisyllabic nonsense word. The first and last syllables both have the vowel [ɪ]. The vowel duration for [i:], [a:], [i] and [a] in Malayalam reported in Jensen and Menon (1972) is summarized in (53b). The target vowels are incorporated in the frame /k__ti/, and the word is embedded in a carrier sentence /i:wa:kə___ena:nə/ 'This word is ___.'

(53) a. Swedish (Lindblom 1967)

[ɪ]: 120ms [iː] 190ms

[a]: 150ms [aː] 225ms

b. Malayalam (Jensen and Menon 1972)

[i]: 99ms [iː] 196ms

[a]: 117ms [aː] 236ms

From these data, we conclude that the durational differences induced by vowel height are very small. They are generally in the range of 20 to 40 msec, depending on the contrastive length of the vowel. Differences in this magnitude are hardly perceivable by listeners. From perceptual studies by Stott (1935), Henry (1948) and Ruhm et al. (1966), Lehiste (1970) concludes that 'in the range of the durations of speech sounds—usually from 30 to 300 msec—the just-noticeable differences in duration are between 10 and 40 msec.' (p.13) This conclusion is corroborated by later studies such as Reinholt Peterson (1976) and Bochner et al. (1988).

The durational differences induced by voicing of the obstruent coda are more varied across languages. Chen (1970) surveys such effects in seven languages reported in the literature. The languages in the survey show a vowel duration difference from 10% (German) to 40% (English). But Keating (1985) documents a study on Polish and Czech and shows that no vowel duration difference exists before a voiceless and a voiced obstruent in these two languages. Therefore, without phonetic details on vowel duration in the tone languages in question, nothing definitive can be said about the durational differences induced by this factor. But Keating (1985) has conjectured that prosodic features such as stress or rhythm in the language might be relevant: languages with phonemic stress like English might have a stronger requirement for balanced syllable duration than languages like Polish where stress falls on a fixed position. Since voiced obstruents generally have shorter closure intervals than voiceless obstruents due to the difficulty to sustain voicing during an oral closure, to achieve a balanced syllable duration, the vowel before a voiced obstruent is necessarily longer than the vowel before a voiceless obstruent. I conjecture that tone languages are more likely to have fixed stress than variable stress, thus behave more like Polish than English. Since pitch is usually one of the major phonetic correlates of stress (Lehiste 1970), it might be difficult to implement contrastive tone and contrastive stress simultaneously, since they may conflict in their desired realization of the pitch. The typology generally confirms this hypothesis. Although many sources lack clear statements on the contrastive status of stress, therefore no specific number or percentage can be given, some trend can still be seen. In the Niger-Congo and Sino-Tibetan phyla to which most of the world's tone languages belong, the majority of the languages have fixed stress. For examples, many Central Bantu languages have penultimate stress, and regular syllables in all Chinese languages are equally stressed. Therefore, it is possible that in these languages, the differences in vowel duration induced by the voicing specification of the following obstruent are small or non-existent, as in Polish and Czech. But again, this claim is subject to corroboration or disconfirmation of future research.

The second reason I would like to suggest for the lack of reflection of these two factors in contour-tone distribution is that within the realm of segmental influences, there are always other factors that exert more influence on vowel duration, and therefore may serve as better predictors for contour distribution.

For vowel height distinctions, since the durational differences caused by them are so small, virtually any other segmental factors that influence duration will be more effective bases for contour restrictions. If no such factor exists, then we have a language which only allows CV syllables. In my typology of tone languages, there is no language that restricts its syllable inventory to CV. Even if such a tone language exists, there is a fair chance that its syllables can only carry level tones, if the vowels in these syllables are truly short.

For voicing distinctions in coda obstruents, we first acknowledge the fact that the presence of coda obstruents usually implies the presence of coda sonorants. This is corroborated by the survey of approximately 400 languages in Gordon (1999a). The majority of the languages in my typology also observes this implicational hierarchy. When the implicational hierarchy holds, the difference in duration of the sonorous portion of the rime between CVR and CVO will be significantly greater than that between CVD (D=voiced obstruent) and CVT (T=voiceless obstruent). For this reason, languages would more likely choose to draw the distinction on contour bearing between CVR and CVO rather than between CVD and CVT. The only attested cases in which the implicational hierarchy does not hold are a number of Chinese dialects where the only syllable types are open syllables and syllables closed by [ʔ] (checked syllables). The voicing distinction in coda obstruents is simply not relevant here. Moreover, in these languages, the vowels in open syllables are always considerably longer phonetically than the vowels in checked syllables. Therefore open vs. checked is usually where the line is drawn with respect to contour bearing.

I have argued in this section that the lack of reflection of vowel height and voicing specification of coda obstruents in contour tone distribution is not an accidental gap, but a systematic one. Two explanations have been entertained. One is that the durational differences induced by these two factors are small in magnitude. The other is that within the realm of segmental compositions, there are always other factors, such as vowel length and sonorancy of the coda, that induce greater durational differences in the sonorous portion of the rime, and thus serve as better predictors for contour distribution.

4.6.3 Languages with No Clearly Documented Contour Tone Restrictions

In the survey, there are 22 languages in which no clear restrictions on contour tones can be established. The names of these languages are given in (54).

(54) No positional restrictions on contour tones (22 languages):

Language phylum	No. of languages	Languages
Afro-Asiatic	1	Moča (Shakicho)
Daic	1	Gelao
Khoisan	2	!Xũ, ǂKhomani Ng'huki
Niger-Congo	4	Abidji, Babungo, Bamileke, Kinande
Nilo-Saharan	1	Toposa
Oto-Manguean	4	Comaltepec Chinantec, Lalana Chinantec, Quiotepec Chinantec, Chiquihuitlan Mazatec
Sino-Tibetan	9	Anren, Apatani, Guiyang, Tanashan Hmong, Lanzhou, Rongmei Naga, Xi'an, Xiangtan, Yinchuan

Among the 22 languages, eight of them—Anren, Gelao, Guiyang, Tanashan Hmong, Lanzhou, Xi'an, Xiangtan, and Yinchuan—only have CV and CVN (N=nasal) in the syllable inventory. Except Gelao, which is a Daic language, the other seven languages here are all Chinese dialects. Given that the CV syllables in Chinese dialects usually have a phonetically long vowel or diphthong, these languages are more like the languages that restrict contour tones to CVV and CVR (see §4.2).

The other fourteen languages have either vowel length contrast or the CVO/CVR distinction. The sources I consulted (see Appendix) either do not specifically mention any contour tone restrictions or claim that contours are unrestricted regarding syllable type or position. But this does not mean that no relation between contour tone and duration is expressed in these languages. It is possible that the field workers' main focus was not phonetic accuracy, and thus they did not specifically record the lengthening of the shorter tone-bearing units (TBUs) such as the vowel in CVO when they carry contour tones, or the partial flattening of contour tones when they occur on shorter TBUs. For example, this has been shown to be the case in Hausa, Luganda, as I have shown in §4.2.2.3. Therefore, careful phonetic studies of these languages may reveal contour tone restrictions much in line with the observations discussed in the previous sections of this work.

4.6.4 Exceptions

In the introduction section of the typology (§4.1), I mentioned that six languages in the typology have contour restrictions in both the expected and unexpected directions. We have seen three of them so far: Lealao Chinantec, Margi, and Zengcheng Chinese. The unexpected restriction is that all three languages only have rising contours. But Lealao Chinantec limits contours to stressed syllables (Mugele 1982), Margi limits contours to monosyllabic words (Hoffman 1963, Williams 1976, Tranel 1992-1994), and Zengcheng Chinese limits contours to CVV and CVR (He 1986, 1987). All these restrictions are predicted by the direct approach, which relates the distribution of contour tones to the duration and sonority of the rime.

The fourth language in this category is Kɔnni (Cahill 1999). As I have shown, Kɔnni exhibits a number of contour restrictions that are durationally based. It limits its contour tones L͡H, H͡L, and H͡!H to word-final position. It further restricts the rising tone L͡H to CVN or CVVN, while allows the falling tone HL to surface on CV. The unexpected distributional property is that, the other falling tone H!H, which has a less drastic pitch fall than HL (impressionistic observation by Cahill, p.c.), has the same restriction as L͡H. Therefore, the final CV syllable can carry H͡L, but cannot carry H͡!H. There might be a historical explanation for this. Suppose the H͡!H contour came from historical H͡LH. Then it is reasonable to assume that in an earlier stage of Kɔnni, the tone H͡LH had a more stringent occurrence restriction than the tone HL. During the course of historical change, the tone H͡LH was simplified to H͡!H, while its occurrence restriction remained. This causes the phonetically unnatural present-day situation in which a contour tone with a lower tonal complexity is more restricted in its distribution than a contour tone with a high *Tonal Complexity*. There could also be a synchronic explanation in terms of the maximum dispersion of contrasts (Flemming 1995) for this. The basic idea is that, on a syllable with short sonorous rime duration, only two tonal contrasts are preserved, and they are distributed at the two ends of the perceptual scale. For the case here, on final syllables, only H͡L and H are allowed, and H͡!H, which lies between H͡L and H on the perceptual scale, is banned. See §7.2 for a formalization of this idea.

The other two languages that have unexpected contour restrictions both belong to the Daic phylum in the language classification. They are Lao (Morev 1979) and Saek (Hudak 1993).

Lao has six tones, as shown in (55).

(55)	1	rising	4	lower-mid level
	2	mid-level	5	low-level
	3	high-falling	6	low-falling

Lao syllables can be open, closed by a sonorant or closed by an obstruent. Vowel length is contrastive in syllables closed by a obstruent. Therefore the syllables types in Lao are CV, CVR, CVO and CVVO. On CV and CVR, all six tones in (55) can occur. On CVO, only tones 1, 2, 3 and 4 occur. And on CVVO, only tones 2, 4, 5 and 6 occur. It is very likely that the vowel in open syllables is phonetically long in Lao, as in other Daic languages (some phonetic data on Standard Thai will be shown in §5.2.3) and historically related Chinese languages. Therefore the lack of contour tone restriction on open syllables does not come as a surprise. What comes as a surprise is that tone 1 (rising) and tone 3 (high-falling) can occur on CVO, but not on CVVO. This violates the implicational hierarchy that states: all else being equal, if a contour tone can occur on a short vowel, then it can occur on a long vowel (see (3a)). Without detailed phonetic description and historical knowledge of this language, I will simply take this as an exception to the implicational hierarchy.

The situation in Saek is very similar to Lao. It also has six tones, as shown in (56).

(56)	1	mid-level with rise at the end	34
	2	low-level	11
	3	mid, falling to low, with glottal constriction	31
	4	high rising-falling	454
	5	high falling	52
	6	mid-level with slight fall, with glottal constriction	32

The syllable inventory in Saek is the same as Lao: CV, CVR, CVO and CVVO. On CV and CVR, all six tones occur. On CVO, only tones 4 and 6 can occur. And on CVVO, only tones 5 and 6 can occur. The surprising fact is: the most complex tone pattern 454 occurs on CVO, but not on CVVO. I again take this as an exception to the proposed implicational hierarchy and await further research to corroborate or disconfirm this position.

4.7 INTERIM CONCLUSION

The discussion of the typological survey of contour tone distribution in this chapter has led to the following conclusions.

First, the result of the survey argues against the general-purpose positional markedness approach to positional restrictions for contour tones. The argument comes from two aspects. The first one is that factors which systematically influence the duration and sonority of the rime also influence contour tone distribution. All such factors identified in Chapter 3 are either shown to affect contour tone distribution, or shown to be unlikely to produce such an effect on independent grounds. Specifically crucial here is the fact that syllables in the final position of a prosodic domain or in a shorter word are shown to be privileged contour tone carriers in some languages, since syllables in these positions are not general-purpose prominent positions—they either only benefit contrasts that specifically require the presence of abundant duration, or are not known to be privileged for any other phonological contrasts, and a general-purpose approach does not provide an explanation for why these positions are privileged particularly for contour tones. The second crucial fact is that word-initial position, which has been shown to be a privileged position for many phonological contrasts, is not specifically privileged for contour tones. I argue that this is precisely because the word-initial position by itself does not lend extra duration to the syllable. A general-purpose positional markedness approach again does not provide an explanation as to why the initial position is perspicuously missing as a privileged position for contour tones.

Second, I have shown that not only factors that serve contrastive purposes, such as segmental composition of a syllable, can influence the distribution of contour tones. Phonetic factors such as final lengthening and durational differences induced by the number of syllables in the word, which are often non-neutralization for length contrast, can also have such an effect. This vitiates the claim that only mora count is relevant in a syllable's ability to carry contours, since the mora is generally used contrastively as a length or weight unit. We need the concept $C_{CONTOUR}$ that encompasses all factors that systematically influence the duration and sonority of the rime, contrastively or not.

Third, we have seen cases in which a binary durational distinction is not sufficient to capture all the facts about contour tone distribution. This is especially likely to happen when multiple durational factors are at play in one language. For example, in Mende, we need to make a four-way distinction: (a) long vowels in monosyllabic words, which can carry a complex contour; (b) long vowels in other positions together with short vowels in monosyllabic words, which can carry a simple rise; (c) short vowels in the final syllable of di- or polysyllabic words, which can carry a simple fall; and (d) short vowels in other positions, which cannot carry contours. In Beijing Chinese, we also need three categories: stressed syllables in the final position, which can carry a complex contour, stressed syllables in other positions, which can carry a simple contour, and unstressed syllables, which cannot carry contours. Examples like these abound in the typology. This further demonstrates the need to incorporate finer-grained durational categories in the analysis of contour tone distribution.

Lastly, languages like Hausa or Pingyao Chinese in which a CVO syllable can carry a contour, but the pitch excursion of the contour is significantly smaller than the contour on CVV or CVR cannot be adequately accounted for if we assume a one-to-one mapping between tones and moras. But this can be easily incorporated into an analysis that refers to concepts such $C_{CONTOUR}$ and tonal complexity, which encode richer phonetic information than contrastive units of length and the number of tonal targets.

Therefore, I conclude that the result of the survey supports either the direct approach or the contrast-specific positional markedness approach to contour tone licensing, both of which espouse the contrast-specificity of positional prominence in a bigger picture. Looking back at the possible interpretations of positional prominence laid out in Chapter 1, we are now left with only two possibilities, as shown in (57).

(57) Possible interpretations of positional prominence

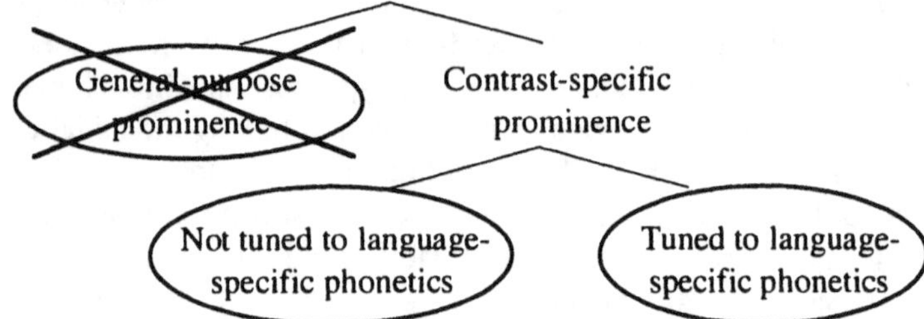

4.8 PROSPECTUS

As I have mentioned in §3.4, the direct approach and the contrast-specific positional markedness approach make two different predictions. One is that the former predicts disjunctive licensing, while the latter does not; the other is that between two positions that can both induce an increase in the $C_{CONTOUR}$ value of a syllable, the former predicts that the position that has a greater degree of influence will always be the one that has a stronger contour licensing ability, while the latter does not predict such correlation. There is in fact evidence in the survey that weighs towards the direct approach on account of the first prediction. There are many languages in which contour tones are licensed by distinct positions. E.g., in Luganda, as we have seen, the falling tone can surface on CVV and CVR (which can potentially be interpreted as CV[+sonorant]), but also on word-final CV. In Maasai, the tonal inventory is H, M, L, H͡L, and the syllable inventory is CV, CVC, CVV, and CVVC; the falling tone can surface on any CVVC and CVV, but also on word-final CV and CVC (Tucker and Mpaayei 1955). In Mende, both the falling tone and the rising tone are licensed by two different factors: the fall can occur on a long vowel or a short vowel in word-final position; the rise can occur on a long vowel or a short vowel in monosyllabic words.

Again, one may appeal to constraint disjunction in the contrast-specific positional markedness approach to derive the disjunctive licensing pattern, as sketched out in §3.4.2. But this mechanism would allow any two positional markedness constraints to be conjoined and thus predict disjunctive licensing by any two strong positions. Take the Mende example, given that [+long], 'word-final', and 'monosyllabic' are all necessary factors to characterize its contour tone licensing, the mechanism predicts that it is potentially possible to have a language Mende' in which a certain contour tone is only licensed in monosyllabic words or word-final syllables (which means word-final syllables, since syllables in monosyllabic words are a subset of word-final syllables), to the exclusion of non-final [+long] vowels, as evidenced by the following constraint ranking: *CONTOUR(¬word-final)∪*CONTOUR(¬monosyllabic) » IDENT(tone) » *CONTOUR(¬ word-final), *CONTOUR(¬monosyllabic), *CONTOUR(-long), *CONTOUR. But presumably, a long vowel in a polysyllabic word is longer than a short vowel in a monosyllabic word. Thus Mende' is a language in which a contour tone can occur on a syllable with shorter duration, but not on a syllable with longer duration. I hypothesize that this type language is unattested.[11] Similarly for Luganda, although we could treat one of the factors as CV[+sonorant], given that CVV and CVR can function as separate contour tone licensers for other languages, the constraint disjunction mechanism potentially predicts that it is possible to have a language Luganda' in which contour tones are licensed on CVR and word-final CV, to the exclusion non-final CVV. And this, I contend, is again unlikely to happen.

The following chapter aims to further tease apart the direct approach and the contrast-specific positional markedness approach by testing the second prediction. I focus on languages in which there are multiple positions that provide phonetically better docking sites for contour tones and see if the correlation 'greater $C_{CONTOUR}$ → greater phonological licensing ability of contour tone' is borne out. Specifically, I discuss a series of phonetic studies on sonorous rime duration in relevant languages and investigate whether the phonetic facts match the phonological patterning. And putting it in a broader perspective, the chapter aims to sort out the two possible interpretations under the contrast-specificity hypothesis of positional prominence shown in (57), i.e., whether phonology is tuned to language-specific phonetics or not. If the answer to the question is 'no', then the speakers' task is only to identify privileged positions for the contrast in question. Under this interpretation, phonology is still to a large extent autonomous, since it is sufficient to encode only the 'structural' properties of the tone-bearing units, such as '[+long] in word-final position', in phonology. There is no need to refer to phonetic categories such as $C_{CONTOUR}$ (CVV-final). If the answer to the question is 'yes', then the speakers not only have to identify privileged positions, but also have to keep track of the language-specific relative power of the conditioning factors. Under this interpretation, phonology must encode more phonetic details than traditionally assumed.

---

[11] But see §5.3 for discussion of possible counter-examples.

CHAPTER 5

The Role of Language-Specific Phonetics in Contour Tone Distribution: Instrumental Studies

5.1 IDENTIFYING RELEVANT LANGUAGES

In the previous chapter, we have established that strong licensing positions for contour tones are contrast-specific. This chapter primarily addresses the different predictions between the direct approach and the contrast-specific positional markedness approach on the comparability of contour tone bearing ability among multiple positions, all of which induce a greater $C_{CONTOUR}$ value. The predictions of these approaches have been laid out in §3.4. They are recapitulated in (1). Furthermore, we will also see more evidence against the moraic approach.

(1) Within a language, when there are multiple factors that induce greater $C_{CONTOUR}$ values:

a. *The direct approach*: their contour tone licensing ability corresponds to the degree of enhancement of $C_{CONTOUR}$: the greater the $C_{CONTOUR}$ value, the greater the contour tone licensing ability.

b. *The contrast-specific positional markedness approach*: any one of the factors may turn out to be the best contour tone licensor, regardless of the degree of phonetic advantage the factor induces as compared to the other factors.

The issue is addressed by instrumental studies of duration in languages with coexisting durational properties that fit the description of P_1 and P_2 in §3.4, i.e., two distinct properties of a syllable that can both induce lengthening of the sonorous portion of the rime. To recapitulate the gist of the argument, if we find languages in which the privileged factor for contour bearing is P_1 despite the fact that syllables endowed with P_1 but not P_2 have a shorter sonorous rime than those endowed with P_2 but not P_1, then we must conclude that the contrast-specific positional markedness approach is the correct one. If, on the other hand, the privileged factor is always the one that induces a greater lengthening effect, or in case of equal lengthening, a longer vocalic component, then we conclude that the direct approach is superior, since it makes exactly this prediction and no others.

Let me first identify the relevant languages. The first type of languages involves stress and final position in a prosodic domain. A language with non-final stress fits the scenario described above: if we take stress to be P_1 and final position to be P_2, the language in question has both syllables with only property P_1—the stressed syllables, and syllables with only property P_2—the final syllables. The clearest cases of this sort are some of the Southern Bantu languages, which have penultimate stress. Specifically, languages which have no vowel length contrasts and restrict their contour distribution solely on the basis of stress are the most relevant. Xhosa is a such a language (Lanham 1958, 1963, Jordan 1966). In many Northern Chinese dialects (e.g., Beijing Chinese), all syllables are equally stressed, but some monosyllabic reduplicative morphemes and functional words can be destressed, and they can occur word-finally. Contour tones are usually restricted to stressed syllables in these languages. They constitute a special case of stress interacting with position: like Xhosa, they can have a stressed penult and an unstressed ultima in a word; but unlike Xhosa in which stress is the marked property of a syllable, stresslessness is the marked property in these languages.

The second pair is a pair of segmental properties. Both contrastive vowel length and sonorancy of the coda consonant influence the sonorous duration of the rime cross-linguistically. For coda sonorancy, this is so not only because a sonorant coda contributes to the sonorous rime duration while an obstruent coda does not, but also because obstruent codas may shorten the duration of the preceding vowel, as in many Chinese dialects. If we take the [+long] feature of the vowel as property P_1 and the [+son] feature of the coda consonant as property P_2, then in a language with both vowel length and coda sonorancy contrasts, syllable CVVO has property P_1 but not P_2, and syllable CVR has property P_2 but not P_1. Among the languages that fit this description, Standard Thai (Abramson 1962, Gandour 1974) and Cantonese (Kao 1971, Li et al. 1995, Gordon 1998) allow fewer contour tones on CVVO than on CVR, while Navajo (Hoijer 1974, Kari 1976, Young and Morgan 1987, 1992) and Somali (Saeed 1982, 1993) do not allow contour tones on CVR, but do on CVVO.

Of all the combinations of factors influencing duration, these two pairs are the most commonly attested that fit the scenario which can differentiate the approaches under consideration: two durational factors cross-classify, yielding syllables that have either properties but not both; and the contour restrictions are based on *one* of these two factors.

Five languages that are representative of the scenarios laid out above, and for which instrumental data are accessible or obtainable, were included in a series of phonetic studies: Xhosa, Beijing Chinese, Standard Thai, Navajo, and Somali. The data sources for these languages are summarized in (2). All data collection was done in the sound booth of the UCLA Phonetics Laboratory. All data analyses were carried out on Kay Elemetrics CSL. The sampling rate for digitization was 20kHz. Spectrograms were made for the speech materials and duration was measured from the spectrograms. In the next section, I lay out the specific hypotheses and document the phonetic results for these five languages. Furthermore, I also discuss the phonetic results on Cantonese in Gordon (1998, 1999a), a language which also fits the criteria above.

(2) Data sources for the phonetic studies:

Language	Source	No. of speakers
Xhosa	UCLA Language Archive	1
Beijing Chinese	Data collection	2
Standard Thai	Data collection	2
Navajo	UCLA Language Archive and data collection	15 (from Archive) 1 (from data collection)
Somali	UCLA Language Archive	1

There is another type of languages that potentially distinguishes the direct approach from the other approaches. These languages have a vowel length contrast, yet contour tones are restricted to word- or utterance-final syllables irrespective of their vowel length. Therefore, the situation here is that the final syllable with a short vowel can carry a contour tone, while non-final syllables with a long vowel cannot. There are two languages of this sort in my survey: Lama (Kenstowicz, Nikiema and Ourso 1988, Ourso 1989, Kenstowicz 1994) and Kɔnni (Cahill 1999). But I do not have any phonetic data on these languages. For further discussion of these languages, see §5.3.

5.2 INSTRUMENTAL STUDIES

5.2.1 Xhosa

5.2.1.1 Hypothesis and Materials

The data pattern of Xhosa has already been discussed in §4.3.2.2. To recapitulate: Xhosa has penultimate word stress, vowel length is non-contrastive except in a few grammatical morphemes, and all syllables are open.[1] There are

---

[1] The nasal /m/ that sometimes seems to be in the coda position is in fact syllabic.

three tones in Xhosa: High (H), Low (L), and Fall (HL̂). There are no distributional restrictions for H and L, but HL̂ is generally restricted to the penult of a content word. A few monosyllabic grammatical prefixes and suffixes can also bear the HL̂ tone, and they do not necessarily occur in the penultimate position of a word. But the vowel in these morphemes is lengthened. In an utterance, especially when spoken quickly, some words lose their penultimate stress, creating the tonal alternation HL̂→H (Lanham 1958, 1963, Jordan 1966). See §4.3.2.2 for examples.

The focus here is the fact that HL̂ is restricted to the penult of a word. The two relevant durational factors here are stress and final position. The two types of syllables directly of interest are the penult and the ultima. The penult is subject to lengthening by virtue of stress, but not by virtue of being at a prosodic boundary. The opposite is true for the ultima. Given that all syllables are open, the vowel alone constitutes the sonorous portion of the rime. I lay out the hypothesis on vowel duration in Xhosa according to the direct approach in (3).

(3) Hypothesis (Xhosa):

The penult has a longer vowel duration than the ultima.

The phonetic data for Xhosa were extracted from a 45-minute analog tape in the UCLA Language Archive. It consists mainly of trisyllabic or tetrasyllabic words read in isolation by one female speaker of Xhosa. Each word has two repetitions. All words extracted for digitization and measurements were trisyllabic. All target syllables—ultima, penult or initial—were open with a level-toned /a/ as the nucleus. The matched vowel quality ensures that any durational differences detected are not induced by vowel quality differences. Level-toned syllables were used to ensure that any durational advantage of the penultimate syllable, if detected, is due to the position per se, not the falling contour it carries, thus avoiding circularity. Fifty-four words were used for the final target, thirty-four for the penultimate target, and forty-four for the initial target. The complete word list is given in (4). In the word list, H is marked with an acute accent /´/, Low is marked with a grave accent /`/, and HL̂ is marked with /ˆ/. The occasional rising tone, marked with /ˇ/, is probably due to morpheme concatenation.

(4) Xhosa word list:

Ultima		Penult		Initial	
pàpáʃà	'make known'	pàpáʃà	'make known'	pàpáʃà	'make known'
ìpákà	'park'	ìpákà	'park'	bàlísà	'enroll'
bàlísà	'enroll'	pʰàkámà	'stand erect'	dàbúlà	'split asunder'
dàbúlà	'split asunder'	vàkálà	'to be audible'	càbúlà	'chafe'
càbúlà	'chafe'	úvàlò	'nervous, anxiety'	kàkʰûlù	'musical forte'
gàlélà	'pour, throw in'	sàkázà	'scattered things'	gàlélà	'pour, throw in'
pʰàkámà	'stand erect'	wálázà	'be careless'	pʰàkámà	'stand erect'
ìkʰâkʰà	'shield, trophy'	íràbà	'rubber'	vàkálà	'to be audible'
vàkálà	'to be audible'	nàkánà	'glimpse'	sàkázà	'scattered things'
sàkázà	'scattered things'	k͡ǁàkázà	'do untidily'	wálázà	'be careless'
úgûtʃá	'combustion'	ámák͡ǁà	'shoulders'	jàlúlà	'roll the eye'
wálázà	'be careless'	úŋk͡ǁàwù	'3-legged ironpot'	màmélà	'listen'
ìlíwá	'precipice'	íŋǀásò	'protest'	nàkánà	'glimpse'
íràbà	'rubber'	íŋ!ájì	'a bald head'	ɲámékà	'attend closely'
làndúlà	'make excuse'	í!ʷàxà	'striped fish'	ǀáɲìlè	'clear'
jàlúlà	'roll the eye'	íŋgàtá	'kind of wild cat'	!ávĭlè	'enquisitive'
màmélà	'listen'	ùmɣàjò	'coursely ground stuff'	ǀʰánílè	'accurate'
nàkánà	'glimpse'			!ʰàjísà	'be proud'
ɲámékà	'attend closely'			k͡ǁàkázà	'do untidily'
íɲândá	'bundle of wood'			ámák͡ǁà	'shoulders'
íŋgàtá	'wild cat'			k͡!àbŭgà	'get burst open'
bùǀâlà	'private'			ŋ͡ǁànélà	'desire earnestly'
!ʰàjísà	'be proud'				
k͡ǁàkázà	'do untidily'				
ámák͡ǁà	'shoulders'				
k͡!àbŭgà	'get burst open'				
ŋ͡ǁànélà	'desire earnestly'				

5.2.1.2 Rusults

The mean duration of /a/ for the three positions is shown in the bar plot in (5). The error bars indicate one standard deviation. The /a/ in the penult has a mean duration of 212ms. The /a/ in the ultima has a considerably shorter duration—132ms. The /a/ in the initial position is yet shorter—99ms. One way ANOVA shows that the effect of position is highly significant ($F(2,131)=242.98$, $p<0.0001$). Fisher's PLSD post-hoc tests show that all pairs of comparison—penult vs. ultima, penult vs. initial, and ultima vs. initial—have a significant effect at the level of $p<0.0001$. Given the limited number of speakers available to Xhosa and the rest of the languages included in the studies,

I only ran statistical tests that treat subjects as a fixed effect, and therefore these tests only allow inference about the subjects included in the study. This is the inevitable limitation of any study that only has a small number of subjects (de Jong and Zawaydeh 1999, Max and Onghena 1999). Any significant effects revealed here must be subject to further tests on data acquired from more subjects which treats the subjects and subjects alone as the independent variable.

(5) Xhosa vowel duration (ms):

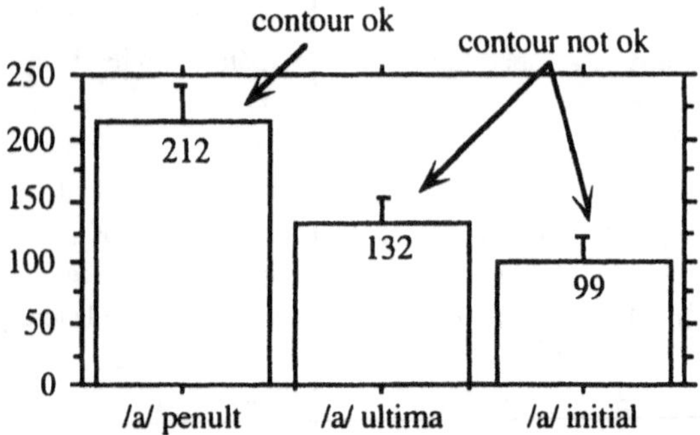

The duration results clearly show that although both stress and final position induce lengthening effect of the syllable nucleus, the effect of stress is significantly greater. One possible objection to this claim is that in the word list, most of the penultimate /a/'s have a H tone, while most of the final /a/'s have a L tone. Therefore the difference between penult and ultima could be due to this tonal difference. I calculated the mean duration of H-toned and L-toned /a/'s in these two positions separately. The results are summarized in (6). As can be seen, although for the penult, the H-toned vowels are longer than the L-toned vowels, the opposite is true for the ultima. Moreover, the durational differences caused by the tonal difference is very small compared to those caused by the positional difference. Thus we can safely conclude that the penult has a significantly longer nucleus than the ultima.

(6) Duration of H-tone and L-tone vowels in Xhosa:

	H	L
Penult	217ms	199ms
Ultima	130ms	132ms

The phonetic hypothesis in (3) is therefore supported by the experimental results: in Xhosa, the lengthening effect induced by stress is greater than that induced by final position. Since it is exactly stress that defines the contour restriction in Xhosa, I conclude that the data in Xhosa are consistent with the direct approach.

5.2.2 Beijing Chinese

5.2.2.1 Hypothesis and Materials

Syllables in Beijing Chinese are either open or closed by a nasal /n/ or /ŋ/. The vowel of an open syllable is either long or a diphthong. Most syllables in Beijing are equally stressed. But some monosyllabic reduplicative morphemes and functional words can be destressed, and they can occur word-finally. There are four lexical tones in Beijing: 55, 35, 213 and 51.[2] Tones 55, 35, and 51 can occur on any regularly stressed syllables. Tone 213 can only occur on a regularly stressed utterance final syllable; non-finally it is realized as 21. On a final destressed syllable however, only level tones can be realized. These syllables are usually described as having the 'neutral tone'. Chao (1948, 1968) gives the following description of its realization under different tonal environments:

(7) Phonetic realization of the neutral tone in Beijing Chinese:

Half-Low after 55:	tʰa˥ tə.˨	'his'
Mid after 35:	ʂeɪ˧˥ tə·˧	'whose'
Half-High after 21:	ni˨˩ tə˙˦	'yours'
Low after 51:	ta˥˩tə.˩	'big one(s)'

The tonal distribution in Beijing Chinese is summarised in (8).

(8) Tonal distribution in Beijing Chinese:

	55, 35, 51	213
Stressed final	√	√
Stressed non-final	√	-
Destressed final	-	-

Focusing our attention to the boldface cases in the table, we can see that Beijing exhibits a situation similar to Xhosa. In a disyllabic word, we may find that the penult is stressed, but the ultima is stressless. Thus the penult is subject

---

2 Tones are marked with Chao letters here. '5' indicates the highest pitch used in lexical tones while '1' indicates the lowest pitch. Contour tones are marked with two juxtaposed numbers. E.g., 51 indicates a falling tone from the highest pitch to the lowest pitch.

to lengthening under stress, while the ultima is subject to final lengthening. We may then lay out the hypothesis on rime duration for Beijing Chinese, as in (9).

(9) Hypothesis (Beijing Chinese):

Non-final regularly stressed syllables have a longer sonorous rime duration than final destressed syllables.

The phonetic data of Beijing Chinese were recorded from two male native speakers—ZJ (the author) and LHY. The speaker read the word *ma55-ma0* ('0' represents a neutral tone) 'mom' with ten repetitions. A level-toned first syllable was selected to avoid circularity. As a means of testing for final lengthening alone, the speakers also read the nonsense word *ma55-ma55* with ten repetitions.

5.2.2.2 Results

The mean vowel duration for the two syllables in *ma55-ma0* is shown in the bar plot in (10a). The vowel in the initial position, which has regular stress, has a mean duration of 204ms. The vowel in the final position, which is destressed, has a considerably shorter mean duration—109ms. The error bars again represent one standard deviation. A two-tail paired t-test shows that this difference is highly significant ($df=15$, $t=12.99$, $p<0.0001$).

The durational data clearly support the phonetic hypothesis in (9). In Beijing Chinese, regularly stressed syllables are significantly longer than final destressed syllables, even though the stressed syllables do not benefit from final lengthening, while the destressed syllables potentially do.

The effect of final lengthening is not immediately obvious in (10a). But it can be observed in durational results obtained from the nonsense word *ma55-ma55*, shown in (10b). As we can see, when the two syllables are equally stressed, the effect of final lengthening is apparent. A two-tail paired t-test shows that this effect is highly significant ($df=15$, $t=-13.39$, $p<0.0001$). Looking back on the contour tone restrictions in Beijing given in (8), we can see that this lengthening effect is responsible for the final stressed syllables' ability to host 213—a complex contour tone.

(10) Beijing Chinese vowel duration:

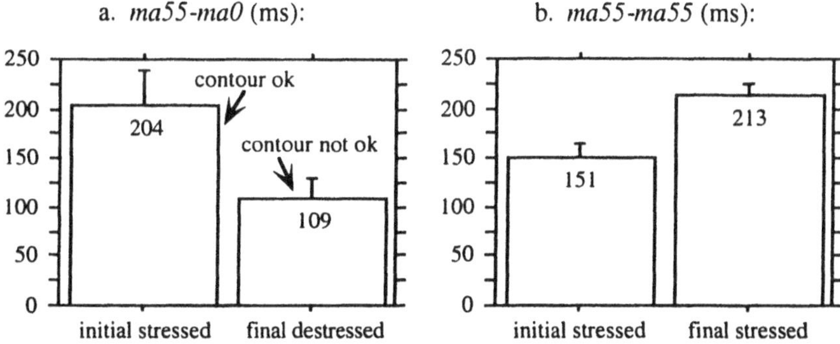

We can also ask the question: does the final destressed syllable benefit from final lengthening at all? To investigate this, the same two speakers were also recorded reading the phrases *shuo55-ma55-ma0* 'scold mother' and *ma55-ma0-shuo55* 'mother says', each with ten repetitions. The vowel durations for *ma0* in these two phrases were measured and compared. The *ma0* in *shuo55-ma55-ma0* has an average vowel duration of 84.7ms, while the *ma0* in *ma55-ma0-shuo55* has an average vowel duration of 84.5ms: the two are practically identical. Not surprisingly, a two-tail paired t-test shows that the difference is not significant ($t=-0.06$, $df=15$, $p>0.05$). Therefore destressed syllables in Beijing Chinese in fact do not benefit from final lengthening, even though regularly stressed syllables do.

At this point, the picture of Beijing Chinese emerges as follows. In the direct approach, the $C_{CONTOUR}$ values that are directly relevant to the contour tone restrictions of Beijing Chinese are $C_{CONTOUR}$(σ-destressed), $C_{CONTOUR}$(σ-stressed-nonfinal), and $C_{CONTOUR}$(σ-stressed-final). From the phonetic results, we can represent their values as x, $x+m$, and $x+m+n$ (x, m, $n>0$) respectively. Among all possible $C_{CONTOUR}$ categories in Beijing Chinese, these are the ones that correspond to different contour bearing abilities: $C_{CONTOUR}$(σ-destressed) can only carry level tones, simple contour tones ok on $C_{CONTOUR}$(σ-stressed-nonfinal), and complex contour 213 ok only on $C_{CONTOUR}$(σ-stressed-final). Clearly, the contour licesning ability of these syllable types is determined by $C_{CONTOUR}$ values: the greater the $C_{CONTOUR}$, the greater the syllable's ability to carry more complex contour tones. For the contrast-specific positional markedness approach, a principled account can be only achieved if one of the parameters is *final lengthening* instead of *the final position*: the final destressed syllable cannot carry contour tones since only *CONTOUR(-stress) and *CONTOUR(¬final-lengthening) outrank IDENT(tone). But by referring to final lengthening, this move amounts to acknowledging the effect of duration.

The final complication that should be mentioned in Beijing Chinese is that the phonetic studies on neutral tones by Lin (1983), Wu and Lin (1989), and

Wang (1996) have shown the the pitches for these tones are not level. Generally, the neutral tones after 55, 35 and 51 are falling to varying degrees, while the neutral tone after 21 is a mid or high-mid level tone. The crucial difference between these pitch changes and real contour tones is that these pitch changes are not used contrastively; i.e., they do not contrast with level tones or each other. These tones have been documented as levels in all phonological literature on Chinese, and this seems to agree with native speakers' intuition on their values. The answer to the discrepancy between the perceived and actual values of these tones may be found in the extremely short duration of destressed syllables—only slightly over 100ms. Greenberg and Zee (1979) show that if the f_0 ramp is only 90ms, the degree of perceived contour will be very small even if the slope of the f_0 ramp is high. They further conjecture that the minimal duration for a substantial percept of dynamic pitch is about 130ms—longer than the sonorous rime duration of destressed syllables in Beijing. This explains why there is no contour percept even though there is f_0 change during the syllable. As for why there is f_0 change at all during such short syllables, I suggest that it results from the interaction between perseverative tonal coarticulation and boundary intonation.

5.2.3 Standard Thai

5.2.3.1 Hypothesis and Materials

Syllables in Standard Thai can be open, closed by an obstruent /p/, /t/, /k/, or /ʔ/, or closed by a nasal /m/, /n/, or /ŋ/. Vowel length is contrastive in closed syllables. Therefore, possible syllable types in Thai are CV, CVN, CVVN, CVO, and CVVO (N=/m, n, ŋ/, O=/p, t, k, ʔ/). I will refer to syllables closed by an obstruent (CVO and CVVO) as checked syllables, and other syllables (CV, CVN, and CVVN) as non-checked syllables. There are five tones in Thai—High (H), Mid (M), Low (L), Fall (H͡L), and Rise (L͡H). On non-checked syllables, all five tones can occur. On CVVO, generally, only H͡L and L occur, but in rare instances, H can also occur (e.g., *nóot* 'note'; *khwɔ́ɔt* 'quart', both English loanwords). On CVO, generally, only H and L occur, but H͡L occurs occasionally (e.g., *kɔ̂ʔ* 'then, consequently') (Gandour 1974, Hudak 1987). This tonal distribution is summarized in (11) (adapted from Gandour 1974).

(11) Tonal distribution in Standard Thai (Gandour 1974):

	H	M	L	H͡L	L͡H
CV	+	+	+	+	+
CVN	+	+	+	+	+
CVVN	+	+	+	+	+
CVVO	(+)	-	+	+	-
CVO	+	-	+	(+)	-

(Parentheses indicate rare occurrence.)

Therefore, the distribution of contour tones in Thai is primarily affected by the checked/non-checked distinction, as non-checked syllables can carry both L͡H and H͡L whether they have a long or a short vowel. But the phonemic status of vowel length is also relevant, since H͡L can occur on CVVO, but usually not on CVO.[3]

Here I focus on the checked/non-checked distinction. The fact that it is L͡H, not H͡L, that is missing from the tonal inventory of checked syllables indicates that this aspect of the tonal distribution may be durationally based, since pitch rises take longer to implement than pitch falls with equal excursion. The two durational factors here are checked vs. non-checked, and short vs. long vowels: it is well known that in many Sino-Tibetan languages, vowels in checked syllables are considerably shorter than non-checked syllables; and apparently, a phonemic long vowel is longer than a phonemic short vowel. The crucial durational comparisons here are then between CV and CVVO, and between CVN and CVVO. The first member of each pair has the advantage of being non-checked, while the second member has the advantage of having a phonemic long vowel. Given the contour distribution facts, I lay out the hypothesis for Thai as in (12).

(12) Hypothesis (Standard Thai):

Non-checked syllables have a longer sonorous rime duration than checked syllables. In particular, CV>CVVO, CVN>CVVO.

---

3 The fact that CVVO primarily carries H͡L and L and CVO primarily carries H and L can be seen from the following historical perspective. In Early Thai (pre-15th century), there was no tonal contrast on checked syllables. Between the 15th and 17th century, a tone split process occurred: on CVVO, the split resulted in a H͡L after a voiced onset and a L after a voiceless onset; on CVO, it resulted in a H after a voiced onset and a L after a voiceless onset (Strecker 1990). Possibly, the reason why a H͡L did not result on CVO was that there was not enough duration for the contour to surface.

Thai data were collected from two native speakers: YS (male) and VV (female). The word list used in the study is given in (13). For each of the five syllable types—CV, CVVN, CVN, CVVO, CVO, four monosyllabic words were included. All words have the nucleus /a/ and are either Mid-toned or Low-toned. The speakers read each word with eight repetitions.

(13) Thai word list:

	IPA	Gloss	IPA	Gloss
CV	bà:	'shoulder'	pà:	'rain forest'
	dà:	'to curse'	pʰà:	'to split'
CVVN	ca:n	'a plate'	cʰa:m	'a bowl'
	cʰa:n	'fiber residue'	kʰà:ŋ	'a spinning top'
CVN	sàn	'to vibrate'	tam	'to pound'
	daŋ	'loud'	tʰam	'to do'
CVVO	kʰà:t	'to be torn'	bà:p	'sin'
	bà:t	'Thai currency'	hà:t	'shore, beach'
CVO	bàt	'ticket, card'	dàp	'extinguish'
	kàt	'to bite'	dàk	'to trap'

5.2.3.2 ***Results***

The sonorous rime duration for the five syllable types are plotted in two separate graphs in (14), one for speaker YS, the other for speaker VV. The gray portion in the bars for CVN and CVVN indicates sonorous duration contributed by the nasal coda.

(14) Thai sonorous rime duration (ms):

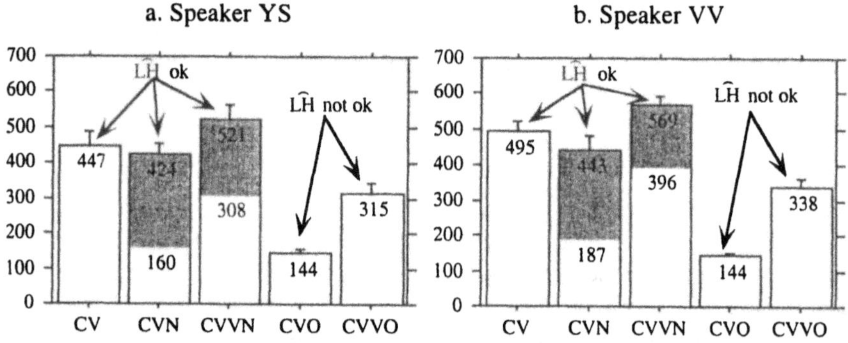

For each speaker, a one-way ANOVA with sonorous rime duration as the dependent variable and syllable type as the independent variable was carried out.

Unsurprisingly, the effect is highly significant for both speakers: for YS, $F(4, 135)=623.3$, $p<0.0001$; for VV, $F(4, 135)=1157.7$, $p<0.0001$. Fisher's PLSD post-hoc tests show that for both speakers, both CV and CVN have a longer sonorous rime duration than CVVO at the significance level of $p<0.0001$.

Therefore, the hypotheses in (12) are supported by the phonetic data. Even though there is no vowel length contrast in open syllables in Thai, the vowel in a CV syllable is phonetically long. It is in fact significantly longer than the long vowel in CVVO. Clearly, the use of 'CV' to characterize these syllables should be taken as conventional; it is misleading with regard to the actual duration. The fact that CVN has a longer sonorous rime duration than CVVO is largely due to the contribution of the overly long nasal coda. For both speakers, the nasal coda in CVN accounts for more than half of its sonorous rime duration. But vowel shortening in checked syllables may also be relevant, as speaker VV shows such effect: the vowel in CVVO is considerably shorter than the vowel in CVVN (338ms vs. 396ms).

Recall that Thai allows both $\widehat{\text{LH}}$ and $\widehat{\text{HL}}$ to occur on a non-checked syllable even when it has a short vowel and does not allow $\widehat{\text{LH}}$ on a checked syllable even when it has a long vowel. The data show that this tonal distribution pattern corresponds closely with the phonetic pattern: a longer sonorous rime duration allows a more 'difficult' contour—$\widehat{\text{LH}}$—to surface. The direct approach to tonal distribution correctly predicts that this is a possible pattern, and does not predict the opposite pattern, in which $\widehat{\text{LH}}$ can surface on CVVO, but not on CV or CVN.

The contrast-specific positional markedness approach cannot rule out the latter pattern in a principled way, because both CVVO and CVN qualify as prominent positions, and there is no a priori reason to rule out the possibility that CVVO is a better contour tone carrier.

The moraic approach also runs into problems here. Given that there is no vowel length contrast in open syllables, there is no structural pressure to posit the vowel in CV to be bimoraic. But one would *have to* assume that the vowel in CVVO is bimoraic in order to characterize its contrast with CVO. Therefore the implicational hierarchy under a structure-only approach would be that a contour tone is allowed on CVVO before it is allowed on CV. This is in contradiction with the distribution of contour tones in Thai.

In §3.2, I mentioned that Standard Thai is one of the languages that could help determine the range of coefficient *a* in the definition of C_{CONTOUR}, which is repeated in (15). This is because the strictest *a* range $1<a<\frac{\text{Dur}(R_1)-\text{Dur}(R_2)}{\text{Dur}(V_2)-\text{Dur}(V_1)}$ is determined by the comparison between $P_1=V_1R_1$ and $P_2=V_2R_2$ where $\text{Dur}(V_1)<\text{Dur}(V_2)$, but $\text{Dur}(V_1)+\text{Dur}(R_1) > \text{Dur}(V_2)+\text{Dur}(R_2)$, and in Standard Thai, this situation is manifested by P_1=VN, P_2=VVO.

(15) $C_{CONTOUR} = a \cdot Dur(V) + Dur(R)$

We can calculate the *a* range from the data of the two speakers. The relevant duration values for each speaker are given in (16).

(16) Speaker YS: $Dur(V_1)=160ms$, $Dur(R_1)=424-160=264ms$;

$Dur(V_2)=315ms$, $Dur(R_2)=0$.

Speaker VV: $Dur(V_1)=187ms$, $Dur(R_1)=443-187=256ms$;

$Dur(V_2)=338ms$, $Dur(R_2)=0$.

Substituting the variables in $1<a<\frac{Dur(R_1)-Dur(R_2)}{Dur(V_2)-Dur(V_1)}$ with the duration values in (16), we get the *a* range from the two speakers, shown in (17).

(17) Speaker YS: $1<a<1.703$

Speaker VV: $1<a<1.695$

Taking the smaller *a* range of the two, we know that $1<a<1.695$.

The calculation here is not meant to show that we have successfully derived the *a* range. Rather, it is meant to demonstrate how to apply the general heuristics discussed in §3.2 to real languages to derive the *a* range. Our approach here is admittedly heuristic, but it is by no means circular. Upon observing a sufficient number of languages, we can hone in on a specific *a* range, and test its validity against further language data. The theory is falsifiable, since it makes concrete predictions about the contour tone bearing ability of syllable types (as indicated by $C_{CONTOUR}$), and the predictions can be tested against the phonological patterning of contour tone distribution in languages.

5.2.4 Cantonese

A data pattern similar to Thai is documented by Gordon (1998) for Cantonese. Possible syllable types in Cantonese are the same as Thai: CV, CVN, CVVN, CVO, and CVVO (N=/m, n, ŋ/, O=/p, t, k/). With both vowel length contrast and the checked/non-checked distinction, the distribution of contour tones in Cantonese is also only affected by the latter factor. In CV, CVN and CVVN, seven different tones, including four contour tones, can occur: 53, 35, 21, 23, 55, 33, 22. But in CVVO and CVO, only level tones 5, 3, and 2 can occur, even when the syllable contains a long vowel.

Gordon's duration data for different syllable types of Cantonese are graphed in (18). Again, the gray portion in the bars for /a:m/ and /am/ indicates sonorous duration contributed by the nasal coda. Similarly to Thai, even though there is no vowel length contrast in open syllables, vowels in open syllables are phonetically long—considerably longer than the phonemic long vowel in CVVO. Also, the sonorous portion of the rime in CVR is considerably longer than that in CVVO.

(18) Cantonese sonorous rime duration (ms):

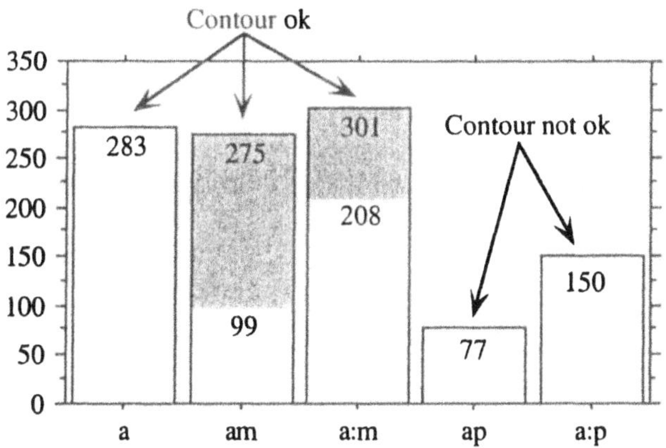

Cantonese may differ from Thai in one respect. In Thai, CVN has a longer sonorous rime duration than CVVO, largely due to the overly long nasal coda, and vowel shortening in checked syllables plays a minor role. But in Cantonese, it is probably the combination of both factors that gives rise to this durational pattern: in (18), we can see that the nasal coda in /am/ accounts for more than half of the sonorous rime duration, and the long vowel in /a:p/ is considerably shorter than that in /a:m/ (150ms vs. 208ms). The more prominent vowel shortening in Cantonese maybe due to the vowel quality differences that accompany the vowel length distinction. For example, in Kao (1971), the long and short versions of /a/ are transcribed as [ɑ:] and [ɐ] respectively. This may give the long vowel more freedom to shorten before an obstruent coda, as the long/short contrast is still safely maintained by their quality difference. Thai, however, does not have quality differences between long and short vowels, and thus must more faithfully preserve the durational distinction between them before an obstruent coda.

I further conjecture that in all languages that favor contour tones on non-checked syllables regardless of the contrastive vowel length status, either a prolonged sonorant coda, or shortening of vowel nucleus in checked syllables, or both, are at play, and this results in non-checked syllables having a significantly longer sonorous rime duration than checked syllables, even when the former has a phonemic short vowel and the latter has a phonemic long vowel.

Just like Standard Thai, Cantonese can be used as another language in our search of an appropriate *a* value for the definition of $C_{CONTOUR}$. The relevant syllable types are again CVN and CVVO, and the relevant duration values are summarized in (19).

(19) $Dur(V_1)$=99ms, $Dur(R_1)$=275-99=176ms;

$Dur(V_2)$=150ms, $Dur(R_2)$=0.

Substituting the variables in $1<a<\frac{Dur(R_1)-Dur(R_2)}{Dur(V_2)-Dur(V_1)}$ with the duration values in (19), we get the *a* range $1<a<3.451$. Therefore, the *a* range that we have obtained from the Thai data ($1<a<1.695$) should be able to account for the Cantonese data; i.e., it will predict that CVN has a greater contour tone bearing ability than CVVO in Cantonese.

5.2.5 Navajo

5.2.5.1 Hypothesis and Materials

The two factors that influence the sonorous rime duration in Thai and Cantonese—phonemic vowel length and coda sonorancy—are also at play in Navajo. The only difference is that in Navajo, vowel length is contrastive in both open and closed syllables, which results in six syllable types: CV, CVO, CVR, CVV, CVVO, and CVVR. But the tonal distribution in Navajo is very different from Thai and Cantonese. Navajo syllables can have four possible tones: High (H), Low (L), Fall (H͡L), and Rise (L͡H), with the contour tones H͡L and L͡H restricted to long vowels and diphthongs, i.e., CVV, CVVO, and CVVR syllables. Therefore, unlike Thai and Cantonese, the factor that determines the contour distribution in Navajo is phonemic vowel length, not coda sonorancy. The tonal distribution in Navajo is summarized in (20).

(20) Tonal distribution in Navajo:

	H	L	HL̂	LĤ
CV	+	+	-	-
CVO	+	+	-	-
CVR	+	+	-	-
CVV	+	+	+	+
CVVO	+	+	+	+
CVVR	+	+	+	+

The crucial phonetic comparisons for contour tone bearing ability are between CVR and CVV, and between CVR and CVVO: CVR benefits from having a sonorant coda, while CVV and CVVO benefit from having a long vowel. Given that a vowel is a better tone bearing segment than a sonorant consonant, we know that CVV and CVVO have greater contour tone bearing ability than CVR as long as their sonorous rime duration is no shorter than CVR's (see §2.2 and §3.2). Thus, the hypothesis for the sonorous rime duration in Navajo under the direct approach crucially differs from that in Cantonese and Thai, as shown in (21).

(21) Hypothesis (Navajo):

> Syllables with a long vowel or diphthong have a longer sonorous rime duration than syllables with a short vowel. In particular, CVV≥CVR, CVVO≥CVR.

One data source of Navajo is two analog audio tapes in the UCLA Language Archive made by Joyce McDonough in the Navajo Mountain area in 1993. Fourteen speakers read a word list after a lead speaker. The dialect they speak was categorized as Western Navajo by McDonough. For each word, there were five tokens from the lead speaker and one from each of the other speakers. The words extracted for use in the durational study included two representative words for each of the following syllables types: CV, CVO, CVR, CVV, CVVO, and CVVR. All words were disyllabic except one. The target syllable was always the second syllable in the disyllabic words and had the vowel /i/ as its nucleus. It was always level-toned. The word list is given in (22). Both practical orthography and IPA transcription are given. High tone is marked with an acute accent /ˊ/. Low tone is not marked. The target syllables are in boldface.

(22) Navajo word list 1 (McDonough tape, 15 speakers):

	Ortho.	IPA	Gloss	Ortho.	IPA	Gloss
CV	sání	sání	'old one'	bizhí	piʒí	'his voice'
CVO	bíni'	píniʔ	'his mind'	bizid	pizit	'his liver'
CVR	bitin	pitʰin	'his ice'	bikin	pikʰin	'his house'
CVV	sáanii	sáanii	'old woman'	kwii	kwii	'here'
CVVO	binii'	piniiʔ	'his face'	bitsii'	pitsʰiiʔ	'his hair'
CVVR	biyiin	pijiin	'his song'	bidziil	bitsiil	'his mountain'

I also collected phonetic data from another native Navajo speaker—EN, who was from the White Horse Lake in New Mexico and speaks an Eastern Navajo dialect. The word list used for EN is given in (23). For each syllable type, two words with /i/ and two words with /a/ were used. All except one target vowels/rimes were in the second syllable of a disyllabic word. The only exception was *'adidiil* 'snowstorm', which was trisyllabic. All target syllables were low-toned. The speaker read each word with eight repetitions.

(23) Navajo word list 2 (data collection, 1 speaker):

	/i/			/a/		
	Ortho.	IPA	Gloss	Ortho.	IPA	Gloss
CV	tł'izi	tł'izi	'little goat'	ncha	n̥cha	'you're crying'
	jádí	tʃátí	'antelope'	shimá	ʃimá	'my mother'
CVO	bibid	pipit	'his stomach'	bíla'	píłaʔ	'his hand'
	'atsi'	atsʰiʔ	'daughter'	bita'	pitʰaʔ	'amidst'
CVR	'ádin	ʔátin	'none'	łikan	łikʰan	'it's sweet'
	bitsin	pitsʰin	'his bone'	sigan	sikan	'dry, skinny'
CVV	tseebíí	tsʰeepíí	'eight'	'ałhaa	ʔałhaa	'to each other'
	bichíí	pitʃíí	'red ochre'	gonaa	konaa	'across'
CVVO	binii'	piniiʔ	'his face'	binaa'	pinaaʔ	'his eyes'
	bitsii'	pitsʰiiʔ	'his hair'	tse'naa'	tsʰeʔnaaʔ	'across'
CVVR	hastiin	hastʰiin	'Mr, sir'	bigaan	pikaan	'his arm'
	'adidiil	ʔatitiil	'snowstorm'	tsé'áán	tsʰéʔáán	'rock cave'

5.2.5.2 Results

The rime duration results obtained from McDonough's tape are plotted in (24). The darker portion in the bars for CVR and CVVR indicates sonorous duration contributed by the sonorant coda. A one-way ANOVA shows that syllable type has a significant effect on the sonorous duration of the rime ($F(5, 222)=208.8$, $p<0.0001$). Fisher's PLSD post-hoc tests show that the difference between CVR and CVVO is not significant ($p>0.05$), but the difference between CVR and CVVO is ($p<0.0001$).

(24) Navajo sonorous rime duration (ms) (McDonough's tape):

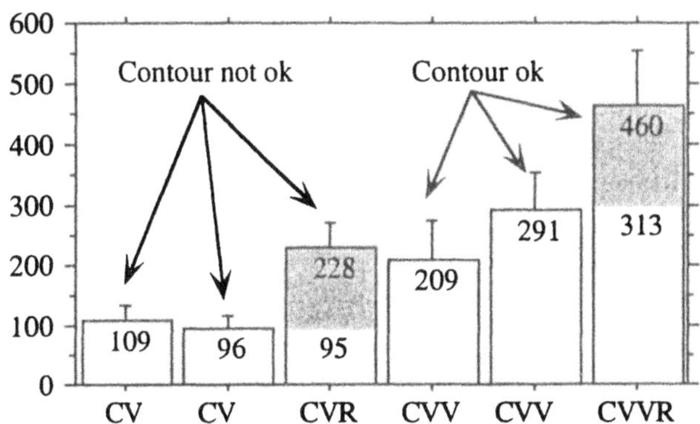

Therefore, the duration data support the phonetic hypothesis in (21): there is no difference in sonorous rime duration between CVR and CVV, and the sonorous rime duration of CVVO is significantly greater than that of CVR. And if we look at the vowel duration in CVR, we can see that it is the shortest of all syllable types—a mere 95ms. More than half of the sonorous duration in a VR rime is contributed by the sonorant coda. The difference in tone-bearing ability between CVR and CVV therefore lies in the difference between a sonorant consonant of 228-95=133ms and a vowel of 209-95=114ms. Although I have no perceptual study to support the hypothesis, it is quite plausible that the winner is the latter.

The duration results obtained from McDonough's tape are confirmed by data collected from EN. The average sonorous duration of the rime and vowel duration for each syllable type are shown in (25). Again, the gray portion in the bars for CVR and CVVR indicates sonorous duration contributed by the sonorant coda. A one-way ANOVA shows that the syllable type has a significant effect on the sonorous rime duration: $F(5, 162)=596.7$, $p<0.0001$. From the plot in (25), we can see that CVR has a comparable sonorous duration in the rime to CVV and CVVO: it is not significantly different from CVVO (Fisher's PLSD post-hoc tests, $p>0.05$); and even though it is marginally greater than CVV (Fisher's PLSD post-hoc tests, $0.01<p<0.05$), the durational difference is only 19ms. Moreover, of the 319ms of sonorous rime duration in CVR, only 152ms is contributed by the vowel. This leaves the comparison in tone-bearing ability between CVR and CVV the comparison between a sonorant consonant of 319-152=167ms and a vowel of 300-152=148ms. I again conjecture that the winner is the latter.

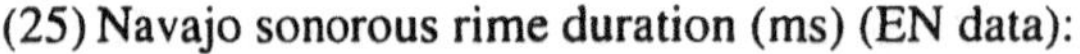
(25) Navajo sonorous rime duration (ms) (EN data):

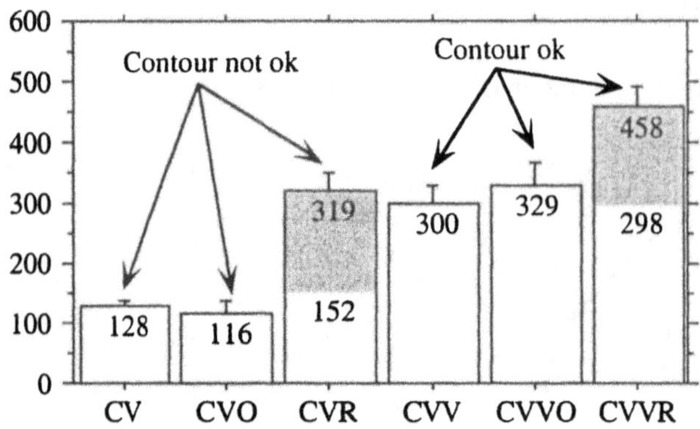

I therefore conclude that the hypothesis in (21) is supported by phonetic data. CVR in Navajo has comparable sonorous rime duration to CVV and CVVO. In light of the fact that the vocalic duration plays a more important role than the duration of the sonorant coda in the definition of $C_{CONTOUR}$ ($C_{CONTOUR} = a \cdot Dur(V)+Dur(R)$, $a>1$), the direct approach, which uses the $C_{CONTOUR}$ value of a syllable to predict its contour bearing behavior, correctly predicts that CVV and CVVO are better suited for contour tone bearing than CVR. A contrast-specific positional markedness approach again does not in principle rule out the possibility that CVR is a better contour tone bearer. But the results here are consistent with the moraic approach, since one may simply posit that only vowels are moraic in Navajo.

Comparing Navajo with Thai and Cantonese, we observe a crucial difference: in Thai and Cantonese, the sonorous rime duration in CVR is considerably longer than that in CVVO, while in Navajo, the two durations are comparable. I further conjecture that the Navajo pattern characterizes the durational pattern for all languages that restrict contour tones to long vowels. In these languages, the sonorant codas do not have a prolonged duration as in Thai, nor do obstruent codas considerably shorten the duration of the nucleus vowel as in Cantonese. Therefore the sonorous duration in CVR is comparable to that in CVVO.

5.2.6 Somali

A preliminary study of Somali (data from UCLA Language Archive), an Afro-Asiatic language, supports the conjecture made at the end of the last section. Somali has vowel length contrasts in both open and closed syllables. Both sonorant and obstruent consonants can occur in coda position. The single contour tone—falling (H͡L)—can only occur on long vowels (Saeed 1982,

1993). Compare the two spectrograms in (26a) and (26b), which depict words *ban* 'plain' and *naak'* 'woman' respectively: the coda nasal in *ban* does not have an excessively long duration, and the coda /k'/ in *naak'* obviously does not shorten the preceding vowel; in fact, the sonorous portion of the rime for these two words has a duration of 257ms and 264ms respectively.

(26) Somali spectrograms:

(a) ban 'plain'

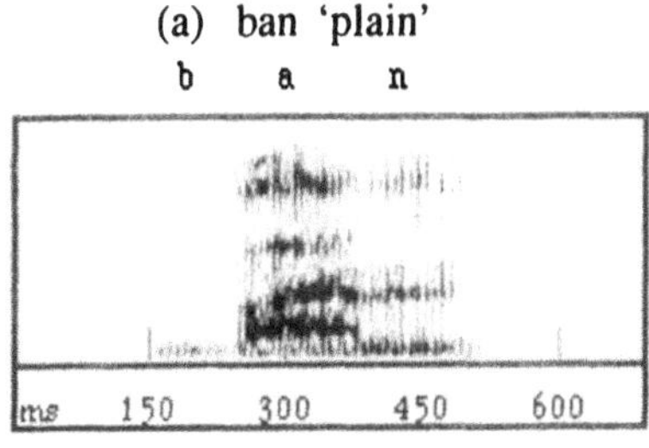

(b) naak' 'woman'

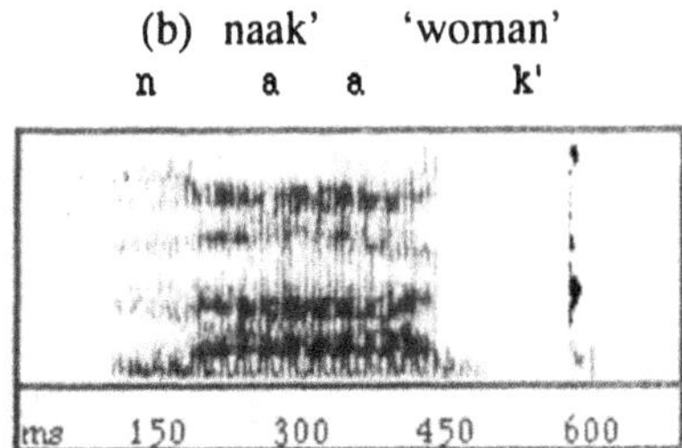

5.3 LAMA AND KƆNNI

I have mentioned in §5.1 that in Lama (Kenstowicz, Nikiema and Ourso 1988, Ourso 1989, Kenstowicz 1994) and Kɔnni (Cahill 1999), contour tones are limited to the final syllable of a word; they cannot occur on non-final syllables even when they have a long vowel. Without phonetic data, we cannot conclude whether a short vowel in final position in these languages is in fact longer than a long vowel in non-final position. But if this is not the case, are these languages problematic for the direct approach to contour tone distribution?

Let us look at the data pattern in Lama first. The presence of a falling contour $\widehat{\text{HL}}$ on a short vowel in final position is shown by the examples in (27a). The avoidance of $\widehat{\text{HL}}$ on a long vowel in non-final position is shown by the examples in (27b): when a long vowel with $\widehat{\text{HL}}$ is followed by a suffix, $\widehat{\text{HL}}$ simplifies to a H. The avoidance of $\widehat{\text{HL}}$ on a short vowel in non-final position is shown by the examples in (27c): when a short vowel with $\widehat{\text{HL}}$ is followed by a suffix, $\widehat{\text{HL}}$ simplifies to a H. Moreover, $\widehat{\text{HL}}$ never surfaces lexically on non-final syllables of any roots. In (27), the underdot indicates that the vowel is [-ATR].

(27) Lama examples:

a. $\widehat{\text{HL}}$ on final CV:

céntị̂	'friend'
nạ̀fậ	'mouse'

b. No $\widehat{\text{HL}}$ on non-final CVV:

náà	'cow'

tẹ̀	'under'
tẹ́	'chez'
náá tẹ̀	'under cow'
náá !tẹ́	'chez cow'

c. No H͡L on non-final CV:

céntị́	'friend'
nâ	Noun Class 2 suffix
céntị́ !nâ	'friends'

A situation like this in fact does not constitute a counterexample to the durational approach even if the final short vowel does not turn out to be longer than the non-final long vowel. The intuition is that a non-final H͡L can be manifested by other means, such as downstepping the following H, or realizing the L tone on the following syllable, but a final H͡L does not have such alternatives. If in the grammar, the constraint that requires the realization of tones (in one way or another) is undominated, then the H͡L on final syllables will have to be realized on the surface even when the syllable has a short vowel, while the H͡L on non-final syllables does not have to surface on the syllable from which it was originated, even when the syllable has a long vowel. This intuition can be captured as follows. Let us posit the constraints in (28). REALIZE-H͡L in (28a) is satisfied in the following three situations: (a) the H͡L contour is preserved on the original syllable; (b) the H͡L contour is simplified to a H, and it is immediately followed by an underlying H tone which surfaces as a downstepped H; (c) the H͡L contour is simplified to a H, and it is immediately followed by an underlying L tone which surfaces as a L tone. The legitimacy of (c) lies in the assumption that the actual realizations of an underlying H͡L-L sequence and H-L sequence are different, despite the fact that they are both transcribed as H-L. The justification for the assumption comes from phonetic studies that show that the peak of a High tone is usually realized on the syllable following its carrier (Xu 1997, 1998, 1999, Myers 1998, Kim 1999). Therefore, it is plausible that the actual realizations of underlying H͡L-L and H-L sequences differ in timing: the f_0 peak is realized later in the latter than in the former. Thus the underlying H͡L-L and H-L sequences are kept distinct. The markedness constraints in (28b) and (28c) ban the H͡L contour on a final short vowel and a non-final long vowel respectively.

(28) a. REALIZE-H͡L: realize the H͡L contour in some fashion.

b. *H͡L-$C_{CONTOUR}$(V-final): no H͡L contour on a final short vowel.

c. *H͡L-$C_{CONTOUR}$(VV-nonfinal): no H͡L contour on a non-final long vowel.

Let us assume that the canonical duration of a non-final long vowel is longer than that of a final short vowel. Then the intrinsic ranking *H͡L-

$C_{CONTOUR}$(V-final) » *H͡L-$C_{CONTOUR}$(VV-nonfinal) holds.[4] But even under this ranking, we can still get the H͡L to surface on a final short vowel, but not on a non-final long vowel. This is achieved by ranking REALIZE-H͡L above both of the tonal markedness constraints. The tableaux in (29) show how this works. In (29a), the H͡L must be realized on the final syllable, as any simplification of it will incur a violation of the REALIZE-H͡L constraint. In (29b), if the L on the final syllable is considered the result of the merger of the L part of the H͡L and the original L of the final syllable, and the surface result is distinct from that of an underlying H-L sequence, then the falling contour is in fact realized in the winning candidate, even though it does not have a surface H͡L in its transcription. In (29c), the winning candidate realizes the H͡L by downstepping the following H, and at the same time avoids the surface H͡L. From these tableaux, we can see that the ranking *H͡L-$C_{CONTOUR}$(V-final) » *H͡L-$C_{CONTOUR}$(VV-nonfinal), which projects from the phonetic assumption that a non-final long vowel is longer than a final short vowel, is inconsequential to the output of the grammar.

(29) a. céntị̂ —> céntị̂

céntị̂	REALIZE-H͡L	*H͡L-$C_{CONTOUR}$(V-final)	*H͡L-$C_{CONTOUR}$(VV-nonfinal)
☞ céntị̂		*	
céntị́	*!		
céntị̀	*!		

b. náà tẹ̀ —> náá tẹ̀

náà tẹ̀	REALIZE-H͡L	*H͡L-$C_{CONTOUR}$(V-final)	*H͡L-$C_{CONTOUR}$(VV-nonfinal)
☞ náá tẹ̀			
náà tẹ̀			*!
náá tệ		*!	

c. náà tẹ́ —> náá ꜝtẹ́

náà tẹ́	REALIZE-H͡L	*H͡L-$C_{CONTOUR}$(V-final)	*H͡L-$C_{CONTOUR}$(VV-nonfinal)
☞ náá ꜝtẹ́			
náà tẹ́			*!

4 For formal definition of the markedness constraints on contour tone realization and their intrinsic rankings, see Chapter 7.

The situation in Kɔnni is similar to that of Lama. Possible syllable types in Lama are CV, CVN, CVV, and CVVN. H͡L can occur on any final syllable, but not on any non-final syllables; L͡H can occur on a final CVN, CVV, and CVVN, but not on any non-final syllables. These are shown by the examples in (30). All noun suffixes in Kɔnni are H-toned. When a noun root with an underlying contour is followed by a suffix, the contour is simplified to a level tone that carries the initial pitch of the underlying contour. The ending pitch of the contour is realized on the suffix, either by assuming that the suffixal H also serves as the H part of L͡H, or by downstepping the suffixal H to manifest the L part of H͡L.

(30) Kɔnni examples:

a. Contour tones on final CV(N):

kʊ́bʊ́bâ	'bowl'
tǎŋ	'stone'

b. No contour tones on non-final CVV(N):

táà	'sister, sg.'
nàáŋ	'chief, sg.'
wá	Noun Class 5 article
táá ꜝwá	'sister, sg.+art.'
nààŋwá	'chief, sg.+art.'

c. No contour tones on non-final CV(N):

tǎŋ	'stone'
rí	Noun Class 1 article
tànní	'stone, sg. +art.'
kʊ́bʊ́bâ	'bowl'
ká	Noun Class 3 article
kʊ́bʊ́báꜝká	'bowl, sg. +art.'

The intuition for Kɔnni is thus similar to that of Lama: a final contour must surface as such since there is no other alternative; a non-final contour, however, can afford to be simplified, since the content of the contour can be realized on the following syllable. The analysis can be captured in OT along the line of (29).

Therefore, I conclude that Lama and Kɔnni will not constitute problems for the durational approach even if a final V turns out to be shorter than a non-final VV. This is because in these languages, non-final contour tones find ways to manifest themselves. Cases that *will* pose a problem for the durational approach are those in which underlying contours on non-final VV simplify to level tones without affecting the tone on the following syllable, while underlying contours on final V are realized faithfully. Under this circumstance, a ranking paradox will emerge, since the former pattern requires *CONTOUR-C$_{\text{CONTOUR}}$(VV-nonfinal) » REALIZE-CONTOUR, while the latter pattern requires REALIZE-CONTOUR » *CONTOUR-$C_{CONTOUR}$(V-final), but the phonetics projects *CONTOUR-$C_{CONTOUR}$(V-final) » *CONTOUR-$C_{CONTOUR}$(VV-nonfinal).

5.4 GENERAL DISCUSSION

The fact that all the phonetic case studies here reveal data patterns consistent with the direct approach constitutes significant evidence for this approach, as this implies that there is no empirical reason for us to adopt the contrast-specific positional markedness approach, which makes less restrictive predictions. The comparison between Navajo/Somali and Thai/Cantonese is especially telling, since their differences in contour tone restrictions correspond precisely to their differences in durational comparison among certain syllable types. The direct approach does not predict situations in which contours are restricted to phonemic long vowels in Thai and Cantonese, or to sonorant-closed syllables in Navajo and Somali. However, the contrast-specific positional markedness approach, which does not encode specific phonetic properties (duration and sonority) of the language in question, makes such incorrect predictions. I have also shown that in Standard Thai and Cantonese, the vowels in open syllables are phonetically long. In a direct approach, their ability to carry a wide array of contour tones follows naturally. A contrast-specific positional markedness approach cannot make this prediction. This also poses a problem for the moraic approach, given that it only refers to phonological length or weight units without acknowledging the relevance of phonetics. This point is further elaborated in the next chapter.

Xhosa and Beijing Chinese illustrate a similar point from the interaction of two different durational parameters—stress and final position in a prosodic domain. It turns out that in both languages, stress plays the decisive role in determining the sonorous duration of the rime and correspondingly the distribution of contour tones. Without a contrasting language in which final position plays the decisive role in the interaction of the same two parameters, the data do not seem as telling as the comparison between Navajo and Thai. But it is possible that stress in general has a greater influence on duration than final position. Then the absence of such languages is indeed predicted by the direct approach, but not by the contrast-specific positional markedness approach.

As for Lama and Kɔnni, without phonetic data, we do not know whether the final short vowels, which can carry a wider range of contour tones than non-final long vowels, are in fact longer than the non-final long vowels. But even if it is not the case, I have shown that the data patterns are still consistent with the direct approach.

Therefore, the phonetic studies documented in this chapter also support the direct approach to contour tone distribution. This means that the speaker not only has to identify positions that specifically benefit $C_{CONTOUR}$, but also has to keep track of the language-specific magnitude of the $C_{CONTOUR}$ advantage induced by these positions. In broader terms, the phonetic results support the direct hypothesis of positional prominence. Going back to the diagram in at the end of last chapter, these results eliminate one of the two remaining phonetic interpretations of positional prominence, as shown in (31). We can now conclude that positional prominence is not only contrast-specific, but also tuned to language-specific phonetics.

(31) Possible interpretations of positional prominence

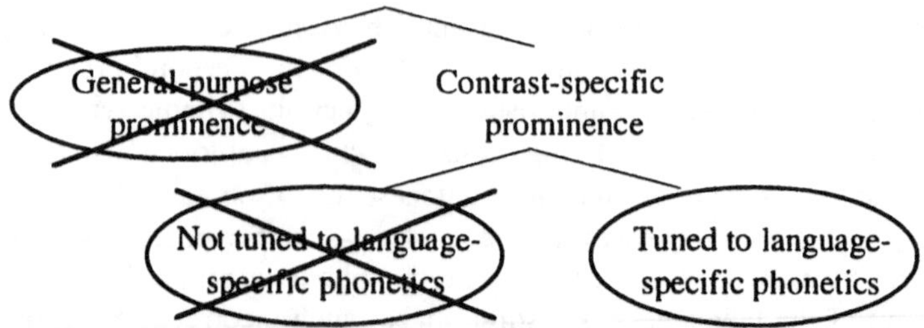

The next chapter serves two purposes. First, it summarizes the arguments against the moraic approach, which have been scattered around in previous chapters. Second, as I have mentioned in §4.4 and §4.5, I will show that the durational advantage of prosodic-final syllables and syllables in shorter words must be referred to in the formal analysis of contour tone distribution, and that their effect cannot be fully captured by the *Generalized Alignment* schema proposed by McCarthy and Prince (1993).

CHAPTER 6

Against Structure-Only Alternatives

The purpose of this chapter is to discuss in more detail the arguments against the structure-only alternatives to contour tone restrictions, especially the moraic approach, which is a general alternative to the direct approach, and tonal melody mapping, which can at least eliminate the need to refer to the durational advantages of prosodic-final syllables and syllables in shorter words, if correct.

For the arguments against the other structure-only approaches—general-purpose and contrast-specific positional markedness, I refer to the reader to Chapters 4 and 5, where they have been laid out in detail, and specifically §4.7 and §5.4, where summaries of the arguments are given.

6.1 THE MORAIC APPROACH

In this section, I discuss the arguments against the moraic approach to contour tone distribution in detail. I first outline the roles of the mora in phonology that previous research has demonstrated. I then show that given the properties of the mora, it is not appropriate for the account of contour tone distribution.

6.1.1 The Roles of the Mora in Phonology

The notion of the mora, or the weight unit, in linguistic theory can be traced back to Trubetzkoy (1939), in which he acknowledged its role in the placement of stress in Classical Latin: '(it) always occurred on the penultimate "mora" before the last syllable, that is, either on the penultimate syllable, if the latter was long, or on the antepenultimate, if the penultimate was short.' (Trubetzkoy 1939, Baltaxe translation 1969, p.174). It was then referred to in McCawley (1968)'s study of Japanese accent to account for the occurrence of different pitches on a single rime, and Newman (1972)'s survey of stress assignment in languages in which the distinction between heavy and light syllables must be made. It was formally introduced as a level of representation in generative phonology in the 1980's. Hyman (1985) proposed the weight unit (WU) *x*, which was equivalent to the mora. McCarthy and Prince (1986) and Hayes (1989) explicitly proposed the mora tier in the representation and argued that the moraic representation was what motivated all the weight-related phenomena such as stress assignment, tone bearing, and compensatory lengthening. For an overview of the history and arguments for the mora, see Broselow (1995).

In essence, the mora plays the following roles in phonological theory.

First, it is used to characterize the weight distinctions. A heavy syllable is represented with two moras while a light syllable with one. Hayes (1989) proposes that a short vowel is underlyingly associated with one mora and a long vowel with two, while a consonant receives a mora by language-specific rules. The moraic representations for CV, CVV, and CVC are given in (1). It is generally assumed that in a particular language, all the weight-related phenomena, such as stress assignment, tone bearing, word minimality, compensatory lengthening, and metrics, will be motivated by the same moraic representations (but see §6.1.6 on moraic inconsistency below).

(1)

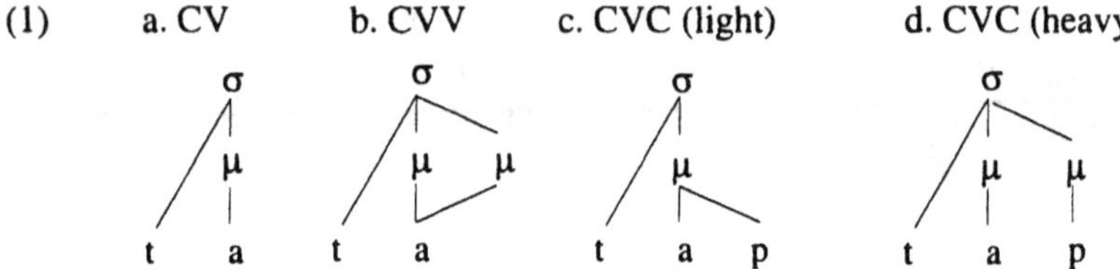

Second, the mora is used to represent segment length. As we have seen in (1), the vowel length distinction can be expressed through a monomoraic vs. bimoraic distinction. The gemination of consonants can also be represented by moraic means. McCarthy and Prince (1986) and Hayes (1989) propose that singleton and geminate consonants differ in that the former is nonmoraic while the latter is monomoraic. Therefore, the moraic representations of /ata/ and /atta/ are as in (2).

(2)

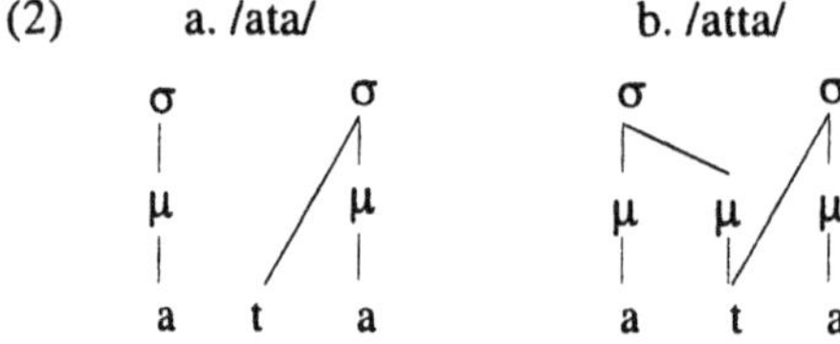

The third role that the mora plays in phonological theory is that it encodes the asymmetries between onsets and rimes in weight-related processes. For example, in stress assignment, the presence of the onset never determines the stressability of the syllable (but see Everett and Everett 1984), while the presence of the coda often does; in compensatory lengthening, the loss of a coda segment triggers lengthening of the nucleus, while the loss of an onset segment rarely does (Hayes 1989); in templatic morphology, the onset of a syllable template is often optional, while the coda rarely is (Broselow 1995). The way in which these asymmetries are expressed in the moraic theory is that onsets are never mora-bearing, while codas may be mora-bearing through language-specific rules.

Given these general roles that the mora plays in phonology, we can evaluate whether it is appropriate for capturing the distribution of contour tones; in other words, whether the distribution of contour tones falls into the realm of processes that the mora can handle.

As I have discussed in §2.4, onset consonants are not tone carriers, even when they are sonorants. Therefore, there exists an onset/rime asymmetry in tone-bearing as well, and we have seen that this can be captured in the moraic theory. In this sense, the mora does seem to be an appropriate representation of a tone-bearing unit. But many problems arise when we try to account all the contour tone distribution phenomena observed in the survey and the phonetic studies. In the following sections (§6.1.2—§6.1.7), I outline the problems that a moraic theory faces in accounting for contour tone distribution.

6.1.2 Advantages of Prosodic-Final Syllables and Syllables in Shorter Words

The survey of contour tone distribution in Chapter 4 has shown that contour tones are more likely to occur on prosodic-final syllables and syllables in shorter words, i.e., words with fewer syllables. These distributional properties can be easily captured in an approach that has direct access to the canonical duration, or the $\mathrm{C_{CONTOUR}}$ property, of the syllable. But it is not clear how the durational advantages of these syllable types can be captured moraically.

For final lengthening, as I have mentioned, even though there are many languages that neutralize vowel length contrast in final position, such as Luganda (Ashton et al. 1954, Tucker 1962, Snoxall 1967, Stevick 1969, Hyman and Katamba 1990, 1993), Tagalog (Schachter and Otanes 1972), Pacific Yupik (Leer 1985), and Mutsun (Okrand 1977), final lengthening is by no means always neutralizing, and the effect of final position on contour tone distribution is not restricted to languages that have neutralizing final lengthening (see §4.4). It is possible that in those languages that do not neutralize vowel length contrasts prosodic-finally, one mora is added to the nucleus of the prosodic final syllable, be it long or short, as shown in (3).

(3) a. CV# b. CVV#

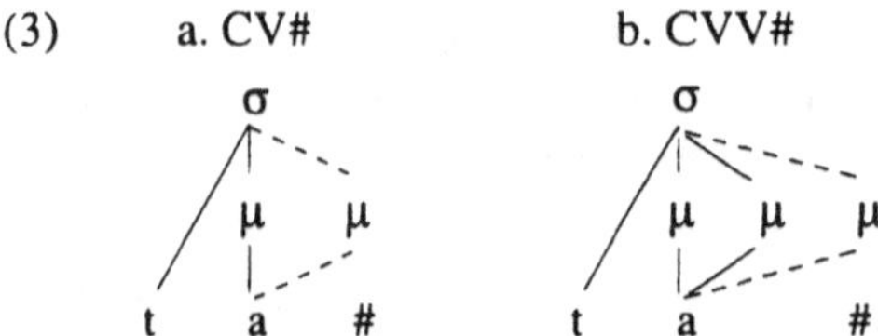

But the mora introduced here is apparently for the purpose of contour tone bearing alone. Hayes (1995)'s survey on stress systems shows that there are few cases in which the final syllable is guaranteed to be stressed regardless whether it is heavy or light, while non-final syllables are only guaranteed stress when they are heavy. Tübatulabal (Voegelin 1935), Aklan (Chai 1971), and Cebuano (Shryock 1993b) are cases of this sort. For example, in Tübatulabal, final syllables and heavy syllables (CV:) are stressed, and every other light syllable (CV) before a heavy syllable is stressed. But cases in which the final syllable is at a disadvantage for attracting stress due to extrametricality of the final consonant or the final syllable abound: English, Estonian, Arabic dialects, Spanish, Romanian, Ancient Greek, Menomini, etc. Comparing the result of the stress survey with that of the contour tone survey in §4.4, which shows the advantage of final position in a great many languages, the discrepancy is hard to miss. This discrepancy cannot be accounted for by the moraic representations in (3) if we assume that the moraic structure is the basis for all weight-related phonological patterning.

For the durational advantage of syllables in shorter words, one may also assume that syllables in shorter words simply have more moras on the weight tier. But this representation runs into the same typological difficulty when it is applied to other weight-related processes. For example, it will predict that a monosyllabic CVV word is heavier than a disyllabic CVCV word, since the former has three moras (two from the long vowel, one from lengthening in monosyllabic words) while the latter has only two. This, I believe, is unattested in either word minimality requirements or metrics. Also, if segmental length contrast, final position, and being in shorter words all contribute moras to the syllable, the number of moras that a syllable has access to will far exceed what is needed to characterize weight-related phenomena other than tone. This is the issue I turn to in the next section.

6.1.3 Levels of Distinction

Given that the primary roles of the mora are to capture the distinctions between long and short segments and between heavy and light syllables, the maximum mora count of a syllable should be two. This is the position taken by McCarthy and Prince (1986) and Steriade (1991). But Hayes (1989) argues that sometimes three levels of weight or length distinction do need to be made. For example, in Estonian, there is a three-way length contrast for vowels (Harms 1962, Tauli 1973); in a dialect of Hindi, superheavy syllables (CVVC, CVCC) behave like a heavy syllable followed by a light syllable; in Persian metrics, superheavy (CVVC, CVCC) and ultraheavy (CVVCC) syllables are scanned as a long position followed by a short position /_ ◡/ (Elwell-Sutton 1976, Hayes 1979). But to the best of my knowledge, no claim has been made to the effect that more than three levels of weight or length distinctions are necessary. As an illustration, the Persian example above shows that an ultraheavy syllable does not have a different metrical scansion from the trimoraic superheavy syllables.

But the contour tone distribution in Mende, as we have seen in §4.5.2.3, shows that four levels of distinction in contour-bearing ability must be made. To recapitulate the Mende pattern: long vowels can carry a complex contour with three pitch targets (L͡H͡L) in monosyllabic words; they can carry a simple contour with two pitch targets (H͡L or L͡H) in other positions. Short vowels can carry either of the simple contours H͡L and L͡H in monosyllabic words; they can carry the falling contour H͡L in the final position of di- or polysyllabic words; they cannot carry contours in other positions. These generalizations were summarized in (45) of Chapter 4, and they are repeated here in (4).

(4) Mende contour tone restrictions:

Vowel length	No. of sylls in word	Syll position in word	L͡H͡L ok?	L͡H ok?	H͡L ok?
VV	1	final	**yes**	**yes**	**yes**
VV	>1	any	no	**yes**	**yes**
V	1	final	no	**yes**	**yes**
V	>1	final	no	no	**yes**
V	>1	non-final	no	no	no

From (4), we can see that the following four levels of contour-bearing ability need to be distinguished: the ability to carry complex contour L͡H͡L; the ability to carry rising contour L͡H; the ability to carry falling contour H͡L; and the inability to carry any contour tones. If one wants to resort to the moraic representation of the syllable to account for the contour tone distribution, one needs to posit up to four moras for the best contour tone bearer. But this goes against what we know about other weight-related phenomena, as I have outlined above. Moreover, now we also have problems explaining the non-existence of supercomplex contour tones with four pitch targets in languages like Mende.

One other problem that the Mende data pose for the moraic approach to contour tone restrictions is how the asymmetry between the falling and rising contours can be captured. Other languages that display the falling-rising asymmetry (see §4.6.1) also pose the same problem. I turn to this issue in the following section.

6.1.4 Differences among Tones with the Same Number of Pitch Targets

The central tenets for the moraic approach to contour tone restrictions are that contour tones are sequences of level tones underlyingly; the tone-bearing unit is the mora; and each mora can host one level tone. These are most explicitly stated in Duanmu (1994b). He argues against the existence of contour tone units, and one of his arguments is that all syllables that can host contour tones are at least bimoraic. Then a rising contour L͡H on a syllable, for example, can be represented as in (5). The segmental materials of the syllable are omitted here.

(5) Representation of a L͡H contour:

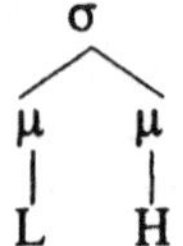

But this representation fails to address two differences in the *Tonal Complexity* scale (see (5)-(7) in Chapter 3): between a falling contour and a rising contour, and between contour tones with the same direction of pitch change, but different pitch excursions.

For the falling vs. rising asymmetry, §4.6.1 has documented that in the survey, there are thirty-seven languages without rising tones, but only three languages without falling tones. There are also languages such as Mende, Kukuya, Gã, Kɔnni, and Tiv, in which rising contours are more restricted in their distribution than falling contours. For example, in Mende, H͡L can occur on the final syllable of disyllabic word while L͡H cannot; in Kɔnni, H͡L can occur on a final CV while L͡H cannot. But this asymmetry cannot be easily captured in the moraic approach, since in this approach, both falling tones are rising tones are sequences of two level tones and thus need two moras to support their realization. Then on a bimoraic syllable, there is no a priori reason why a falling tone can occur while a rising tone cannot.

One may posit specific restrictions for the occurrence of rising tones such that they can only occur on trimoraic syllables. But then all the problems identified in §6.1.2 and §6.1.3 ensue: in the case of rising tones being restricted to final syllable or syllables in shorter words, it will be an ad hoc remedy for the contour tone problem and cannot be extended to other weight-related phenomena; in languages like Mende, it will create a situation in which quadrimoraic syllables are necessary.

For the pitch excursion differences, they are best illustrated by Pingyao Chinese (Hou 1980, 1982a, 1982b), which I discuss in details in Zhang (1998, 1999). I recapitulate the arguments here.

Syllables in Pingyao are in the shape of CV, CVŋ, or CVʔ. The vowel in CV is either a diphthong or phonetically long, and the vowel in CVʔ is very short. The former is usually more than twice as long as the latter (Zhang 1998). I will hence write open syllables as CVV. Hou (1980) reports five tones for monosyllables in Pingyao: 13, 23, 35, 53, 54. Tones 13, 35, and 53 only occur on CVV and CVŋ syllables; tones 23 and 54 only occur on CVʔ syllables and are called checked tones or short tones. Examples in (6) show lexical items that carry these tones.

(6) Pingyao examples:

13	pu	'to hatch'	iŋ	'overcast'
23	pʌʔ	'to push aside'	xuʌʔ	'hair'
35	pu	'cloth'	tuŋ	'to move'
53	pu	'to mend'	tiŋ	'nap'
54	pʌʔ	'a musical instrument'	xuʌʔ	'to live'

Hou (1980) argues that tones 23 and 54 are allotones of 13 and 53 respectively, not only because of their phonetic similarities, but also because the allotones of an underlying tone have the same tone sandhi behavior. They are realized with a lesser pitch excursion because of the short duration of the CVʔ syllables. Tone sandhi behavior in Pingyao is syntactically conditioned. Words in different syntactic configurations have different tone sandhi forms even if they have the same base form. Tone sandhi behavior of disyllabic words of predicate-object or subject-predicate configuration in Pingyao is summarized in (7). The leftmost column and the top row show the base forms of the first and second syllables respectively. The body of the table indicates the sandhi forms of the disyllabic words. Checked tones are underlined for easy identification.

(7)

$\sigma_1 \backslash \sigma_2$	13	23	35	53	54
13	13-13	13-23	31-35	35-423	35-423
23	23-13	23-23	32-35	45-423	45-423
35	13-13	13-23	31-35	35-423	35-423
53	53-13	53-23	53-35	35-423	35-423
54	54-13	54-23	54-35	45-423	45-423

Disyllabic words with syntactic configurations other than predicate-object or subject-predicate, such as modifier-noun, verb-verb, noun-noun, and predicate-adjunct, have different tone sandhi behavior. It is given in the table in (8).

(8)

$\sigma_1\backslash\sigma_2$	13	23	35	53	54
13	31-35	31-45	13-13	31-53	31-54
23	32-35	32-45	23-13	32-53	32-54
35	35-53	35-54	35-53	35-53	35-54
53	53-13	53-23	53-35	**53-53**	53-54
54	54-13	54-23	54-35	**45-53**	54-54

For an account of the tone sandhi behavior, see Zhang (1999). But let us just notice here that in both types of tone sandhi, 13 and 23 have exactly the same behavior, so do 53 and 54, except the pair in boldface in (8), which I simply take as an exception. The difference in pitch excursion between the non-checked and checked tones in the sandhi forms can again be attributed to the durational difference between CVV, CVŋ on the one hand and CVʔ on the other.

Therefore, from the tone sandhi pattern, we conclude that 23 and 54 are indeed allophonic realizations of 13 and 53 on CVʔ syllables. The question now becomes, how do we account for the reduction of pitch excursion on a short syllable.

It is not clear that the moraic representation can help us here. We have the same problem as the falling vs. rising asymmetry: both the reduced and unreduced contour tones have two pitch targets, thus should be represented as two level tones; this determines that both need at least bimoraic syllables to be realized; given that CVʔ must be bimoraic, just as CVV and CVŋ in Pingyao, why is there a need to reduce the pitch excursion at all? Let us look at two proposals.

The first proposal is to posit the syllable types CVV and CVR to be trimoraic and CVO to be bimoraic, as in (9). In this proposal, sonorant codas are moraic, but obstruent codas are not. We then restrict contour tones with pronounced pitch excursion to syllables of this sort. But then, we are left without an explanation for why there are no complex contour tones with three tonal targets in this language, since they should be perfectly licensed on the trimoraic CVV and CVR syllables.

(9)

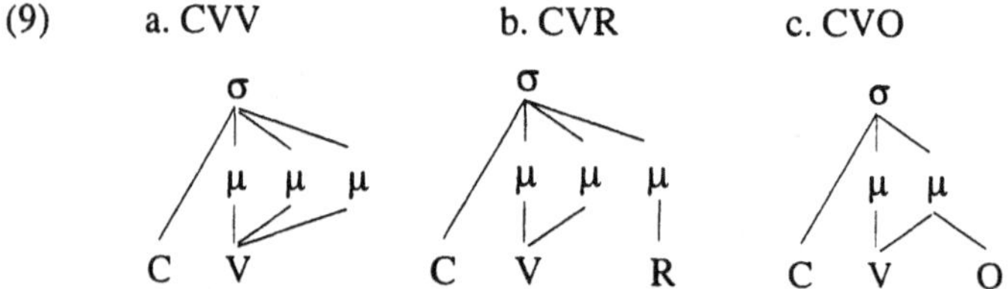

Another proposal is given in Duanmu (1990, 1994b). He argues that in isolation, syllables in Chinese dialects are generally bimoraic: the vowel in CV is lengthened; the coda consonant, whether it is a sonorant or an obstruent, always contributes a mora to the syllable. The usual lack of contour tones on CVO syllables is due to low-level phonetic reasons: since the obstruent coda in Chinese is usually unreleased, a tone cannot be phonetically realized on it, even though it may be underlyingly linked to the mora that the coda contributes. The proposed moraic representations for CVV, CVR, and CVO are shown in (10).

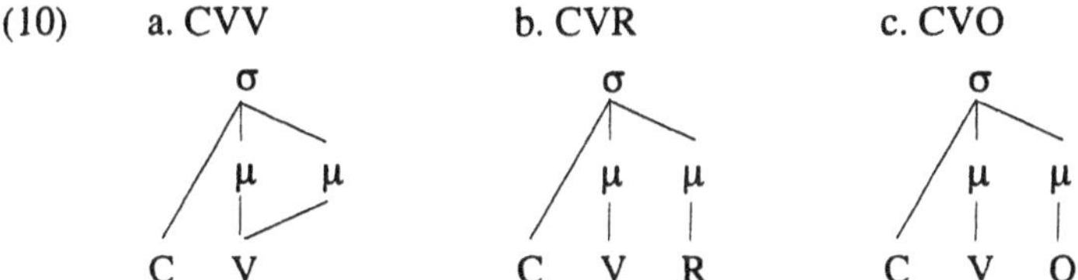

In languages like Pingyao, which allows contour tones on CVO, Duanmu argues that the vowel on CVO is lengthened to bimoraic. This allows the two levels tones that comprise the contour tone to be both realized phonetically. But this essentially leaves the smaller pitch excursion of the contour tones on CVO unaccounted for. Duanmu (p.c.) has suggested two possible solutions.

First, the vowels in CVV and CVR may also be lengthened, which will render all syllable types trimoraic, as shown in (11). But then, the problem again becomes why complex contours do not occur in CVV and CVR syllables in this language: there is no reason why the lengthening of the vowel in CVV and CVR should not license one more pitch target as in CVO.

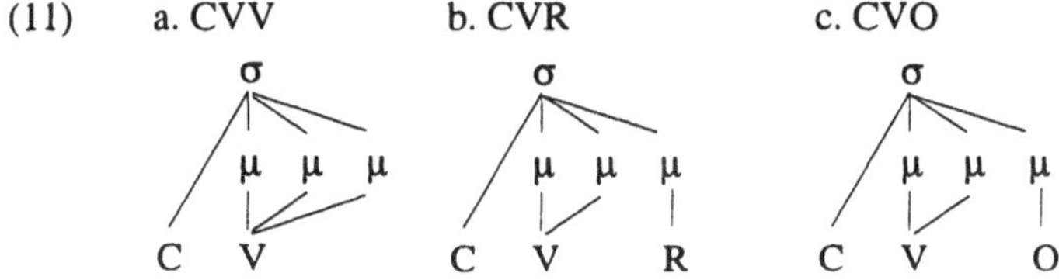

Second, the pitch excursion reduction is a phonetic effect, i.e., it falls outside the realm of phonology. Even though the vowel in CVO is bimoraic, it is phonetically shorter than the bimoraic vowel in open syllables. This phonetic shortening gives rise to a phonetic contour flattening effect on CVO. Yip (1995), though she disagrees with Duanmu's view that the mora is the tone-bearing unit and that there is no contour tone unit, seems to endorse the phonetic nature of the partial contour flattening. I have two objections to this view.

First, from the survey, it is clear that different languages adopt different strategies to resolve the conflict between a sharp pitch excursion and a short duration. Some languages flatten the contour completely, like Xhosa, which reduces the underlying falling contour to a level tone on unstressed syllables. Some languages flatten the contour partially, like Pingyao Chinese. Some languages lengthen the rime duration, like Mitla Zapotec: Briggs (1961) reports that the contour tones H͡L and L͡H can occur on diphthongs as well as single vowels. But when L͡H occurs on a single vowel, the vowel is lengthened (Briggs 1961). Yet some other languages implement both partial flattening and lengthening, like Hausa (see §4.2.2.3). Therefore, it at best falls under the rubric of linguistic phonetics, in the sense of Keating (1985, 1988a, b) and Cohn (1990, 1993). But as I will argue in Chapter 7 later on, the dichotomy between phonology and linguistic phonetics is neither valid nor necessary. It is not valid in the sense that the account of phonological patterning sometimes crucially relies on phonetic information. It is not necessary in the sense that the categorical vs. gradient nature of the so-called phonological vs. phonetic processes can fall out from a sufficiently articulate theory of phonology without committing ourselves to this dichotomy.

Second, from the Pingyao data alone, it is conceivable to consider 23 and 54 to be incomplete phonetic realizations of 13 and 53 on a short duration. But there are many languages, especially in Sino-Tibetan, in which the tones on CVO generally have smaller pitch excursions than those on CVV and CVR, but there is no clear resemblance between the two sets of tones in either phonetic similarity or sandhi behavior.

For example, in Xiamen (Chen 2000), a Min dialect of Chinese, five tones can occur on CV and CVR syllables—44, 24, 53, 21, and 22, and two tones can occur on CVO syllables—32 and 4. It is not immediately obvious whether the small fall 32 on CVO is a natural phonetic reduction of any of the tones on CVV and CVR. Moreover, if we look at the tone sandhi behavior of Xiamen, we can see that 32 behaves quite differently from the tones on CV and CVR. Xiamen tone sandhi is sensitive to prosodic context, but not to tonal context. So each tone in non-phrase-final position is changed into another tone regardless of the tone following it, as schematically shown in (12). We can verify that 32 does not behave similarly to any tones on CVV and CVR.

(12) Xiamen tone sandhi:

a. On CVV and CVR:

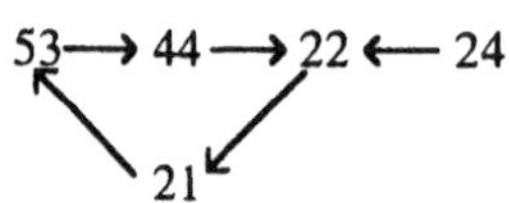

b. On CVO:
4 → 21
32 → 4 for syllables ending in p, t, k
→ 53 for syllables ending in ʔ

In Changzhou (Wang 1988), a northern Wu dialect of Chinese, five tones can occur on CVV and CVR—55, 13, 523, 24, and 45, and two tones can occur on CVO—23 and 5. The small rise 23 on CVO looks like an incomplete phonetic realization of either 13 or 24, which can occur on CVV and CVR. But if we look at the tone sandhi behavior of Changzhou, shown in (13), we can see that 23 does not behave similarly to either 13 or 24. In the table, tones on CVO are underlined for easy identification.

(13) Changzhou tone sandhi:

$\sigma_1\backslash\sigma_2$	23	5	55	13	45
23	2-5		1-13		
13	11-3		11-33		
24	11-24		11-24		

These examples illustrate that the smaller pitch excursion on CVO cannot always be the result of phonetic implementation. In other words, it cannot be taken as the phonetic reduction of contour tones that can occur on CVV and CVR, since these tones behave independently from other tones in phonological processes such as tone sandhi. Therefore, it is up to the phonology to rule out pronounced pitch excursions on CVO syllables, not just phonetic implementation. Moreover, Zhang (1998) shows that the durational property of the syllables, such as the shortness of CVO, can play a role in determining the sandhi behavior of the tones they carry (see Zhang 1998 for accounts of Yangqu, Shuozhou, and Changzhou tone sandhi). This also indicates that the durational property of the syllable and the properties of tones as a consequence of it cannot only be left in the realm of phonetics; they are relevant to phonological patterning and thus must be accessible in phonology.

6.1.5 The Size of Tonal Inventory of Different Syllable Types

If we look back at the Pingyao data in (6), we will notice that not only do CVʔ syllables have contour tones with smaller pitch excursion, they also have fewer contour tones. The rising contour 35, which can occur on CVV and CVR, has no counterpart in the tonal inventory of CVO. This is a very common phenomenon in Chinese dialects. In those dialects with CVO syllables (which include most of Wu, Min, Jin, Yue, and Hakka dialects), there are usually a maximum of two contrastive tones on CVO, but four to six on CVV and CVR. Often times, the tones that occur on CVO are contour tones, as the Pingyao and Xiamen cases that we have seen. So the difference in the size of tonal inventory of different syllable types cannot simply result from a contour vs. level distinction. Then what is the basis for this difference?

The moraic approach does not have much to say about this difference. As long as the structural requirement for a contour tone—two moras—is met on CVO, as it has to be, given the presence of contour tones on this syllable type, the theory itself provides no explanation as to why one contour tone can occur while another cannot.

This is a problem for the direct approach as well. The situation is the same: if the C_{CONTOUR} value of a syllable is high enough for one contour tone to surface, why does another contour tone with the same tonal complexity fail to surface? But the direct approach is a phonetically more articulate theory. It allows the phonology to access phonetic details. One type of phonetic detail that the phonology could conceivably have access to is the perceptual distance between two contrasting phonological entities, and here, the relevant phonological entities are tones. Flemming (1995) and Kirchner (1997) have both proposed to introduce constraints that require a minimum distance between phonological contrasts into the phonological system, Flemming by MINDIST, Kirchner by POLAR. Take MINDIST for instance, it is a series of intrinsically ranked constraints MINDIST=M (MINDIST=1 » MINDIST=2 » MINDIST=3...), which requires phonological contrasts to be *M* 'steps' apart. When it is interleaved with another series of intrinsically ranked constraints MAINTAIN-N-CONTRASTS (MAINTAIN-1-CONTRAST » MAINTAIN-2-CONTRASTS » MAINTAIN-3-CONTRASTS...), which requires the maintenance of *N* contrasts, the constraint hierarchy ensures that the resulting members of an inventory are kept a maximum perceptual distance apart from each other. Adopting the MINDIST and MAINTAIN-N-CONTRASTS into the direct approach, we may assume that given the shorter duration on CVO than CVV and CVR, the perceptual distance between the same tones on CVO is smaller than that on CVV and CVR. This determines that we will only be able to maintain fewer tonal contrasts on CVO than CVV and CVR.

Let us assume that on the canonical duration of CVV or CVR, adjacent tones in 13, 35, and 53 are at a distance of two steps along a linear perceptual scale: 13 and 35 are two steps from each other, so are 35 and 53; 13 and 53 are four steps apart. Intuitively, this is because 13 and 35 differ in average pitch height, 35 and 53 differ in pitch change direction, and 13 and 53 differ in both parameters. On the canonical duration of CVO however, the adjacent tones in 13, 35, and 53 are only at a distance of one step, due to the shortness of the CVO duration. The constraint ranking in (14) will then ensure that 13, 35, and 53 will be the tonal inventory on CVV and CVR, while 13 and 53 will be the tonal inventory on CVO.

(14) MAINTAIN-1-CONTRAST » MINDIST=1 » MINDIST=2 » MAINTAIN-2-CONTRASTS » MINDIST=3 » MAINTAIN-3-CONTRASTS

The tableaux in (15) show how the inventories are derived. In (15a), since the tones 13-35-53 are two steps apart on the perceptual scale, they only violate the lowest ranked MINDIST constraint here: MINDIST=3; and keeping all of them will only violate the lowest ranked MAINTAIN-N-CONTRASTS constraint here: MAINTAIN-3-CONTRASTS. Having one more tone in the inventory will violate MINDIST=2, and having one fewer tone in the inventory will violate MAINTAIN-2-CONTRASTS, both of which outrank MINDIST=3 and MAINTAIN-3-CONTRASTS. Thus 13-35-53 is the optimal tonal inventory of CVV and CVR. In (15b) however, since 13-35-53 are only one step apart on the perceptual scale due to the short duration, having all of them in the inventory will violate MINDIST=2. Removing 35 from the inventory will result in a violation of MAINTAIN-2-CONTRASTS, but satisfy MINDIST=2. Given that MINDIST=2 » MAINTAIN-2-CONTRASTS, we conclude that 13-53 is the optimal tonal inventory of CVO. Notice that this system is essentially Pingyao's system.

(15) a. On CVV and CVR: 13-35-53

	MT 1 CNTRST	MINDIS =1	MINDIS =2	MT 2 CNTRSTS	MINDIS =3	MT 3 CNTRSTS
13-53				*!		*
13-35				*!	*	*
☞ 13-35-53					*	*
13-35-55-53			*!		*	

b. On CVO: 13-53

	MT 1 CNTRST	MINDIS =1	MINDIS =2	MT 2 CNTRSTS	MINDIS =3	MT 3 CNTRSTS
☞ 13-53				*	*	*
13-35			*!	*	*	*
13-35-53			*!		*	*
13-35-55-53		*!	*		*	

Boersma (1998) argues that the maximal dispersion of phonological contrasts on a certain dimension is the result of the interaction among three locally ranked functional constraint families: *GESTURE, which bans articulatory gestures; PARSE, which requires the underlying value of features to appear in the surface form; and *CATEG, which bans the categorization of a feature to a certain value. For details of the proposal, see Boersma (1998).

All in all, the point here is that, given its phonetically rich nature, it is possible for the direct approach to adopt these proposals, which all require the reference to phonetic details, to account for the difference in tonal inventory size of different syllable types. For the purely representational approach based on the mora, it is not clear how this issue can be addressed.

6.1.6 Moraic Inconsistency

The next problem that a moraic approach faces is moraic inconsistency. As I have mentioned, the strong position of the moraic theory of weight predicts that all weight-related phenomena in a particular language are accounted for by the same moraic representation. Although this strong position is shown to be supported in a handful of languages, like Cairene Arabic, in which the behavior of stress, word-minimality, and vowel shortening converges to the same moraic representation (McCarthy and Prince 1986), it has been pointed out to be problematic in languages like Lithuanian, Classical Greek, Tübatulabal, Yawelmani, and other languages by Hyman (1985), Archangeli (1991), Crowhurst (1991), Steriade (1991), Broselow (1995), and most recently, Gordon (1998, 1999a).

For example, in Lithuanian (Steriade 1991), monosyllabic roots consisting of only a short open syllable are not allowed; but syllables closed by an obstruent coda, such as *lip* 'rise, climb' are sufficient to satisfy the root minimality requirement. This indicates that if the minimality requirement is two moras, then an obstruent coda must be counted as moraic. But Zec (1988) argues that if we look at other weight-related processes in the language, an obstruent coda should not be counted as moraic. First, in accent distribution, the rising tone accent can only occur on CVV and CVR syllables, but not on CVO. Second, in the formation of infinitive verbs, there is a requirement for the stem to be bimoraic. The vowel is lengthened in CVO stems, but it remains short in CVR stems, indicating that CVR stems are bimoraic, while CVO stems are not. Third, a long vowel is shortened when it is followed by a tautosyllabic sonorant, but not when it is followed by a tautosyllabic ostruent.

In Classical Greek (Attic) (Steriade 1991), CVCC is as heavy as CVVC and CVV for recessive accent assignment, quantitative meter, and word minimality requirement, indicating that the final consonants in CVCC must contribute at least one mora to the syllable. But from the distribution of a High tone that appears on the last syllable of words followed by enclitics, Steriade argues that only vowels are tone-bearing segments in Classical Greek. Her argument goes as follows: the placement of the High tone is blocked when the word has penultimate accent and the penult is either CV or CVC, and this is due to the OCP, which disallows two adjacent High tones; but when the word has penultimate accent and the penult is CVV, the High tone surfaces on the final syllable, and this is because the second vowel in the penult carries a Low tone, which breaks up the High-High sequence. The examples in (16) show that the High tone surfaces when the penult is CVV, but it is blocked when the penult is CV or CVC.

(16) a. High tone surfaces:

óikos	'house'
óikós tis	'some house'
dóoron	'gift'
dóorón tis	'some gift'

b. High tone blocked:

phílos	'friend'
phílos tis	'some friend'
éntha	'there'
éntha te	'and there'

In Yawelmani, Archangeli (1991) shows that mapping a CVC root to a bimoraic morphological template results in the lengthening of the vowel, which indicates that the coda consonant is nonmoraic; but long vowels shorten in closed syllables, which could be interpreted as a bimoraic limit on the syllable and consequently leads to the conclusion that the coda consonant is moraic.

Various proposals have been made to deal with the moraic inconsistency problem, mostly notably, rule ordering and multileveled representations.

For example, for Classical Greek, Hyman (1985) proposes a margin creation rule, which applies after the accent assignment but before the mapping of the High tone, changing the representation in (17a) to that in (17b), i.e., associating the coda consonant to the mora contributed by the vowel and removing its own mora. This rule ordering ensures that the coda consonant is moraic in accent assignment, but nonmoraic in High tone mapping.

(17) a. Before the margin creation rule:

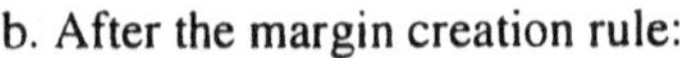

b. After the margin creation rule:

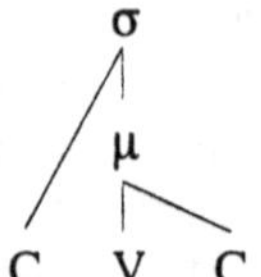

Archangeli (1991) proposes a similar solution to the moraic inconsistency in Yawelmani. She orders Weight-by-Position, which assigns a mora to a coda consonant, after templatic mapping, but before vowel shortening, thus accounting for both the lengthening and the shortening.

Hayes (1995), on the other hand, proposes that moras form a grid within the syllable, with the height of the column determined by the sonority of the segment it is associated with. A sample set of moraic representations for CVV, CVC, and CV in a language that involves moraic inconsistencies of the coda consonant is given in (18). In this conception, processes that treat CVC as bimoraic refer to the lower layer of the grid, while processes that treat CVC as monomoraic refer to the higher layer of the grid.

(18) a. CVV b. CVC c. CV

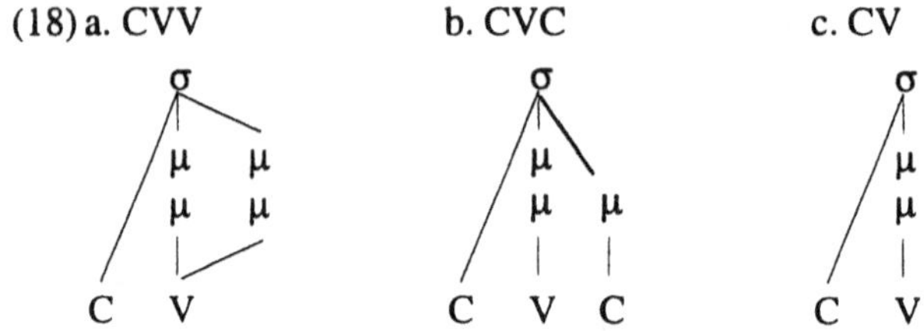

Adopting a claim in Steriade (1991), Hayes further conjectures that syllable-external prosodic requirements such as footing, word minimality, and tonal docking generally refer to the higher layer, while syllable-internal requirements such as mora population limits generally refer to the lower layer.

My major objection to the rule-ordering approach is its arbitrariness. Given that there is no a prior principle that states which rules should apply before which other rules, it is equally likely for the margin creation rule, for example, to occur before stress assignment but after tone mapping, and before tone mapping but after stress assignment. Therefore the theory does not predict any asymmetry among processes in treating the weight of a syllable type. For example, it is just as likely for CVO to be considered heavy for tone but light for stress as the other way around. But this turns out not to be true. Gordon (1998, 1999a) has pointed out that it is much more likely for a CVO syllable to be counted as heavy for stress than for tone. His survey shows that of 41 languages with weight-sensitive contour tone distribution, only two of them (4.8%) treat CVO as heavy; all others requires either CVV or CVR for contour tones to surface. But of 69 languages with weight-sensitive stress, 28 of them (40.6%) treat CVO as heavy—a much higher percentage than weight-sensitive tone. Gordon's result on contour tones is corroborated by my survey: a total of 104 languages require either CVV or CVR for contour tones to be realized, while only four languages allow contour tones on CVO (see §4.2).

Hayes' solution to the problem does make predictions about the correlation between processes and the segmental content of the moraic projection by making the distinction between syllable-external and syllable-internal processes. But given that stress assignment and contour tone distribution should both be considered syllable-external processes, we are still left without an explanation for the asymmetry between these two processes in their treatment of the CVO syllables.

I believe that the different treatment of CVC, especially CVO, among different weight-related processes lies in the different phonetic requirements of these processes. This line has been explicitly pursued by Gordon (1999a). He lays out the possible phonetic bases for six weight-related processes —quantitative stress assignment, contour tone licensing, compensatory lengthening, metrics, syllable templates, and word minimality, as summarized in (19), and argues that these phonetic bases are the driving forces for the phonological patterning of these processes. In particular, he argues that for quantitative stress assignment, it is the total energy of the rime that determines the ability of the syllable to attract stress, while for contour tone restrictions, it is the total *sonorant* energy of the rime that is crucial. The fact that it is more frequent for the world's languages to treat CVO as heavy for stress than for tone is determined by the necessity of sonorancy (i.e., presence of energy in the second to fourth harmonics) for tonal perception, but not for stress.

(19) Different weight-related processes and their phonetic considerations:

Weight-related processes	Phonetic bases
Quantitative stress assignment	Total perceptual energy of the rime[1]
Contour tone licensing	Total sonorant energy of the rime
Compensatory lengthening	Rime duration
Metrics	Rime duration[2]
Syllable templates	Syllable isochrony
Word minimality	CVV, CVC ok: duration CVV ok: support of a minimal intonational contour[3]

While agreeing with Gordon's position that weight-related phenomena are process-specific, not language-specific, and that the process-specificity of the weight criteria is determined by the difference in phonetic consideration among these processes, I disagree with him in the phonetic bases for contour tone licensing. Gordon (1999a) argues that a coda sonorant can be tone-bearing only if it has a long enough duration (p.109), but he doesn't specify how long is 'long enough'. He then goes on to conclude that the total sonorant energy of the rime is the indicator for a syllable's tone-bearing ability. I have argued in §3.2, §5.2.3, and §5.2.4 that the contour tone bearing ability of a syllable is proportional to the $C_{CONTOUR}$ value of the syllable, which is calculated as

---

[1] The total perceptual energy of the rime is calculated by Gordon as follows. First, the average amplitude (RMS) in decibels of the target vowel and coda consonant was calculated relative to a reference vowel. Second, the relative RMS of each segment was converted to a value representing perceived loudness. Third, the relative loudness value for each segment was multiplied by the segment duration, yielding the perceptual energy value of the segment. Finally, the perceptual energy values of the rime segments are added together, yielding the total perceptual energy of the rime (Gordon 1999a: p.170).

[2] Gordon (1999a) does not specifically discuss the phonetic basis for the heavy/light distinction in metrics. But given that the weight criteria for metrics and compensatory lengthening are always consistent with each other within a language (p.248), and he argues that the phonetic basis for compensatory lengthening is rime duration, I assume that the weight criterion for metrics is also dependent on rime duration.

[3] This is only one of the possible phonetic bases that Gordon (1999a) provides for word minimality. Other possibilities include: content words must possess sufficient amount of energy to increase their perceptual salience; the total material in a morpheme should be maximized to increase its chances of being recovered from the signal; a short open syllable is disallowed to avoid neutralization in the face of stress, final lengthening, and the greater duration induced by being in a word with fewer syllables.

$C_{CONTOUR} = a \cdot \mathrm{Dur(V)} + \mathrm{Dur(R)}$, with the a value in the range $1<a<1.695$. This is on the one hand more specific and hence more empirically testable than Gordon's conclusion, on the other hand, it could also potentially make different predictions than Gordon's theory.

First, given the range of a, I predict that the role of the vocalic component of the rime is not that much greater than that of the sonorant coda in the evaluation of the tone-bearing ability. This is intuitive since the crucial harmonics for tonal perception are present in sonorant consonants, just as in vowels. But in Gordon's theory, the vocalic component of the rime will play a much greater role than the sonorant coda, since one expects that the total energy of a vowel will be much greater than that of a sonorant consonant (probably more than twice as much). Therefore, these two approaches can be potentially distinguished by languages like Standard Thai and Cantonese, in which CVVO and CVR are in competition for which one is a better contour tone bearer. Unfortunately, Gordon (1999a) does not provide total sonorant energy data for the Cantonese stimuli in his experiment, and the Standard Thai stimuli recorded in my experiment were not designed in a way that the total sonorant energy relative to a reference vowel could be calculated, as Gordon's theory requires (see Footnote 1 on p.144). Thus the issue has to be left for future investigation.

Second, my approach does not take into consideration the differences among vowels of different sonority, e.g., different height, or sonorant consonants of different sonority, e.g., glides and nasals, in the evaluation of contour tone bearing ability. This is intuitive since the major difference in the amplitude of the harmonic structure lies in the difference between vowels and consonants, thus the differences among vowels or among consonants are unlikely to play a role in tonal perception. But Gordon's theory does take into account these differences since it is that total sonorant energy that is being calculated. Unfortunately, I again do not have the relevant data to test the different predictions of the two approaches and must leave the issue to future research.[4]

Another crucial difference between Gordon's approach and mine is that Gordon's system of phonology does not directly encode phonetic details. Rather, the phonetics is mediated through phonological entities such as the X slot. Therefore, in his account of contour tone distribution, he uses constraints such as

---

[4] Gordon's theory also has a component that evaluates the complexity of the weight criteria, which will complicate the comparison between his theory and mine. But taking into account of phonological complexity still does not allow the reversal of the phonetics, i.e., taking syllable type A as a better contour tone bearer than syllable type B despite the fact that syllable B has a greater total sonorant energy, only because this will result in a simpler grammar. Therefore his predictions can still be compared to mine against actual data.

the ones in (20), and posits constraint rankings as the ones in (21) ('»' indicates fixed rankings, the arrow indicates language-specific rankings).

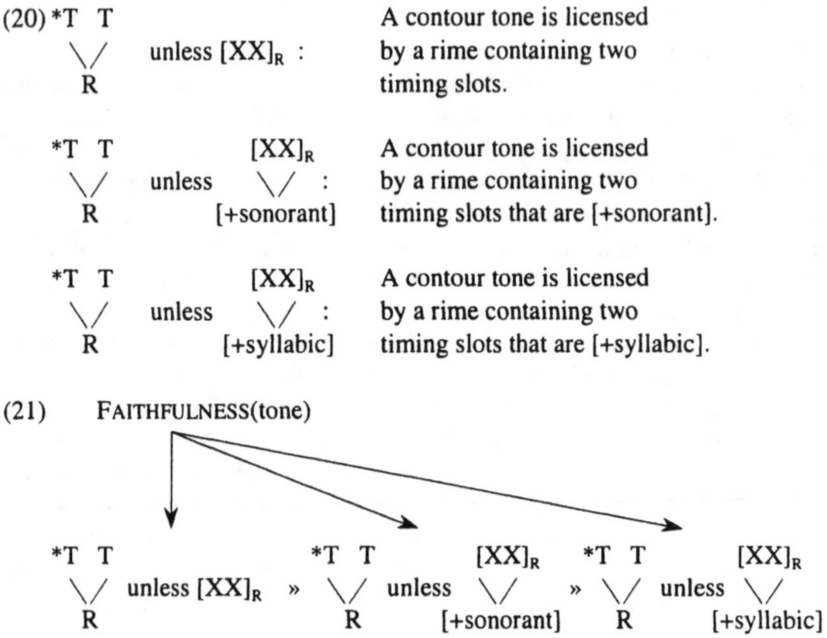

But as I have argued in earlier in this chapter (§6.1.3—§6.1.5), the richness of the phonetic influence on phonological patterning such as contour tone restrictions far exceeds what Gordon's phonological account in (20) and (21) inherently predicts. Therefore, my position is that the phonetic details must be directly encoded in phonology instead of being mediated by phonological entities such as the X slots. The complete theoretic apparatus is spelled out in Chapters 7 and 8.

6.1.7 Indirect Evidence: Diphthong Distribution

The last argument against the moraic approach to contour tone restrictions is an indirect one from the distribution of diphthongs, which I discuss in detail in Zhang (2001).

Diphthongs are similar to contour tones in the following ways: articulatorily, a diphthong involves hitting two articulatory targets within a syllable nucleus (Lehiste and Peterson 1961, Ladefoged 2001), and a contour tone involves hitting two vocal fold configurations (Hirano et al. 1969, Lindqvist 1972, Ohala 1978); auditorily, a diphthong involves the perception of two different vocalic qualities and the transition between the two within one syllable (Gay 1968, 1970, Gerber 1971, Jha 1985), and a contour tone involves the perception of two different pitches and the transition between the two (Gandour 1978, 1981, 1983). Crucially, diphthongs differ from VC sequences in that they behave as phonological units instead of sequences of segments, and the transition between the two vocalic components in a diphthong plays an important role in its identification (Gay 1968, 1970, Gerber 1971, Jha 1985). These properties determine that just like contour tones, diphthongs need ample duration to be realized, because the muscle contraction that is necessary for an articulatory movement needs time to be implemented (Collier, Bell-Berti, and Raphael 1982), and the perception of the acoustic gliding portion, which is crucial for the identification of diphthongs, also needs a minimal duration (Bladon 1985, He 1985). If we assume that the duration of a syllable is inherent to its prosodic properties, such as stress, position in a prosodic domain, etc.; in particular, there are maximum duration restrictions for a syllable in different prosodic positions, then the direct approach to positional prominence predicts that, similar to contour tones, diphthongs should occur more freely in positions with longer inherent duration; and the longer the duration, the more likely diphthongs can occur in the position.

This prediction was borne out in a survey of forty-two languages, as reported in Zhang (2001). The genetic composition of the survey is given in (22). Of the forty-two languages, twenty-one show a preference for diphthongs to occur in open syllables,[5] eighteen languages show a preference for them to occur in stressed syllables, and thirteen languages show a preference for them to occur in word- or phrase-final syllables.

[5] Precautions were taken to ensure that any dispreference to have diphthongs in closed syllables was not due to the avoidance of superheavy syllables or complex codas. For example, if a phonemic long vowel can occur in closed syllables while a diphthong cannot, or if the diphthongs that can occur in closed syllables is a proper subset of those that can occur in open syllables, then the diphthong restriction is not due to the avoidance of superheavy syllables, since superheavy syllables are allowed in the language in question; if the occurrence of rising diphthongs (diphthongs that rise in sonority) is more restricted in closed syllables, then it is not due to coda conditions.

(22) Genetic composition of the diphthong distribution survey in Zhang (2001):

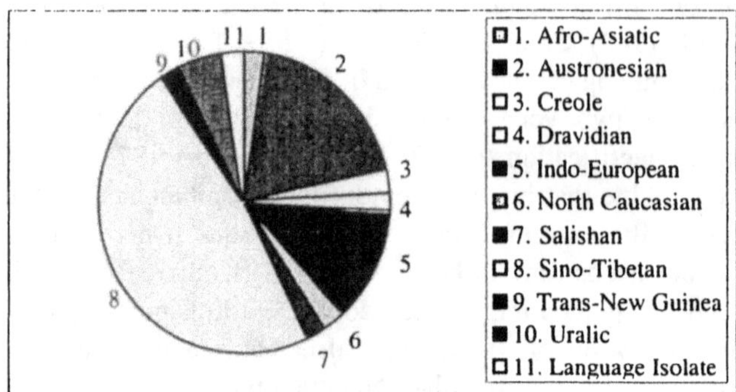

Moreover, in a series of phonetic studies on syllable duration, I show in Zhang (2001) that, similar to contour tones, when there are multiple durational factors in competition for being the preferred diphthong licenser, it is the one that induces the greatest lengthening that wins out.

Clearly, these apparent parallels between the distribution of contour tones and that of diphthongs are expected, and can be readily captured, in the direct approach: given that in both contour tones and diphthongs, duration plays an important role in their articulation and perception, and phonological patterning directly reflects the role of phonetics by referring to phonetic properties such as duration, it is no accident that contour tones and diphthongs behave similarly in their distribution.

But the similarities do not fall out so easily if a moraic approach is taken to account for the contour tone distribution. If we take tone as a suprasegmental feature, it is possible for us to imagine that the wellformedness of a tonal representation is dependent on the weight tier, which is projected from the segmental tier. But for diphthongs, which are on the segmental tier and project moras themselves, it is not clear where the restrictions on their occurrence would come from. Apparently they do not come from the lack of moras, since they project moras themselves. Then no matter where they come from, the account is necessarily different from that for contour tone restrictions. Hence the similarities between diphthong and contour tone restrictions are left without an explanation. One may argue that the mora count of a syllable does not only depend on its segmental material, but also on its prosodic properties such as stress and proximity to prosodic boundaries. Therefore, there are restrictions on the maximal number of moras that are allowed on a certain position; e.g., unstressed syllables can have only one mora. Then even when a diphthong is able to project two moras itself, it will not surface on an unstressed syllable if the constraint against a bimoraic unstressed syllable is highly ranked in an OT grammar. This move seems to allow an explanation for diphthong distribution in moraic terms, but it also exposes the explanation to all the criticisms to the moraic approach to contour tone distribution outlined in the previous sections, such as too many predicted levels of distinction, inability to capture the size differences among diphthong inventories in different positions, and moraic inconsistency. For example, Zhang (2001) shows that, similar to the contour tone cases, diphthong restrictions are not only reflected in the total absence of diphthongs, but also in the number of diphthongs that are allowed in the position in question. Therefore the criticisms for using the moras to account for contour tone distribution in §6.1.5 will hold here too.

The evidence against the moraic approach to contour tone distribution provided here is admittedly indirect. But the similarities between contour tone and diphthong restrictions clearly indicate that they should be accounted for in similar fashions, and as argued above, the moraic approach does not seem to be an ideal candidate for a unified approach for both phenomena.

6.1.8 Local Conclusion

In this section, I have argued against the moraic approach to contour tone distribution. I have shown that this approach cannot provide a satisfactory account for a four-way distinction in tone-bearing ability, or the distributional restrictions of contour tones with different pitch excursions, or the size differences among contour tone inventories in different positions, all of which were attested in the contour tone survey discussed in Chapter 4. And given that the mora is being used as the unified weight unit for all weight-related phenomena, it also faces the moraic inconsistency problem. Zhang (2001)'s study on diphthong distribution is cited as a piece of indirect evidence that the moraic approach is not appropriate for contour tone distribution, as it cannot be easily extended to the distribution of diphthongs, which patterns similarly to that of contour tones.

6.2 THE MELODY MAPPING APPROACH

As I have mentioned before, for the attraction of contour tones to prosodic-final syllables and syllables in shorter words, an intuitively possible alternative is to use the notion of tone melodies and the *Generalized Alignment* schema proposed by McCarthy and Prince (1993). If this alternative is viable, then maybe we do not need to refer to the durational advantages in prosodic-final syllables and syllables in shorter words. This section formally explores this alternative.

6.2.1 Two Types of Tone Languages

The basic tenet of autosegmental phonology is that phonological representations are tiered. An autosegmental representation of tone assumes that tones and tone-bearing units (TBUs) occupy different tiers in the phonological representation and are linked together either underlyingly or during the derivation from input to output (Leben 1971, 1973, 1978, Goldsmith 1976, Williams 1976, Clements and Ford 1979, Halle and Vergnaud 1982, Pulleyblank 1986, among others).

We can in principle distinguish two types of tone languages. The first type is languages in which the association between tones and tone-bearing units is non-distinctive. Assuming the Obligatory Contour Principle (OCP) in the lexicon (Odden 1986), this means that for a set number of tone-bearing units and a specific tonal melody, there is a unique way in which these elements on the two tiers are associated. Consequently, there is no contrast between trisyllabic High-Low-Low and High-High-Low, or disyllabic Low-High and Low-Rise, etc., as shown in (23).

(23) Non-distinctive association: no contrast between—

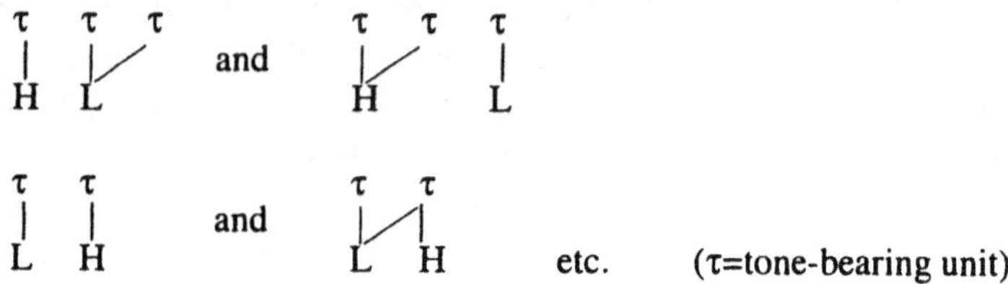

From a derivational point of view, this tonal pattern can be construed as follows: tones and tone-bearing units are unassociated underlying; during the derivation, tones are mapped to tone-bearing units according to the *Association Conventions* and *Well-formedness Condition* envisioned by Leben (1971, 1973, 1978), Goldsmith (1976), Pulleyblank (1986), and others.

(24) a. *Association Conventions*:

Map a sequence of tones onto a sequence of tone-bearing units,
(a) from left to right;
(b) in a one-to-one relation.

b. *Well-formedness Condition*:
Association lines do not cross. (Pulleyblank 1986: p.11)

From an Optimality-Theoretic perspective, we may entertain the following constraints in (25) (MAX(tone) and IDENT(tone) after McCarthy and Prince 1993, 1995).

(25) a. MAX(tone): if T is a tone in the input, then T has an identical correspondent in the output.

b. IDENT(tone): if α is a tone-bearing unit in the input and β is a correspondent of α in the output, then the tonal specification of α must be identical to the tonal specification of β.

c. Tonal markedness constraints on tonal shape, melody, and association; e.g.,

$*\widehat{T_1T_2}$: no two tones can be mapped onto a single tone-bearing unit.

$*T_1T_2T_3$-WORD: no tonal melody $T_1T_2T_3$ can surface on a word.

ALIGN(Tone, L, Word, L): align the left edge of a tone with the left edge of a word.

*FLOAT: all tones are associated with some segmental material in the output.

The lack of distinctive tonal association can be accounted for by ranking MAX(tone) and tonal markedness constraints over IDENT(tone). This is due to the fact that IDENT(tone) is the only constraint that enforces the distinctiveness of tonal association, and if it is outranked by tonal markedness constraints that require a particular mode of association, then the association will be rendered non-distinctive. And to ensure that not all conceivable tones in the *Rich Base* (Prince and Smolensky 1993, Smolensky 1996) are realized on the surface, MAX(tone) must still be outranked by some tonal markedness constraints. This general schema of constraint ranking for non-distinctive tonal association is summarized in (26).

(26) Constraint ranking for non-distinctive tonal association:

Some tonal markedness constraints
⇓
MAX(tone)
⇓
Some other tonal markedness constraints
⇓
IDENT(tone)

An example of this type of languages is given in §6.2.2, and the constraints and their ranking will be more clearly motivated there.

The second type of languages are those in which the association between tones and tone-bearing units *is* distinctive. Obviously, this means that for a set number of tone-bearing units and a specific tonal melody, there is more than one way in which these elements on the two tiers can be associated. The association thus serves a contrastive function in these languages, and consequently, contrasts between trisyllabic High-Low-Low and High-High-Low, or disyllabic Low-High and Low-Rise, for example, are attested, as shown in (27).

(27) Distinctive association: contrast between—

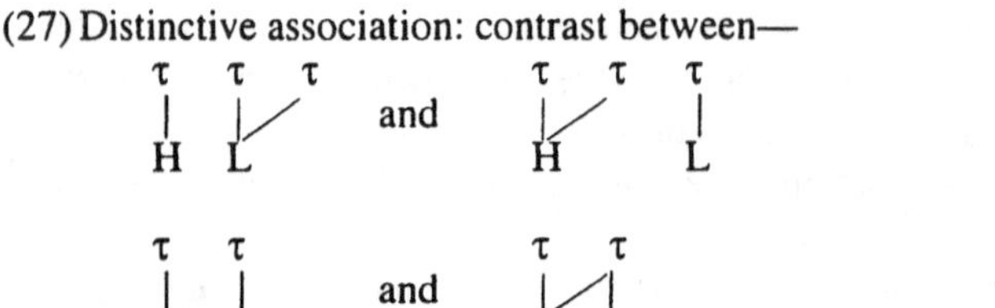

etc. (τ=tone-bearing unit)

From a derivational perspective, this tonal pattern can be construed as the presence of prelinking in the underlying representation, and then the execution of the *Association Conventions*, abiding by the *Well-formedness Condition*. The derivation in (28) exemplifies how the contrast between trisyllabic HLL and HHL is rendered in this type of language.

(28)

τ τ τ H L	τ τ τ H L	UR
τ τ τ H L	τ τ τ H L	*Association Conventions* and *Well-formedness Condition*
τ τ τ H L	τ τ τ H L	SR

From an Optimality-Theoretic perspective, the analysis will necessarily involve the promotion of the IDENT(tone) constraint over some tonal markedness constraints, notably constraints on tonal association like ALIGN-L. Under this ranking, the tonal association in the underlying representation must be preserved sometimes, giving rise to the contrastiveness of the association. The general scheme of constraint ranking for distinctive tonal association is given in (29). 'Some other tonal markedness constraints' necessarily include constraints on tonal association such as ALIGN-L.

(29) Constraint ranking for distinctive tonal association:

Some tonal markedness constraints

⇓

MAX(tone), IDENT(tone)

⇓

Some other tonal markedness constraints

An example of this type of languages will be given later in §6.2.3, and the constraints and their ranking will be more clearly motivated there.

As we can see, in the OT interpretations of the two types of languages, it is not entirely clear that we need the notion of tonal melody. For languages with non-distinctive tonal association, whether the tones and tone-bearing units are associated underlyingly is not crucial to the output of the grammar, since the low ranking of IDENT(tone) will cause all the unwanted underlying associations to be lost in the output in any event. In fact, if we consider the addition of association lines from the input to the output to be a violation of DEP(Association), we should opt for the representation *with* the associations in the input according to *Lexicon Optimization* (Prince and Smolensky 1993). This move might render the notion of tonal melody vacuous, since if lexical tones are always associated with the TBU's underlyingly, they should then be considered properties of the TBU's, in other words, syllables or moras. For languages with distinctive tonal association, given that some underlying associations must be necessarily present, there seems to be even less of a reason to consider tonal melody a relevant notion.

But the tonal melody does have its merits. First of all, on the lexical level, the tonal melody does seem to be a relevant notion in languages that truly limit the number of tonal combinations that can occur on a word. Even though in the previous chapter, we have shown that Mende (§4.5.2.3) does not in fact limits its tonal melodies to the ones proposed by Leben, and that its limitations are phonetically motivated rather than accidental, we still have Kukuya (§4.5.2.4), for which we do not have strong counterevidence so far for the five tonal melodies proposed by Paulian (1974). Granted that we do not find the HLH pattern for trisyllabic words or more complicated tonal patterns for tetrasyllabic or even longer words, we must consider constraints such as *HLH-WORD, *HLHL-WORD to be relevant constraints for Kukuya, and in this we find the justification for tonal melodies. Although intuitively, this seems more likely to be the property of non-distinctive tonal association, it can occur in both type of languages, since even though languages with distinctive tonal association do tend to allow more tonal melodies to surface (e.g., Mende), it is not necessarily the case. It is a priori possible to find a language that only allows Low-High-High and Low-Low-High but nothing else on trisyllabic words.

Second, tonal melodies are useful in languages in which grammatical information is carried by floating tones or tonal melodies. For instance, in Tiv, each verb tense is marked with one of two tonal melodies—a High melody or a Low melody (Abraham 1940, Arnott 1964, McCawley 1970, Goldsmith 1976). The two melodies for the General Past realized on one, two, or three-syllable words, as argued for in Goldsmith (1976), are given in (30).

(30) Tiv General Past tense:

	σ	σσ	σσσ
High melody !HL	!H	!HL	!HLL
Low melody L	L	LL	LLL

Third, tonal melodies are also useful in languages in which the tone sandhi behavior of polysyllabic words is determined by the lexical tone of one of the syllables. Many Wu and Min dialects of Chinese are examples of this sort. We have seen a simplified account of Shanghai Chinese in §4.5.2.1. The formulation is repeated in (31). In a way, the disyllabic compound has a 'tonal melody' that is determined by the tone of the first syllable.

(31) σ_1 [T_1 T_2] σ_2 [T_3 T_4] → σ_1 | T_1 σ_2 | T_2

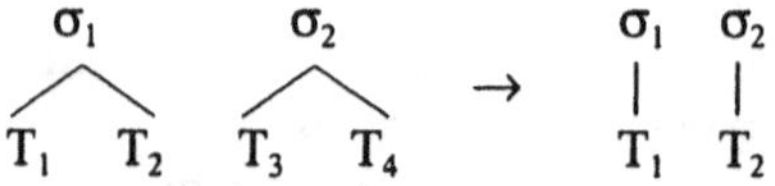

As I have shown in the survey of contour tone distribution, whether the tonal association is distinctive or not, there is a tendency for contour tones to be attracted to the final syllable of a prosodic domain and to syllables in shorter words: for non-distinctive tonal association, Kukuya (§4.5.2.4); for distinctive tonal association, Mende (§4.5.2.3). The goal of this section is to show that for both types of languages, we need to specifically refer to the durational advantage these parameters induce ($C_{CONTOUR}$(σ-final), $C_{CONTOUR}$(σ-short-word)). Since the data in this section do not differentiate the direct approach, which refers to the durational categories of different syllable types, and a structural-only approach, which only refers to the syllable types, I opt for the simpler notation of the structure-only approach and only write σ_{final} and $\sigma_{short\text{-}word}$ when the need arises. But given that the direct approach has been motivated in the previous chapters, this should only be taken as a notational simplification, not an argument for the structure-only approach. I will start the discussion from languages with non-distinctive tonal association.

6.2.2 Non-Distinctive Tonal Association—An Analysis of Kukuya

6.2.2.1 Kukuya and Pseudo-Kukuya

Let us recall that in Kukuya, there are five tonal melodies: L, H, LH, HL, and LHL. These melodies are mapped onto words of various lengths (from one to three syllables, as given in Paulian 1974). Examples of Kukuya are repeated in (32).

(32) Kukuya examples:

	σ	σσ	σσσ
H	bá 'oil palms'	bágá 'show knives'	bálágá 'fence'
L	bà 'grasshopper killer'	bàlà 'to build'	bàlàgà 'to change route'
HL	kâ 'to pick'	kálà 'paralytic'	kálàgà 'to be entangled'
LH	sǎ 'weaving knot'	sàmí 'conversation'	**mʷàrəgí** 'younger brother'
LHL	bvı̃̂ 'he falls'	pàlı̂ 'he goes out'	kàlə́gì 'he turns around'

Apparently, the mapping of tones to syllables conforms to the one-to-one, left-to-right *Association Conventions* and the no-crossing *Well-formedness Condition* except for the pattern in bold in the table—LLH in a trisyllabic word—which seems to require a right-to-left mapping of the tonal melody. But the generalization regarding contour tone distribution holds true for both the general and the exceptional cases: the complex contour LHL and the rising contour LH can only occur on monosyllabic words; and the falling contour HL can only occur on monosyllabic words or the final syllable of disyllabic words. Hyman (1987) and Zoll (1996) have subsequently provided analyses for the exceptional pattern, Hyman by prelinking the High tone to the final syllable, Zoll by positing a constraint LICENSE(H) which penalizes a surface High on a non-final position. Given that neither of these analyses bears on the issue of contour tones, I simply consider the trisyllabic Low-Low-High pattern to be an exception, and in the following analysis, I consider instead Pseudo-Kukuya, which has an exceptionless mapping of one, two, or three tones onto mono-, di-, or trisyllabic words according to the *Association Conventions* and *Well-formedness Condition*. The tonal melodies abide by the Obligatory Contour Principle. Therefore, T_1=H or L, T_1T_2=HL or LH, $T_1T_2T_3$=HLH or LHL. The tonal patterns of Pseudo-Kukuya are summarized in (33).

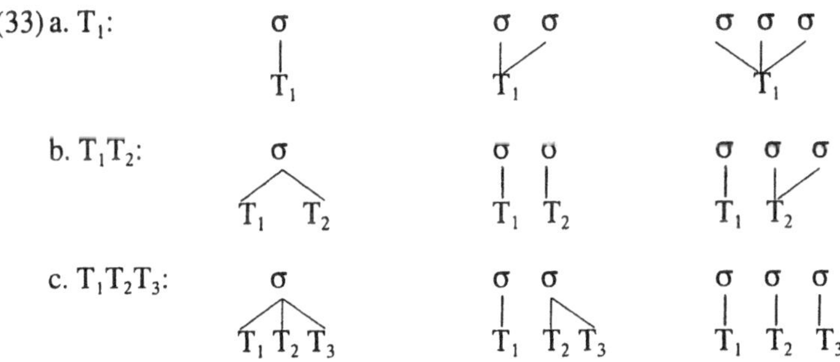

6.2.2.2 *First Try:* ALIGN-L *and* ALIGN-R

As I have discussed in §6.2.1, in the Optimality-Theoretic framework, the relevant faithfulness constraints to consider here are MAX(tone) and IDENT(tone). For languages with non-distinctive tonal association, MAX(tone) is highly ranked—it is in fact only outranked by undominated markedness constraints on tonal contours allowed on a single syllable and tonal melodies allowed in words, e.g., $*T_1T_2T_3T_4$ and $*T_1T_2T_3T_4$-WORD. Moreover, IDENT(tone) is lowly ranked, and this renders the associations in the underlying representation non-crucial. In the following analyses, for reasons of simplicity, I only consider underlying forms that do not have any associations between tones and syllables. I also assume that *FLOAT is undominated. Therefore if a tone is in the output, it must be linked.

To achieve the gravitation of contours to the final syllable, our first attempt is to use an ALIGN constraint which requires tones to align to the right edge of the word, as defined in (34). This is a gradient constraint. If the right edge of a tone is separated from the right edge of the word by *n* syllables, the constraint accumulates *n* violations.

(34) ALIGN (Tone, R, Word, R) (abbr. ALIGN-R):

The right edge of a tone must align with the right edge of a word.

As a reminder of the purpose of this chapter: if this scheme can indeed capture the desired effects of contour tone distribution, then no mention of the final syllable as a privileged contour bearer is needed in the analysis, and the argument for the contrast-specificity of positional prominence based on this effect might be lost.

The effect of the ALIGN-R constraint can be seen in the tableau in (35). The winner, which has a contour on the final syllable, satisfies ALIGN-R better than the losing candidate, which has a contour on the initial syllable.

(35)

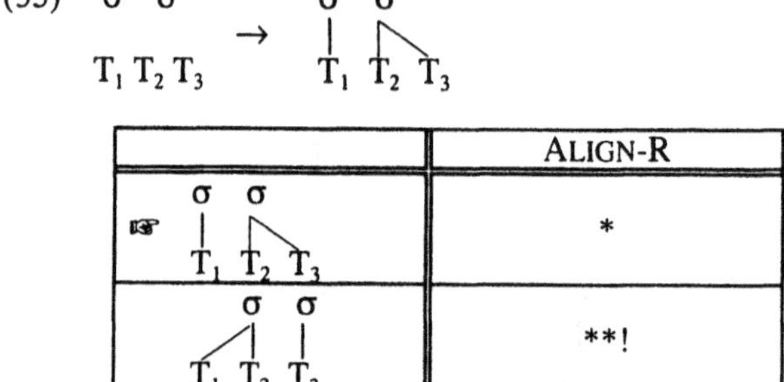

	ALIGN-R
☞ σ σ (T_1 T_2 T_3)	*
σ σ (T_1 T_2 T_3)	**!

We must also posit markedness constraints against contour tones to rule out the possibility of aligning all the tones to the rightmost syllable. These constraints are defined in (36). Obviously, these constraints must outrank ALIGN-R. The tableaux in (37) show that unnecessary contours are avoided.

(36) a. $*T_1T_2$: no $\widehat{HL}$ or $\widehat{LH}$ contour is allowed on any syllable.

b. $*T_1T_2T_3$: no $\widehat{HLH}$ or $\widehat{LHL}$ contour is allowed on any syllable.

(37) a. σ σ / T_1 T_2 T_3 → σ σ (σ₁–T_1; σ₂–T_2 T_3)

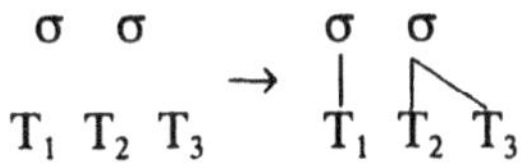

	$*T_1T_2T_3$	ALIGN-R
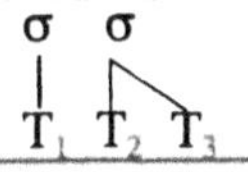 ☞ σ σ (σ₁–T_1; σ₂–T_2 T_3)		*
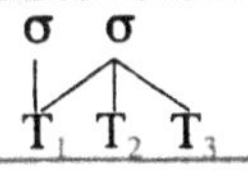 σ σ (σ₁–T_1 T_2; σ₂–T_2 T_3)	*!	

b. σ σ / T_1 T_2 → σ σ (σ₁–T_1; σ₂–T_2)

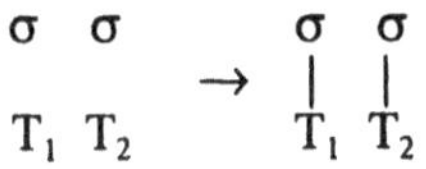

	$*T_1T_2$	ALIGN-R
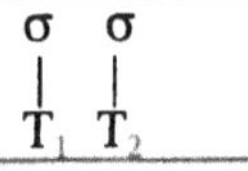 ☞ σ σ (σ₁–T_1; σ₂–T_2)		*
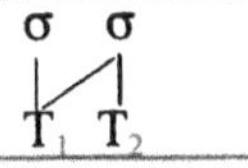 σ σ (σ₁–T_1; σ₂–T_1 T_2)	*!	

Therefore, we are led to the following constraint ranking, shown in (38).

(38) Interim ranking:

$*T_1T_2T_3T_4$, etc.
⇓
MAX(tone)
⇓
$*T_1T_2T_3$, $*T_1T_2$
⇓
ALIGN-R
⇓
IDENT(tone)

But this constraint ranking makes the wrong prediction for two tones mapping onto three syllables. This is shown in (39).

(39) σ σ σ → σ σ σ
T_1 T_2 → T_1 T_2 (T_1 linked to first σ; T_2 linked to second and third σ)

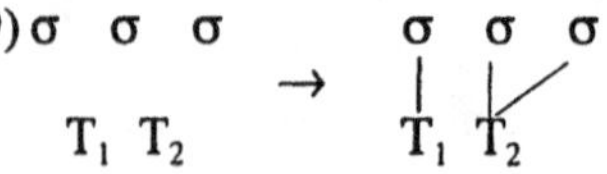

	ALIGN-R
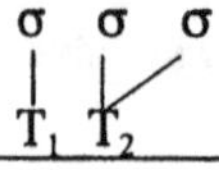 σ σ σ / T_1 T_2 (T_1–σ₁; T_2–σ₂σ₃)	**!
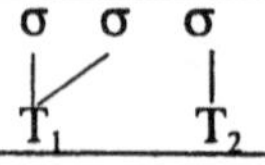 ☛ σ σ σ / T_1 T_2 (T_1–σ₁σ₂; T_2–σ₃)	*

The winning candidate is the one that realizes T_1 on the first two syllables and T_2 on the last syllable. It satisfies ALIGN-R better than the actual output since the right edge of T_1 is closer to the right edge of the word.

We may try to remedy the situation by positing an ALIGN-L constraint, as defined in (40). As ALIGN-R, it is also a gradient constraint. If we rank ALIGN-L over ALIGN-R, we derive the correct output for (39), as shown in (41).

(40) ALIGN (Tone, L, Word, L) (abbr. ALIGN-L):

The left edge of a tone must align with the left edge of a word.

(41) σ σ σ → σ σ σ
T_1 T_2 → T_1 T_2 (T_1 linked to first σ; T_2 linked to second and third σ)

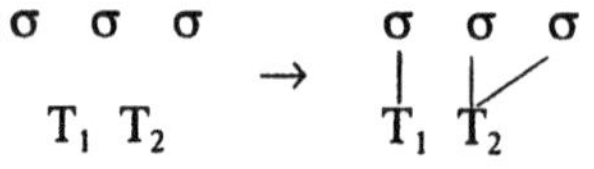

	ALIGN-L	ALIGN-R
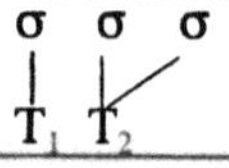 ☞ σ σ σ / T_1 T_2 (T_1–σ₁; T_2–σ₂σ₃)	*	**
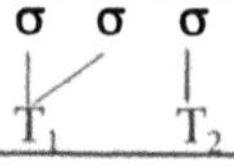 σ σ σ / T_1 T_2 (T_1–σ₁σ₂; T_2–σ₃)	**!	*

But we observe immediately that the tableaux in (37) now give the wrong result. E.g., when three tones are mapped onto two syllables, the contour tone now occurs on the initial syllable instead of the final one, as illustrated in (42).

(42) σ σ → σ σ
T_1 T_2 T_3 → T_1 T_2 T_3 (T_1 linked to first σ; T_2 T_3 linked to second σ)

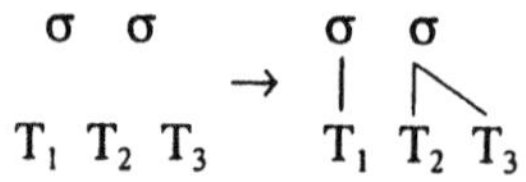

	ALIGN-L	ALIGN-R
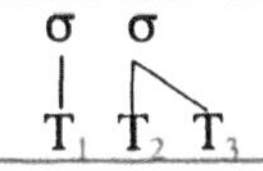 σ σ T_1 T_2 T_3	**!	*
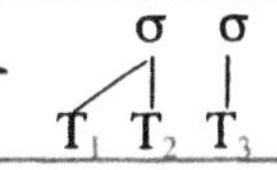 ☞ σ σ T_1 T_2 T_3	*	**

I argue that the problem here is a conceptual one rather than a technical one. The conflict lies between the left-to-right mapping mechanism, which requires a higher ranking of ALIGN-L, and the attraction of contours to the final syllable, which requires a higher ranking of ALIGN-R. Therefore, in order for the analysis to work, the desired effect of *one* of the ALIGN constraints must be achieved by other means.

6.2.2.3 *Second Try: ALIGN-L and* $*T_1T_2\text{-}\sigma_{nonfinal}$

I propose that the solution to the problem is to eliminate ALIGN-R from the constraint composition and achieve the same effect by referring to the final syllable in the word as a privileged position for contour-bearing. The failure of simply using ALIGN and markedness constraints without referring to privileged positions already constitutes one argument for such a move. Moreover, for ALIGN-L, we can find motivation for it in numerous psycholinguistic studies which illustrate the importance of word-initial position in lexical access and word recognition. For example, Brown and McNeill (1966) show that in a tip-of-the-tongue state, the initial segment in a word has a higher rate of being recalled by subjects than other segments; Horowitz et al. (1968) and Horowitz et al. (1969) show that utterance-initial materials provide better cues for word recognition and lexical retrieval than medial or final materials; and a series of studies by Marslen-Wilson and colleagues illustrate the significance of beginnings of words in psycholinguistic tasks such as close-shadowing and cross-modal priming (Marslen-Wilson and Welsh 1978, Marslen-Wilson and Tyler 1980, Marslen-Wilson and Zwitserlood 1989, among others, summarized in Marslen-Wilson 1989). But for ALIGN-R, no such motivation can be found. Of course, having only the ALIGN-L constraint opens up the possibility of crowding all the tones onto the first syllable, and I argue that its force is counteracted by the preference to have contour tones on prosodic-final syllables, which have longer duration due to final lengthening. Then intuitively, the irresolvable conflict mentioned above becomes a resolvable one: tones prefer to occur closer to the left edge of the word for the ease of processing, but contour tones prefer to occur on the final syllable because of its extended duration.

To capture this effect, we split the $*T_1T_2T_3$ and $*T_1T_2$ constraints into the following constraints, as in (43).

(43) a. $*T_1T_2\text{-}\sigma_{nonfinal}$: no $\widehat{HL}$ or $\widehat{LH}$ contour is allowed on a non-final syllable.
b. $*T_1T_2$: no $\widehat{HL}$ or $\widehat{LH}$ contour is allowed on any syllable.
c. $*T_1T_2T_3\text{-}\sigma_{nonfinal}$: no $\widehat{HLH}$ or $\widehat{LHL}$ contour is allowed on a non-final syllable.
d. $*T_1T_2T_3$: no $\widehat{HLH}$ or $\widehat{LHL}$ contour is allowed on any syllable.

The constraints in (43) observes the intrinsic rankings in (44), as suggested by the *Pāṇini's Theorem* of constraint ranking (Prince and Smolensky 1993). The gist of the theorem is that if for any underlying representation, its violation of constraint *A* implies the same or a greater number of violations of constraint *B*, then constraint *A* must intrisincally outrank constraint *B*, since otherwise, constraint *A* will never have any effect in the grammar. The intrinsic rankings in (44) are derived from the fact that the violation of $*T_1T_2T_3\text{-}\sigma_{nonfinal}$ and $*T_1T_2\text{-}\sigma_{nonfinal}$ implies the violation of $*T_1T_2T_3$ and $*T_1T_2$ respectively. This type of rankings has also been assumed in the literature on positional markedness (Alderete et al. 1996, Zoll 1998, and Steriade 1999, among others).

(44) a. $*T_1T_2T_3\text{-}\sigma_{nonfinal} \gg *T_1T_2T_3$.

b. $*T_1T_2\text{-}\sigma_{nonfinal} \gg *T_1T_2$.

The tableau in (45) illustrates the effect of ALIGN-L: when two tones are mapped onto three syllables, the second tone is mapped onto the last two syllables, since it fares better with ALIGN-L than the alternative, which maps the first tone to the first two syllables.

(45) σ σ σ → σ σ σ
T_1 T_2 → T_1 T_2 (T_1 linked to the first σ; T_2 linked to the second and third σ)

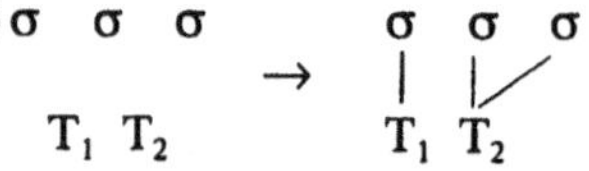

	ALIGN-L
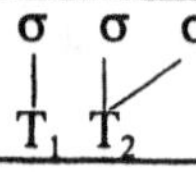 ☞ σ σ σ: T_1 → σ₁; T_2 → σ₂, σ₃	*
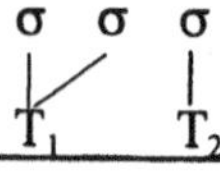 σ σ σ: T_1 → σ₁, σ₂; T_2 → σ₃	**!

For three tones mapping onto two syllables, we posit the ranking in (46).

(46) $*T_1T_2T_3\text{-}\sigma_{nonfinal}$, $*T_1T_2\text{-}\sigma_{nonfinal} \gg$ ALIGN-L

The high ranking of $*T_1T_2T_3\text{-}\sigma_{\text{nonfinal}}$ and $*T_1T_2\text{-}\sigma_{\text{nonfinal}}$ ensures that the contour tone occurs on the final syllable, as shown in (47). The second candidate in this tableau, even though fares better with ALIGN-L, loses for violating the more highly ranked $*T_1T_2\text{-}\sigma_{\text{nonfinal}}$. The third candidate in the tableau unsurprisingly loses for violating $*T_1T_2T_3\text{-}\sigma_{\text{nonfinal}}$.

(47) σ σ → σ σ

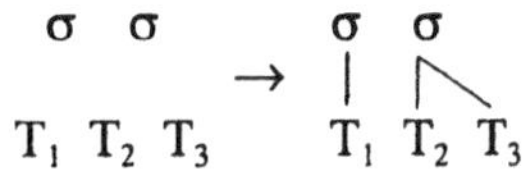

T_1 T_2 T_3 T_1 T_2 T_3 .

	$*T_1T_2T_3\text{-}\sigma_{\text{nonfinal}}$	$*T_1T_2\text{-}\sigma_{\text{nonfinal}}$	$*T_1T_2T_3$	$*T_1T_2$	ALIGN-L
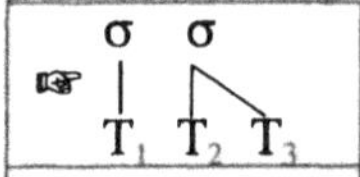 ☞ σ σ T_1 T_2 T_3				*	**
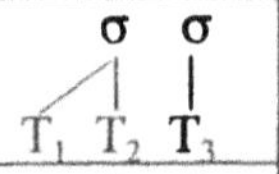 σ σ T_1 T_2 T_3		*!		*	*
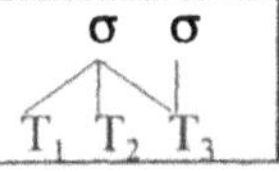 σ σ T_1 T_2 T_3	*!	*	*	*	

There is no need to establish any ranking between ALIGN-L and $*T_1T_2T_3$, $*T_1T_2$, since any attempt to satisfy ALIGN-L at the expense of $*T_1T_2T_3$ or $*T_1T_2$ will also violate $*T_1T_2T_3\text{-}\sigma_{\text{nonfinal}}$ or $*T_1T_2\text{-}\sigma_{\text{nonfinal}}$, which are more highly ranked than ALIGN-L. Max(tone) is still highly ranked in the grammar, and it is only outranked by undominated tonal markedness constraints such as $*T_1T_2T_3T_4$ and $*T_1T_2T_3T_4$-WORD. Therefore, the constraint ranking emerges as in (48). This ranking derives all the correct output patterns for Pseudo-Kukuya.

(48) Complete ranking:

$*T_1T_2T_3T_4$, etc

⇓

MAX(tone), $*T_1T_2T_3\text{-}\sigma_{\text{nonfinal}}$, $*T_1T_2\text{-}\sigma_{\text{nonfinal}}$

⇓

$*T_1T_2T_3$, $*T_1T_2$, ALIGN-L

⇓

IDENT(tone)

Therefore, I conclude that the durational advantage of the final position in a prosodic domain must be referred to as a privileged contour carrier in languages with non-distinctive tonal association. One way in which this privilege can be manifested in the grammar is in the form of $*T_1T_2\text{-}\sigma_{\text{nonfinal}}$, which, in this section, is the short form for $*T_1T_2\text{-}C_{\text{CONTOUR}}(\sigma\text{-nonfinal})$. Again, I opted for the former formulation here partly because it is notationally simpler, partly because the data discussed in this section do not directly motivate the less traditional latter approach.

The data pattern of Pseudo-Kukuya does not establish the need to refer to word length to account for the fact that syllables in shorter words are more tolerant of contour tones. For example, that the complex contour LHL can occur on monosyllabic words, but not on syllables of disyllabic words can be due to the fact that LHL is a possible tonal melody while HLHL is not, as shown in (49). Therefore the data pattern can be captured by positing a high-ranking *HLHL-WORD constraint, and no specific mention of word length is necessary.

(49)

But if HLHL *is* a possible tonal melody in the language, specifically, if it can be found on polysyllabic words, but not on disyllabic words, as shown in (50), then it is justified to say that the lack of L͡HL on syllables in disyllabic words is due to a high-ranking constraint in the nature of *LHL-$\sigma_{\text{disyllabic}}$, which intrinsically outranks *LHL-$\sigma_{\text{monosyllabic}}$. Then when the tonal faithfulness constraint MAX(tone) intervenes between the two, L͡HL will be able to surface on monosyllabic words, but not on syllables in disyllabic words. Mende, whose analysis I will discuss in §6.2.3, illustrates this point.

(50)

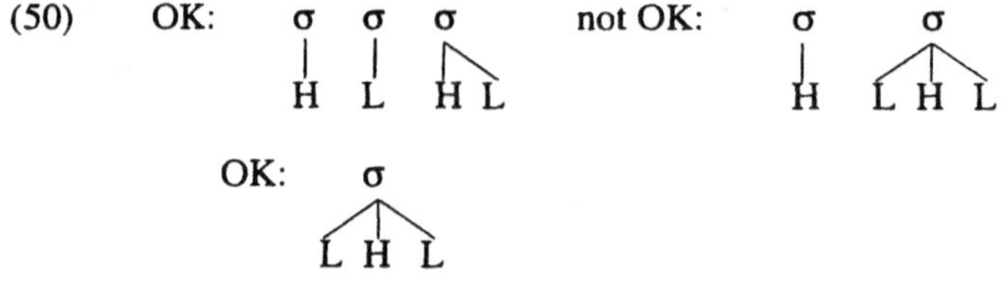

6.2.2.4 *Zoll (1997)*

A similar approach to the attraction of contour tones on the final syllable has been proposed by Zoll (1997). In her account, the effect is captured by constraint ALIGN-R(contour). Her account is different from the one advanced above in two respects.

First, using an ALIGN constraint implies that the closer the contour is to the prosodic boundary, the better the constraint is satisfied. Therefore we would expect that all else being equal, the penult is a better docking site for contours than the antepenult. But according to the result of the survey documented in Chapter 4, this is not the case. It seems that the distinction is of an 'all or nothing' nature: my survey only finds final preference for contour tones, but not penultimate or antepenultimate preference, when all else is equal. Therefore, licensing constraints such as $*T_1T_2T_3\text{-}\sigma_{nonfinal}$ and $*T_1T_2\text{-}\sigma_{nonfinal}$, which directly refer to non-final syllables, are better suited for the task. Zoll, in her 1996 dissertation, in fact realizes this problem and proposes a constraint COINCIDE, which requires a marked structure to coincide with a strong constituent.

Second, Zoll's account does not encode the rationale for having contours on the final syllable, while the account I propose clearly states that the durational advantage is crucial to the contour licensing conditions. This is done either by assuming that speakers form tonal markedness constraints by encoding durational categories directly in the analysis. Under Zoll (1997)'s account, it should be equally possible to have a high ranking ALIGN-L(CONTOUR) constraint, which will have the effect of attracting contours to the initial syllable when all else is equal. This is unattested in the survey. And given Zoll (1996)'s COINCIDE approach does not provide specific predictors for where the 'strong constituent' is, there is no a priori reason for us to rule out any non-final positions, especially the initial position, to constitute a strong constituent for contour tones.

6.2.3 Distinctive Tonal Association—An Analysis of Mende

The distinctiveness of tonal association in Mende is established through examples in (41) in Chapter 4 which show the contrasts between HL and H$\widehat{\text{HL}}$ on disyllabic words as well as the contrasts between HLL and HHL, between LHH and LLH on trisyllabic words. Moreover, Dwyer's works have also shown that tonal patterns other than the ones proposed by Leben, such as HLH and HLHL, as also attested (see (40) in Chapter 4). These findings, together with Leben's observations, provide the complete picture of the tonal patterns in Mende: the tonal restrictions are in principle the restrictions on the distribution of contour tones. The table in (45) in Chapter 4, which summarizes these restrictions, is repeated in (51).

(51) Mende contour tone restrictions:

Vowel length	No. of sylls in word	Syll position in word	$\widehat{\text{LHL}}$ ok?	$\widehat{\text{LH}}$ ok?	$\widehat{\text{HL}}$ ok?
VV	1	final	yes	yes	yes
VV	>1	any	no	yes	yes
V	1	final	no	yes	yes
V	>1	final	no	no	yes
V	>1	non-final	no	no	no

From this table, we can see that the contour limitations in Mende are largely due to durational restrictions instead of restrictions on tonal melodies. For example, LHL can occur on long vowels in monosyllabic words, but not in disyllabic words. This is not due to the lack of HLHL patterns, as is the case in Kukuya. Rather, HLHL can occur on trisyllabic words as in náfàlê 'raphia clothed clown' (see (41) in Chapter 4). But it does not occur on disyllabic words, nor does LLHL occur on disyllabic words—with IDENT(tone) ranked over alignment constraints as discussed in §6.2.1, this would have been entirely possible. Both of these scenarios would result in a LHL contour, as shown in (52).

(52)

```
σ   σ              σ   σ
|  /|\              \ /|\
H L H L              L H L
```

For now, I propose to account for the tonal patterns in Mende with the following constraint family defined in (53).

(53) *CONTOUR$_i$-σ_j: contour *i* cannot occur on syllable type *j*.

Again, σ_j here is the shorthand for $C_{CONTOUR}(\sigma_j)$.

The constraints in this constraint family are intrinsically ranked, according to the two ranking principles in (54).

(54) a. If the sonorous portion of the rime in σ_m is longer than σ_j, then *CONTOUR$_i$-σ_j » *CONTOUR$_i$-σ_m.

b. If contour$_i$ is higher on the *Tonal Complexity* scale than contour$_n$, then *CONTOUR$_i$-σ_j » *CONTOUR$_n$-σ_j.

The principle in (54a) ensures that a contour tone is allowed on a longer syllable before it is allowed on a shorter syllable, and the principle in (54b) ensures that a syllable allows a contour that requires a shorter duration before it allows a contour that requires a longer duration. Both of these principles are projected from phonetics and reflect the implicational hierarchies established in the typological survey. More discussion of such intrinsic rankings projected from phonetics is given in Chapter 7, where the formal theoretical apparatus for capturing contour tone distribution is spelled out.

Specifically for Mende, the relevant contour types, in descending *Tonal Complexity*, are LHL, LH, and HL. The sonorous rime duration of the syllables in Mende is systematically affected by three parameters: vowel length (σ_{VV}>σ_V), position of the syllable in the word (σ_{final}>$\sigma_{nonfinal}$), and syllable count in the word ($\sigma_{monosyllabic}$>$\sigma_{polysyllabic}$, where 'polysyllabic' here represents two or more syllables). If we assume that long vowels are longer than short vowels in any situation, then the syllable types in Mende can be ordered in the descending sonorous rime duration as: $\sigma_{VV\text{-monosyllabic}}$, $\sigma_{VV\text{-polysyllabic-final}}$, $\sigma_{VV\text{-polysyllabic-nonfinal}}$, $\sigma_{V\text{-}}$

$_{\text{monosyllabic}}$, $\sigma_{\text{V-polysyllabic-final}}$, and $\sigma_{\text{V-polysyllabic-nonfinal}}$. Therefore, the relevant constraints in the *CONTOUR$_i$-σ_j constraint family and their intrinsic rankings in Mende can be shown as in (55). In (55), MS=monosyllabic, PS=polysyllabic, F=final, NF=nonfinal.

(55) Mende *CONTOUR$_i$-σ_j constraint family:

*L͡HL-$\sigma_{\text{V-PS-NF}}$	»	*L͡HL-$\sigma_{\text{V-PS-F}}$	»	*L͡HL-$\sigma_{\text{V-MS}}$	»	*L͡HL-$\sigma_{\text{VV-PS-NF}}$	»	*L͡HL-$\sigma_{\text{VV-PS-F}}$	»	*L͡HL-$\sigma_{\text{VV-MS}}$
∨∨		∨∨		∨∨		∨∨		∨∨		∨∨
*L͡H-$\sigma_{\text{V-PS-NF}}$	»	*L͡H-$\sigma_{\text{V-PS-F}}$	»	*L͡H-$\sigma_{\text{V-MS}}$	»	*L͡H-$\sigma_{\text{VV-PS-NF}}$	»	*L͡H-$\sigma_{\text{VV-PS-F}}$	»	*L͡H-$\sigma_{\text{VV-MS}}$
∨∨		∨∨		∨∨		∨∨		∨∨		∨∨
*H͡L-$\sigma_{\text{V-PS-NF}}$	»	*H͡L-$\sigma_{\text{V-PS-F}}$	»	*H͡L-$\sigma_{\text{V-MS}}$	»	*H͡L-$\sigma_{\text{VV-PS-NF}}$	»	*H͡L-$\sigma_{\text{VV-PS-F}}$	»	*H͡L-$\sigma_{\text{VV-MS}}$

The remaining task for the Mende account is to rank the tonal faithfulness constraints MAX(tone) and IDENT(tone) against the *CONTOUR$_i$-σ_j constraint family. Given that for Mende, all the tonal restrictions can be captured by markedness constraints on the tonal shape on a syllable, the effect of tonal melody constraints, even if such constraints exist, will be unseen. Then the MAX(tone) constraint will not be able to preserve more underlying tonal patterns than the IDENT(tone) constraint, nor vice versa. I therefore rank them on the same tier. Then according to the table in (51), for L͡HL, since it can only occur on a long vowel in a monosyllabic word, for the first row of markedness constraints in (55), the faithfulness constraints should be ranked just above *L͡HL-$\sigma_{\text{VV-MS}}$; for L͡H, since it cannot occur on a short vowel in polysyllabic words, for the second row of markedness constraints, the faithfulness constraints should be ranked just below *L͡H-$\sigma_{\text{V-PS-F}}$; and for H͡L, since it is only restricted from occurring on the non-final syllable of a polysyllabic word, for the third row of markedness constraints, the faithfulness constraints should be ranked just below *H͡L-$\sigma_{\text{V-PS-NF}}$. The complete ranking of Mende is summarized in (56). Given that Mende has distinctive tonal association, the ALIGN-L constraint is ranked on a lower tier of the hierarchy.

(56) Mende ranking:

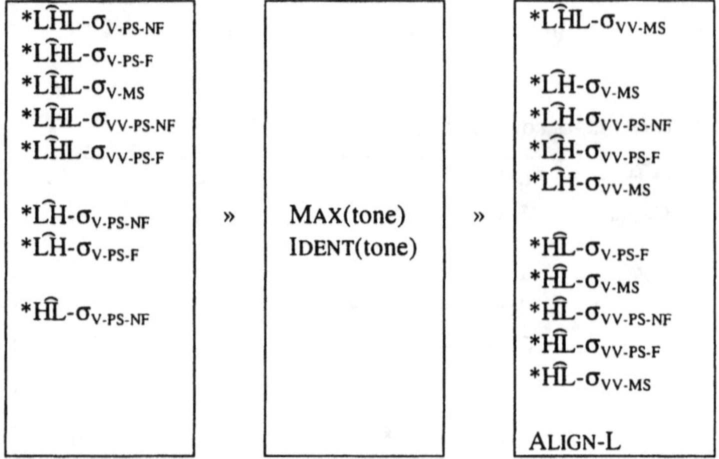

The tableaux in (57) serve as an illustration of how the ranking in (56) works. Tableaux (57a) and (57b) show that if the prelinking in the input results in the output a contour tone in a position that is banned by a constraint on the top tier of the hierarchy, e.g., LĤL or L͡H on either syllable in a disyllable, then the prelinking is not preserved in the output, since IDENT(tone) is outranked by these tonal markedness constraints. Tableaux (57c) and (57d) illustrate that if the prelinking does not result in a violation of the high-ranking markedness constraints in the output, then the prelinking is preserved, sometimes at the cost of the ALIGN-L constraint.

(57) a.

	*LĤL-$\sigma_{VV\text{-}PS\text{-}F}$	IDENT(tone)	*H͡L-$\sigma_{V\text{-}PS\text{-}F}$	ALIGN-L
σ σ / L H L (H and L linked to second σ, L and H to first)	*!			**
☞ σ σ / L H L (L to first σ; H L to second σ)		*	*	**

b. σ σ / L H L → σ σ / L H L

	*L͡H-$\sigma_{V\text{-}PS\text{-}NF}$	IDENT(tone)	*H͡L-$\sigma_{V\text{-}PS\text{-}F}$	ALIGN-L
σ σ (L H L: L, H → σ1; H, L → σ2)	*!			*
☞ σ σ (L → σ1; H L → σ2)		*	*	**

c. σ σ, H L (H linked to σ1) → σ σ, H L (H → σ1, σ2; L → σ2)

	*L͡H-$\sigma_{V\text{-}PS\text{-}NF}$	IDENT(tone)	*H͡L-$\sigma_{V\text{-}PS\text{-}F}$	ALIGN-L
☞ σ σ (H → σ1, σ2; L → σ2)			*	*
σ σ (H → σ1; L → σ2)		*!		*

d. σ σ σ, H L (H linked to σ1) → σ σ σ (H → σ1, σ2; L → σ3)

	*H͡L-$\sigma_{V\text{-}PS\text{-}NF}$	IDENT(tone)	*H͡L-$\sigma_{V\text{-}PS\text{-}F}$	ALIGN-L
☞ σ σ σ (H → σ1, σ2; L → σ3)				**
σ σ σ (H → σ1; L → σ2, σ3)		*!		*
σ σ σ (H → σ1, σ2; L → σ2, σ3)	*!			*

I have thus shown that for a representative language with distinctive tonal association, the analysis must refer to the final position as well as the syllable count in the word in order to account for its distribution of contour tones.

Of course, there is the question whether all languages with distinctive tonal association behave like Mende, namely, the contour restrictions can only be accounted for by constraints of the nature *CONTOUR$_i$-σ_j, not by constraints on tonal melodies such as *HLHL-WORD. As I have mentioned, this is not in principle the case. For example, we can imagine a language that only allows Low-High-High and Low-Low-High but nothing else on trisyllabic words, and a language like this can be accounted for by the constraints and constraint ranking in (58). The constraints on the top tier, by outranking MAX(tone) and IDENT(tone), ensure that other tonal melodies do not occur, and the LH melody does not create contour tones. But the fact that MAX(tone) and IDENT(tone) outrank ALIGN-L ensures that the melody LH can derive both LLH and LHH on trisyllables by a linking difference in the input.

(58) *FLOAT, *CONTOUR, *L-WD, *H-WD, *HL-WD, *HLH-WD, etc.
⇓
MAX(tone), IDENT(tone)
⇓
ALIGN-L

The tableaux in (59) illustrate how the constraint ranking works. In (59a), when the prelinking in the input results in a contour tone in the output, the link is not preserved due to the ranking *CONTOUR » IDENT(tone). In (59b), when the prelinking in the input does not result in a contour tone in the output, the link is preserved due to the ranking IDENT(tone) » ALIGN-L. In (59c), when there is no prelinking in the input, the tonal melody matches to the syllables from left to right. Crucially, let us observe that in this hypothetical system, there is no need to refer to the durational disadvantage of non-final syllables.

(59) a. σ σ σ / L H → σ σ σ / L H

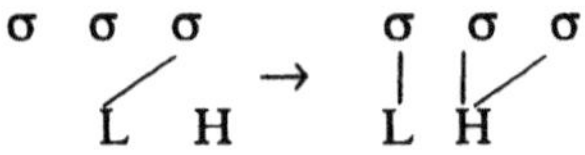

	*CONTOUR	IDENT(tone)	ALIGN-L
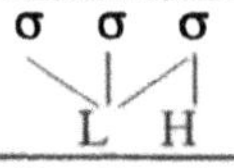 σ σ σ / L H	*!		**
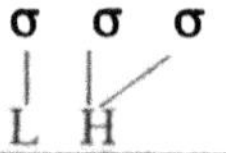 ☞ σ σ σ / L H		*	*

b. σ σ σ / L H → σ σ σ / L H

	*CONTOUR	IDENT(tone)	ALIGN-L
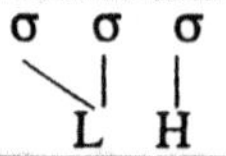 ☞ σ σ σ / L H			**
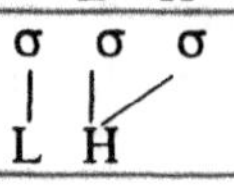 σ σ σ / L H		*!	*

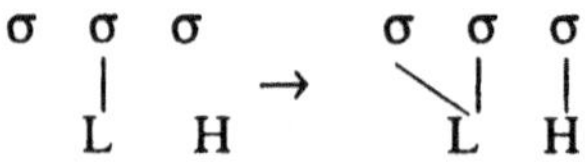

c. σ σ σ → σ σ σ
L H → L H (L linked to first σ; H linked to second and third σ)

	*CONTOUR	IDENT(tone)	ALIGN-L
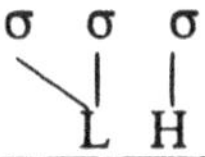 σ σ σ (L linked to first and second σ; H linked to third σ)			**!
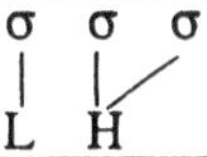 ☞ σ σ σ (L linked to first σ; H linked to second and third σ)			*

But this type of languages is simply not attested in my survey. Rather, languages with distinctive tonal association behave more or less like Mende. It is not entirely clear to me why languages with only a LLH and LHH contrast on trisyllabic words are not attested. Perhaps this is due to the consideration of distance between contrasts, à la Flemming (1995): languages tend to construct tonal contrasts in words using different tonal melodies before resorting to different tonal associations, since the former render more salient differences among words.

The point here is that it is typically the case that in languages with distinctive tonal association, the contour restrictions are usually not explicable by restrictions on tonal melodies on the word; instead, their account must resort to reference to the durational advantage induced by being in the final position of a word or a shorter word for contour bearing.

6.2.4 Local Conclusion

In this section, I have formally explored the possibility of explaining the gravitation of contour tones to final position of a prosodic domain and shorter words by using the notion of tonal melody and alignment constraints without specifically referring to the durational property of these syllables. The conclusion is that in both languages with and without distinctive tonal association, the analysis cannot completely do without referring to the durational advantage these properties induce for contour bearing. Therefore, I claim that the durational advantage that these positions have must be relevant for the phonological analyses of contour tone restrictions.

6.3 INTERIM CONCLUSION

In this chapter, I have discussed arguments against the structural alternatives to contour tone restrictions, especially the moraic approach and the tone mapping approach. In the next two chapters, I lay out the theoretic apparatus in the direct approach to contour tone restrictions and provide analyses for representative languages.

CHAPTER 7

A Phonetically-Driven Optimality-Theoretic Approach

The aim of this chapter is to formalize the direct approach defended in the previous sections and provide a theoretical apparatus in which its predictions are made specific and directly testable against data.

7.1 SETTING THE STAGE

7.1.1 Positional Faithfulness vs. Positional Markedness

The theoretical framework I adopt here is Optimality Theory (Prince and Smolensky 1993). The central idea to be expressed is that distributional restrictions on contour tones are directly related to the duration and sonority, or $C_{CONTOUR}$, of the rime.

In Chapter 1—Chapter 5 of the book, I have been using positional markedness to characterize these restrictions, in both the structure-only contrast-specific approaches and the direct approach. Basically, this approach singles out the markedness constraint specific to non-prominent positions from context-free markedness and ranks positional markedness over context-free markedness. Then when a relevant faithfulness constraint is ranked between these two constraints, the marked value will be able to surface in the prominent position, but not elsewhere. For contour tone restrictions per se, we identify positions with smaller $C_{CONTOUR}$ values and impose stronger markedness conditions upon them by the ranking *CONTOUR-$C_{CONTOUR}$(P) » IDENT(tone) » *CONTOUR, where P is a position with a smaller $C_{CONTOUR}$ value.

But there is another way in which positional prominence can be captured in OT—positional faithfulness (Alderete 1995, Jun 1995, Steriade 1995, Beckman 1997, among others). Its basic idea is to single out the faithfulness constraint specific to a prominent position from context-free faithfulness and rank positional faithfulness over context-free faithfulness. Then when a relevant markedness constraint is ranked between these two constraints, the marked value will be able to surface in the prominent position, but not elsewhere.

To illustrate the basic mechanism of positional faithfulness, let us again assume the following neutralization pattern: feature F is only contrastive ([+F] and [-F]) in position P, elsewhere it is realized as [-F]. We posit the constraints as in (1). As we can see, unlike positional markedness, which refers to the weak positions ¬P in the markedness constraint, positional faithfulness refers to P positions in the faithfulness constraint, as in (1c).

(1) a. IDENT(F): let α be a segment in the input, and β be any correspondent of α in the output; if α is [γF], then β is [γF].
b. *[+F]: no [+F] is allowed in the output.
c IDENT-P(F): let β be a segment in position P_1 in the output, and α be any correspondent of β in the input; if β is [γF], then α is [γF].

With the constraint ranking in (2), we can generate the correct data pattern for the realization of F, as illustrated in the tableaux in (3).

(2) Constraint ranking: IDENT-P(F) » *[+F] » IDENT(F)

(3) a. [+F] is faithfully realized in P:

[+F] in P	IDENT-P(F)	*[+F]	IDENT(F)
☞ [+F]		*	
[-F]	*!		*

b. [+F] is realized as [-F] elsewhere:

[+F] in ¬P	IDENT-P(F)	*[+F]	IDENT(F)
[+F]		*!	
☞ [-F]			*

For contour tone restrictions per se, we can identify positions with greater $C_{CONTOUR}$ values and impose stronger faithfulness conditions upon them by the ranking IDENT-$C_{CONTOUR}$(P)(tone) » *CONTOUR » IDENT(tone), where P is a position with a greater $C_{CONTOUR}$ value.

There are in fact good reasons to believe that positional markedness is a more appropriate approach for contour tone restrictions. Zoll (1998) argues that only positional markedness can account for cases in which a marked structure arises through augmentation of an input, and the marked structure only surfaces in a strong position, since positional faithfulness would block the augmentation in strong positions, but not weak positions, thus creating the marked structure only in weak positions. The case she discusses in detail is Guugu Yimidhirr

(Kager 1995). In this language, a long vowel can only occur in the first two syllables of a word. Some suffixes trigger vowel lengthening on the final vowel of their base, but this lengthening is blocked if the base is trisyllabic or longer, i.e., if the lengthening would create a long vowel outside the domain (=first two syllables of a word) in which it could be licensed. She rightly argues that positional faithfulness cannot block the lengthening in a trisyllabic or longer base and provides a positional markedness account for the distribution of long vowels in this language.

We find parallels to this scenario in some synchronic tonal processes involving contour tones.

One synchronic scenario that will specifically motivate a positional markedness treatment of contour tone restrictions is as follows: a tonal process (tone sandhi, floating tone docking, etc.) creates a contour tone on the target syllable; but it only does so when the target syllable has a long enough duration to host the contour; when the target syllable does not have a sufficient duration, the tonal process is blocked. Thus we have a situation in which the tone on a short duration is faithfulness preserved, while the tone on a long duration is altered by the tonal process, counter to the prediction of positional faithfulness.

This scenario can be found in a number of Chinese dialects.

In Suzhou, a Northern Wu dialect of Chinese (Ye 1979, Ye and Sheng 1996), there are five contrastive tones on CV and CVR syllables—44, 13, 52, 412, 31, and two contrastive tones on CVO syllables—level tones 5 and 3. Again, the vowel in CV is phonetically long, and the vowel in CVO is very short. Ye uses two numbers to mark the tones on CV and CVR, even when the tone is a level tone, but only uses one number to mark the tones on CVO. This perhaps reflects the rime duration difference between checked (CVO) and non-checked (CV and CVR) syllables. One sandhi process in Suzhou involves a CVO syllable with a 3 tone and the following syllable: it changes the tone of a following CV or CVR into 31 regardless of its underlying tone, but it does not change the tone of a following CVO. This is summarized in (4). Some examples are given in (5).

(4) Suzhou tone sandhi:

$\sigma_1\backslash\sigma_2$	44 CV(R)	13 CV(R)	52 CV(R)	412 CV(R)	31 CV(R)	5 CVO	3 CVO
3 CVO	3-31					3-5	3-3

(5) a.

3-44 → 3-31	zəʔ ten	sɛ three	'thirteen'
3-13 → 3-31	loʔ green	zo tea	'green tea'
3-52 → 3-31	zəʔ ten	tɕiʏ nine	'nineteen'
3-412 → 3-31	bɑʔ white	tsʰɛ vegetable	'Chinese cabbage'
3-31 → 3-31	moʔ wood	doŋ barrel	'wooden barrel'

b.

3-5 → 3-5	laʔ wax	tsoʔ candle	'wax candle'
3-3 → 3-3	loʔ six	ŋəʔ month	'June'

Let us see how this tone sandhi pattern can be captured in a positional markedness approach. I posit the constraints in (6). Constraints (6a)—(6c) are the ones necessary for positional markedness, while constraint (6d) requires that the tone following a tone 3 be changed to 31. I also assume that there is an undominated constraint IDENT(tone, 3) which requires the tone 3 to be preserved in the output.

(6) a. *CONTOUR-$C_{CONTOUR}$(CVO): no contour tone is allowed on a syllable with the $C_{CONTOUR}$ of CVO.
b. *CONTOUR: no contour tone is allowed on any syllable.
c. IDENT(tone): let α be a syllable in the input, and β be any correspondent of α in the output; if α is has tone T, then β has tone T.
d. ALIGN(3, R, 31, L): the right edge of a tone 3 must be aligned to the left edge of 31.

Given that a contour tone 31 can occur on CVV and CVR, we know that ALIGN(3, R, 31, L) » IDENT(tone). This is illustrated in the tableau in (7).

(7) zəʔ^{3} sɛ^{44} → zəʔ^{3} sɛ^{31}

zəʔ^{3} sɛ^{44}	ALIGN(3, R, 31, L)	IDENT(tone)
zəʔ^{3} sɛ^{44}	*!	
☞ zəʔ^{3} sɛ^{31}		*

Given that the contour tone 31 cannot occur on CVO, we know that *CONTOUR-C$_{CONTOUR}$(CVO) » ALIGN(3, R, 31, L). This is illustrated in the tableau in (8).

(8) laʔ^{3} tsoʔ^{5} —> laʔ^{3} tsoʔ^{5}

laʔ^{3} tsoʔ^{5}	*CONTOUR-C$_{CONTOUR}$(CVO)	ALIGN(3, R, 31, L)	IDENT(tone)
☞ laʔ^{3} tsoʔ^{5}		*	
laʔ^{3} tsoʔ^{31}	*!		*

Therefore, with the constraint ranking in (9), the tone sandhi pattern in Suzhou given in (4) can be accounted for.

(9) *CONTOUR-C$_{CONTOUR}$(CVO) » ALIGN(3, R, 31, L) » IDENT(tone) » *CONTOUR

But let us now see whether a positional faithfulness can equally account for the sandhi data. The constraints we use are given in (10). I again assume an undominated constraint IDENT(tone, 3).

(10) a. IDENT-C$_{CONTOUR}$(CVV, CVR)(tone): let β be a syllable that has the C$_{CONTOUR}$ value of CVV or CVR in the output, and α be any correspondent of β in the input; if β has tone T, then α has tone T.
b. IDENT(tone): let α be a syllable in the input, and β be any correspondent of α in the output; if α is has tone T, then β has tone T.
c. *CONTOUR: no contour tone is allowed on any syllable.
d. ALIGN(3, R, 31, L): the right edge of a tone 3 must be aligned to the left edge of 31.

Since contour tones can occur on CVV and CVR, but not on CVO, we derive the ranking IDENT-C$_{CONTOUR}$(CVV, CVR)(tone) » *CONTOUR » IDENT(tone).

Since the tone on a CVV or CVR syllable is changed to 31 after 3, we know that ALIGN(3, R, 31, L) » IDENT-C$_{CONTOUR}$(CVV, CVR)(tone), as shown in the tableau in (11).

(11) zəʔ^{3} sɛ^{44} —> zəʔ^{3} sɛ^{31}

zəʔ^{3} sɛ^{44}	ALIGN(3, R, 31, L)	IDENT-C$_{CONTOUR}$(CVV, CVR)(tone)
zəʔ^{3} sɛ^{44}	*!	
☞ zəʔ^{3} sɛ^{31}		*

But then we will not be able to predict the blocking of the tone sandhi on CVO, as illustrated in the tableau in (12). The candidate that chooses the 31 on CVO wins out since it only violates the lowly ranked *CONTOUR and IDENT(tone). The fully faithful candidate, which should be the winner, loses the competition by violating the highest ranked ALIGN(3, R, 31, L).

(12) laʔ^{3} tsoʔ^{5} —> laʔ^{3} tsoʔ^{5}

laʔ^{3} tsoʔ^{5}	ALIGN (3, R, 31, L)	IDENT-C$_{CONTOUR}$ (CVV,CVR)(tone)	*CONTOUR	IDENT (tone)
laʔ^{3} tsoʔ^{5}	*!			
☞ laʔ^{3} tsoʔ^{31}			*	*

Therefore, Suzhou tone sandhi is a parallel case to Guugu Yimidhirr vowel length alternation, and it demonstrates the need for positional markedness in the account of contour tone distribution.

A few other Chinese dialects have tone sandhi behavior similar to Suzhou. In another Northern Wu dialect Ningbo (Chan 1985), there are three contrastive tones on TV or TVR syllables (T represents a voiceless obstruent)—53, 424, 33, and only one tone on TVO—5.[1] The tones 424 and 5 trigger the tone sandhi as in (13).

(13) Ningbo tone sandhi:

$\sigma_1\backslash\sigma_2$	53 CV(R)	424 CV(R)	33 CV(R)	5 CVO
424 CV(R)		42-42		42-4
5 CVO		5-35		5-5

As we can see, sandhi tones 42 and 35 can occur on CV or CVR syllables, but cannot occur on CVO, presumably due to its short duration. If we assume that the second tone 4 in 42-4 is not distinct from the second tone 5 in 5-5, then we can conclude that these sandhi processes are simply blocked when the target syllable is CVO in order to avoid contour tones on a short duration.

---

1 The tones on DV and DVR are 35, 313, 213, and the tone on DVO is 34. Their sandhi pattern is not relevant for the point made here.

In Xinzhou, a Jin dialect of Chinese (Wen and Zhang 1994), the tones on CV and CVR are 313, 31, 53, and the tone on CVO is always 2. The tone 53 changes the tone of the following CV or CVR into 31, but does not change the 2 on CVO, as shown in (14). This is the same pattern as in Suzhou and Ningbo.

(14) Xinzhou tone sandhi:

$\sigma_1 \backslash \sigma_2$	313 CV(R)	31 CV(R)	53 CV(R)	2 CVO
53 CV(R)		53-31		53-2

I argue that these tone sandhi processes in Suzhou, Ningbo, and Xinzhou clearly motivate a positional markedness approach for contour tone restrictions.[2]

---

[2] Another possible synchronic process that will motivate positional markedness is the behavior of floating tone docking. The scenario is as follows: a floating tone creates a contour tone by docking onto a syllable, but it only does so when the syllable has sufficient duration; when the syllable is too short, the docking of the floating is blocked and the syllable surfaces with its original tone. I do not have an example of this sort, but it looks like a reasonable system and I believe the lack of an example is due to the limitation of my knowledge. The argument for positional markedness here is slightly different from the one in the tone sandhi cases. Let me review it briefly here.

Let us suppose that a floating H tone associated with a grammatical morpheme docks onto the initial syllable of the base. If the initial syllable is stressed and carries a L tone, a $\widehat{HL}$ surfaces as the result of the floating tone docking. But if the initial syllable is unstressed and carries a L tone, floating tone docking is blocked and the L tone surfaces as is.

In a positional markedness approach, we entertain the following constraints in (1).

(1) a. REALIZEMORPHEME: the floating tone morpheme must be realized in the output.

b. *CONTOUR-$C_{CONTOUR}$(-stress): no contour tone is allowed on a syllable with the $C_{CONTOUR}$ of an unstressed syllable.

c. *CONTOUR: no contour tone is allowed on any syllable.

d. IDENT(tone): let α be a syllable in the input, and β be any correspondent of α in the output; if α is has tone T, then β has tone T.

e. MAX(tone): let α be a syllable in the input, and β be any correspondent of α in the output; if α is has tone T, then tone T must be at least part of the realization of β.

Since the floating H tone docks onto a stressed L-toned syllable to create a $\widehat{HL}$ contour, we know that REALIZEMORPHEME, MAX(tone) » IDENT(tone), *CONTOUR, as shown in the tableau in (2).

(2) ´+ 'σ̀ —> 'σ̂

´+ 'σ̀ —> 'σ̂	MAX(tone)	REALMORPH	IDENT(tone)	*CONTOUR
☞ 'σ̂			*	*
'σ́	*!		*	
'σ̀		*!		

Since the floating H does not dock onto an unstressed syllable with a L tone, we know that *CONTOUR-$C_{CONTOUR}$(-stress), MAX(tone) » REALIZEMORPHEME, as shown in the tableau in (3).

(3) ´+ σ̀ —> σ̀

´+ σ̀ —> σ̀	*CONTOUR- (-stress)	MAX (tone)	REAL MORPH	IDENT (tone)	*CONTOUR
σ̂	*!			*	*
σ́		*!		*	
☞ σ̀			*		

Therefore, the following ranking captures the pattern of the floating H docking in this hypothetical language: *CONTOUR-$C_{CONTOUR}$(-stress), MAX(tone) » REALIZE-MORPHEME » IDENT(tone), *CONTOUR.

Let us now consider the positional faithfulness approach. The constraints are given in (4).

(4) a. REALIZEMORPHEME: the floating tone morpheme must be realized in the output.

b. IDENT-$C_{CONTOUR}$(stress)(tone): let β be a syllable that has the $C_{CONTOUR}$ value of a stressed syllable in the output, and α be any correspondent of β in the input; if β has tone T, then α has tone T.

c. MAX-$C_{CONTOUR}$(stress)(tone): let α be a syllable that has the $C_{CONTOUR}$ value of a stressed syllable in the input, and β be any correspondent of α in the output; if α is has tone T, then tone T must be at least part of the realization of β.

d. IDENT(tone): let α be a syllable in the input, and β be any correspondent of α in the output; if α is has tone T, then β has tone T.

e. MAX(tone): let α be a syllable in the input, and β be any correspondent of α in the output; if α is has tone T, then tone T must be at least part of the realization of β.

f. *CONTOUR: no contour tone is allowed on any syllable.

Since the floating H tone docks onto a stressed L-toned syllable to create a HL contour, we know that REALIZEMORPHEME, MAX-$C_{CONTOUR}$(stress)(tone) » IDENT-$C_{CONTOUR}$(stress)(tone), *CONTOUR, as shown in the tableau in (5).

Therefore, in the remaining sections of the book, I will use continue using positional markedness in the formal analysis of contour tone restrictions, only now it is a well-motivated choice.

---

(5) ´+ 'σ̀ —> 'σ̂

´+ 'σ̀ —> 'σ̂	MAX-(stress) (tone)	REAL MORPH	IDENT-(stress) (tone)	*CONTOUR
☞ 'σ̂			*	*
'σ́	*!		*	
'σ̀		*!		

But this ranking will never be able to predict blocking of the floating H docking. Let us see why. Since REALIZEMORPHEME » IDENT-$\text{C}_{\text{CONTOUR}}$(stress)(tone), and from the positional faithfulness ranking, we know that IDENT-$\text{C}_{\text{CONTOUR}}$(stress)(tone) » IDENT(tone), we conclude that IDENT(tone) is at the bottom of the hierarchy. MAX(tone), however, has two possible rankings that will produce different results. If MAX(tone) » *CONTOUR, the ranking predicts a H͡L contour on unstressed syllables, as shown in the tableau in (6). If *CONTOUR » MAX(tone), the ranking predicts that the floating H will replace the L tone on an unstressed syllable, as shown in the tableau in (7). But no ranking will rank REALIZEMORPHEME, which the blocking candidate violates, low enough to allow the blocking candidate to win.

(6) ´+ σ̀ —> σ̂

´+ σ̀ —> σ̀	REALMORPH	MAX(tone)	*CONTOUR	IDENT(tone)
☞ σ̂			*	*
σ́		*!		*
σ̀	*!			

(7) ´+ σ̀ —> σ́

´+ σ̀ —> σ̀	REALMORPH	*CONTOUR	MAX(tone)	IDENT(tone)
σ̂		*!		*
☞ σ́			*	*
σ̀	*!			

Therefore, the difference between floating tone docking and the tone sandhi processes discussed in the text is that for floating tone docking, given that the relevant constraint is to realize the floating tone rather than to change the target syllable into a certain tone, a positional faithfulness approach is able to prevent the contour tone from occurring on a non-prominent syllable, but it is still not able to completely block the floating tone docking from applying, and I assume that complete blocking is an entirely possible outcome.

7.1.2 Overview of the Theoretical Apparatus

The patterns of contour tone distribution that the theoretical apparatus must capture are the following. First, the distribution of contour tones depends on the on a phonetic index of the rime—$C_{CONTOUR}$; the lower the $C_{CONTOUR}$ values, the more limited distribution the contour tones will have on the rime. Second, when a contour tone encounters a syllable with insufficient tone bearing ability, there is a wide range of cross-linguistic variation with respect to the strategy taken to avoid the violation of a highly ranked tonal markedness constraint: the syllable may be lengthened, the contour tone may be flattened, or both; and the lengthening and flattening can be neutralizing and non-neutralizing.

Therefore, I posit three families of constraints: markedness constraints against certain contour tones on rimes with certain $C_{CONTOUR}$ values—*CONTOUR(*T*)-$C_{CONTOUR}$(*R*), markedness constraints against having extra duration on the syllable—*DUR, and faithfulness constraints on tonal realization—PRES(tone). Each of these constraint families has a set of intrinsic rankings. For *CONTOUR(*T*)-$C_{CONTOUR}$(*R*), when the $C_{CONTOUR}$ value is the same, the ban on a contour with higher tonal complexity is ranked above the ban on a contour with lower tonal complexity; when the contour is the same, the ban of the contour on a lower $C_{CONTOUR}$ value is ranked above its ban on a higher $C_{CONTOUR}$ value. For *DUR, the ban on a greater amount of extra duration is ranked above the ban on a smaller amount of extra duration. And for PRES(tone), a greater perceptual deviation from the input tone is penalized more severely than a smaller perceptual deviation.

The interaction of these three families of constraints gives rise to the attested patterns of contour tone restriction: when *DUR and PRES(tone) are highly ranked and all relevant tonal markedness constraints *CONTOUR(*T*)-$C_{CONTOUR}$(*R*) are lowly ranked, the contour tone is faithfully realized on the rime without flattening or lengthening; when some *DUR constraints are outranked by the relevant tonal markedness constraints while all PRES(tone) are still highly ranked, the contour tone is faithfully realized upon lengthening of the rime; when some PRES(tone) constraints are outranked by the relevant tonal markedness constraints while all *DUR are highly ranked, the contour tone is partially or completely flattened; and when some *DUR and some PRES(tone) constraints are outranked by the relevant tonal markedness constraints simultaneously, the contour tone is partially flattened, and at the same time, the rime is lengthened. These scenarios are summarized in (15). All these scenarios are attested in real languages.

(15) Constraint rankings and predicted patterns (overview):

Output	Constraint ranking
a. Faithful:	PRES(T), *DUR ⇓ *CONTOUR(*T*)-$C_{CONTOUR}$(*R*)
b. Contour reduction:	*DUR, *CONTOUR(*T*)-$C_{CONTOUR}$(*R*) ⇓ some PRES(T)
c. Rime lengthening:	PRES(T), *CONTOUR(*T*)-$C_{CONTOUR}$(*R*) ⇓ some *DUR
d. Contour reduction and rime lengthening:	some *DUR, some PRES(T), *CONTOUR(*T*)-$C_{CONTOUR}$(*R*) ⇓ some other *DUR, some other PRES(T)

In the following sections of this chapter, I formally define these three constraint families and discuss their interactions in detail.

7.2 CONSTRAINTS AND THEIR INTRINSIC RANKINGS PROJECTED FROM PHONETICS

7.2.1 *CONTOUR(x)-$C_{CONTOUR}$(y)

I formally define a series of positional markedness constraints *CONTOUR(x)-$C_{CONTOUR}$(y) as follows:

(16) *CONTOUR(x_i)-$C_{CONTOUR}$(y_j):

no contour tone x_i is allowed on a syllable with the $C_{CONTOUR}$ value of syllable y_j or smaller.

If we subscribe to the view that intrinsic constraint rankings projected from phonetics are the way to formally encode the role of phonetics in phonology, then the *CONTOUR(x_i)-$C_{CONTOUR}$(y_j) constraints observe the intrinsic ranking in (17). This ranking reflects the speaker's knowledge that a structure that is phonetically more demanding is banned before a structure that is less so.

(17) If $C_{CONTOUR}(y_a) > C_{CONTOUR}(y_b)$,

then *Contour(x_i)-$C_{CONTOUR}$(y_b) » *Contour(x_i)-$C_{CONTOUR}$(y_a).

We can identify another set of intrinsic rankings for the constraints in (16), as shown in (18). It expresses the fact that a syllable is able to host a tone with a lower complexity before it can host a tone with a higher complexity.

(18) If contour tone x_m is higher on the *Tonal Complexity* scale than contour tone x_n, then *CONTOUR(x_m)-$C_{\text{CONTOUR}}(y_j)$ » *CONTOUR(x_n)-$C_{\text{CONTOUR}}(y_j)$.

From the definition of the *Tonal Complexity* scale ((5) and (7) in §3.2), the ranking principle in (18) can be made more specific as in (19).

(19) For any two tones T_1 and T_2, suppose T_1 has *m* pitch targets and T_2 has *n* pitch targets; the cumulative falling excursions for T_1 and T_2 are Δf_{F_1} and Δf_{F_2} respectively, and the cumulative rising excursions for T_1 and T_2 are Δf_{R_1} and Δf_{R_2} respectively. *CONTOUR(T_1)-$C_{\text{CONTOUR}}(y_j)$ » *CONTOUR(T_2)-$C_{\text{CONTOUR}}(y_j)$ iff:

a. $m>n$, $\Delta f_{F_1} \geq \Delta f_{F_2}$, and $\Delta f_{R_1} \geq \Delta f_{R_2}$;
b. $m=n$, $\Delta f_{F_1} \geq \Delta f_{F_2}$, and $\Delta f_{R_1} \geq \Delta f_{R_2}$ ('=' holds for at most one of the comparisons);
c. $m=n$, $\Delta f_{F_1}+\Delta f_{R_1}=\Delta f_{F_2}+\Delta f_{R_2}$, and $\Delta f_{R_1} \geq \Delta f_{R_2}$.

Tonal complexity is determined by the following factors: the number of pitch targets, the overall pitch excursion, and the direction of the pitch change. The conditions in (19) are the ones that determine that T_1 is higher on the *Tonal Complexity* scale than T_2: (19a) states that T_1 has more pitch targets and T_1's cumulative falling excursion and rising excursion are both no smaller than those of T_2's; (19b) states that T_1 and T_2 have the same number of pitch targets, and at least one of T_1's cumulative falling excursion and rising excursion is greater than that of T_2's, and the other one is no smaller than that of T_2's; (19c) states that T_1 and T_2 have the same number of pitch targets and the same overall pitch excursion, but the cumulative rising excursion in T_1 is greater than that in T_2.

To capture the role of phonetics in phonology by intrinsic rankings of constraints determined by phonetic scales has been commonly practiced in the OT literature. Prince and Smolensky (1993) explicitly express this idea in their discussion of the universal peak and margin hierarchies based on the sonority scale. Other advocates of the idea include Jun (1995), who illustrates the necessity of intrinsic rankings among faithfulness constraints on place features in account for place assimilation, basing the argument on the production and perception of consonants at different places; Steriade (1999), who argues for a series of intrinsically-ranked licensing constraints which requires the reference to perceptual cues for laryngeal features in analyzing cross-linguistic laryngeal neutralization patterns; Kirchner (1998), who shows that consonant lenition patterns observed cross-linguistically are the result of the interaction between faithfulness and an intrinsically ranked constraint hierarchy banning effort expenditure; Boersma (1998), who argues for a production grammar and a perception grammar, both of which are constructed from intrinsically ranked constraints based on functional principles; etc.

To visualize the effect of tonal complexity and $C_{CONTOUR}$ on the ranking of these constraints, let us assume that every constraint is associated with a *Ranking Value*, with a higher *Ranking Value* indicating a higher constraint ranking. Then the *Ranking Value* of the constraint *CONTOUR(x)-$C_{CONTOUR}(y)$ can be considered a function of the tonal complexity of x—$TC(x)$, and the $C_{CONTOUR}$ value of y—$C_{CONTOUR}(y)$, as shown in (20).

(20) *Ranking Value* of *CONTOUR(x)-$C_{CONTOUR}(y) = f_{RV}(TC(x), C_{CONTOUR}(y))$

From (17) and (18), we know that f_{RV} increases when $TC(x)$ increase, but decreases when $C_{CONTOUR}(y)$ increases. The function f_{RV} can be schematically plotted in a 3-D space as in (21).

(21) The *Ranking Value* of *CONTOUR(x)-$C_{CONTOUR}(y)$ as a function of $TC(x)$ and $C_{CONTOUR}(y)$:

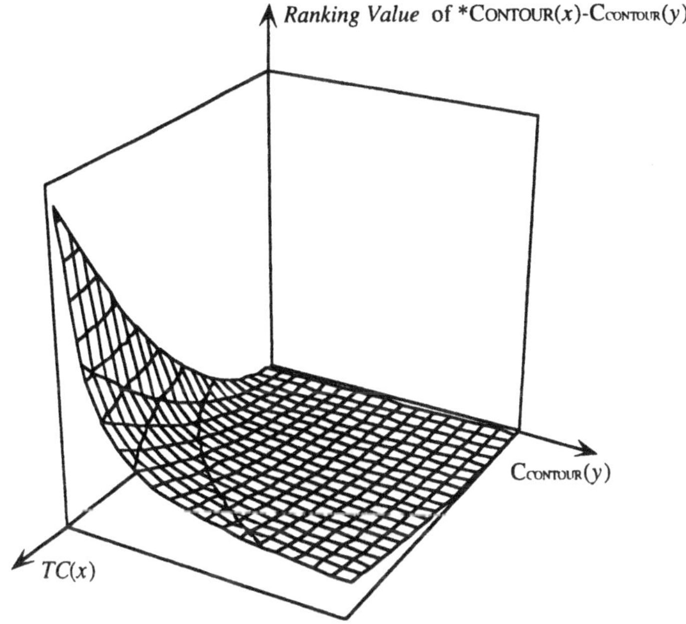

But let me emphasize that the graph in (21) is only a schematic. Crucially, for two constraints whose relevant components do not stand in the relationships described in (17)—(19), and no ranking between the two constraints can be deduced by transitivity through a third constraint, I do not claim that there is an intrinsic ranking between them, and their ranking should be determined on a language-specific basis. In other words, *CONTOUR(x_i)-C$_{CONTOUR}$(y_i) and *CONTOUR(x_j)-C$_{CONTOUR}$(y_j) are intrinsically ranked only under the following three conditions: (a) x_i=x_j; (b) y_i=y_j; (c) x_i>x_j and y_i<y_j. The general claim here is that intrinsic rankings can only be determined locally or transitively. This has been proposed as the *Local-Ranking Principle* by Boersma (1998).

7.2.2 *DURATION

When an underlying tonal contour on a certain syllable type in a certain prosodic position causes the violation of a *CONTOUR(x)-C$_{CONTOUR}$(y) constraint, three approaches can be taken to resolve the violation: increasing the C$_{CONTOUR}$ value of the syllable, flattening out the pitch excursion, or both. Theoretically, there are various ways to increase the C$_{CONTOUR}$ value of the syllable: increasing the sonorous rime duration, changing its sonorant coda into a vowel, making the syllable in question stressed, etc. The factorial typology with the *CONTOUR(x)-C$_{CONTOUR}$(y) constraints and IDENT(long), IDENT(syllabic), IDENT(stress) should predict all these patterns. But in reality, I have not seen cases in which the sonorant coda is changed to a vowel or the stress is shifted in order to accommodate a contour tone. Lengthening of the sonorous rime duration seems to be the only option. This is admittedly a problem that my theory does not address. Two proposals may be entertained to block the unattested changes. One is the P-map proposal by Steriade (2001b), in which she claims that correspondence constraints are intrinsically ranked according to a perceptual map: if the perceptual distance from the input is greater for output No. 1 than for output No.2, then the correspondence constraint that penalizes the change from the input to output No.1 outranks the constraint that penalizes the change to output No.2. If it can be shown that the changes of the vocalic and stress features of the syllable are perceptually more costly than the change of sonorous rime duration, then the former two approaches will not be explored by languages. The other proposal is made by Wilson (2000), in which he argues that markedness constraints are targeted, i.e., they only favor fixes of the marked structure that are perceptually minimally distinct from the marked structure. Then again, if changing the sonorous rime duration is a perceptually less costly fix to the violation of *CONTOUR(x)-C$_{CONTOUR}$(y) than changing the vocalic or stress feature of the syllable, the latter two options will not be explored by languages. Both Steriade's and Wilson's approaches crucially hinge on the difference in perceptual cost between changing the sonorous rime duration and changing the vocalic and stress features of the syllable. I leave the verification of this hypothesis for future research.

In short, languages explore three possibilities to resolve a *CONTOUR(x)-C$_{\text{CONTOUR}}$(y) violation: lengthening the rime, flattening out the contour, or both. For lengthening, both neutralizing and non-neutralizing lengthenings are attested. For non-neutralizing lengthening, Mitla Zapotec lengthens syllables that carry the rising tone, but does not do so when the syllables carry the falling tone (Briggs 1961). For neutralizing lengthening, in Gã, a [-long] vowel becomes [+long] when it carries a rising tone, but stays [-long] when it carries a falling tone (Paster 1999). For contour tone flattening, it can also be both neutralizing and non-neutralizing. For non-neutralizing flattening, we have seen that in Pingyao Chinese, contour tones 53 and 13, which can be fully realized on CV (with a phonetically long vowl) and CVR syllables, have partial realizations 54 and 23 on CVO syllables (Hou 1980, 1982a, b). For neutralizing flattening, Xhosa does not allow its only contour tone—H͡L—on unstressed syllables, and a H͡L tone is realized as H when the stress is removed (Lanham 1958, 1963, Jordan 1966). For the combination of rime lengthening and contour flattening, it is always non-neutralizing. For example, Hausa partially flattens the falling contour on CVO as compared to CVV and CVR, and at the same time lengthens the CVO syllable that carries the contour.

These resolutions obviously do not come at no costs: lengthening the duration slows down the speed of communication and must be penalized by markedness constraints against the extra time spent; flattening out the contour jeopardizes tonal contrasts and must be penalized by faithfulness constraints on tones. In this section, I first tackle the markedness constraints on duration. The tonal faithfulness constraints are discussed in the next section.

As a first approximation, I define the constraint *DURATION (abbr. *DUR) as in (22).

(22) *DUR: minimize the duration of a rime.

*DUR requires the minimization of a rime's duration. But of course, to have a duration of zero, which is the best way to satisfy the constraint, is not the way to go. I assume that for every segment x in a prosodic environment independent of tone, there is a minimum duration associated with it under the canonical speaking rate and style, and these minimum duration requirements must be met. The prosodic environment here includes segment length, stress, proximity to prosodic boundaries, number of syllables in the word, etc. In OT terms, I posit the constraints in (23) that enforce the realization of these minimum durations.

(23) DUR(x_{env})≥MIN(x_{env}): for any segment x in a certain prosodic environment, its duration in the canonical speaking rate and style cannot be less than a certain minimum value—MIN(x_{env}).

We must also assume that under the canonical speaking rate and style, all DUR(x_{env})≥MIN(x_{env}) constraints universally outrank *DUR, since this is the only way to ensure that the mininum duration requirements are respected. Under this ranking, *DUR will only rule out candidates that have extra duration than the minimum duration. For example, let us suppose that the minimum duration for a segment *x* is *d*, and *d* induces *n* violations of *DUR. From the tableau in (24), we can see that any attempt to reduce the number of violations for *DUR will necessarily cause the violation of the more highly ranked DUR(x_{env})≥MIN(x_{env}). But *DUR rules out any attempt to lengthen the segment, which will induce more than *n* violations of this constraint.

(24)

x_{env}	DUR(x_{env})≥MIN(x_{env})	*DUR
☞ DUR(x_{env})=d		*****
DUR(x_{env})=d-d_0	*!	****
DUR(x_{env})=d+d_0		******!

For reasons of simplicity, I reinterpret *DUR as in (25) and only assess violations for it when any segment of the syllable is longer than its minimum duration.

(25) *DUR (reinterpretation): for each segment *x* of a rime Rin a certain prosodic environment, the duration of *x* is no greater than the minimum duration of *x* in this prosodic environment.

Under this conception, the number of violations of the constraint is counted cumulatively. Therefore, if for rime VC_1C_2, V and C_2 are longer, but C_1 is shorter, than their minimum duration respectively, the number of violations for *DUR is determined by the combination of the degrees to which V and C_2 are longer than their minimum duration. The shorter duration of C_1 does not reduce the number of violations of *DUR. To make this more concrete, let us assume that under the standard speaking rate and style, every extra 30ms induces one violation of *DUR. For segments /a/, /l/, and /m/, their minimum durations are 120ms, 100ms, and 80ms respectively, and for an output candidate syllable [alm], the durations of its components are 150ms, 70ms, and 120ms, then the candidate incurs 2 violations of *DUR—one due to [a], one due to [m].

But, like the markedness constraints *CONTOUR(x)-$C_{CONTOUR}$(y), I split the *DUR constraint into a constraint family, as in (26).

(26) *DUR(τ): the cumulative duration in excess of the minimum duration for each segment of a rime in the prosodic environment in question cannot be τ or more. (τ>0)

Again, the constraints in (26) have an intrinsic ranking projected from the phonetic scale, as show in (27).

(27) If $\tau_i > \tau_j$, then *DUR(τ_i) » *DUR(τ_j)

If we consider the ranking value of * DUR(τ) to be a function of τ ($\tau>0$), with a higher Ranking Value indicating a higher ranking, then according to (27), this function is monotonically increasing, as shown schematically in (28).

(28) The *Ranking Value* of *DUR(τ) as a function of τ:

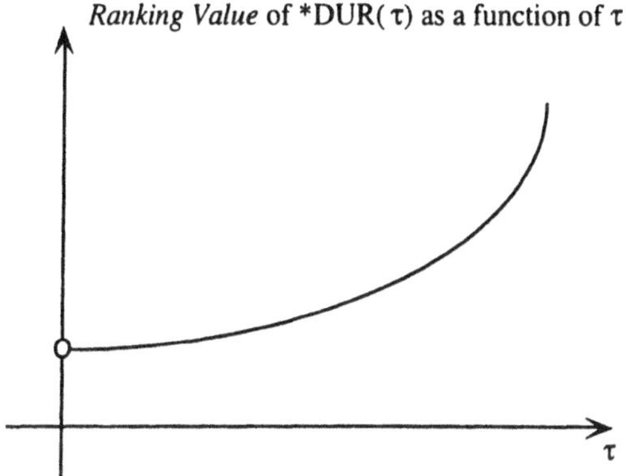

The idea of minimum duration for a segment has been explicitly discussed in Klatt (1973) and Allen et al. (1987) in their works on text-to-speech synthesis. They also discuss how the actual duration of a segment is determined by its prosodic context. For example, Allen et al. uses the following formula in (29) to predict the actual duration of a segment:

(29) *DUR*=((*INHDUR*-*MINDUR*)×*PRCNT*)/100+*MINDUR* (Allen et al.: p. 93)

In the formula, *DUR* is the actual duration of the segment in a certain prosodic context; *INHDUR* and *MINDUR* are the inherent duration and minimum duration of the segment respectively; and *PRCNT* is a percentage adjustment to duration determined by prosodic rules such as final lengthening, emphatic lengthening, polysyllabic shortening, unstressed shortening, etc.

The theoretical apparatus explored here is in a way similar to their system. I also posit a minimum duration for a segment and require that it be respected in the output, and I also allow the prosodic environment of the segment to induce lengthening from its minimum duration. The difference is that in my theoretical apparatus, all these are done in an Optimality-Theoretic framework.

7.2.3 PRESERVE(tone)

I discuss the formulation of the tonal faithfulness constraints in this section. Again, as a first approximation, I define PRESERVE(tone) (abbr. PRES(T)) as in (30). It is a tonal faithfulness constraint that penalizes deviation from the underlying tonal specification in the output.

(30) PRES(T): an input tone T_I must have an output correspondent T_O, and T_O must preserve all the pitch characteristics of T_I.

Clearly, we need to define how the violations for this constraint are assigned, which means that we need to define how to assess deviations from the canonical 'pitch characteristics'.

I consider all perceptually salient properties of tone to be potential 'pitch characteristics' that define PRES(T). Specifically relevant for the interaction of tone and duration, studies by Gandour (1978, 1981, 1983) and Gandour and Harshman (1978) have shown that the pitch excursion and the direction of slope are both relevant for the perception of contour tones. Apparently, the number of pitch targets in a contour, e.g., L͡HL vs. H͡L and L͡H, is perceptually relevant as well, as all languages that have complex contours such as L͡HL or H͡LH distinguish them from simple contours such as H͡L and L͡H.

I start by devising a similarity scale among all relevant simple contour and level tones with respect to tone *t* with a duration *d*. The tones I consider solely differ in pitch excursion and/or direction of slope from *t*. Although the average pitch and length of the tone are both perceptually relevant for contour tones, the former is not directly relevant for the interaction of tone and duration, and the latter is being evaluated by *DUR.

Let us assume that the beginning pitch and the end pitch for *t* are T_1 and T_2 respectively. I first define the pitch excursion of *t* as in (31).

(31) Pitch excursion of a simple contour tone *t*: $\Delta f_t = T_2 - T_1$

Under this definition, if $T_2 > T_1$, then *t* is a rising tone; if $T_2 < T_1$, then *t* is a falling tone; and if $T_2 = T_1$, then *t* is a level tone.

In order to evaluate the perceptual distance between tone *t* and other simple tones with the same average pitch and duration, let us consider two number series $a_1, a_2, a_3, \ldots, a_n$, and $b_1, b_2, b_3, \ldots, b_m$, which I term *Differential Limen Scales* with respect to tone *t*. The a_i series is further termed the *Rising Differential Limen Scale*, and it has the properties in (32). The b_i series is furthered termed the *Falling Differential Limen Scale*, and it has the properties in (33).

(32) a. *Rising Differential Limen Scale:* $0<a_1<a_2<a_3< \ldots <a_n$.

b. a_1 is the minimum pitch excursion difference required to distinguish a tone *t'* from tone *t* when $\Delta f_{t'}>\Delta f_t$.

c. $a_n+\Delta f_t$ is the maximum pitch rise used linguistically in any human language.

d. For $1<k\leq n$, the pitch excursion difference between $a_k+\Delta f_t$ and $a_{k-1}+\Delta f_t$ is the smallest perceivable by listeners.

(33) a. *Falling Differential Limen Scale:* $0<b_1<b_2<b_3< \ldots <b_m$.

b. b_1 is the minimum pitch excursion difference required to distinguish a tone *t"* from tone *t* when $\Delta f_{t''}<\Delta f_t$.

c. $|\Delta f_t-b_m|$ is the maximum pitch fall used linguistically in any human language.

d. For $1<k\leq m$, the pitch excursion difference between Δf_t-b_k and Δf_t-b_{k-1} is the smallest perceivable by listeners.

Let us suppose that a simple contour or level tone *c* has a pitch excursion Δf_c. I define a function $\mathbb{S}_t$ that returns the similarity value between any such *c* and the tone *t* above, as in (34).

(34)
$$\mathbb{S}_t(c) = \begin{cases} i \text{ if } \Delta f_c>\Delta f_t \text{ and } a_i\leq\Delta f_c-\Delta f_t<a_{i+1}\ (1\leq i<n). \\ j \text{ if } \Delta f_c<\Delta f_t \text{ and } b_j\leq\Delta f_t-\Delta f_c<b_{j+1}\ (1\leq j<m). \end{cases}$$

By way of an example, let us consider a falling tone 53 in Chao letters and its similarity function $\mathbb{S}_{53}$. For concreteness only, let us suppose that a change in the number of 1 in Chao letters is the minimum difference perceivable by listeners, which renders $a_1=1$, $a_2=2$, $a_3=3$, etc., and $b_1=1$, $b_2=2$, etc. Then $\mathbb{S}_{53}(54)=a_1=1$, $\mathbb{S}_{53}(55)=a_2=2$, $\mathbb{S}_{53}(35)=a_4=4$, $\mathbb{S}_{53}(52)=b_1=1$, etc.

We can also include complex contours with more than two pitch targets in the domain of the similarity function $\mathbb{S}_t$. Let me first formally define *Turning Point*, *Complex Contour Tone*, and *Simple Contour Tone* as in (35).

(35) a. *Turning Point*: consider a tone *t* with duration *d* as a series of time points d_0, d_1, ..., d_n, each of which is associated with a pitch value $p(d_0)$, $p(d_1)$, ..., $p(d_n)$. The distance between adjacent time points is infinitely small. The time point d_i is a *Turning Point* if and only if: $p(d_i) > p(d_{i-1})$ and $p(d_i) > p(d_{i+1})$; or $p(d_i) < p(d_{i-1})$ and $p(d_i) < p(d_{i+1})$.

b. *Complex Contour Tone*: a tone *t* is a *Complex Contour Tone* if and only if there is at least one *Turning Point* in the duration of *t*.

c. *Simple Contour Tone*: a tone *t* is a *Simple Contour Tone* if and only if there is no *Turning Point* in the duration of *t*.

Then to compute the similarity between a complex contour tone and a simple contour tone with the same duration, we can decompose the complex contour tone into simple contour tones according to where the turning points lie, make comparisons of these simple contours with the corresponding parts of the simple contour tone, and sum the similarity values together. Let me illustrate this with an example. Consider a complex contour with three tonal targets $T_3T_4T_5$, which has the same duration as a simple contour tone T_1T_2. There is one turning point during the complex contour—the time point when T_4 is realized. We decompose the complex contour into two portions—T_3T_4 and T_4T_5—and compare them with the corresponding portions in tone T_1T_2—T_1c and cT_2, as shown in (36).

(36) The similarity between a complex contour tone and a simple contour tone:

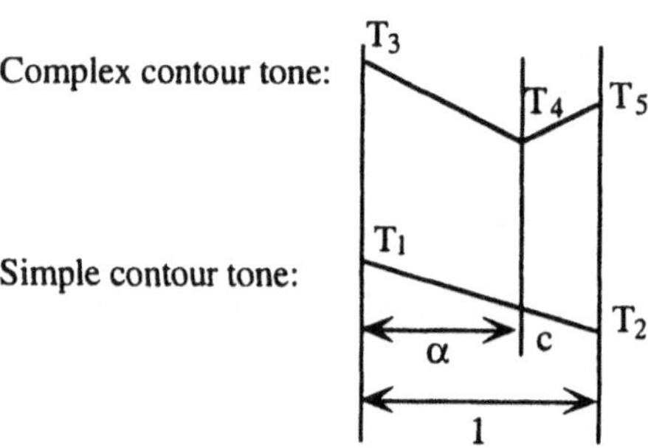

Given that T_1c and T_3T_4 are both simple contours, their similarity can be computed in the same method as laid out in (32)—(34); i.e., we can first define the *Differential Limen Scales* with respect to tone T_1c, then define accordingly a function $\mathbb{S}_{T_1c}$ that returns the similarity value between T_1c and another tone, and from that we know the similarity between T_1c and T_3T_4—$\mathbb{S}_{T_1c}(T_3T_4)$. We can similarly compute the similarity between cT_2 and T_4T_5—$\mathbb{S}_{cT_2}(T_4T_5)$.

Suppose that $\mathbb{S}_{T_1c}(T_3T_4)=i$ and $\mathbb{S}_{cT_2}(T_4T_5)=j$, then the value of $\mathbb{S}_{T_1T_2}(T_3T_4T_5)$ is defined as in (37). Intuitively, this means that the similarity between a simple contour and a complex contour with the same duration is the sum of similarities between the simple components of the complex contour and their corresponding parts in time in the simple contour.

(37) $\mathbb{S}_{T_1T_2}(T_3T_4T_5) = i+j$

One more issue needs to be addressed before we leave the subject. We need to know the value of *c* in (36) to calculate the similarity between T_1c and T_3T_4 and that between T_3T_4 and T_4T_5. If T_3T_4 accounts for a fraction α ($0<\alpha<1$) of entire tone duration, and T_4T_5 accounts for the rest of the tone duration, as shown in (36), then the value of *c* can be calculated as in (38).

(38) $c = (1-\alpha)T_1+\alpha T_2$

With the similarity functions, we can split the PRES(T) constraint into a constraint family with an intrinsic ranking, as shown in (39).

(39) $\forall i$, $1 \leq i \leq n$, $\exists$ constraint PRES(T, *i*), defined as:

> an input tone T_I must have an output correspondent T_O, and T_O must satisfy the condition $\mathbb{S}_{T_I}(T_O)<i$.

The intrinsic ranking in this family of constraints is given in (40). It is consistent with the P-map approach advocated by Steriade (2001b), since in this hierarchy, the candidate that deviates the most from the input will be penalized by the highest ranking constraint.

(40) PRES(T, *n*) » PRES(T, *n-1*) » ... » PRES(T, *2*) » PRES(T, *1*).

Plainly, the values in the similarity functions given here are abstract and hypothetical. The hypotheses are made according to our current knowledge of tonal perception and must be tested against actual similarity judgments. The approach of taking the just noticeable difference as the step size is a conservative one, in the sense that it does not run the risk of missing any distinctions that may be linguistically relevant. But of course, it seems that it runs the risk of having excess power and overgeneration, and thus needs to be trimmed back when certain distinctions are shown to be universally irrelevant linguistically. I would like to argue that this approach on the one hand is necessary for capturing all the contour tone restriction patterns, on the other hand does not a priori vastly overgenerate.

To see the necessity of such phonetic details in phonology, we have seen that languages do show sensitivity to the size and direction of pitch excursion.

For example, in Pingyao Chinese, contour tones on CVO syllables have smaller pitch excursion than those on CVV and CVR; in Hausa, contour tones on CVO not only have smaller pitch excursion, but also lengthen the vowel in the syllable; in Kanakuru (Newman 1974) and Ngizim (Schuh 1971), rising tones are more likely to flatten than falling tones in Kanakuru (Newman 1974) and Ngizim (Schuh 1971). As argued in Chapter 6, these phenomena cannot receive satisfactory accounts in structural alternatives that only make distinctions between the presence and absence of tonal contours.

To address the overgeneration problem, let us first briefly review the psychoacoustic results on the just noticeable difference between tones.

Studies have generally shown that listeners are extremely good at distinguishing successively presented level pure tones when they differ in frequency. For example, Harris (1952) showed that it was not uncommon for the frequency differential limens of pure tones to be less than 1Hz. Flanagan and Saslow (1958), using synthetic vowels in the frequency range of a male speaker, reported the differential limen to be between 0.3-0.5Hz, and this result was replicated by Klatt (1973). Some studies have reported higher differential limens for frequency. For example, Issachenko and Schädlich (1970) found that with resynthesized vowels, the frequency differential limen is around 5% of the base frequency of 150Hz.

To distinguish a pitch change from a steady pitch, Pollack (1968) reported that listeners could better detect a pitch change if the duration of the pitch change was longer or if the rate of the pitch change was greater, and he showed that the threshold of pitch change was linearly proportional to the total frequency difference between the initial and the end pitches, which was the multiplication of rate by duration. For example, the minimally detectable pitch change was around 2.5-3% of a starting frequency of 125Hz, and this held true for pitch durations of 0.5, 1, 2, and 4s. The threshold of pitch change in speech-like signals has been studied by Rossi (1971, 1978) and Klatt (1973). Klatt reported a minimum slope of 12Hz/s with a duration of 250ms, while Rossi reported greater minimum slopes: 890Hz/s with 50ms, 250Hz/s with 100ms, and 95Hz/s with 200ms.

Finally, to distinguish two pitch changes, Pollack (1968), using a central frequency of 707Hz, reported differential thresholds of two pitch changes from 0.1ms to 870ms in terms of the quotient of the their rates of change in Hz/s. He showed that the minimum quotient was around 2 for longer durations and could be considerably higher (up to 30) for shorter durations. Nabelek and Hirsh (1969), in a more comprehensive study, reported slightly lower differential thresholds. Klatt (1973) studied the differential thresholds of pitch changes in speech-like signals and reported that listeners could distinguish a 135Hz to 105Hz f_0 fall from a 139Hz to 101Hz f_0 fall, both with a 250ms duration. The differential threshold here, if converted to the quotient of rates of change (1.27), was even better than the results in Pollack (1968) and Nabelek and Hirsh (1969).

In short, we can see that in psychoacoustic experiments involving either pure tones or tones carried by speech-like signals, listeners' ability to distinguish different tones is very high. But 't Hart (1981), and 't Hart et al. (1990) have rightly pointed out that the just noticeable differences in psychoacoustic studies are usually elicited under extreme conditions in which the subject's only task is to listen to one particular difference in controlled environments; but the perception of actual speech requires the listener to perform multiple tasks simultaneously. We therefore should expect the just noticeable differences in real speech to be considerably higher than those elicited in psychoacoustic experiments.

This point has been explicitly addressed in experiments by 't Hart (1981), 't Hart et al. (1990), Rietveld and Gussenhoven (1985), Harris and Umeda (1987), and Ross et al. (1992). 't Hart (1981) studied the differential threshold for pitch changes on a target syllable in real speech utterances in Dutch and reported only differences of more than 3 semitones (around 20-30Hz in the speech range) play a role in communicative functions. Rietveld and Gussenhoven (1985) put 't Hart's claim to test in a linguistically oriented task—one which required the listener to decide which of the two accents that differed in f_0 excursion size was more prominent. They concluded that a difference of 1.5 semitones is sufficient to cause a difference in the perception of prominence. Harris and Umeda (1984) showed that the differential limens for f_0 in naturally spoken sentences were between 10 and 50 times greater than those found with sustained synthetic vowels, and the differential limens varied significantly depending on the complexity of the stimulus and the speaker. Ross et al. (1992), in their study of 'tone latitude'—the tolerance of imprecision in the realization of lexical tones—in Taiwanese, showed that the tone latitude was about 1.9 semitones for average f_0, 2.0 semitones for initial f_0, and 29 semitones/s for f_0 slope. The differential thresholds obtained in these experiments were considerably higher than those obtained in the psychoacoustic experiments discussed earlier.

Therefore, the overgeneration problem in taking the just noticeable difference as the step size to construct the faithfulness constraints PRES(tone) might not be as serious as one might originally have thought. This is due to the fact that in real speech, the just noticeable differences among tones may be considerably higher than those elicited under extremely clean conditions in psychoacoustic studies.

The overgeneration problem may also be addressed from the other side; i.e., the cross-linguistic variation in phonetic realization that the theory is able to predict might not be overgeneration. With more detailed phonetic studies, we may find that many patterns that seemed to be overgenerated by the factorial typology of a phonetically rich system are in fact attested. A growing body of phonetic literature has shown that many phonetic processes that were thought to be universal exhibit cross-linguistic variation, and these variations are not random—they usually tie into the phonological system of the language in question (Magen 1984, Keating 1988a, b, Keating and Cohn 1988, Manuel 1990, Flemming 1997). It would be then premature to conclude that the factorial typology of phonetically rich system vastly overgenerates.

7.3 ASSUMPTIONS MADE IN THE MODEL

So far I have laid out the constraints and any intrinsic ranking needed for capturing the interaction between contour tone restrictions and phonetic properties, especially duration and sonority, of the rime. I have already acknowledged that some of the parameters in constraint definitions, e.g., the values in the similarity matrix for tonal faithfulness, are to a certain extent hypothetical. The improvement of the model will rely on the perception research of tone and detailed cross-linguistic phonetic documentation of tonal realization.

This theoretical apparatus has also made the following four assumptions.

Canonicality. I assume that the canonical speaking rate and style are the basis on which the grammar is constructed. The concepts of C_{CONTOUR} value is calculated from the canonical duration of the sonorous portion of the rime. The assumption is necessary since the duration of the syllable and the pitch range of the speaker vary under different speaking rates and styles, and the 'tolerance level' for tone slope varies too. The assumption is justified since given that the standard mode of speech is what language users are most frequently exposed to and most frequently utilize, it is reasonable to assume that it is under this mode that contrastive values and allophonic relationships are established.

Normalization. The second assumption is that speakers are able to normalize different values for duration and pitch across speaking rates and styles. This assumption is necessary since only under this assumption, can we account for the stability of the phonological system across speaking rates and styles in such a phonetically rich phonology. Let us look at it this way. In order for the phonological system to be the same in a slower speaking rate and a faster speaking rate, we want to make sure that the same phonological entity in the two speaking rates, e.g., a $\widehat{\text{HL}}$ contour on CVO, to be treated the same way in the grammar. But if the speaker did not have the ability to normalize, but took the phonetic values in the inputs, outputs, and constraints as absolute values, then a $\widehat{\text{HL}}$ contour on CVO would violate a higher ranked *CONTOUR(x_i)-$C_{\text{CONTOUR}}(y_j)$ constraint in the fast speech grammar that it would not violate in the slow speech grammar. Then the phonological system in the two speaking rates would be different, since the same phonological entity is treated differently in the two rates by the grammar. This does not a priori preclude the possibility of different phonological behavior in different speaking rates and styles. It is still possible for particular speech styles to be associated with constraints that are specific to them, e.g., constraints that refer to the realization of affective signaling or constraints that refer to absolute duration instead of normalized duration to express physiological limitations, etc. A number of languages with different phonological patterns in different speech rates have been reported in the literature. For example, Ao (1993) discusses the different tone sandhi patterns under different speech rates in Nantong Chinese (cited in Yip, to appear); Harris (1969) and Giannelli and Savoia (1979) document different consonant lenition patterns under different speech rates in Mexico City Spanish and Florentine Italian respectively (cited in Kirchner 1998). But given the overall stability of the phonological system in the face of the fluctuation of speaking rates and styles, I believe that normalization is a necessary assumption here.

This assumption is justified by ample phonetic evidence on speakers' knowledge of normalization. For example, many perceptual studies show that the speaking rate of the stimuli influences listeners' perceptual boundary between two segments if this boundary is dependent on duration (Port 1979, Miller and Liberman 1979, Miller and Grosjean 1981, Pols 1986). For an extensive review of related issues, see Perkell and Klatt (eds.) (1986). For additional studies on tone normalization, see Leather (1983), Moore C. (1995), Moore and Jongman (1997).

Awareness of phonetic details. Thirdly, I have assumed that speakers are aware of phonetic details in the sense that they can influence phonological patterning. Two types of phonetic details are assumed here: the C_{CONTOUR} value of a syllable, which indicates its contour tone bearing ability and is determined by the canonical duration of the vowel and sonorant coda (if any) of the syllable; and the pitch characteristics of a tone, which include all perceptually salient properties of tone, such as pitch excursion, the direction of slope, the number of pitch targets, etc. Moreover, I assume that all just noticeable differences in tone in real speech are relevant in the evaluation of faithfulness or correspondence in phonology. These assumptions are necessary since I have argued from both the survey of contour tone restrictions and phonetic studies of relevant languages that phonetics must play a more important in phonology than we traditionally acknowledged in order to limit the predictions of the theory to only allow patterns that are attested. These assumptions are justified since as I have argued above, the theory based on them does not necessarily vastly overgenerate in terms of its predictions.

Contrast constraints. Finally, I assume that there are contrast constraints in the system. The question is: if phonetic details such as a minute change of duration or pitch excursion can be included in phonological representations, how do phonological contrasts emerge from the ultra-rich representations? After all, along a phonetic dimension, only a small number of contrasts will emerge in any given language.

This issue has already been brought up in §6.1.1.5 when I discussed the difference in tonal inventory size on syllables with different duration. Flemming (1995)'s idea of MINDIST was used to illustrate how to explain the smaller tonal inventory on syllables with shorter duration. Kirchner (1997)'s and Boersma

(1998)'s proposals were also mentioned.

The issue here is similar in nature to the one discussed in §6.1.1.5. To make the question more concrete: if a contour tone 51 is allowed on one type of syllables, how do we make sure that we do not automatically allow 52, 53, 54, etc., which have less pitch excursion, in the tonal inventory on that type of syllables? The constraints introduced in §7.2.1—§7.2.3 cannot ensure that. I assume that it is the same contrast constraints that account for the smaller inventory size on syllables with shorter duration that will achieve this effect.

By way of an example, let us recall that in the survey of contour tone distribution, we have seen languages in which a certain syllable type can carry a contour of relatively great tonal complexity, but not one with less tonal complexity, although the tone with less tonal complexity might occur on a different syllable type with greater duration. For example, in Kɔnni, a final CV syllable can carry a $\widehat{\text{HL}}$ contour, but not a $\widehat{\text{H!}}$H contour, which presumably has a less pronounced pitch excursion; but a final CVV or CVN syllable can carry $\widehat{\text{H!}}$H as well as $\widehat{\text{HL}}$. Again, these phenomena are not explicable by the constraint families introduced in the previous sections. This is because, when the duration is constant, the permissible pitch excursion is purely determined by the *CONTOUR(x_i)-C_{CONTOUR}(y_j) constraints. The intrinsic ranking among the *CONTOUR(x_i)-C_{CONTOUR}(y_j) constraints determines that if a contour of higher tonal complexity is allowed on the duration in question, a contour of lower tonal complexity will be too.

Tonal discrimination studies discussed in §7.2.3 (Pollack 1968, Rossi 1971, 1978, Klatt 1973) have shown that a contour tone can be better discriminated from another contour tone or a level tone when the duration of the tone carrier is longer. Therefore, to distinguish a contour tone from other tones, the required pitch difference is greater on a relatively short duration than on a relatively long duration. So the intuition behind Kɔnni's pattern is that, on a short syllable, certain pitch contours might not have enough pitch differences from other tones, and are therefore reanalyzed by listeners as other tones; but on a longer syllable, these contours are more likely to be differentiated from other tones, and when they are, their contour specification will be able to surface in the output.

This intuition can be formally captured as follows. For syllable type σ, there is a series of MINDIST constraints as defined in (41a), with an intrinsic ranking as in (41b).

(41) a. For $i \geq 1$, MINDIST-σ(tone)=i is defined as:
the distance between any two tones in the tonal inventory on σ must be at least i steps.
b. If $i>j$, then MINDIST-σ(tone)=j » MINDIST-σ(tone)=i.

For a different syllable type σ', there is a parallel series of MINDIST-σ'(tone)=i constraints, and they observe the intrinsic ranking with the constraints on syllable type σ in (42). This ranking reflects the perceptual fact that for the same descending pitch slope, it is easier for it to be perceived as a falling contour on a longer duration than on a shorter duration.

(42) If Duration(σ)>Duration(σ'),

then MINDIST-σ'(tone)=*i* » MINDIST-σ(tone)=*i*.

Let us assume that the distance between a H͡L slope and a level tone is two 'steps' and the distance between a H͡!H slope and a level tone is one 'step'. Let us also assume the presence of MAINTAIN-N-CONTRASTS constraints (see §6.1.1.5). Then the Kɔnni pattern mentioned above can be captured by the ranking in (43), as illustrated in the tableaux in (44).

(43) MAINTAIN-2-CONTRASTS, MINDIST-(CV-final)(tone)=2
⇓
MAINTAIN-3-CONTRASTS
⇓
MINDIST-(CVV, CVN-final)(tone)=2

(44) a. On final CVV and CVN—H͡L, H͡!H, and H:

	MNTN 2 CNTRST	MINDIST-CV =2	MNTN 3 CNTRST	MINDIST-CVV, CVN =2
☞ H͡L-H͡!H-H				*
H͡L-H			*!	
H͡!H-H			*!	*
H	*!		*	

b. On final CV—H͡L and H:

	MNTN 2 CNTRST	MINDIST-CV =2	MNTN 3 CNTRST	MINDIST-CVV, CVN =2
H͡L-H͡!H-H		*!		
☞ H͡L-H			*	
H͡!H-H		*!	*	
H	*!		*	

In (44a), we see that H͡!H contrasts with H͡L and H on final CVV and CVN. This is because the MINDIST constraint that requires the fall and level to be two steps apart on CVV and CVN is lowly ranked. In (44b), we see that H͡!H does not occur on final CV. And this is because the MINDIST constraint that requires the fall and level to be two steps apart on CV is highly ranked.

The above is just an illustration of how the contrast constraints rule out candidates that do not stand in enough distance from other contrasts in the system, but are otherwise wellformed. The exact way in which the contrast constraints should be formulated falls outside the scope of this work. For more comprehensive treatments of this issue, see Flemming (1995) and Boersma (1998). In the remaining part of the book, I assume that some form of the contrast constraints is present in the phonological system, since in a phonetically rich system that I argue for, only with this assumption can we avoid situations in which two phonetically very similar entities stand in contrast.

7.4 FACTORIAL TYPOLOGY

To have a basic understanding of what kinds of languages the model predicts, let us consider the possible fates of an underlying contour tone that are predicted by the factorial typology of the proposed constraint families.

Suppose that in language *L*, there exists an underlying contour tone *T* with a pitch excursion of Δf under the standard speaking rate and style. Let us see what the possible predictions of the grammar are when the contour encounters a rime *R* whose $C_{CONTOUR}$ value is *c* and whose minimum sonorous rime duration is *d*. The predicted input-output mapping may be the characterization of either alternation or static phonotactic requirement. The latter construal requires the assumption of the *Richness of the Base* (Prince and Smolensky 1993, Smolensky 1996).

During the discussion of the factorial typology, since the only attested way to increase a syllable's $C_{CONTOUR}$ value from the input to the output is to lengthen its sonorous rime duration, as discussed in §7.2.2, for candidates that differ from the input in $C_{CONTOUR}$ value, I only consider those that manipulate the sonorous rime duration, and I use the sonorous rime duration *d* instead of directly referring to the $C_{CONTOUR}$ value *c* in the candidates. Again, I refer the interested reader to Steriade (2001b) and Wilson (2000) for possible ways of eliminating other fixes.

7.4.1 No Change Necessary

The first possibility is that the PRES(tone) and *DUR constraint families outrank *CONTOUR(*T*)-$C_{CONTOUR}$(*R*) en masse. Under this ranking, the contour faithfully surfaces on the given rime without lengthening. This is because any flattening of the contour or lengthening of the sonorous rime duration in order to satisfy *CONTOUR(*T*)-$C_{CONTOUR}$(*R*) will incur violations in the higher ranking PRES(TONE) or *DUR constraint families, as illustrated by the tableau in (45).

(45) $T_{\Delta f}, R_d \rightarrow \Delta f, d$

$T_{\Delta f}, R_d$	PRES(tone)	*DUR	*CONTOUR(*T*)-C$_{CONTOUR}$(*R*)
faithful: ☞ $\Delta f, d$			*
contour reduction: Δf-f_0, d	*!		
rime lengthening: Δf, $d+d_0$		*!	

This ranking also predicts that on a rime *R'* with a greater C$_{CONTOUR}$ value than *c*, Δf will also be faithfully realized, since the constraint *CONTOUR(*T*)-C$_{CONTOUR}$(*R'*) will be even lower ranked than *CONTOUR(*T*)-C$_{CONTOUR}$(*R*). This is consistent with the implicational hierarchies established in the typological survey of contour tone distribution, since the implicational hierarchies all show that if a contour can occur on a syllable with a shorter canonical duration, then it can also occur on a syllable with a longer canonical duration. And indeed, languages of this sort are attested in the survey. As I have discussed in §4.6.3, a number of languages in the survey do not exhibit any restrictions for the occurrence of contour tones. For example, !Xũ (Doke 1925, Heikkinen 1986, Snyman 1970), ǂKhomani (Doke 1937), and a number of Chinantec languages allow all tones on all syllable types, be they open or checked, long-vowelled or short-vowelled. Although most of the sources I consulted on these languages do not give phonetic details of tone and duration, thus it is possible that the contour tones on shorter syllable types are somewhat flattened, or these syllables are somewhat lengthened, there is some phonetic documentation on Lalana Chinantec (Mugele 1982) which shows that the same contour tone exhibits relative stability of onset and endpoint on different syllable types, and the same syllable type exhibits relatively stable duration when carrying different tones.

7.4.2 Partial Contour Reduction

The second possibility is that *CONTOUR(*T*)-C$_{CONTOUR}$(*R*) outranks some, but not all PRES(tone) constraints, but the *DUR constraint family en masse is still undominated. Under this ranking, the contour is flattened to satisfy the *CONTOUR(*T*)-C$_{CONTOUR}$(*R*) constraint, but no extra duration can be added to the sonorous portion of the rime. This is illustrated in the tableau in (46).

(46) $T_{\Delta f}$, R_d → Δf-f_0, d

$T_{\Delta f}$, R_d	*DUR	*CONTOUR(*T*)-$C_{CONTOUR}(R)$	PRES(tone)
faithful: Δf, d		*!	
contour reduction: ☞ Δf-f_0, d			*
rime lengthening: Δf, d+d_0	*!		

This ranking also predicts that on a rime *R'* with a greater $C_{CONTOUR}$ value than *c*, Δf will be more faithfully realized, i.e. realized with less or no reduction of the pitch excursion. This is because the relevant *CONTOUR(*x*)-$C_{CONTOUR}(y)$ constraint *CONTOUR(*T*)-$C_{CONTOUR}(R')$ will be lower ranked than *CONTOUR(*T*)-$C_{CONTOUR}(R)$, and this will allow more PRES(tone) constraints to exert influence on the output form. This, again, is consistent with the implicational hierarchy established in the typological survey in Chapter 4. It reflects the pattern in which certain contour tones can have a full realization on syllables with longer sonorous rime duration, but are partially flattened on syllables with shorter sonorous rime duration. Pingyao Chinese's flattening of 53 and 13 on CVO syllables to 54 and 23 is an example of this sort.

7.4.3 Complete Contour Reduction

The third possibility is to have all *CONTOUR(*x*)-$C_{CONTOUR}(R)$ and *DUR constraints outrank all the relevant PRES(tone) constraints. That is, *CONTOUR(δ)-$C_{CONTOUR}(R)$, where δ represents the smallest pitch excursion, outranks the PRES(tone, *i*) constraint that penalizes changing the tone *T* to a level tone. This ranking predicts that the tone *T* will be flattened all the way to a level tone. This is illustrated in the tableau in (47).

(47) $T_{\Delta f}, R_d \rightarrow 0, d$

$T_{\Delta f}, R_d$	*DUR	*CONTOUR(δ)-$C_{CONTOUR}(R)$	PRES(tone, i)
faithful: $\Delta f, d$		*!	
partial contour reduction: $\Delta f\text{-}f_0, d$		*!	
complete contour reduction: ☞ $0, d$			*
rime lengthening: $\Delta f, d+d_0$	*!		

For the same reason as the ranking for partial contour reduction, this ranking still predicts that on a rime R' with a greater $C_{CONTOUR}$ value than c, Δf will be more faithfully realized, i.e. realized with less or no reduction of the pitch excursion: *CONTOUR(δ)-$C_{CONTOUR}(R')$ will be lower ranked than *CONTOUR(δ)-$C_{CONTOUR}(R)$, and this will allow more PRES(T) constraints to exert influence on the output form. This is yet again consistent with the implicational hierarchy established in the typological survey in Chapter 4. In fact, this is the most commonly attested pattern of contour tone restrictions in languages, i.e., certain contour tones cannot occur on syllables with low $C_{CONTOUR}$ values. We have seen many examples of this sort, e.g., Xhosa's restriction of contour tones to stressed syllables, Navajo's restriction of contour tones to long vowels, Cantonese's restriction of contour tones to non-checked syllables, etc.

7.4.4 Interim Summary

The scenarios described in §7.4.1-§7.4.3 can be summarized in the schematic graph in (48). In the graph, the x-axis represents tonal candidates. Since all *DUR constraints are always ranked on the top tier in the scenarios described so far, I only consider candidates that respect these constraints, i.e., candidates with no lengthening. The leftmost candidate on the x-axis is the most faithfulness to the input, with no flattening at all—(Δf, d). The rightmost candidate is the one with complete flattening—(0, d). d is the sonorous rime duration of the candidate rime, and it is the same in all the candidates considered here. The y-axis represents constraint ranking—the higher the y value, the higher the ranking. The curves in the graph represent the highest ranked constraints in the *CONTOUR(x)-$C_{CONTOUR}(R)$ and PRES(tone, i) families that the candidates on the x-axis violate.

(48) Interaction of *CONTOUR(x)-$C_{CONTOUR}$(R) and PRES(tone, i) yielding different degrees of contour reduction:

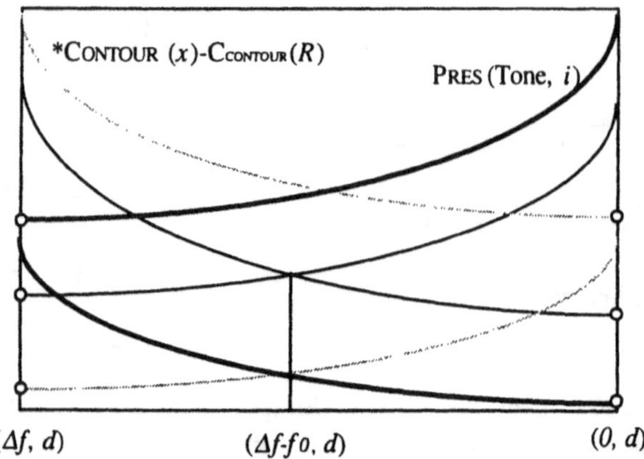

The thick black lines in the graph indicate the ranking of the two constraint families that ensures the faithful realization of the pitch excursion Δf, which is the leftmost candidate on the x-axis. The highest ranked constraint it violates is *CONTOUR(T)-$C_{CONTOUR}$(R). Any other candidate towards the right, which deviates from the input, will induce the violation of a higher ranked PRES(tone, i) constraint.

The thin black lines indicate the ranking that produces partial reduction of the contour to Δf-f_0, which is the candidate on the x-axis that corresponds to the point of intersection of the two curves. Any candidate towards the left violates a higher ranked *CONTOUR(x)-$C_{CONTOUR}$(R) constraint, and any candidate towards the right violates a higher ranked PRES(tone, i) constraint.

The gray lines indicate the ranking that forces complete reduction of the contour tone to a level tone, which is the rightmost candidate on the x-axis. The highest ranked constraint it violates is the highest ranked PRES(tone, i) constraint. Any other candidate towards the left, which deviates less from the input, will induce the violation of a higher ranked *CONTOUR(x)-$C_{CONTOUR}$(R) constraint.

7.4.5 Non-Neutralizing Lengthening

The fourth possibility is that *CONTOUR(T)-$C_{CONTOUR}$(R) outranks some *DUR constraints, but the PRES(tone) constraint family *en masse* is undominated. Under this ranking, the tone-bearing portion of the rime is lengthened to satisfy the *CONTOUR(T)-$C_{CONTOUR}$(R) constraint, but the contour must be faithfully realized, as illustrated by the tableau in (49).

(49) $T_{\Delta f}, R_d \rightarrow \Delta f, d+d_0$

$T_{\Delta f}, R_d$	PRES(tone)	*CONTOUR(*T*)-$C_{CONTOUR}(R)$	*DUR
faithful: $\Delta f, d$		*!	
contour reduction: $\Delta f\text{-}f_0, d$	*!		
rime lengthening: ☞ $\Delta f, d+d_0$			*

This ranking also predicts that on a rime *R'* with a greater $C_{CONTOUR}$ value, there will be a lesser degree of lengthening or no lengthening at all depending on what the sonorous rime duration is. And this again is consistent with the implicational hierarchies established in the typological survey in Chapter 4. This pattern does not seem prevalent in the survey. But as mentioned before, this may be due to the fact that the primary attention has been devoted to documenting the restrictions of contour tones on certain syllable types in the data sources, so when a syllable type is able to carry a certain contour, the durational change of the syllable is considered a phonetic side-effect and has escaped the attention of many. We do have a few examples in which this pattern is instantiated. For example, in Mitla Zapotec (Briggs 1961), a rising tone lengthens the duration of its carrier, and in Wuyi Chinese, a CVO syllable is drastically lengthened to carry a complex contour 213. Also, in Ngizim and Musey, even though CVO syllables can carry contour tones, their duration is reported impressionistically to be longer than when carry a level tone (Schuh p.c., Shryock p.c.).

7.4.6 Neutralizing Lengthening

It is also possible that the lengthening is neutralizing. Let us suppose that the minimum durations for a short vowel and a long vowel are *d* and *2d* respectively. Then when *CONTOUR(*T*)-$C_{CONTOUR}(V_{2d-\delta})$ (with δ being a very short duration) outranks *DUR(*d*), while all PRES(tone) constraints are still ranked on top, the ranking predicts neutralizing lengthening when the tone *T* occurs on a short vowel. This is illustrated in the tableau in (50). The first candidate, with no contour flattening and no lengthening, violates the highly ranked *CONTOUR(*T*)-$C_{CONTOUR}(V_{2d-\delta})$; the second candidate, with contour flattening, violates at least one of the highly ranked PRES(tone) constraints. The third candidate, with insufficient lengthening, still violates the constraint *CONTOUR(*T*)-$C_{CONTOUR}(V_{2d-\delta})$. The last candidate, with sufficient lengthening, only violates the lowly ranked *DUR constraints, and is therefore the winner.

(50) $T_{\Delta f}, V_d \rightarrow \Delta f, V_{2d}$

$T_{\Delta f}, V_d$	PRES(tone)	*CONTOUR(T)-$C_{CONTOUR}(V_{2d\text{-}\delta})$	*DUR(d)
$\Delta f, V_d$		*!	
$\Delta f\text{-}f_0, V_d$	*!		
$\Delta f, V_{2d\text{-}\delta}$		*!	
☞ $\Delta f, V_{2d}$			*

This ranking also predicts that on a long vowel, the tone T can be faithfully realized. This pattern is attested in Gã. There is a vowel length contrast in this language. But when a rising tone is co-occurs with a short vowel due to morphological concatenation, neutralizing lengthening (Paster 1999).

7.4.7 Interim Summary

The scenarios described in §7.4.5—§7.4.6 can be summarized in the schematic graph in (51). In the graph, the x-axis represents durational candidates. Since all PRES(tone) constraints are always ranked on the top tier in these scenarios, I only consider candidates that respect these constraints, i.e., candidates with no contour reduction. The leftmost candidate on the x-axis is the most faithful to the input, with no lengthening at all—($\Delta f, d$). The rightmost candidate is the one with neutralizing lengthening—($\Delta f, 2d$). The y-axis represents constraint ranking—the higher the y value, the higher the ranking. The curves in the graph represent the highest ranked constraints in the *CONTOUR(T)-$C_{CONTOUR}(x)$ and *DUR families that the candidates violate.

(51) Interaction of *CONTOUR(T)-$C_{CONTOUR}(x)$ and *DU R yielding different degrees of lengthening:

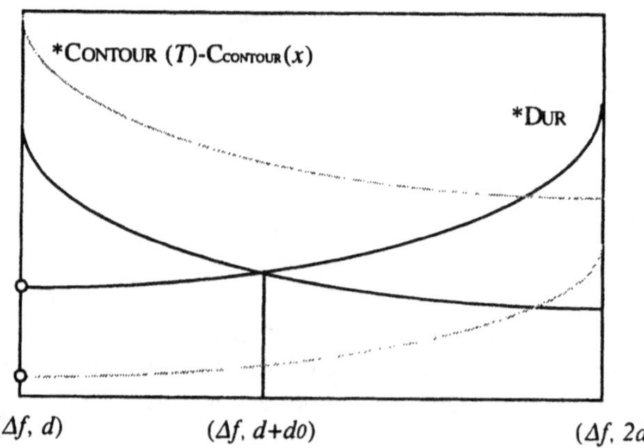

The black lines in the graph indicate the ranking of the two constraint families that produces partial lengthening of the vowel to $d+d_0$, which is the candidate on the x-axis that corresponds to the point of intersection of the two curves. Any candidate towards the left violates a higher ranked *CONTOUR(T)-$C_{CONTOUR}(x)$ constraint, and any candidate towards the right violates a higher ranked *DUR constraint.

The gray lines indicate the ranking that forces neutralizing lengthening, which is the rightmost candidate on the x-axis. The highest ranked constraint it violates is the highest ranked *DUR constraint. Any other candidate towards the left, which lengthens less from the input, will induce the violation of a higher ranked *CONTOUR(T)-$C_{CONTOUR}(x)$ constraint.

7.4.8 Contour Reduction + Rime Lengthening

The last possibility is that *CONTOUR(T)-$C_{CONTOUR}(R)$ outranks some *DUR constraints and some PRES(tone) constraints. Under this ranking, the avoidance of the *CONTOUR(T)-$C_{CONTOUR}(R)$ constraint violation is achieved by contour reduction and rime lengthening simultaneously.

To illustrate this, let us assume the following: $f_0>f_1$, $d_0>d_1$, $\mathbb{S}_T(\Delta f\text{-}f_0)=i$ (meaning that the pitch excursion $\Delta f\text{-}f_0$ is i steps away from tone T, which has the pitch excursion Δf, see §7.4.4), and $\mathbb{S}_T(\Delta f\text{-}f_1)=j$ (meaning that the pitch excursion $\Delta f\text{-}f_1$ is j steps away from tone T). Given that $f_0>f_1$, we know that $i>j$, meaning that $\Delta f\text{-}f_1$ is perceptually closer to tone T than $\Delta f\text{-}f_0$. Based on the intrinsic rankings among the *DUR (§7.2.2) and PRES(tone) (§7.2.3) constraint families respectively, these relations render the intrinsic rankings shown in (52).

(52) a. *DUR(d_0) » *DUR(d_1)

b. PRES(T, i) » PRES(T, j)

If *CONTOUR(T)-$C_{CONTOUR}(R)$ is ranked on a par with *DUR(d_0) and PRES(T, i), but outranks *DUR(d_1) and PRES(T, j), then the winning candidate will have a flattened contour $\Delta f\text{-}f_1$ and a lengthened duration $d+d_1$. Just flattening the contour to satisfy the *CONTOUR(T)-$C_{CONTOUR}(R)$ constraint is too costly for the PRES(T) constraint family as it incurs a violation of the highly ranked PRES(T, i); and just lengthening the rime is too costly for the *DUR constraint family as it incurs a violation of the highly ranked *DUR(d_0). The tableau in (53) illustrates these arguments.

(53) $T_{\Delta f}, R_d$ —> Δf-f_1, $d+d_1$

$T_{\Delta f}, R_d$	PRES (T, *i*)	*DUR (d_0)	*CONTOUR(*T*)-C$_{CONTOUR}$(*R*)	PRES (T, *j*)	*DUR (d_1)
faithful: $\Delta f, d$			*!		
lots of contour reduction: Δf-f_0, d	*!			*	
lots of rime lengthening: Δf, $d+d_0$		*!			*
some reduction, some lengthening: ☞ Δf-f_1, $d+d_1$				*	*

This ranking also predicts that on a rime *R'* with a duration longer than *d*, there will be a lesser degree of flattening, or a lesser degree of lengthening, or both, depending on the ranking among the lower-ranked *CONTOUR(*x*)-C$_{CONTOUR}$(*y*), PRES(tone), and *DUR constraints. This is consistent with the implicational hierarchies established in the survey. This pattern is instantiated by Hausa, which shows both partial contour flattening and rime lengthening when a CVO syllable carries a falling contour, as shown by the phonetic data in §4.2.2.3. The factorial typology clearly predicts many variations of this pattern, but this pattern does not seem prevalent in the survey. An explanation is surely needed. I again conjecture that this might be due to the close-to-exclusive attention to the distributional facts about contours and the lack of detailed phonetic documentation of many languages. Upon closer scrutiny of the phonetic realization of tonal contours and duration of rimes that carry them, many such patterns might emerge and the range of variation predicted by the typology can be tested against these phonetic data.

7.4.9 Summary

To visualize the interaction of the three families of constraints, let us consider a 3-D space. The *x*-*y* plane represents candidates for the input ($T_{\Delta f}$, R_d). The origin is the faithful candidate (Δf, *d*). The *x*-axis represents the amount of rime lengthening, and the *y*-axis represents the amount of contour reduction. The *z*-axis represents constraint ranking. Again, the higher the *z* value, the higher the ranking.

Let us consider three planes in this space *CONTOUR-C$_{CONTOUR}$(*x*, *y*), *DUR(*x*, *y*), and PRES(tone)(*x*, *y*) that represent the highest ranked constraint in the *CONTOUR-$C_{CONTOUR}$, *DUR, and PRES(tone) families respectively that the candidates on the *x*-*y* plane violate. These planes should have the following characteristics.

For the *CONTOUR-$C_{CONTOUR}(x, y)$ plane, it has the highest value at the origin of the space, and it decreases monotonically when *x* increases or when *y* increases. This means that the faithful candidate violates the highest ranked *CONTOUR-$C_{CONTOUR}$ constraint, and reducing the tonal contour and lengthening the rime will both help resolving the violation of this highly ranked tonal markedness constraint. This plane is schematically shown in (54).

(54) The *CONTOUR-$C_{CONTOUR}(x, y)$ plane:

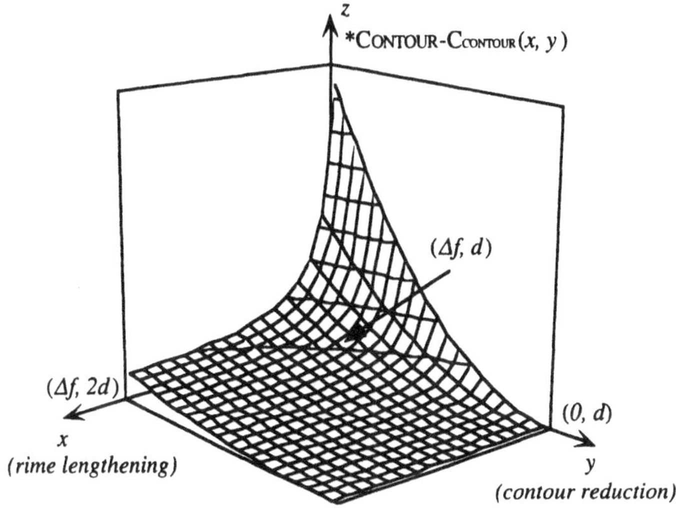

For the *DUR(*x*, *y*) plane, its value increases when *x* increases, but is constant with respect to *y*. This means that the more lengthening the candidate has, the higher *DUR constraint it violates. But *DUR is insensitive to contour reduction. This plane is schematically shown in (55).

(55) The *DUR(*x*, *y*) plane:

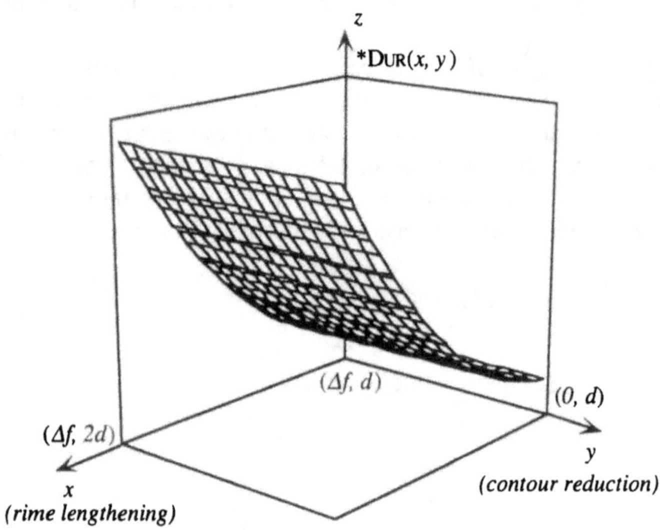

For the PRES(tone)(*x*, *y*) plane, its value increases when *y* increases, but is constant with respect to *x*. This means that the more contour reduction the candidate has, the higher PRES(tone) constraint it violates. But PRES(tone) is insensitive to rime lengthening. This plane is schematically shown in (56). Notice that the candidates that do not have any contour reduction do not violate PRES(tone) constraints.

(56) The PRES(tone)(*x*, *y*) plane:

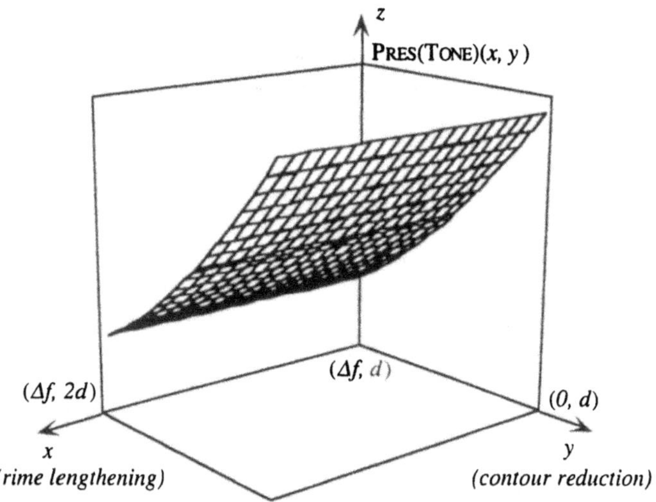

To find the optimal candidate is to find the minimum value of the function in (57).

(57) $z = f(x, y) = max$(*CONTOUR-$C_{\text{CONTOUR}}(x, y)$, *DUR(x, y), PRES(tone)(x, y))

This function is plotted from two different angles in (58). The optimal candidate $(\Delta f\text{-}f_1, d+d_1)$ is indicated in both graphs.

(58) $z = max$(*CONTOUR-$C_{\text{CONTOUR}}(x, y)$, *DUR(x, y), PRES(tone)(x, y)):

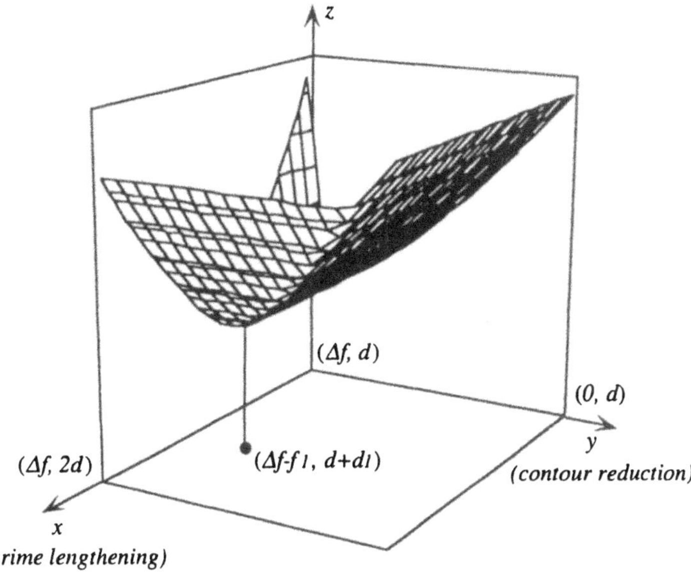

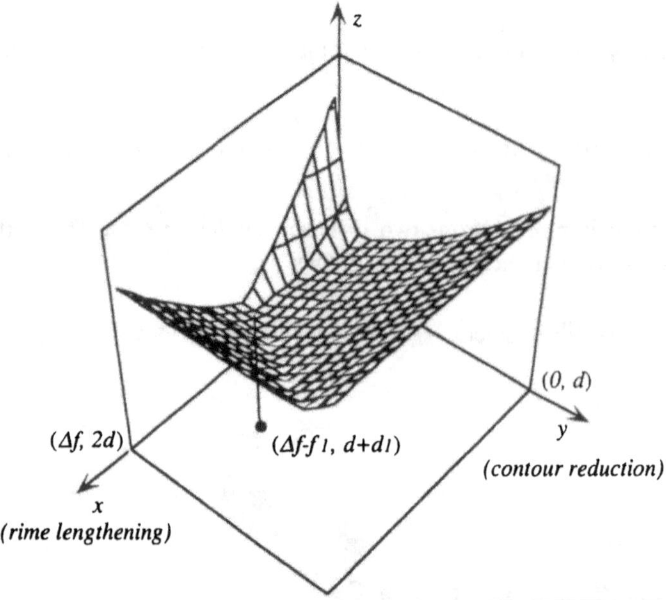

We can prove that the point of intersection of the three planes is the point where the highest constraint that the candidate violates is the lowest as compared to all other candidates. Let us suppose that the three planes intersect at point (x_0, y_0, z_0). That is to say, max(*CONTOUR-C$_{\text{CONTOUR}}(x_0, y_0)$, *DUR$(x_0, y_0)$, PRES(tone)$(x_0, y_0)$) $= z_0$. For a different candidate (x_1, y_1), if *CONTOUR-C$_{\text{CONTOUR}}(x_1, y_1) < z_0$, then $x_1>x_0$ or $y_1>y_0$. But when $x_1>x_0$, *DUR$(x_1, y_1) >$ *DUR$(x_0, y_0) = z_0$; and when $y_1>y_0$. PRES(tone)$(x_1, y_1) >$ PRES(tone)$(x_0, y_0) = z_0$. Therefore, max(*CONTOUR-C$_{\text{CONTOUR}}(x_1, y_1)$, *DUR$(x_1, y_1)$, PRES(tone)$(x_1, y_1)$) $> z_0$. Thus we have proved that the projection of the point of intersection of the three planes on the x-y plane—(x_0, y_0)—indeed represents the winning candidate.

As we have seen, the interaction of these three families of constraints yields six possible outputs for contour tone T on rime R. This is summarized in (59).

(59) Outputs of $T_{\Delta f}$, R_d generated by the factorial typology:

Output	Constraint ranking	Example languages
a. Faithful: Δf, d	PRES(T), *DUR ⇓ *CONTOUR(T)-C$_{CONTOUR}$(R)	Lalana Chinantec, !Xũ, ǂKhomani
b. Partial contour reduction: Δf-f_0, d	*DUR, *CONTOUR(T)-C$_{CONTOUR}$(R) ⇓ some PRES(T)	Pingyao Chinese
c. Complete contour reduction: 0, d	*DUR, *CONTOUR(δ)-C$_{CONTOUR}$(R) ⇓ PRES(T, i)	Xhosa, Navajo
d. Non-neutralizing lengthening: Δf, $d+d_0$	PRES(T), *CONTOUR(T)-C$_{CONTOUR}$(R) ⇓ some *DUR	Mitla Zapotec, Wuyi Chinese
e. Neutralizing lengthening: Δf, $2d$	PRES(T), *CONTOUR(T)-C$_{CONTOUR}$($V_{2d-\delta}$) ⇓ *DUR(d)	Gã
f. Reduction and lengthening: Δf-f_1, $d+d_1$	some *DUR, some PRES(T), *CONTOUR(T)-C$_{CONTOUR}$(R) ⇓ some other *DUR, some other PRES(T)	Hausa

In the following chapter, I provide detailed analyses for the contour restrictions in Pingyao Chinese, Xhosa, Mitla Zapotec, Gã, and Hausa, each representing a distinct contour restriction pattern. The purpose of the analyses is two-fold. Firstly, they provide a more complete picture of how the proposed theoretical apparatus can be used to capture positional prominence patterns regarding contour tones. Secondly, they provide reassurance that the theoretical apparatus can indeed capture the desired contour tone patterns.

CHAPTER 8

Case Studies

8.1 PINGYAO CHINESE

As I have discussed in §6.1.1.4, syllables in Pingyao Chinese are in the shape of CV, CVŋ, or CVʔ. The vowel in CV is either a diphthong or phonetically long, and the vowel in CVʔ is very short. The former is usually more than twice as long as the latter. I henceforth write CV syllables as CVV. The vowel in CVŋ has comparable duration to the vowel in CVʔ (Zhang 1998). On CVV and CVŋ, three tones can occur: 13, 35, and 53; on CVʔ, 13 and 53 can occur, but they are partially flattened to 23 and 54 (Hou 1980, 1982a, b). Some Pingyao examples are repeated in (1).

(1) Pingyao examples:

puu^{13}	'to hatch'	puu^{35}	'cloth'	puu^{53}	'to mend'
$p\text{ʌ}ʔ^{23}$	'to push aside'	$p\text{ʌ}ʔ^{54}$	'a musical instrument'		

I focus on the partial flattening of the contour tones 13 and 53 on CVʔ syllables here. What needs to be explained is: (a) 13 and 53 can occur on CVV and CVŋ syllables; and (b) they must be flattened to 23 and 54 on CVʔ syllables. I discuss the 13~23 alternation in detail. The 53~54 alternation can be accounted for similarly.

Suppose that under the canonical speaking rate and style, the minimum sonorous rime duration for CVV and CVŋ is $d+d_0$ (Zhang 1998 reports that the sonorous rime duration for these syllable types is comparable), and the minimum sonorous rime duration for CVʔ is d. From the definition of $C_{CONTOUR}$ (§3.2), we know that the $C_{CONTOUR}$ values of the three syllable types observe the order $C_{CONTOUR}(CVV) > C_{CONTOUR}(CVŋ) > C_{CONTOUR}(CVʔ)$. The first '>' sign is due to the fact that CVV and CVŋ have comparable sonorous rime duration, but CVV has a greater vocalic component than CVŋ. The second '>' sign is due to the fact that CVŋ has longer sonorous rime duration than CVʔ.

Let us now consider the crucial constraints for Pingyao Chinese from the three constraints families—*CONTOUR-$C_{CONTOUR}$, *DUR, and PRES(T).

From the *CONTOUR-$C_{CONTOUR}$ family, the crucial constraints are shown in (2). These constraints observe the intrinsic ranking in (3).

(2) a. *CONTOUR(13)-$C_{CONTOUR}$(CVV)
b. *CONTOUR(13)-$C_{CONTOUR}$(CVŋ)
c. *CONTOUR(13)-$C_{CONTOUR}$(CVʔ)
d. *CONTOUR(23)-$C_{CONTOUR}$(CVV)
e. *CONTOUR(23)-$C_{CONTOUR}$(CVŋ)
f. *CONTOUR(23)-$C_{CONTOUR}$(CVʔ)

(3) *CONTOUR(13)-$C_{CONTOUR}$(CVʔ) ⇒ *CONTOUR(23)-$C_{CONTOUR}$(CVʔ)
⇓ ⇓
*CONTOUR(13)-$C_{CONTOUR}$(CVŋ) ⇒ *CONTOUR(23)-$C_{CONTOUR}$(CVŋ)
⇓ ⇓
*CONTOUR(13)-$C_{CONTOUR}$(CVV) ⇒ *CONTOUR(23)-$C_{CONTOUR}$(CVV)

From the *DUR family, since we know that no lengthening occurs in Pingyao, we conclude that the entire *DUR family is ranked on top. I will simply use *DUR as a shorthand for the constraint family.

To define the crucial constraints from the PRES(T) family, let us suppose that $S_{13}(23)=i$, meaning that 23 is i steps away from 13 on the perceptual scale. Then the crucial PRES(T) constraints are the ones given in (4), and their intrinsic ranking is given in (5).

(4) a. PRES(T, i): do not reduce 13 to 23.
b. PRES(T, 1): 13 must be faithfully realized.

(5) PRES(T, i) » PRES(T, 1)

Let us now see what the necessary rankings among these constraints are in order to arrive at the Pingyao pattern.

First, since 13 can be faithfully realized on CVV and CVŋ, we know that PRES(T, 1) » *CONTOUR(13)-$C_{CONTOUR}$(CVŋ) » *CONTOUR(13)-$C_{CONTOUR}$(CVV). Second, since on CVʔ, 13 is partially flattened to 23, but not to anything with an even smaller pitch excursion, we know that PRES(T, $i+1$), *CONTOUR(13)-$C_{CONTOUR}$(CVʔ) » PRES(T, i), *CONTOUR(23)-$C_{CONTOUR}$(CVʔ). Therefore, the crucial ranking for Pingyao is as in (6), and this ranking does not contradict the intrinsic ranking in (3).

(6) Crucial ranking for Pingyao Chinese:

*DUR, *CONTOUR(13)-C$_{\text{CONTOUR}}$(CVʔ), PRES(T, *i*+*1*)

⇓ (from *DUR, *CONTOUR(13)-C$_{\text{CONTOUR}}$(CVʔ)) … ⇓ (from PRES(T, *i*+*1*))

PRES(T, *i*) … *CONTOUR(23)-C$_{\text{CONTOUR}}$(CVʔ)

⇓

PRES(T, *1*)

⇓

*CONTOUR(13)-C$_{\text{CONTOUR}}$(CVŋ)

⇓

*CONTOUR(13)-C$_{\text{CONTOUR}}$(CVV)

The tableau in (7a) illustrates how the faithful rendition of 13 is derived on CVV. The tableau in (7b) illustrates how the partial reduction of 13 to 23 is derived on CVʔ. For both tableaux, we assume that the entire *DUR family is ranked on top, and we only consider candidates that do not have lengthening.

(7) a. /puu^{13}/ → [puu^{13}]

puu^{13}	PRES(T, *1*)	*CONTOUR(13)-C$_{\text{CONTOUR}}$(CVV)
☞ puu^{13}		*
puu^{23}	*!	
puu^{33}	*!	

b. /pʌʔ^{13}/ —> [pʌʔ^{23}]

pʌʔ^{13}	PRES (T, *i*+*1*)	*CONTOUR(13)- C$_{\text{CONTOUR}}$(CVʔ)	PRES (T, *i*)	*CONTOUR(23)- C$_{\text{CONTOUR}}$(CVʔ)
pʌʔ^{13}		*!		*
☞ pʌʔ^{23}			*	*
pʌʔ^{33}	*!		*	

The behavior of tone 53 on the two different syllable types (CVV and CVŋ vs. CVʔ) can be similarly accounted for.

Pingyao Chinese is an example language that has partial contour reduction. To see how we get complete contour reduction, let us look at Xhosa.

8.2 XHOSA

To recapitulate the data pattern in Xhosa: there is penultimate stress and no contrastive vowel length. All syllables are open. The only contour tone in the language—$\widehat{\text{HL}}$—is restricted to the stressed syllable of the word. The phonetic study I conducted has shown that syllables are drastically lengthened under stress, but only moderately so in final position. When the penultimate stress of a word is lost in the utterance, if the originally stressed syllable carried $\widehat{\mathrm{HL}}$, it is simplified to H, as shown in the example in (8).

(8) Xhosa tonal alternation:

ísìɓâyà 'sheep fold'
ísìɓáyá ésìkhûlù 'big sheep fold'

Therefore, the distributional properties to be explained in Xhosa are the following: (a) stressed syllables can carry $\widehat{\mathrm{HL}}$; (b) final syllables cannot carry $\widehat{\mathrm{HL}}$; and (c) other syllables cannot carry $\widehat{\mathrm{HL}}$. As for the tonal alternation in (8), the theory developed here will only predict that $\widehat{\mathrm{HL}}$ must be flattened to a level tone. I assume that there are other constraints in the language that force a H to surface, not a L.

In the phonetic study of Xhosa that I reported in §5.2.1, I found that both prosodic-final and stressed syllables were lengthened, but the effect of stress lengthening was significantly greater than that of final lengthening. Therefore we may suppose that under the canonical speaking rate and style, the minimum sonorous rime duration for a stressed syllable, a final syllable, and an unstressed non-final syllable is $d+d_0+d_1$, $d+d_0$ and d respectively. From the definition of $C_{CONTOUR}$ (§3.2), we know that the $C_{CONTOUR}$ values of the three syllable types observe the order $C_{CONTOUR}(\sigma_{stressed}) > C_{CONTOUR}(\sigma_{final}) > C_{CONTOUR}(\sigma_{unstressed\text{-}nonfinal})$.

Let us now consider the crucial constraints for Xhosa from the three constraints families—*CONTOUR-$C_{CONTOUR}$, *DUR, and PRES(T).

From the *CONTOUR-$C_{CONTOUR}$ family, the crucial constraints are shown in (9). 'δ' in (9d-f) indicates a small pitch excursion, and these constraints ban any contour tones on the specified syllable type. The constraints in (9) observe the intrinsic ranking in (10).

(9) a. *CONTOUR($\widehat{\mathrm{HL}}$)-$C_{CONTOUR}(\sigma_{stressed})$
b. *CONTOUR($\widehat{\mathrm{HL}}$)-$C_{CONTOUR}(\sigma_{final})$
c. *CONTOUR($\widehat{\mathrm{HL}}$)-$C_{CONTOUR}(\sigma_{unstressed\text{-}nonfinal})$
d. *CONTOUR(δ)-$C_{CONTOUR}(\sigma_{stressed})$
e. *CONTOUR(δ)-$C_{CONTOUR}(\sigma_{final})$
f. *CONTOUR(δ)-$C_{CONTOUR}(\sigma_{unstressed\text{-}nonfinal})$

(10)
*CONTOUR($\widehat{\mathrm{HL}}$)-$C_{CONTOUR}(\sigma_{unstressed\text{-}nonfinal})$ ⇒ *CONTOUR(δ)-$C_{CONTOUR}(\sigma_{unstressed\text{-}nonfinal})$
⇓ ⇓
*CONTOUR($\widehat{\mathrm{HL}}$)-$C_{CONTOUR}(\sigma_{final})$ ⇒ *CONTOUR(δ)-$C_{CONTOUR}(\sigma_{final})$
⇓ ⇓
*CONTOUR($\widehat{\mathrm{HL}}$)-$C_{CONTOUR}(\sigma_{stressed})$ ⇒ *CONTOUR(δ)-$C_{CONTOUR}(\sigma_{stressed})$

To determine the status of the *DUR family, I carried out a phonetic study to test the hypothesis that the stressed syllables in Xhosa are not lengthened when they carry a falling tone. Durational measurements of 16 tokens of Xhosa words with $\widehat{\text{HL}}$ on a penultimate CV syllable showed a mean duration of 207ms for the vowel in the penult. It is not significantly different from a level-toned penult with matched segmental conditions (36 tokens, mean duration 212ms), as shown by a one-way ANOVA: $F(1,50)=.330$, $p=$n.s. Since no lengthening occurs in Xhosa, we rank the entire *DUR family on top, and I use *DUR as a shorthand for the constraint family.

To define the crucial constraints from the PRES(T) family, let us suppose that $\mathbb{S}_{\widehat{\text{HL}}}(\text{H})=i$, meaning that H is *i* steps away from $\widehat{\text{HL}}$ on the perceptual scale. Then the crucial PRES(T) constraints are the ones given in (11), and their intrinsic ranking is given in (12).

(11) a. PRES(T, *i*): do not reduce $\widehat{\text{HL}}$ to H.

b. PRES(T, *1*): $\widehat{\text{HL}}$ must be faithfully realized.

(12) PRES(T, *i*) » PRES(T, *1*)

Let us now see what the necessary rankings among these constraints are in order to arrive at the Xhosa pattern.

First, since $\widehat{\text{HL}}$ can be faithfully realized on a stressed syllable, we know that PRES(T, *1*) » *CONTOUR($\widehat{\text{HL}}$)-$C_{\text{CONTOUR}}(\sigma_{\text{stressed}})$. Second, since on an unstressed syllable, $\widehat{\text{HL}}$ is flattened to H, we know that *CONTOUR(δ)-$C_{\text{CONTOUR}}(\sigma_{\text{unstressed-nonfinal}})$ » *CONTOUR(δ)-$C_{\text{CONTOUR}}(\sigma_{\text{final}})$ » PRES(T, *i*). Therefore, the crucial ranking for Xhosa is as in (13), and this ranking does not contradict the intrinsic ranking in (10).

(13) Crucial ranking for Xhosa:

*DUR, *CONTOUR(δ)-$C_{\text{CONTOUR}}(\sigma_{\text{unstressed-nonfinal}})$
⇓
*CONTOUR(δ)-$C_{\text{CONTOUR}}(\sigma_{\text{final}})$
⇓
PRES(T, *i*)
⇓
PRES(T, *1*)
⇓
*CONTOUR($\widehat{\text{HL}}$)-$C_{\text{CONTOUR}}(\sigma_{\text{stressed}})$

The tableau in (14a) illustrates how the faithful rendition of $\widehat{\text{HL}}$ is derived on a stressed syllable. The tableau in (14b) illustrates how the complete reduction of $\widehat{\text{HL}}$ to H is derived when the syllable loses its stress. For both tableaux, we assume that the entire *DUR family is ranked on top, and we only consider candidates that do not have lengthening. Stress is indicated in boldface.

(14) a. /ísìɓâyà/ → [ísìɓâyà]

ísìɓâyà	PRES(T, *1*)	*CONTOUR(HL)-$C_{CONTOUR}(\sigma_{stressed})$
☞ ísìɓâyà		*
ísìɓá¯yà	*!	
ísìɓáyà	*!	

b. /ísìɓâyá ésìkhûlù/ → [ísìɓáyá ésìkhûlù]

ísìɓâyá ésìkhûlù	*CONTOUR(*δ*)-$C_{CONTOUR}(\sigma_{unstressed\text{-}nonfinal})$	PRES(T, *i*)
ísìɓâyá ésìkhûlu	*!	
ísìɓá¯yá ésìkhûlu	*!	
☞ ísìɓáyá ésìkhûlù		*

In (14a), the candidate with a faithful realization of the falling contour on the stressed syllable [ɓa] is the winner, since it only violates the lowly ranked constraint *CONTOUR(HL)-$C_{CONTOUR}(\sigma_{stressed})$. Flattening the contour to HM or H, as the second and third candidates show, violates the higher ranked PRES(T, *1*) and makes the candidates lose. In (14b) however, the candidate with a complete contour reduction to H on the syllable [ɓa], which has lost its stress, is the winner, since PRES (T, *i*) is ranked lower than the relevant tonal markedness constraint here—*CONTOUR(*δ*)-$C_{CONTOUR}(\sigma_{unstressed\text{-}nonfinal})$. Any other candidate with a lesser degree of flattening, even though it will fare better with PRES (T, *i*), will lose for violating the highly ranked tonal markedness constraint.

We may also imagine a hypothetical input with a HL contour on the final syllable of a word. The HL contour will also be flattened to a level tone due to the ranking *CONTOUR(*δ*)-$C_{CONTOUR}(\sigma_{final})$ » PRES (T, *i*).

The difference then between Xhosa, which has complete contour reduction, and Pingyao Chinese, which has partial contour reduction, lies in the different interactions between the PRES(tone) and *CONTOUR-$C_{CONTOUR}$ constraint families. In Xhosa, the constraints that ban contour tones on syllables with short sonorous rime duration are so highly ranked that they must be respected even at the cost of faithfulness violations when completely flattening the contour. But in Pingyao Chinese, the two constraint families interleave in such a way that result in a compromise—the partial flattening of the contour avoids violations of both the highly ranked *CONTOUR-$C_{CONTOUR}$ constraints and the highly ranked PRES(tone) constraints.

8.3 MITLA ZAPOTEC

Syllables in Mitla Zapotec can be either open or closed. The nucleus of the syllable is either a single vowel or a diphthong. There is no vowel length contrast. There are four tones in Mitla Zapotec: H, L, L͡H, H͡L. The contour tones can occur on single vowels as well as diphthongs, but when a single vowel carries L͡H, it is lengthened (Briggs 1961).

Therefore, the contour tone patterning that needs to be explained in Mitla Zapotec includes the following: (a) both H͡L and L͡H can occur on CVV; (b) H͡L can occur on CV, but L͡H can only occur on CV upon lengthening of the vowel.

Let us assume that in the canonical speaking rate and style, a single vowel has a minimum duration of d, and when it carries L͡H, it is lengthened to $d+d_0$, and I write $V^{\bullet}$ to represent the lengthened vowel. A diphthong has a minimum duration of $2d$, and $2d>d+d_0$. I further assume that L͡H and H͡L only differ in their slope direction, but have the same amount of pitch excursion—Δf.

The crucial constraints from the *CONTOUR-$C_{CONTOUR}$ family for Mitla Zapotec are shown in (15).

(15) a. *CONTOUR(L͡H)-$C_{CONTOUR}$(CV)
 b. *CONTOUR(L͡H)-$C_{CONTOUR}$(CV$^{\bullet}$)
 c. *CONTOUR(L͡H)-$C_{CONTOUR}$(CVV)
 d. *CONTOUR(H͡L)-$C_{CONTOUR}$(CV)
 e. *CONTOUR(H͡L)-$C_{CONTOUR}$(CV$^{\bullet}$)
 f. *CONTOUR(H͡L)-$C_{CONTOUR}$(CVV)

Since the rising tone L͡H has a higher tonal complexity than the falling tone H͡L when they have the same pitch excursion (see §3.2), we have the intrinsic ranking among these constraints as shown in (16).

(16)			
	*CONTOUR(L͡H)-$C_{CONTOUR}$(CV)	⇒	*CONTOUR(H͡L)-$C_{CONTOUR}$(CV)
	⇓		⇓
	*CONTOUR(L͡H)-$C_{CONTOUR}$(CV$^{\bullet}$)	⇒	*CONTOUR(H͡L)-$C_{CONTOUR}$(CV$^{\bullet}$)
	⇓		⇓
	*CONTOUR(L͡H)-$C_{CONTOUR}$(CVV)	⇒	*CONTOUR(H͡L)-$C_{CONTOUR}$(CVV)

The crucial *DUR constraints for Mitla Zapotec are given in (17). The first constraint penalizes a lengthening of d_0 from the minimum duration; and with δ representing a small duration, the second constraint penalizes any lengthening that is more than d_0, and the third constraint penalizes any lengthening at all.

(17) a. *DUR(d_0)

b. *DUR(d_0+δ)

c. *DUR(δ)

Since contour reduction is not an option that Mitla Zapotec explores, we know that the entire PRES(tone) constraint family is ranked on the top of the hierarchy. I will use PRES(tone) as a shorthand for the constraint family here.

To see the crucial ranking of these constraints for the Mitla Zapotec pattern, let us first observe that both H͡L and L͡H can occur on CVV, from which we know that *DUR(δ) » *CONTOUR(L͡H)-$C_{CONTOUR}$(CVV) » *Contour(H͡L)-$C_{CONTOUR}$(CVV); let us then observe that H͡L can occur on CV without lengthening, from which we know that *DUR(δ) » *CONTOUR(H͡L)-$C_{CONTOUR}$(CV); lastly, let us observe that L͡H can only occur on CV upon vowel lengthening, and from this we know that *DUR(d_0+ δ), *CONTOUR(L͡H)-$C_{CONTOUR}$(CV) » *DUR(d_0), *CONTOUR(L͡H)-$C_{CONTOUR}$(CV•). Therefore, the crucial ranking for Mitla Zapotec is as in (18), and this ranking does not contradict the intrinsic ranking in (16).

(18) Crucial ranking for Mitla Zapotec:

*PRES(tone), *CONTOUR(L͡H)-$C_{CONTOUR}$(CV), *DUR(d_0+δ)

⇓ ⇓

*DUR(d_0) *CONTOUR(L͡H)-$C_{CONTOUR}$(CV•)

⇓

*DUR(δ)

⇓

*CONTOUR(L͡H)-$C_{CONTOUR}$(CVV), *Contour(H͡L)-$C_{CONTOUR}$(CV)

⇓

*Contour(H͡L)-$C_{CONTOUR}$(CVV)

The tableau in (19a) illustrates how the faithful realization of H͡L is derived on a short vowel, and the tableau in (19b) illustrates how the vowel lengthening is derived when the short vowel carries L͡H. For both tableaux, we assume that the entire *PRES(tone) family is ranked on top, and we only consider candidates that do not reduce the contour. Again, I use V• to represent a single vowel that is lengthened to d+d_0. I use VV to represent a single vowel that is lengthened to the duration of a diphthong.

(19) a. V̂ → V̂

V̂	*DUR(δ)	*CONTOUR(H͡L)-$C_{CONTOUR}$(CV)
☞ V̂		*
V̂•	*!	
V́V̀	*!	

b. V̌ → V̌•

V̌	*DUR ($d_0+\delta$)	*CONTOUR(L͡H) -$C_{CONTOUR}$(CV)	*DUR(d_0)	*CONTOUR(L͡H)-$C_{CONTOUR}$(CV•)
V̌		*!		*
☞ V̌•			*	*
VV́	*!		*	

In the analysis here, I made the assumption that both the falling and rising contours are faithfully rendered on single vowels. This is of course subject to confirmation or rejection by empirical tests. The crucial question would be: do these contour tones have the same pitch excursion on single vowels as on diphthongs? If the falling and rising excursions are smaller on single vowels than on diphthongs, the analysis needs to be revised, and the revision would involve lowering the PRES(tone) constraints in the constraint hierarchy. This, then, would be a similar scenario to the data pattern in Hausa, whose analysis I discuss in §8.5.

8.4 GÃ

Except on very rare occasions where a nasal consonant can occur as a coda, syllables in Gã are all open. There is vowel length contrast, and there are four tones—H, L, L͡H, H͡L. On non-phrase-final syllables, L͡H and H͡L can only occur when the syllable has a on long vowel nucleus; on phrase-final syllables, H͡L can occur on syllables with a short vowel, but L͡H cannot. When a L͡H contour is created on a short vowel by morphological concatenation, the short vowel is lengthened to a long vowel (Paster 1999). The example in (20a) illustrates that a short vowel can carry H͡L. The example in (20b) illustrates the lengthening of a final short vowel to a long vowel when it carries L͡H.

(20) a. he → hê 'to buy'
HL

b. cha → chàá 'dig!'
L H
'dig' imperative

Therefore, the contour tone restrictions that need to be explained in Gã are the following: (a) L͡H and H͡L cannot occur on non-phrase-final short vowels; (b)

H͡L can occur on phrase-final short vowels without lengthening the vowel; (c) L͡H can occur on phrase-final short vowels only upon neutralizing lengthening.

Let us assume that in the canonical speaking rate and style, the minimum duration for a non-final short vowel, a non-final long vowel, a final short vowel, and a final long vowel is d, $2d$, $d+d_0$ ($d_0<d$, i.e., I assume that a final short vowel is shorter than a non-final long vowel), and $2d+d_l$ respectively. I further assume that L͡H and H͡L only differ in their slope direction, but have the same amount of pitch excursion—Δf.

The crucial constraints from the *CONTOUR-$C_{CONTOUR}$ family for Gã are shown in (21). To avoid long constraint names, I use 'CON' as a shorthand for 'CONTOUR' in (21) and subsequent tableaux. For clarity, in the constraints, I write the minimum duration of the vowel in the prosodic environment to represent the syllable's $C_{CONTOUR}$ value. So for example, '*CON(L͡H)-($d+d_0$)' means '*CON(L͡H)-C_{CON}(CV_{final})'. In the constraint, δ_R represents a small pitch rise, δ_F represents a small pitch fall, and δ_D represents a small duration. Their usage will become clear later on.

(21) a. *CON(L͡H)-($2d$): no L͡H on vowels with a duration of non-final long vowels.

b. *CON(L͡H)-($2d+d_l$): no L͡H on vowels with a duration of final long vowels.

c. *CON(L͡H)-($2d-\delta_D$): no L͡H on vowels with a duration that is shorter than the duration of non-final long vowels.

d. *CON(δ_R)-($2d-\delta_D$): no pitch rise on vowels with a duration that is shorter than the duration of non-final long vowels.

e. *CON(δ_F)-(d): no pitch fall on vowels with a duration of non-final short vowels.

f. *CON(H͡L)-($d+d_0$): no H͡L on vowels with a duration of final short vowels.

g. *CON(H͡L)-($2d$): no H͡L on vowels with a duration of non-final long vowels.

h. *CON(H͡L)-($2d+d_l$): no H͡L on vowels with a duration of non-final long vowels.

Given that the rising tone L͡H has a higher tonal complexity than the falling tone H͡L when they have the same pitch excursion (see §3.2), we have the intrinsic ranking among these constraints as shown in (22).

(22) *CON(L͡H)-($2d$-δ_D) ⇒ *CON(δ_R)-($2d$-δ_D)

⇓ *CON(H͡L)-(d+d_0)

⇓

*CON(L͡H)-($2d$) ⇒ *CON(H͡L)-($2d$)

⇓ ⇓

*CON(L͡H)-($2d$+d_1) ⇒ *CON(H͡L)-($2d$+d_1)

The crucial *DUR constraints for Gã are given in (23). The first constraint penalizes a lengthening of d from the minimum duration. The second constraint penalizes a lengthening of d-d_0 from the minimum duration, which is the amount of lengthening that a final short vowel has to undergo in order to carry a rising tone. With δ representing a small duration, the third constraint penalizes any lengthening this is greater than d-d_0, and the last candidate penalizes any lengthening at all.

(23) a. *DUR(d)

b. *DUR(d-d_0)

c. *DUR(d-d_0+δ)

d. *DUR(δ)

Since H͡L and L͡H cannot occur on a non-final short vowel, I assume that they are neutralized to a level tone, e.g., H. Suppose that S_{HL}(H)=i, and S_{LH}(H)=j, meaning that H is i steps away from both H͡L and j steps from L͡H on the perceptual scales. Then the crucial PRES(T) constraints are the ones given in (24), and their intrinsic rankings are given in (25).

(24) a. PRES(H͡L, i): do not reduce H͡L to H.

b. PRES(H͡L, 1): H͡L must be faithfully realized.

c. PRES(L͡H, j): do not reduce L͡H to H.

d. PRES(L͡H, 1): L͡H must be faithfully realized.

(25) PRES(H͡L, i) » PRES(H͡L, 1)

PRES(L͡H, j) » PRES(L͡H, 1)

Now we proceed to determine the crucial rankings among these constraints for Gã.

Let us first look at the behavior of the falling tone H͡L. First, since it can occur on a long vowel without flattening or lengthening, we know that *DUR(δ), PRES(H͡L, 1) » *CON(H͡L)-($2d$) » *CON(H͡L)-($2d$+d_1). Second, since it can occur on a phrase-final short vowel without flattening or lengthening, we know that *DUR(δ), PRES(H͡L, 1) » *CON(H͡L)-(d+d_0). Third, since it is flattened to a level tone on non-final syllables, we know that the following ranking can capture this pattern: *CON(δ_F)-(d), *DUR(δ) » PRES($\widehat{\text{HL}}$, i) (cf. Xhosa in §8.2). Therefore, the constraint hierarchy relevant to the falling tone is as in (26).

(26)

$$\begin{array}{c} *\text{CON}(\delta_F)\text{-}(d),\ *\text{DUR}(\delta) \\ \Downarrow \\ \text{PRES}(\widehat{\text{HL}}, i) \\ \Downarrow \\ \text{PRES}(\widehat{\text{HL}}, 1) \\ \Downarrow \\ *\text{CON}(\widehat{\text{HL}})\text{-}(d+d_0) \\ \Downarrow \\ *\text{CON}(\widehat{\text{HL}})\text{-}(2d) \\ \Downarrow \\ *\text{CON}(\widehat{\text{HL}})\text{-}(2d+d_1) \end{array}$$

Let us now look at the behavior of the rising tone $\widehat{\text{LH}}$. First, since it can occur on a long vowel without flattening or lengthening, we know that *DUR(δ), PRES($\widehat{\text{LH}}$, 1) » *CON($\widehat{\text{LH}}$)-($2d$) » *CON($\widehat{\text{LH}}$)-($2d+d_1$). Second, since it can occur on a phrase-final short vowel upon neutralizing lengthening, we know that PRES($\widehat{\text{LH}}$, 1), *DUR(d-$d_0+\delta$), *CON($\widehat{\text{LH}}$)-($2d$-δ) » *DUR(d-d_0), *CON($\widehat{\text{LH}}$)-($2d$). This ranking is illustrated in the tableau in (27). The first candidate, which is the faithful candidate, loses for violating the highly ranked *CON($\widehat{\text{LH}}$)-($2d$-δ), since it has a $\widehat{\text{LH}}$ tone on duration $d+d_0$, which is smaller than $2d$-δ. The third candidate loses due to extra lengthening, which causes the violation of the highly ranked *DUR(d-$d_0+\delta$). The fourth candidate loses due to insufficient lengthening and the candidate still violates *CO N($\widehat{\text{LH}}$)-($2d$-δ). The last candidate, which flatten the contour to $\widehat{\text{LM}}$, loses due to the violation of the tonal faithfulness constraint PRES($\widehat{\text{LH}}$, 1), which is highly ranked. The second candidate is the winner here since it only violates constraints in the lower stratum.

(27) $\check{V}_{d+do} \rightarrow \check{V}_{2d}$

$\check{V}_{d+do}$	PRES ($\widehat{\text{LH}}$, 1)	*DUR (d-$d_0+\delta$)	*CON($\widehat{\text{LH}}$)-($2d$-δ)	*DUR (d-d_0)	*CON($\widehat{\text{LH}}$)-($2d$)
$\check{V}_{d+do}$			*!		*
☞ $\check{V}_{2d}$				*	*
$\check{V}_{2d+\delta}$		*!		*	
$\check{V}_{2d-\delta}$			*!		*
$\check{V}_{d+do}$	*!				

Third, since $\widehat{\text{LH}}$ is flattened to a level tone on non-final syllables, but does not lengthen the vowel to a duration of $2d$, which we know is able to carry $\widehat{\text{LH}}$, the following constraint hierarchy accounts for the pattern and does not contradict the constraint hierarchy that has already been established: *CON(δ_R)-($2d$-δ), *DUR(d) » PRES(L͡H, j). This ranking is illustrated in the tableau in (28). The first, fourth, and fifth candidates all have a rising excursion on a duration less than $2d$, hence violate the highly ranked constraint *CON(δ_R)-($2d$-δ), which penalizes exact this. The third candidate, which lengthens the vowel to a duration of $2d$, violates the highly ranked *DUR(d). The second candidate, which completely flattens the rising contour, only violates the lowly ranked PRES(L͡H, j) and is therefore the winner.

(28) $\check{V}_d \rightarrow \acute{V}_d$

$\check{V}_d$	*CON(δ_R)-($2d$-δ)	*DUR(d)	PRES(L͡H, j)
$\check{V}_d$	*!		
☞ $\acute{V}_d$			*
$\check{V}_{2d}$		*!	
$\check{V}_{2d\text{-}\delta}$	*!		
$\check{V}_d$	*!		

Therefore, the constraint hierarchy relevant to the rising tone is as in (29).

(29)

*CON(L͡H)-($2d$-δ)
⇓
*CON(δ_R)-($2d$-δ), *DUR(d)
⇓
*DUR(d-d_0+δ)
⇓
PRES(L͡H, j)
⇓
PRES(L͡H, 1)
⇓
*DUR(d-d_0)
⇓
*DUR(δ)
⇓
*CON(L͡H)-($2d$)
⇓
*CON(L͡H)-($2d$+d_1)

Together with the constraint hierarchy for the falling tone, the complete constraint hierarchy for Gã is given in (30).

(30) Constraint ranking for Gã:

*CON(L͡H)-($2d$-δ)
⇓
*CON(δ_R)-($2d$-δ), *DUR(d)
⇓
*DUR(d-d_0+δ)
⇓
PRES(L͡H, j)
⇓
PRES(L͡H, 1)
⇓
*DUR(d-d_0)
⇓

*CON(δ_F)-(d)	⇒	*DUR(δ)	⇒	PRES(H͡L, i)
		⇓		⇓
		*CON(L͡H)-($2d$)		PRES(H͡L, 1)
		⇓		⇓
		*CON(L͡H)-($2d$+d_1)		*CON(H͡L)-(d+d_0)
				⇓
				*CON(H͡L)-($2d$)
				⇓
				*CON(H͡L)-($2d$+d_1)

Gã illustrates three types of asymmetry in contour tone patterning. First, long vowels are better contour tone carriers than short vowels. This is shown by the free occurrence of contour tones on long vowels and the restriction of contour tones on short vowels to phrase-final position. In the theoretical apparatus, this is captured by the intrinsic ranking among the *CONTOUR-$\mathrm{C_{CONTOUR}}$ constraints. Second, phrase-final vowels are better contour tone carriers than non-phrase-final vowels. This is shown by the facts that H͡L can occur on a final short vowel, and that L͡H can occur on a final short vowel upon neutralizing lengthening; the former is because the effect of final lengthening allows the falling tone to surface, and the latter is because the effect of final lengthening makes the extra duration needed for carrying the rising tone shorter (only an extra duration of d-d_0 is needed if the vowel is phrase-final, but an extra duration of d is needed if the vowel is phrase-medial). In the theoretical apparatus, this is captured by taking into account the effect of final lengthening in the *CONTOUR-$\mathrm{C_{CONTOUR}}$ constraints and the intrinsic ranking among *DUR constraints. Third, rising tones place a higher durational demand than falling tones. This is shown by the neutralizing lengthening that a phrase-final short vowel must undergo when it carries a rising tone. In the theoretical apparatus, this is captured by taking into account the difference in *Tonal Complexity* (see §3.2) between rising tones and falling tones and incorporating it in the grammar by way of positing intrinsic rankings among the *CONTOUR-C$_{CONTOUR}$ constraints that observe this difference.

Gã is also meant to be an illustration of how neutralizing lengthening is derived. As discussed in the factorial typology (§7.4.6), under the assumption that the short and long vowels have the duration d and $2d$ respectively, the crucial ranking for neutralizing lengthening is *CONTOUR(T)-C$_{CONTOUR}$($V_{2d\text{-}\delta}$) » *DUR(d). The crucial ranking here for Gã is *CONTOUR(L͡H)-C$_{CONTOUR}$($V_{2d\text{-}\delta}$) » *DUR(d-d_0). The highest *DUR constraint that is violated by the length-neutralizing candidate is only *DUR(d-d_0), not *DUR(d), because the short vowel in question is in phrase-final position, and final lengthening has already contributed a duration of d_0 to it.

8.5 HAUSA

Hausa syllables can be open or closed, and there is vowel length contrast in open syllables. There are three lexical tones in Hausa—H, L and H͡L. H and L tones can occur on all syllable types—CVV, CVR, CVO and CV, while H͡L can only occur on CVV, CVR and CVO. As the phonetic study discussed in §4.2.2.3 shows, the ability of CVO to carry the falling contour is contingent on two conditions: the vowel in CVO is significantly longer when it carries a falling tone than when it carries a level tone, and the falling pitch excursion on CVO is significantly smaller than that on CVV and CVR.

Therefore a more accurate description on the contour distribution in Hausa is: H͡L can freely occur on CVV and CVR; it can also occur on CVO upon lengthening of the vowel and reduction of the pitch excursion; it cannot occur on CV syllables.

Let us leave aside the CV syllables for a moment and account for the behavior of H͡L on CVV, CVR, and CVO first. Suppose that under the canonical speaking rate and style, the minimum sonorous rime duration for CVO is d, and the minimum sonorous rime duration for CVV and CVR is d+d_0+d_1. When CVO is lengthened to carry H͡L, the duration is lengthened to d+d_0, and I write CV˙O to represent the lengthened syllable. I further assume that the falling pitch excursion is Δf on CVV and CVR, but only Δf-f_0 ($0<f_0<\Delta f$) on CVO, and I write H͡M to represent the partial contour reduction.

Let us now consider the crucial constraints for Hausa from the three constraints families—*CONTOUR-C$_{CONTOUR}$, *DUR, and PRES(T).

From the *CONTOUR-C$_{CONTOUR}$ family, the crucial constraints are shown in (31). These constraints observe the intrinsic ranking in (32).

(31) a. *CONTOUR(H͡L)-C$_{CONTOUR}$(CVV)

b. *CONTOUR(H͡L)-C$_{CONTOUR}$(CVR)

c. *CONTOUR(H͡L)-C$_{CONTOUR}$(CV˙O)

d. *CONTOUR($\widehat{HL}$)-$C_{CONTOUR}$(CVO)

e. *CONTOUR($\widehat{HM}$)-$C_{CONTOUR}$(CV'O)

f. *CONTOUR($\widehat{HM}$)-$C_{CONTOUR}$(CVO)

(32) *CONTOUR($\widehat{HL}$)-$C_{CONTOUR}$(CVO) ⇒ * CONTOUR($\widehat{HM}$)-$C_{CONTOUR}$(CVO)
⇓ ⇓
*CONTOUR($\widehat{HL}$)-$C_{CONTOUR}$(CV'O) ⇒ *CONTOUR($\widehat{HM}$)-$C_{CONTOUR}$(CV'O)
⇓
*CONTOUR($\widehat{HL}$)-$C_{CONTOUR}$(CVR)
⇓
*CONTOUR($\widehat{HL}$)-$C_{CONTOUR}$(CVV)

The crucial *DUR constraints for Hausa are given in (33). The first constraint penalizes a lengthening of d_0 from the minimum duration; and with δ representing a small duration, the second constraint penalizes any lengthening that is more than d_0, and the third constraint penalizes any lengthening at all. These constraints observe the intrinsic ranking in (34).

(33) a. *DUR(d_0)

b. *DUR($d_0+\delta$)

c. *DUR(δ)

(34) *DUR($d_0+\delta$) » *DUR(d_0) » *DUR(δ)

To define the crucial constraints from the PRES(T) family, let us suppose that $\mathbb{S}_{\Delta f}(\Delta f\text{-}f_0)=i$, meaning that the partially flattened tone $\Delta f\text{-}f_0$ is i steps away from Δf on the perceptual scale. Then PRES(T, i), as defined in (35a), is a relevant constraint for Hausa. It bans flattening the falling tone to $\Delta f\text{-}f_0$. Moreover, PRES(T, $i+1$), which bans a greater degree of flattening than to $\Delta f\text{-}f_0$, and PRES(T, 1), which bans any attempts to flatten the falling contour, are also relevant, and they are defined in (35b) and (35c). The intrinsic ranking among these three constraints is shown in (36).

(35) a. PRES(T, i): do not reduce Δf to $\Delta f\text{-}f_0$.

b. PRES(T, $i+1$): do not reduce Δf to $\Delta f\text{-}f_1$. ($f_1>f_0$, $\mathbb{S}_{\Delta f}(\Delta f\text{-}f_1)=i+1$)

c. PRES(T, 1): Δf must be faithfully realized.

(36) PRES(T, $i+1$) » PRES(T, i) » PRES(T, 1).

Let us now see what the necessary rankings among these constraints are to arrive at the contour distribution pattern for Hausa.

First, we know that $\widehat{\text{HL}}$ can occur faithfully on CVV and CVR without lengthening the rime. The lack of lengthening in CVV when it carries $\widehat{\text{HL}}$ is supported phonetic data. The three disyllabic words of Hausa shown in (37), each with a high-toned long vowel in the first syllable, were recorded from the same speaker that participated in the other Hausa experiments, each with five repetitions.

(37) máárì 'to slap someone'
náákù 'yours (pl.)'
náámà 'meat'

Duration measurements show that the long vowels in the first syllable of these words have an average duration of 249ms. Compared to the 247ms derived from long vowels with a falling tone in comparable contexts, it is apparently not significantly different from it. This is confirmed by a one-way ANOVA: $F(1, 28)=0.058$, p=n.s. I assume that the rime in CVR is not lengthened either when it carries $\widehat{\text{HL}}$.

From this we deduce the ranking *DUR(δ), PRES(T, *1*) » *CONTOUR($\widehat{\text{HL}}$)-C_{CONTOUR}(CVR) » *CONTOUR($\widehat{\text{HL}}$)-C_{CONTOUR}(CVV). This is illustrated by the tableau in (38), which shows the derivation of a $\widehat{\text{HL}}$ tone on a CVV syllable. The winning candidate only violates the lowly ranked tonal markedness constraint. Flattening the contour, as the second candidate shows, and lengthening the vowel, as the third candidate shows, violate the highly ranked PRES(T) and *DUR constraints respectively.

(38) /CV́V̀/ —> [CV́V̀]

CV́V̀	*DUR(δ)	PRES(T, *1*)	*CONTOUR($\widehat{\text{HL}}$)-C_{CONTOUR}(CVV)
☞ CV́V̀			*
CV́V̄		*!	
CV́V̂V̀	*!		

Second, to account for the fact that $\widehat{\text{HL}}$ cannot occur on CVO with its canonical duration d, but can occur on a lengthened duration $d+d_0$ when its excursion is partially flattened, we need the ranking *CONTOUR($\widehat{\text{HM}}$)-C_{CONTOUR}(CVO), *CONTOUR($\widehat{\text{HL}}$)-C_{CONTOUR}(CV·O), *DUR($d_0+\delta$), PRES(T, $i+1$) » *CONTOUR($\widehat{\text{HM}}$)-C_{CONTOUR}(CV·O), *DUR(d_0), Pres(T, i). This is illustrated in the tableau in (39). The first candidate, which is the faithful candidate, violates *CONTOUR($\widehat{\text{HL}}$)-C_{CONTOUR}(CVO), which outranks *CONTOUR($\widehat{\text{HM}}$)-

C

$\mathrm{C_{CONTOUR}}$(CVO) by the intrinsic ranking given in (32). The second candidate, with partial lengthening but no flattening, violates *CONTOUR(H͡L)-$\mathrm{C_{CONTOUR}}$(CV·O). The third candidate, with partial flattening but no lengthening, violates *CONTOUR(H͡M)-$\mathrm{C_{CONTOUR}}$(CVO). The fourth candidate, with excessive lengthening, violates *DUR(d_0+δ). And the fifth candidate, with excessive flattening, violates PRES(T, i+1). These constraints that the above candidates violate outrank the constraints that the winner, which executes the right amount of contour flattening and rime lengthening, violates: *CONTOUR(H͡M)-$\mathrm{C_{CONTOUR}}$(CV·O), *DUR(d_0), and PRES(T, i).

(39) /CV̂O/ —> [CV̂·O]

CV̂O	*H͡L-CVO	*H͡M-CVO	*H͡L-CV·O	*DUR (d_0+δ)	PRES (T, i+1)	*H͡M-CV·O	*DUR (d_0)	PRES (T, i)
CV̂O	*!							
CV̂·O			*!				*	
CV̂O		*!				*		*
CV́V̀O				*!			*	
CV́O					*!			*
☞CV̂·O						*	*	*

The crucial constraint rankings for Hausa are summarized in (40). These rankings do not contradict the intrinsic rankings established above.

(40) Crucial ranking for Hausa:

*CONTOUR(H͡L)-$\mathrm{C_{CONTOUR}}$(CVO)

⇓

*CONTOUR(H͡M)-$\mathrm{C_{CONTOUR}}$(CVO), *CONTOUR(H͡L)-$\mathrm{C_{CONTOUR}}$(CV·O)
*DUR(d_0+δ), PRES(T, i+1)

⇓ ⇓

*DUR(d_0), PRES(T, i) *CONTOUR(H͡M)-$\mathrm{C_{CONTOUR}}$(CV·O)

⇓

*DUR(δ), PRES(T, 1)

⇓

*CONTOUR(H͡L)-$\mathrm{C_{CONTOUR}}$(CVR)

⇓

*CONTOUR(H͡L)-$\mathrm{C_{CONTOUR}}$(CVV)

One remaining question regarding Hausa is why CV syllables do not lengthen to carry the falling contour. From tableau (39), if a CV syllable also has a minimum vowel duration of d, it should be able to lengthen just as a CVO syllable, so that it can carry a partially flattened H͡L. Gordon (1998) provides some insight into this question: since there is vowel length contrast in open syllables while there is no such contrast in closed syllables, CVO has more freedom in subphonemic lengthening than CV because such lengthening does not jeopardize any contrast in CVO, but could potentially do so in CV. To capture this effect then, we need to distinguish two kinds of *DUR constraints: one whose violation reduces the difference between two durational contrasts and one whose violation does not. For example, *DUR(CV, d_0) belongs to the former group and *DUR(CVO, d_0) belongs to the latter group, since lengthening the vowel duration by d_0 in CV reduces the durational difference between CV and CVV by d_0, but lengthening the vowel duration in CVO does not reduce the durational difference between any contrastive pair. These two constraints are universally ranked: *DUR(CV, d_0) » *DUR(CVO, d_0).

Let us suppose that $\mathbb{S}_{\Delta f}(0)=j$ ($j>i$). Then since complete contour flattening was chosen as the solution, *DUR(CV, d_0) » PRES(T, j). This is illustrated by the mini-tableau in (41).

(41) Complete flattening of H͡L on CV: /CV̂/ → [CV́].

CV̂	*DUR(CV, d_0)	PRES(T, j)
CV̂•	*!	
☞ CV́		*

Given the intrinsic ranking PRES(T, j) » PRES(T, i), the constraint ranking for Hausa should be revised as in (42). This ranking derives all the contour distribution patterns in Hausa.

(42) Crucial ranking for Hausa (revised):

*CONTOUR(H͡L)-$C_{CONTOUR}$(CVO), *DUR(CV, d_0), PRES(T, j)

⇓

*CONTOUR(H͡M)-$C_{CONTOUR}$(CVO), *CONTOUR(H͡L)-$C_{CONTOUR}$(CV•O)
*DUR(d_0+δ), PRES(T, i+1)

⇓ ⇓

*DUR(CVO, d_0), PRES(T, i) *CONTOUR(H͡M)-$C_{CONTOUR}$(CV•O)

⇓

*DUR(δ), PRES(T, 1)

⇓

*CONTOUR(H͡L)-$C_{CONTOUR}$(CVR)

⇓

*CONTOUR(H͡L)-$C_{CONTOUR}$(CVV)

In summary, as discussed in the factorial typology, Hausa instantiates the pattern in which, on a certain syllable type, a contour tone is realized as a partially flattened pitch excursion on a lengthened rime. The OT grammar that derives it has the crucial tonal markedness constraint ranked on a par with some high-ranking *DUR and PRES(T) constraints. Consequently, the tonal markedness constraint will outrank some other *DUR and PRES(T) constraints. Then to satisfy the markedness constraint, the language chooses to simultaneously violate the lower-ranking *DUR and PRES(T) constraints, creating the part flattening, part lengthening data pattern.

8.6 LOCAL CONCLUSION

In this chapter, I have provided an analysis for one representative language for each of the five major patterns predicted by the factorial typology discussed in Chapter 7. In summary, the restriction of contour tones to syllables with greater $C_{CONTOUR}$ values (such as in Pingyao Chinese and Xhosa) is captured by the high-ranking of the relevant *CONTOUR-$C_{CONTOUR}$ constraints and *DUR constraints. Allowing contours on syllables with smaller original $C_{CONTOUR}$ values upon rime lengthening (such as in Mitla Zapotec and Gã) is captured by the high-ranking of *CONTOUR-$C_{CONTOUR}$ constraints and PRES(T) constraints. And finally, allowing contours on syllables with smaller original $C_{CONTOUR}$ values upon both partial contour flattening and rime lengthening (such as in Hausa) is captured by interleaving the *CONTOUR-$C_{CONTOUR}$ constraints with *DUR and PRES(T) constraints.

CHAPTER 9

Conclusion

I have addressed the following two general questions for phonology in this book: (a) Are positional prominence effects contrast-specific? (b) For a specific phonological contrast, is its positional prominence behavior tuned to language-specific phonetic patterns?

The phonological entity that I used to address these two questions is contour tones. Contour tones are particularly suitable for this task for the following two reasons.

First, according to the phonetic properties of contour tones, we know clearly that the duration of the sonorous portion of the rime is the most crucial factor for the production and perception of contour tones. This provides us with a testing ground for the contrast specificity of positional prominence, because we can then compare the distribution of contour tones with the distribution of other phonological features whose production and perception do not crucially rely on the abundance of sonorous rime duration—if contour tones are found to occur more freely in positions with longer sonorous rime duration, while the abundance of this duration is not a necessary condition for the occurrence of the phonological features in comparison, it can be taken as evidence for the contrast specificity of positional prominence; otherwise positional prominence is likely to be general-purpose, i.e., feature-blind.

Second, there exist multiple phonological factors that affect the duration of the sonorous portion of the rime, and the effect of these factors can be of different magnitudes. Crucially, the difference in magnitude among these phonological factors can be language-specific. This then provides us with an opportunity to address the question whether the differences in the magnitude of phonetic advantage result in differences in phonological patterning regarding positional prominence, since if in the face of the same phonological factors that affect sonorous rime duration, the distribution of contour tones accords to the language-specific magnitudes of the durational advantage induced by these factors, we will have an argument for the relevance of such phonetic details in positional prominence, and possibly phonological patterning in general. Otherwise we must conclude that the magnitude of phonetic advantage induced by the prominent position is not relevant to the phonological patterning of positional prominence.

In a typological survey of 187 languages, I found that the distribution of contour tones in a language correlates closely with the duration of the sonorous portion of the rime of different syllable types. Syllable types which have longer sonorous duration of the rime, e.g., long-vowelled, sonorant-closed, stressed, final in a prosodic domain, and being in a shorter word, are more likely to carry contour tones. This, I argue, constitutes strong support for the contrast specificity of positional prominence, since we know that final position is not a prominent position for many other phonological contrasts that do not crucially require the presence of abundant duration, e.g., [±cor] in consonants, [±high] in vowels; and initial position, which is a prominent position for many other phonological contrasts, does not much benefit contour tones, precisely because it does not provide any extra duration.

In phonetic studies of languages with the same multiple factors that induce rime lengthening, I found that contour tones always favor the factor with the greatest lengthening, even though different languages have different factors that induce the greatest lengthening. This, I argue, is evidence for the relevance of phonetic details such as the non-contrastive durational properties of different syllable types in different positions in phonological patterning.

To provide a formal account for the effects of duration and sonority on the distribution of contour tones, I propose theoretical apparatus couched in Optimality Theory. Given the wide range of cross-linguistic variations on the phonetic realization of contour tones on different types of syllables and the relevance of detailed durational properties in the distribution of contour tones shown by the phonetic studies, the theoretical apparatus necessarily encodes many phonetic details. But it is shown that the apparatus only predicts general patterns that observe the implicational hierarchies established in the contour-tone survey. It is also shown that the proposed analysis can account for both the 'phonological' effect such as the neutralization of tone and length and the 'phonetic', albeit language-specific, effect of partial contour reduction and rime lengthening.

Appendix: Data Sources for Languages in the Survey

Note: Non-italic language names in parentheses indicate aliases to the language. Italic language names in parentheses indicate the specific dialects of the language being described by the references.

Name	Classification	References
!Xóõ	Khoisan, Southern Africa, Southern, Hua	Maingard (1958), Miller-Ockhuizen (1998), Traill (1975, 1985, 1994)
!Xũ (Kung-Ekoka)	Khoisan, Southern Africa, Northern	Doke (1925), Heikkinen (1986), Snyman (1970)
Abidji	Niger-Congo, Atlantic-Congo, Volta-Congo, Kwa, Nyo, Agneby	Tresbarats (1990)
Acoma (Western Keres)	Keres	Miller (1965)
Agaw (Awiya)	Afro-Asiatic, Cushitic, Central, Southern	Hetzron (1969)
Aghem	Niger-Congo, Atlantic-Congo, Volta-Congo, Benue-Congo, Bantoid, Southern, Wide Grassfields, Narrow Grassfields	Hyman (1979)
Anren	Sino-Tibetan, Chinese, Xiang	Chen M.-H. (1995)
Apache (*Western*)	Na-Dene, Nuclear Na-Dene, Athapaskan-Eyak, Athapaskan, Apachean	Potter (1997), Potter, Dawson, de Reuss and Ladefoged (2000)
Apatani	Sino-Tibetan, Tibeto-Burman, Baric, Mirish	Abraham (1985)

Babungo (Vengo)	Niger-Congo, Atlantic-Congo, Volta-Congo, Benue-Congo, Bantoid, Southern, Wide-Grassfields, Narrow Grassfields	Schaub (1985)
Bamileke	Niger-Congo, Atlantic-Congo, Volta-Congo, Benue-Congo, Bantoid, Southern, Wide-Grassfields, Narrow Grassfields	Voorhoeve (1971)
Bandi	Niger-Congo, Mande, Western	Mugele and Rodewald (1991)
Bari	Nilo-Saharan, Eastern Sudanic, Nilotic, Eastern, Bari	Yokwe (1987)
Beijing	Sino-Tibetan, Chinese, Mandarin	Chao (1948, 1968), Dow (1972, 1974)
Beja (Bedawi)	Afro-Asiatic, Cushitic, North	Hudson (1973)
Bolanci (Bole)	Afro-Asiatic, Chadic, West, A	Gimba (1998), Schuh (1991)
Brao	Austro-Asiatic, Mon-Khmer, Eastern Mon-Khmer, Bahnaric, West Bahnaric	Keller (1976)
Bugan	Austro-Asiatic, Mon-Khmer, Unclassified	Li J.-F. (1996)
Caddo	Caddoan, Southern	Chafe (1976)
Camus	Nilo-Saharan, Eastern Sudanic, Nilotic, Eastern, Lotuxo-Maa, Ongamo-Maa	Heine (1980)
Cantonese	Sino-Tibetan, Chinese, Yue	Gordon (1998), Kao (1971), Li, Chen and Mai (1995)
Chaga (*Kivunjo*)	Niger-Congo, Atlantic-Congo, Volta-Congo, Benue-Congo, Bantoid, Southern, Narrow Bantu, Central, D	McHugh (1990a, b)
Chaga (*Machame*)	Niger-Congo, Atlantic-Congo, Volta-Congo, Benue-Congo, Bantoid, Southern, Narrow Bantu, Central, D	Sharp (1954)
Changzhi	Sino-Tibetan, Chinese, Jinyu	Hou (1983, 1985)
Changzhou	Sino-Tibetan, Chinese, Wu	Wang P. (1988)
Chaoyang	Sino-Tibetan, Chinese, Min Nan	Zhang S.-Y.(1979, 1980)
Chengdu	Sino-Tibetan, Chinese, Mandarin	Cui (1997)

Cherokee (*Oklahoma*)	Iroquoian, Southern Iroquoian	Munro (1996a, b), Wright (1996)
Chichewa	Niger-Congo, Atlantic-Congo, Volta-Congo, Benue-Congo, Bantoid, Southern, Narrow Bantu, Central, N	Trihart (1976)
Chilcotin	Na-Dene, Nuclear Na-Dene, Athapaskan-Eyak, Athapaskan, Canadian, Carrier-Chilcotin	Cook (1989)
Chin (*Tiddim, Tedim*)	Sino-Tibetan, Tibeto-Burman, Baric, Kuki-Naga, Kuki-Chin, Northern	Weidert (1987)
Chinantec (*Comaltepec*)	Oto-Manguean, Chinantecan	Anderson, Martínez and Pace (1990), Pace (1990)
Chinantec (*Lalama*)	Oto-Manguean, Chinantecan	Mugele (1982)
Chinantec (*Lealao*)	Oto-Manguean, Chinantecan	Rupp (1990)
Chinantec (*Quiotepec*)	Oto-Manguean, Chinantecan	Gardner and Merrifield (1990), Robbins (1961)
Chongming	Sino-Tibetan, Chinese, Wu	Zhang H.-Y. (1979, 1980)
Ciyao	Niger-Congo, Atlantic-Congo, Volta-Congo, Benue-Congo, Bantoid, Southern, Narrow Bantu, Central, P	Hyman and Ngunga (1994), Mtenje (1993), Sanderson (1954), Whiteley (1966)
Crow	Siouan, Siouan Proper	Kaschube (1954, 1967)
Datooga	Nilo-Saharan, Eastern Sudanic, Nilotic, Southern	Rottland (1983)
Dholuo (Luo)	Nilo-Saharan, Eastern Sudanic, Nilotic, Western	Okoth-Okombo (1982), Omondi (1982)
Didinga	Nilo-Saharan, Eastern Sudanic, Eastern, Surmic, South	Odden (1983)
Dong (*Southern*)	Daic, Kam-Sui	Long and Zheng (1998)
Elmolo	Afro-Asiatic, Cushitic, East, Western Omo-Tana	Heine (1980)
Etung	Niger-Congo, Atlantic-Congo, Volta-Congo, Benue-Congo, Bantoid, Southern, Ekoid	Edmondson and Bendor-Samuel (1966)
Fuzhou	Sino-Tibetan, Chinese, Min Dong	Liang and Feng (1996)

Gã (Ga)	Niger-Congo, Atlantic-Congo, Volta-Congo, Kwa, Nyo, Ga-Dangme	Paster (1999)
Galla (Booran Oromo)	Afro-Asiatic, Cushitic, Eastern, Oromo	Owens (1980)
Gelao	Daic, Kadai	He (1983)
Guiyang	Sino-Tibetan, Chinese, Mandarin	Li L. (1997)
Haikou	Sino-Tibetan, Chinese, Min Nan	Chen (1997)
Hausa	Afro-Asiatic, Chadic, West, A	Newman (1986, 1990)
Haya	Niger-Congo, Atlantic-Congo, Volta-Congo, Benue-Congo, Bantoid, Southern, Narrow Bantu, Central, J	Byarushengo et al. (1976), Hyman and Byarushengo (1984)
Hefei	Sino-Tibetan, Chinese, Mandarin	Li J. (1997)
Hmong (*Tananshan*)	Miao-Yao, Miao	Miao Language Team (1972)
Huojia	Sino-Tibetan, Chinese, Mandarin	He (1979)
Igbo	Niger-Congo, Atlantic-Congo, Volta-Congo, Benue-Congo, Igboid	Clark (1983, 1990), Green and Igwe (1963), Liberman et al. (1993)
Jemez (Towa)	Kiowa Tanoan, Kiowa-Towa	Bell (1993)
Ju|'hoasi (Kung-Tsumkwe)	Khoisan, Southern Africa, Northern	Dicksens (1994), Elderkin (1988), Maingard (1957), Miller-Ockhuizen (1998), Snyman (1975)
Kambari	Niger-Congo, Atlantic-Congo, Volta-Congo, Benue-Congo, Kainji, Western	Meeusssen (1970)
Kanakuru	Afro-Asiatic, Chadic, West, A	Newman (1974)
Kenyang	Niger-Congo, Atlantic-Congo, Volta-Congo, Benue-Congo, Bantoid, Southern, Mamfe, Central	Odden (1988)
Khamti	Daic, Tai, Southwestern, East Central	Weidert (1977)
Kikuyu	Niger-Congo, Atlantic-Congo, Volta-Congo, Benue-Congo, Bantoid, Southern, Narrow Bantu, Central, E	Armstrong (1940), Ford (1975), Pratt (1972)

Kimbundu	Niger-Congo, Atlantic-Congo, Volta-Congo, Benue-Congo, Bantoid, Southern, Narrow Bantu, Central, R	Arvanites (1976)
Kinande	Niger-Congo, Atlantic-Congo, Volta-Congo, Benue-Congo, Bantoid, Southern, Narrow Bantu, Central, J	Mutaka (1994)
Kinyarwanda	Niger-Congo, Atlantic-Congo, Volta-Congo, Benue-Congo, Bantoid, Southern, Narrow Bantu, Central, J	Kimenyi (1976, 1979)
Kiowa	Kiowa Tanoan, Kiowa-Towa	Watkins (1984)
Kisi (Kissi)	Niger-Congo, Atlantic-Congo, Atlantic, Southern, Mel	Childs (1995)
Kitsai	Caddoan, Northern	Bucca and Lesser (1969)
Konni	Niger-Congo, Atlantic-Congo, Volta-Congo, North, Gur, Central, Northern	Cahill (1999)
Korana	Khoisan, Southern Africa, Central, Nama	Beach (1938)
Kpele	Niger-Congo, Mande, Western	Meeussen (1970)
Kru (*Nana*)	Niger-Congo, Atlantic-Congo, Volta-Congo, Kru	Elimelech (1974)
Kru (*Wobe*)	Niger-Congo, Atlantic-Congo, Volta-Congo, Kru	Bearth and Link (1980)
Kunming	Sino-Tibetan, Chinese, Mandarin	Mao (1997)
Kukuya (Southern Teke)	Niger-Congo, Atlantic-Congo, Volta-Congo, Benue-Congo, Bantoid, Southern, Narrow Bantu, Northwest, B	Paulian (1974), Hyman (1987)
Lahu	Sino-Tibetan, Tibeto-Burman, Burmese-Lolo, Lolo, Southern	Burling (1967), Chang (1986), Maran (1971), Matisoff (1973a)
Lakkja	Miao-Yao, Yao	Mao and Zhou (1972), Mao et al. (1982)
Lama	Niger-Congo, Atlantic-Congo, Volta-Congo, North, Gur, Central, Southern	Kenstowicz, Nikiema and Ourso (1988), Ourso (1989), Kenstowicz (1994)

Lamba	Niger-Congo, Atlantic-Congo, Volta-Congo, Benue-Congo, Bantoid, Southern, Narrow Bantu, Central, M	Bickmore (1995)
Lango	Nilo-Saharan, Eastern Sudanic, Nilotic, Western	Noonan (1992)
Lanzhou	Sino-Tibetan, Chinese, Mandarin	Wang and Zhao (1997)
Lao	Daic, Tai, Southwestern, East Central	Morev (1979)
Lisu	Sino-Tibetan, Tibeto-Burman, Burmese-Lolo, Lolo, Northern	Burling (1967), Maran (1971), Xu et al. (1986)
Lithuanian	Indo-European, Baltic	Kenstowicz (1972), Young (1991)
Logo	Nilo-Saharan, Central Sudanic, East	Goyvaerts (1983)
Lokele	Niger-Congo, Atlantic-Congo, Volta-Congo, Benue-Congo, Bantoid, Southern, Narrow Bantu, Northwest, C	Carrington (1943)
Luganda	Niger-Congo, Atlantic-Congo, Volta-Congo, Benue-Congo, Bantoid, Southern, Narrow Bantu, Central, J	Ashton et al. (1954), Hyman and Katamba (1990,1993), Snoxall (1967), Stevick (1969), Tucker (1962)
Lulubo	Nilo-Saharan, Central Sudanic, East	Anderson (1987)
Lushai	Sino-Tibetan, Tibeto-Burman, Baric, Kuki-Naga, Kuki-Chin, Central	Weidert (1975, 1987)
Lüsi	Sino-Tibetan, Chinese, Wu	Lu (1994)
Maasai	Nilo-Saharan, Eastern Sudanic, Nilotic, Eastern, Lotuxo-Maa, Ongamo-Maa	Tucker and Mpaayei (1955)
Makonde (*Chimahuta*)	Niger-Congo, Atlantic-Congo, Volta-Congo, Benue-Congo, Bantoid, Southern, Narrow Bantu, Central, P	Odden (1990)
Makonde (*Chimaraba*)	Niger-Congo, Atlantic-Congo, Volta-Congo, Benue-Congo, Bantoid, Southern, Narrow Bantu, Central, P	Odden (1990)
Maonan	Daic, Kam-Sui	Liang (1980)

Margi	Afro-Asiatic, Chadic, Biu-Mandara, A	Hoffman (1963), Williams (1976), Tranel (1992-1994)
Mazatec (*Chiquihuitlan*)	Oto-Manguean, Popolocan, Mazatecan	Jamieson (1977)
Mbum	Niger-Congo, Atlantic-Congo, Volta-Congo, North, Adamawa-Ubangi	Meeussen (1970)
Meidob	Nilo-Saharan, Eastern Sudanic, Eastern, Nubian, Western	Thelwall (1983b)
Mende	Niger-Congo, Mande, Western	Brown (1982), Conteh et al. (1983), Cowper and Rice (1985), Dwyer (1971, 1978, 1985), Innes (1963, 1969), Leben (1971, 1973, 1978), Spears (1967), Ward (1944)
Mianmin	Trans-New Guinea, Main Section, Central and Western, Central and South New Guinea-Kutubuan, Central and South New Guinea, Ok, Mountain	Smith and Weston (1974)
Mixtec (*Jicaltepec*)	Oto-Manguean, Mixtecan, Mixtec-Cuicatec	Bradley (1970)
Mjen (Mien)	Miao-Yao, Yao	Mao and Zhou (1972), Mao et al. (1982)
Mocha (Shakicho)	Afro-Asiatic, Omotic, North	Leslau (1958)
Mumuye (*Zing*)	Niger-Congo, Atlantic-Congo, Volta-Congo, North, Adamawa-Ubangi	Shimuzu (1983)
Muong	Austro-Asiatic, Mon-Khmer, Viet-Muong, Muong	Barker (1966, 1968)
Musey	Afro-Asiatic, Chadic, Masa	Shryock (1993a, 1996)
Naga (*Chang*)	Sino-Tibetan, Tibeto-Burman, Baric, Konyak-Bodo-Garo, Konyak	Weidert (1987)
Naga (*Rongmei*)	Sino-Tibetan, Tibeto-Burman, Baric, Kuki-Naga, Naga	Weidert (1987)
Nama	Khoisan, Southern Africa, Central, Nama	Beach (1938), Davey (1977), Hagman (1977)

Nanchang	Sino-Tibetan, Chinese, Gan	Xiong (1979)
Nandi (Kalenjin)	Nilo-Saharan, Eastern Sudanic, Nilotic, Southern, Kalenjin, Nandi-Markweta	Creider (1980), Tucker (1964)
Nanjing	Sino-Tibetan, Chinese, Mandarin	Liu (1997)
Naro	Khoisan, Southern Africa, Central, Tshu-Khwe, Southwest	Visser (1998)
Navajo (Navaho)	Na-Dene, Nuclear Na-Dene, Athapaskan-Eyak, Athapaskan, Apachean	Wall and Morgan (1958), Sapir and Hoijer (1967), Hoijer (1974), Kari (1976), Young and Morgan (1992)
Ng'huki (*ǂKhomani*)	Khoisan, Southern Africa, Southern, !Kwi	Doke (1937)
Ngamambo	Niger-Congo, Atlantic-Congo, Volta-Congo, Benue-Congo, Bantoid, Southern, Wide-Grassfields, Narrow Grassfields	Asongwed and Hyman (1976)
Ngazija	Niger-Congo, Atlantic-Congo, Volta-Congo, Benue-Congo, Bantoid, Southern, Narrow Bantu, Central, G	Tucker (1970)
Ngie	Niger-Congo, Atlantic-Congo, Volta-Congo, Benue-Congo, Bantoid, Southern, Wide-Grassfields, Narrow Grassfields	Hombert (1976a)
Ngizim	Afro-Asiatic, Chadic, West, B	Schuh (1971, 1981)
Ngumbi (Kombe)	Niger-Congo, Atlantic-Congo, Volta-Congo, Benue-Congo, Bantoid, Southern, Narrow Bantu, Northwest, C	Elimelech (1976)
Ningbo	Sino-Tibetan, Chinese, Wu	Chen N.-P. (1985)
Nubi	Creole, Arabic based	Heine (1982)
Nupe	Niger-Congo, Atlantic-Congo, Volta-Congo, Benue-Congo, Nupoid	Meeussen (1970)
Ocaina (Huitoto)	Witotoan, Witoto, Ocaina	Agnew and Pike (1957)

Ólusamia	Niger-Congo, Atlantic-Congo, Volta-Congo, Benue-Congo, Bantoid, Southern, Narrow Bantu, Central, J	Chagas (1976)
Päkot (Pökoot)	Nilo-Saharan, Eastern Sudanic, Nilotic, Southern, Kalenjin, Pokot	Tucker (1964)
Pingyang	Sino-Tibetan, Chinese, Wu	Chen (1979)
Pingyao	Sino-Tibetan, Chinese, Jinyu	Hou (1980, 1982a, b)
Pirahã (Mura-Pirahã)	Mura	Everett and Everett (1984), Everett (1986, 1988)
Popoloca (*Tlacoyalco*)	Oto-Manguean, Popolocan, Chocho-Popolocan	Stark and Machin (1977)
Punu	Miao-Yao, Miao	Mao and Zhou (1972), Mao et al. (1982)
Rendille	Afro-Asiatic, Cushitic, East, Rendille-Boni	Heine (1980)
Runyankore (Nkore)	Niger-Congo, Atlantic-Congo, Volta-Congo, Benue-Congo, Bantoid, Southern, Narrow Bantu, Central, J	Johnson (1976)
Saek	Daic, Tai, Northern	Hudak (1993)
Samburu (*Chamus*)	Nilo-Saharan, Eastern Sudanic, Nilotic, Eastern	Heine (1980)
Sandawe	Khoisan, Sandawe	Elderkin (1998)
Sarcee (Sarsi)	Na-Dene, Nuclear Na-Dene, Athapaskan-Eyak, Athapaskan, Canadian, Sarcee	Cook (1984)
Sayanci	Afro-Asiatic, Chadic, West, B	Schneeberg (1971)
Sechuana	Niger-Congo, Atlantic-Congo, Volta-Congo, Benue-Congo, Bantoid, Southern, Narrow Bantu, Central, S	Jones (1928)
Sekani	Na-Dene, Nuclear Na-Dene, Athapaskan-Eyak, Athapaskan, Canadian, Beaver-Sekani	Hargus (1988)
Shanghai	Sino-Tibetan, Chinese, Wu	You (1994), Zee and Maddieson (1979)
Shantou	Sino-Tibetan, Chinese, Min Nan	Shi (1997)
Shexian	Sino-Tibetan, Chinese, Huizhou	Meng (1997)

Shi	Niger-Congo, Atlantic-Congo, Volta-Congo, Benue-Congo, Bantoid, Southern, Narrow Bantu, Central, J	Polak-Bynon (1975)
Shuozhou	Sino-Tibetan, Chinese, Jinyu	Jiang (1991)
Siane	Trans-New Guinea, Main Section, Central and Western, East New Guinea Highlands, East-Central	James (1981), Kenstowicz (1994)
So (Thavung)	Austro-Asiatic, Mon-Khmer, Viet-Muong, Thavung	Suwilai (1996)
Somali	Afro-Asiatic, Cushitic, East	Saeed (1982, 1993)
Sre	Austro-Asiatic, Mon-Khmer, Eastern Mon-Khmer, Bahnaric, South Bahnaric	Manley (1972)
Suzhou	Sino-Tibetan, Chinese, Wu	Xie (1982), Ye (1979), Ye and Sheng (1996)
Thai (*Ron Phibun*)	Daic, Tai, Southwestern, Southern	Thompson (1998)
Thai (*Songkhla*)	Daic, Tai, Southwestern, Southern	Henderson (1959)
Thai (*Standard*)	Daic, Tai, Southwestern, East Central	Abramson (1962), Davies (1979), Gandour (1974)
Taishan	Sino-Tibetan, Chinese, Yue	Cheng (1973)
Tibetan (*Lhasa*)	Sino-Tibetan, Tibeto-Burman, Bodic, Bodish, Tibetan	Duanmu (1992), Hu et al. (1982), Jin (1983)
Tibetan (*Rgyalthang*)	Sino-Tibetan, Tibeto-Burman, Bodic, Bodish, Tibetan	Hongladarom (1996), Wang (1996)
Tiv	Niger-Congo, Atlantic-Congo, Volta-Congo, Benue-Congo, Bantoid, Southern, Tivoid	Abraham (1940), Arnott (1964), McCawley (1970), Pulleyblank (1986)
Toposa	Nilo-Saharan, Eastern Sudanic, Nilotic, Eastern	Dimmendaal (1983c)
Trique (*San Andrés Chichahuaxtla*)	Oto-Manguean, Mixtecan, Trique	Hollenbach (1977)
Trique (*San Juan Copala*)	Oto-Manguean, Mixtecan, Trique	Hollenbach (1977)
Tunxi	Sino-Tibetan, Chinese, Huizhou	Qian (1997)

Turkana	Nilo-Saharan, Eastern Sudanic, Nilotic, Eastern	Dimmendaal (1981, 1983a, b, c)
Venda	Niger-Congo, Atlantic-Congo, Volta-Congo, Benue-Congo, Bantoid, Southern, Narrow Bantu, Central, S	Cassimjee (1983, 1987), Kenstowicz (1994)
Vietnamese	Austro-Asiatic, Mon-Khmer, Viet-Muong, Vietnamese	Han (1969), Nguyen (1970)
Wenling	Sino-Tibetan, Chinese, Wu	Li (1979)
Wuhan	Sino-Tibetan, Chinese, Mandarin	Liu and Xiang (1997)
Wuyi	Sino-Tibetan, Chinese, Wu	Fu (1984)
Xhosa	Niger-Congo, Atlantic-Congo, Volta-Congo, Benue-Congo, Bantoid, Southern, Narrow Bantu, Central, S, Nguni	Claughton (1983), Jordan (1966), Lanham (1958, 1963)
Xi'an	Sino-Tibetan, Chinese, Mandarin	Wang (1997)
Xiangtan	Sino-Tibetan, Chinese, Xiang	Zeng (1997)
Xining	Sino-Tibetan, Chinese, Mandarin	Zhang C.-C. (1997)
Xinzhou	Sino-Tibetan, Chinese, Jinyu	Wen (1985), Wen and Zhang (1994)
Yanggu	Sino-Tibetan, Chinese, Mandarin	Dong (1993)
Yangqu	Sino-Tibetan, Chinese, Jinyu	Meng (1991)
Yinchuan	Sino-Tibetan, Chinese, Mandarin	Gao and Zhang (1997)
Yong	Daic, Tai, Southwestern	Davies (1979)
Yoruba	Niger-Congo, Atlantic-Congo, Volta-Congo, Benue-Congo, Defoid, Yoruboid	Abraham (1958), Courtenay (1971), Hombert (1976b), La Velle (1974), Laniran (1992)
Yudu	Sino-Tibetan, Chinese, Hakka	Xie (1992)
Zapotec (*Isthmus*)	Oto-Manguean, Zapotecan, Zapotec	Pickett (1967)
Zapotec (*Macuitianguis*)	Oto-Manguean, Zapotecan, Zapotec	Broadwell and Zhang (1999)
Zapotec (*Mitla*)	Oto-Manguean, Zapotecan, Zapotec	Briggs (1961)
Zapotec (*Sierra Juarez*)	Oto-Manguean, Zapotecan, Zapotec	Bickmore and Broadwell (1998), Marks (1976), Nellis and Nellis (1983)
Zengcheng	Sino-Tibetan, Chinese, Yue	He (1986, 1987)
Zhangping	Sino-Tibetan, Chinese, Min Nan	Zhang (1982a, b, 1983)

Zhenjiang	Sino-Tibetan, Chinese, Mandarin	Zhang (1985)
Zulu	Niger-Congo, Atlantic-Congo, Volta-Congo, Benue-Congo, Bantoid, Southern, Narrow Bantu, Central, S, Nguni	Cope (1959, 1970)

References

Abraham, P.T. (1985). *Apatani grammar. CIIL (Central Institute of Indian Languages) Grammar Series* 12. Manasgangotri, Mysore-570 006.

Abraham, Roy Clive (1940). *The principles of Tiv.* Crown Agents for the Colonies London, UK.

——— (1958). *Dictionary of modern Yoruba.* University of London Press Ltd. London, UK.

Abramson, Arthur S. (1962). *The vowels and tones of Standard Thai: Acoustical measurements and experiments.* Publication 20, Indiana University Research Center in Anthropology, Folkflore and Linguistics. *International Journal of American Linguistics* 28.2, part III.

Adams, Corinne and R.R. Munro (1978). In search of the acoustic correlates of stress: fundamental frequency, amplitude, and duration in the connected utterance of some native and non-native speakers of English. *Phonetica* 35: 125-156.

Agnew, Arlene and Euelyn G. Pike (1957). Phonemes of Ocaina (Huitoto). *International Journal of American Linguistics* 23.1: 24-27.

Alderete, John (1995). *Faithfulness to prosodic heads.* Rutgers Optimality Archive, ROA-94-0000.

———, Jill Beckman, Laura Benua, Amalia Gnanadesikan, John McCarthy, and Susanne Urbanczyk (1996). *Reduplication and segmental unmarkedness.* Ms., University of Massachusetts, Amherst.

Allen, Jonathan, M. Sharon Hunnicutt, and Dennis Klatt, with Robert C. Armstrong and David Pisoni (1987). *From text to speech: The MITalk system.* Cambridge University Press, Cambridge, UK.

Anderson, Judi Lynn, Isaac H. Martínez and Wanda Pace (1990). Comaltepec Chinantec tone. In William R. Merrifield and Calvin R. Rensch (eds.), *Syllables, tone and verb paradigms. Studies in Chinantec Languages* 4: 3-20. Summer Institute of Linguistics and the University of Texas at Arlington Publications in Linguistics, Publication, No. 95.

Anderson, Torben (1987). An outline of Lulubo phonology. *Studies in African Linguistics* 18.1: 39-65.

Ao, Benjamin (1993). *Phonetics and phonology of Nantong Chinese.* Ph.D. dissertation, The Ohio State University.

Archangeli, Diana (1991). Syllabification and prosodic templates in Yawelmani. *Natural Language and Linguistic Theory* 9: 231-283.

Armstrong, Lilias E. (1940). *The phonetic and tonal structure of Kikuyu*. Oxford University Press, London, UK.

Arnold, G.E. (1961). Physiology and pathology of the cricothyroid muscle. *Laryngoscope* 71: 687-753.

Arnott, David W. (1964). Downstep in the Tiv verbal system. *African Language Studies* 5: 34-51.

Arvanites, Linda (1976). Kimbundu nominals: Tone patterns in two contexts. In Larry M. Hyman (ed.), *Studies in Bantu Tonology, Southern California Occasional Papers in Linguistics*, No. 3: 131-140.

Ashton, E.O., E.M.K. Mulira, E.G.M. Ndawula and A.N. Tucker (1954). *A Luganda grammar*. Longmans, Green and Co., London, New York, Toronto.

Asongwed, Tah and Larry M. Hyman (1976). Morphotonology of the Ngamambo noun. In Larry M. Hyman (ed.), *Studies in Bantu tonology, Southern California Occasional Papers in Linguistics* 3: 23-56.

Bao, Zhiming (1990). *On the nature of tone*. Ph.D. dissertation, MIT.

Barker, Milton E. (1966). Vietnamese-Muong tone correspondences. In Norman H. Zide (ed.), *Studies in comparative Austroasiatic linguistics*: 9-27. The Hague, Mouton & Co.

——— (1968). The phonemes of Mu'ong. *Studies in Linguistics* 20, 59-62.

Beach, D.M. (1924). The science of tonetics and its application to Bantu languages. *Bantu Studies* 2: 75-106.

——— (1938). *The phonetics of the Hottentot languages*. W. Heffer & Sons Ltd., Cambridge, UK.

Bearth, Thomas and Christa Link (1980). The tone puzzle of Wobe. *Studies in African Linguistics* 11.2: 147-207.

Beckman, Jill (1997). *Positional faithfulness*. Ph.D. dissertation, University of Massachusetts, Amherst.

Beckman, Mary E. and Jan Edwards (1990). Lengthening and shortening and the nature of prosodic constituency. In John Kingston and Mary E. Beckman (eds.), *Papers in the laboratory phonology I: Between the grammar and the physics of speech*: 152-178. Cambridge University Press, Cambridge, UK.

Bell, Alan (1993). Jemez tones and stress. *Colorado Research in Linguistics* 12: 26-34.

Bender, M. Lionel (1983). Majang phonology and morphology. In M. Lionel Bender (ed.), *Nilo-Saharan language studies*: 114-147. Michigan State University, East Lansing, MI.

Bendor, Byron W. (1971). Micronesian languages. In Thomas A. Sebeok, J. Donald Bowen, Isidore Dyen, George W. Grace, Stephan A. Wurm, and Geoffrey N. O'Grady (eds.), *Current trends in linguistics, Vol. 8: Linguistics in Oceania*: 426-265. Mouton, The Hague, The Netherlands.

Benett, Tina (1976). Tonally irregular verbs in Chishona. In Larry M. Hyman (ed.), *Studies in Bantu tonology, Southern California Occasional Papers in Linguistics* 3: 287-319.

Bernard, H. Russell (1966). Otomi tones. *Anthropological Linguistics* 8.9: 15-19.

Bickmore, Lee (1995). Tone and stress in Lamba. *Phonology* 12.3: 307-341.

——— and Aaron Broadwell (1998). High tone docking in Sierra Juárez Zapotec. *International Journal of American Linguistics* 64.1: 37-67.

Black, John W (1970). The magnitude of pitch inflection. *Proceedings of the 6th International Congress of Phonetic Sciences*: 177-181. Prague.

Bladon, Anthony (1985). Diphthongs: A case study of dynamic auditory processing. In *Speech Communication*, Vol. 4, Nos. 1-3, Special issue in honour of Ludmilla Andreevna Chistovich: 145-154.

——— (1986). Phonetics for hearers. In Graham McGregor (ed.), *Language for hearers*: 1-24. Pergamon Press, Oxford, UK; New York, NY, USA.

——— and Ameen Al-Bamerni (1976). Coarticulation resistance in English /l/. *Journal of Phonetics* 4: 137-150.

Bochner, Joseph H., Karen B. Snell and Douglas J. MacKenzie (1988). Duration discrimination of speech and tonal complex stimuli by normally hearing and hearing-impaired listeners. *Journal of the Acoustical Society of America* 84: 493-500.

Boersma, Paul (1998). *Functional phonology: Formalizing the interaction between articulatory and perceptual drives*. Holland Academic Graphics, The Hague, The Netherlands.

Borden, Gloria J., Katherine S. Harris and Lawrence J. Raphael (1994). *Speech science primer: Physiology, acoustics and perception of speech*, 3rd edition. Williams and Wilkins, Baltimore, MD.

Bradley, C. Henry (1970). *A linguistic sketch of Jicaltepec Mixtec. Summer Institute of Linguistics Publications in Linguistics and Related Fields*, Publication, No. 25.

Briggs, Elinor (1961). *Mitla Zapotec grammar*. Instituto Linguistico de Verano, Mexico.

Broadwell, Aaron and Jie Zhang (1999). *Tonal alignment constraints and the nature of evaluation*. Paper presented at the 73rd Annual Meeting of Linguistic Society of America, Los Angeles.

Broselow, Ellen (1995). Skeletal positions and moras. In John A. Goldsmith (ed.), *Handbook of phonological theory*: 175-205. Blackwell Publishers, Oxford, UK.

Browman, Catherine and Louis Goldstein (1995). Gestural syllable position effects in American English. In Fredericka Bell-Berti and Lawrence J. Raphael (eds.), *Producing speech: A festschrift for Katherine Safford Harris*: 19-34. American Institute of Physics Press, New York, NY.

Brown, R. and D. McNeill (1966). The 'tip-of the-tongue' phenomenon. *Journal of Verbal Learning and Verbal Behavior* 5: 325–337.

Brown, S. (1982). *A Mende grammar with tones*. U.C.C. Literature Bureau, Bo—Sierra Leone.

Bucca, Salvador and Alexander Lesser (1969). Kitsai phonology and morphophonemics. *International Journal of American Linguistics* 35.1: 7-19.

Burling, Robbins (1967). *Proto Lolo-Burmese. Indiana University Publication in Anthropology and Linguistics*, Publication 43. University of Indiana Press, Bloomington, Indiana. The Hague, Mouton & Co.

Byarushengo, Ernest R., Larry M. Hyman and Sarah Tenenbaum (1976). Tone accent and assertion in Haya. In Larry M. Hyman (ed.), *Studies in Bantu tonology, Southern California Occasional Papers in Linguistics* 3: 183-205.

Cahill, Michael (1999). *Aspects of the morphology and phonology of Kɔnni*. Ph.D. dissertation, The Ohio State University.

Carrington, J.F. (1943). The tonal structure of Kele (Lokele). *African Studies* 2: 193-209.

Cassimjee, Farida (1983). An autosegmental analysis of Venda nominal tonology. *Studies in the Linguistic Sciences* 13.1: 43-72.

——— (1987). *An autosegmental analysis of Venda tonology*. Ph.D. dissertation, University of Illinois, Urbana Champaign.

Chafe, Wallace L. (1976). *The Caddoan, Iroquoian and Siouan languages*. The Hague, Mouton & Co.

Chagas, Jeremy E. (1976). The tonal structure of Ólusamia. In Larry M. Hyman (ed.), *Studies in Bantu Tonology, Southern California Occasional Papers in Linguistics*, No. 3: 217-240.

Chai, Nemia M. (1971). *A grammar of Aklan*. Ph.D. dissertation, University of Pennsylvania, Philadelphia.

Chan, Marjorie Kit-Man (1985). *Fuzhou phonology: A non-linear analysis of tone and stress*. Ph.D. dissertation, University of Washington.

Chan, Ningping (1985). Tone sandhi phenomenon in Ninponese. *Fangyan* (Dialects) 1985: 15-27.

Chang, Hongen (1986). *Lahuyu jianzhi* (A grammatical sketch of the Lahu language). *Zhongguo shaoshu minzu yuyan jianzhi congshu* (A collection of grammatical sketches of the minority languages in China). Minzu Chubanshe (The Nationality Publishing House), Beijing.

Chao, Yuen Ren (1948). *Mandarin primer: An intensive course in spoken Chinese*. Harvard University Press, Cambridge, MA.

——— (1968). *A grammar of spoken Chinese*. University of California Press, Berkeley and Los Angeles, CA.

Chen, Cheng-Rong (1979). Pingyang fangyan jilüe (A sketch of the Pingyang dialects). *Fangyan* (Dialects) 1979.1: 47-74.

Chen, Hongmai (1997). *Haikouhua yindang* (The sound record of Haikou). Jing-Yi Hou (ed.), *Xiandai hanyu fangyan yinku* (The sound archives of modern Chinese dialects). Shanghai Jiaoyu Chubanshe (Shanghai Education Publishing House), Shanghai.

Chen, Manhua (1995). *Anren fangyan* (The Anren dialect). Beijing Yuyan Xueyuan Chubanshe (Beijing Language Institute Press), Beijing.

Chen, Matthew Y. (1970). Vowel length variation as a function of the voicing of the consonant environment. *Phonetica* 22: 129-159.

——— (2000). *Tone sandhi: Patterns across Chinese dialects*. Cambridge University Press, Cambridge, UK.

Cheng, Teresa M. (1973). The phonology of Taishan. *Journal of Chinese Linguistics* 1.2: 256-322.

Childs, G. Tucker (1995). *A grammar of Kisi—A southern Atlantic language. Mouton Grammar Library* 16. Mouton de Gruyter, Berlin, New York.

Cho, Taehong, and Patricia Keating (2001). Articulatory and acoustic studies of domain-initial strengthening in Korean. *Journal of Phonetics* 29: 155-190.

Choi, John (1992). *Phonetic underspecification and target interpolation: An acoustic study of Marshallese vowel allophony*. Ph.D. dissertation, UCLA. Distributed as *UCLA Working Papers in Phonetics* 82.

Clark, Mary M. (1983). On the distribution of contour tones. *Proceedings of WCCFL* 2: 44-55.

——— (1990). *The tonal system of Igbo. Publications in African languages and linguistics* 10. Foris Publication, Dordrecht.

Claughton, John S. (1983). *The tones of Xhosa inflections. Communication* no. 13. Dept. of African Languages, Rhodes University, Grahamstown.

Clements, George N. (1984). Principles of tone assignment in Kikuyu. In George N. Clements and John Goldsmith (eds.), Autosegmental studies in Bantu tone: 281-339. Foris Publications, Dordrecht.

——— and Kevin C. Ford (1979). Kikuyu tone shift and its synchronic consequences. *Linguistic Inquiry* 10: 95-108.

Cohn, Abigail C. (1990). *Phonetic and phonological rules of nasalisation*. Ph.D. dissertation, UCLA. Distributed as *UCLA Working Papers in Phonetics* 76.

——— (1993). Nasalisation in English: Phonology or phonetics. *Phonology* 10: 43-81.

Cole, Ronald A. and Jola Jakimik (1978). Understanding speech: How words are heard. In Geoffrey Underwood (ed.), *Strategies of information processing*: 67-116. Academic Press, London, UK.

Collier, René, Fredericka Bell-Berti, and Lawrence J. Raphael (1982). Some acoustic and physiological observations on diphthongs. *Language and Speech* 25: 305-323.

Collins, Laura (1972). *Luganda (Language of Uganda)*. Ms., UCLA.

Comrie, Bernard (1981). *The languages of the Soviet Union*. Cambridge University Press, Cambridge, UK.

Connine, Cynthia M., Charles Clifton Jr., and Anne Cutler (1987). Effects of lexical stress on phonetic categorization. *Phonetica* 44: 133-146.

Conteh, Patrick, Elizabeth Cowper, Deborah James, Keren Rice and Michael Szamosi (1983). A Reanalysis of tone in Mende. In Jonathan Kaye, Hilda Koopman, Dominique Sportiche and André Dugas (eds.), *Current approaches to African linguistics* 2: 127-137. Foris Publications, Dordrecht, The Netherlands; Cinnaminson, NJ, USA.

Cook, Eung-Do (1971). Vowels and tones in Sarcee. *Language* 47: 164-79.

——— (1984). *A Sarcee grammar*. University of Britich Columbia Press, Vancouver.

——— (1989). Chilcotin tone and verb paradigms. In Eung-Do Cook and Keren D. Rice (eds.), *Athapaskan linguistics: Current perspectives on a language family*: 145-198. Mouton de Gruyter, Berlin, New York.

Cooper, William E. and Jeanne Paccia-Cooper (1980). *Syntax and speech*. Harvard University Press, Cambridge, MA.

Cope, A.T. (1959). Zulu tonology. *Afrika und Übersee* 43: 190-200.

——— (1970). Zulu tonal morphology. *Journal of African Languages* 9, Part 3: 111-152.

Cornyn, William S. (1964). *Outline of Burmese grammar. Language* 20.4, *Supplement. Language Dissertation*, No. 38.

Courtenay, Karen (1971). Yoruba: A 'terraced-level' language with three tonemes. *Studies in African Linguistics* 2.3: 239-255.

Cowper, Elizabeth and Keren Rice (1985). The destruction of tonal structure in Mende. *Studies in African Linguistics*, Supplement 9: 57-62.

Creider, Chet A. (1980). Studies in Kalenjin nominal tonology. Bernd Heine, Wilhem J.G. Möhlig and Franz Rottland (eds.), *Language and dialect atlas of Kenya, Supplement* 3. Dietrich Reimer Verlag, Berlin.

Crowhurst, Megan (1991). Demorafication in Tübatulabal: Evidence from initial reduplication and stress. In T. Sherer (ed.), *Proceedings of NELS 21*. GLSA Publications, Amherst, MA.

——— and Mark Hewitt (1997). *Boolean operations and constraint interaction in Optimality Theory*. Rutgers Optimality Archive, ROA-229-1197.

Cui, Rong-Chang (1997). *Chengduhua yindang* (The sound record of Chengdu). Jing-Yi Hou (ed.), *Xiandai hanyu fangyan yinku* (The sound archives of modern Chinese dialects). Shanghai Jiaoyu Chubanshe (Shanghai Education Press), Shanghai, China.

Cutler, Anne and Donald J. Foss (1977). On the role of sentence stress in sentence processing. *Language and Speech* 20: 1-10.

Davey, A.S. (1977). Some remarks on tonal realization in Nama--A preliminary survey. In J.W. Snyman (ed.), *Bushman and Hottentot Linguistic Studies* 1977: 52-61. University of South Africa, Pretoria, South Africa.

Davies, Somchit (1979). A comparative study of Yong and Standard Thai. In Theraphan L. Thongkum, Vichin Panupong, Prancee Kullavanijaya, M.R. Kalaya Tingsabadh (eds.), *Studies in Tai and Mon-Khmer phonetics and phonology: In honour of Eugénie J.A. Henderson*: 26-48. Chulalongkorn University Press, Bangkok.

Dickens, Patrick J. (1994). *English-Ju|'hoan--Ju|'hoan-English dictionary*. Rüdiger Köppe Verlag, Köln, Germany.

Dimmendaal, Gerrit J. (1981). Non-voiced vowels in Turkana: A Nilo-Saharan feature? In F. Rottland (ed.), *Collected seminar papers 1979-80*. Nairobi University.

——— (1983a). *The Turkana language*. *Publication in African Languages and Linguistics* 2. Foris Publications, Dordrecht and Cinnaminson.

——— (1983b). Topics in a grammar of Turkana. In M. Lionel Bender (ed.), *Nilo-Saharan language studies*: 239-271. Michigan State University.

Doke Clement M. (1925). An Outline of the phonetics of the language of the Chū̥: Bushmen of North-West Kalahari. *Bantu Studies* 2.3: 129-165.

——— (1926). *The phonetics of the Zulu language*. Witwatersrand University Press, Johannesburg, South Africa.

——— (1937). An outline of ǂKhomani Bushman phonetics. In J.D. Rheinallt Jones and C.M. Doke (eds.), *Bushmen of the Southern Kalahari*: 61-88. Witwatersrand University Press, Johannesburg, South Africa.

Donegan, Patricia J. (1985). *On the natural phonology of vowels*. Garland Publishing Inc., New York, NY, USA; London, UK.

——— and David Stampe (1979). The study of natural phonology. In Daniel A. Dinnsen (ed.), *Current approaches to phonological theory*: 126-173. Indiana University Press, Bloomington, IN.

Dong, Shao-Ke (1993). Shandong Yanggu fangyan de biandiao (Tone sandhi in the Yanggu dialect of Shandong Province). *Fangyan* (Dialects) 1993.1: 57-58.

Dow, Francis D.M. (1972). *An outline of Mandarin phonetics.* Australian National University Press, Canberra, Australia.

——— (1984). *An introduction to the pronunciation of Chinese.* Dept. of Chinese, University of Edinburgh.

Duanmu, San (1990). *A formal study of syllable, tone, stress and domain in Chinese languages.* Ph.D. dissertation, MIT.

——— (1992). An autosegmental analysis of tone in four Tibetan languages. *Linguistics of the Tibeto-Burman Area* 15.1: 65-91.

——— (1994a). Syllabic weight and syllabic duration: A correlation between phonology and phonetics. *Phonology* 11: 1-24.

——— (1994b). Against contour tones. *Linguistic Inquiry* 25: 555-608.

Dwyer, David (1971). Mende tone. *Studies in African Linguistics* 2.2: 117-130.

——— (1978). What sort of tone language is Mende? *Studies in African Linguistics* 9.2: 167-208.

——— (1985). A segmental, automelodic view of Mende tone. *Studies in African Linguistics*, Supplement 9: 90-94.

Edmondson, T. and J.T. Bendor-Samuel (1966). Tone patterns of Etung. *Journal of African Languages* 5, Part 1: 1-6.

Edwards, Jan, Mary E. Beckman and Janet Fletcher (1991). The articulatory kinematics of final lengthening. *Journal of the Acoustical Society of America* 89: 369-382.

Elderkin, Edward D. (1988). Patterns of sound in Northern Khoisan. *African Languages and Cultures* 1.2: 123-48.

——— (1998). Sandawe stems. In Mathias Schladt (ed.), *Language, identity, and conceptualization among the Khoisan*: 15-33. Rüdiger Köppe Verlag, Köln.

Elimelech, Baruch (1974). On the reality of underlying contour tones. *UCLA Working Papers in Phonetics* 27: 74-83.

——— (1976). Noun tonology in Kombe. In Larry M. Hyman (ed.), *Studies in Bantu tonology, Southern California Occasional Papers in Linguistics* 3: 113-130.

Elwell-Sutton, Laurence Paul (1976). *The Persian metres.* Cambridge University Press, Cambridge, UK.

Enrico, John (1991). *The lexical phonology of Masset Haida. Alaska Native Language Center Research Papers*, No. 8. University of Alaska, Fairbanks, AL.

Erickson, Donna, Thomas Baer, and Katherine S. Harris (1983). The role of the strap muscles in pitch lowering. In D.M. Bless and J.H. Abbs (eds.), *Vocal fold physiology: Contemporary research and clinical issue*: 279-285. College-Hill Press, San Diego, CA.

Everett, Daniel (1986). Pirahã. In Desmond C. Derbyshine and Geoffrey K. Pullum (eds.), *Handbook of Amazonian languages*, Vol. 1: 200-326. Mouton de Gruyter, Berlin, New York, Amsterdam.

——— (1988). Metrical structure in Pirahã phonology. *Natural Language and Linguistic Theory* 6.2: 207-246.

——— and Keren Everett (1984). On the relevance of syllable onsets to stress placement. *Linguistic Inquiry* 15.4: 705-711.

Feldman, David M. (1967). Outline of a comparison of the segmental phonemes of Brazilian Portuguese and American Spanish. *Linguistics* 29: 44-57.

——— (1972). On utterance-final [ɨ] and [ɰ̥] in Portuguese. In Albert Valdman (ed.), *Papers in linguistics and phonetics to the memory of Pierre Delattre*: 129-141. Mouton, The Hague, The Netherlands; Paris, France.

Flanagan, J.L. and M.G. Saslow (1958). Pitch discrimination for synthetic vowels. *Journal of the Acoustical Society of America* 30: 435-442.

Flemming, Edward (1995). *Auditory representations in phonology*. Ph.D. dissertation, UCLA.

——— (1997). Phonetic optimization: Compromise in speech production. *University of Maryland Working Papers in Linguistics 5: Selected Phonology Papers from H-OT-'97*.

Ford, K.C. (1975). The tones of nouns in Kikiyu. *Studies in African Linguistics* 6.1: 49-64.

Fortune, George (1955). *An analytical grammar of Shona*. Longmans, Green and Co., London, UK.

Fougeron, Cécile (1999). Articulatory properties of initial segments in several prosodic constituents in French. *UCLA Working Papers in Phonetics* 97: 74-99.

Fry, D.B. (1955). Duration and intensity as physical correlates of linguistic stress. *Journal of the Acoustical Society of America* 27: 765-768.

Fu, Guotong (1984). Wuyi fangyan de liandu biandiao (Tone Sandhi in the Wuyi dialect). *Fangyan* (Dialects) 1984.2: 109-127.

Gandour, Jackson T. (1974). The glottal stop in Siamese: Predictability in phonological description. *UCLA Working Papers in Phonetics* 27: 84-91.

——— (1978). The perception of tone. In Victoria A. Fromkin (ed.), *Tone: A linguistic survey*: 41-76. Academic Press, New York, NY.

——— (1981). Perceptual dimensions of tone: Evidence from Cantonese. *Journal of Chinese Linguistics* 9: 20-36.

——— (1983). Tone perception in Far Eastern languages. *Journal of Phonetics* 11: 149-175.

——— and Richard A. Harshman (1978). Crosslanguage differencs in tone perception: A multidimensional scaling investigation. *Language and Speech* 21: 1-33.

———, Eva Gårding and Kristina Lindell (1978). Tone in Northern Kammu: A perceptual investigation. *Acta Orientalia* 39: 181-189.

Gao, Baotai and Ansheng Zhang (1997). *Yinchuanhua yindang* (The sound record of Yinchuan). Jing-Yi Hou (ed.), *Xiandai hanyu fangyan yinku (The sound archives of modern Chinese dialects)*. Shanghai Jiaoyu Chubanshe (Shanghai Education Publishing House), Shanghai.

Gardner, Richard and William R. Merrifield (1990). Quiotepec Chinantec tone. In William R. Merrifield and Calvin R. Rensch (eds.), *Syllables, tone and verb paradigms. Studies in Chinantec languages* 4: 91-105. *Summer Institute of Linguistics and the University of Texas at Arlington Publications in Linguistics*, Publication, No. 95.

Gårding, Eva and Kristina Lindell (1977). Tones in Northern Kammu: A phonetic investigation. *Acta Orientalia* 38: 321-332.

Gay, Thomas (1968). Effect of Speaking rate on diphthong formant movements. *Journal of the Acoustical Society of America* 44: 1570-1573.

——— (1970). A perceptual study of American English diphthongs. *Language and Speech* 13: 65-88.

Gerber, Sanford E. (1971). Perception of segmented diphthongs. In André Rigault and René Charbonneau (eds.), *Proceedings of the Seventh International Congress of Phonetic Sciences*: 479-492. Mouton, The Hague, The Netherlands.

Giannelli, L. and L. Savoia (1979). Indelbolimento consonantico in Toscana. *Revista Italiana di Diallettologia* 2: 23-58.

Gilley, Leoma G. (1992). *An autosegmental approach to Shilluk phonology*. Summer Institute of Linguistics, Arlington, TX.

Gimba, Alhaji M. (1998). *Low tone raising in Bole*. MA thesis, Univeristy of California, Los Angeles.

Goldsmith, John (1976). *Autosegmental phonology*. Ph.D. dissertation, MIT. Reproduced by the Indiana University Linguistics Club.

——— (1985). Vowel harmony in Khalkha Mongolian, Yaka, Finnish and Hungarian. *Phonology Yearbook* 2: 253-75.

Gordon, Kent H. (1976). *Phonology of Dhangar-Kurux*. Tribhuvan University Press, Kathmandu.

Gordon, Matthew (1998). The process specific nature of weight: the case of contour tone restrictions. In Kimary N Shahin, Susan Blake, and Eun-Sook Kim (eds.), *Proceedings of WCCFL 17*. GLSA Publications, Amherst, MA.

——— (1999a). *Syllable weight: Phonetics, phonology, and typology*. Ph.D. dissertation, UCLA.

——— (1999b). *The tonal basis for weight asymmetries in final position*. Paper presented at 73rd Annual Meeting of LSA, Los Angeles, CA.

Goyvaerts, D.L. (1983). Some aspects of Logo phonology and morphology. In M. Lionel Bender (ed.), *Nilo-Saharan language studies*: 272-280. Michigan State University.

Green, Margaret M. and G.E. Igwe (1963). *A descriptive grammar of Igbo*. Akademie-Verlag, Berlin.

Greenberg, Steven and Eric Zee (1979). On the perception of contour tones. *UCLA Working Papers in Phonetics* 45: 150-164.

Grimes, Barbara F. (1996). *Ethnologue: Languages of the world* (13th edition). Summer Institute of Linguistics, Dallas, TX.

Hagman, Roy S. (1977). *Nama Hottentot grammar. Language Science Monographs* 15. Indiana University, Bloomington, IN.

Haiman, John (1972). Phonological targets and unmarked structures. *Language* 48: 365–377.

Hall, Robert A., Jr. (1943). The unit phonemes of Brazilian Portuguese. *Studies in Linguistics* 1: 1-6.

Halle, Morris and Jean-Roger Vergnaud (1982). On the framework of autosegmental phonology. In Harry van der Hulst and Norval Smith (eds.), *The structure of phonological representations (part I)*: 65-82. Foris Publications, Dordrecht, The Netherlands.

Hamilton, Philip (1996). *Phonetic constraints and markedness in the phonotactics of Australian aboriginal languages*. Ph.D. dissertation, University of Toronto. Distributed as *Toronto Working Papers in Linguistics, Dissertation Series* 7.

Han, Mieko S. (1969). *Vietnamese tones. Studies in the phonology of Asian languages* VIII. Acoustic Phonetic Research Laboratory, University of Southern California.

Hargus, Sharon (1988). *The lexical phonology of Sekani.* Garland Publishing Inc., New York and London.

Harms, Robert T. (1962). *Estonian Grammar.* Indiana University Publications. Uralic and Altaic Series, Vol. 12. Mouton, The Hague, The Netherlands.

Harris, J.D. (1952). Pitch discrimination. *Journal of the Acoustical Society of America* 24: 750-755.

Harris, James (1969). *Spanish phonology.* MIT Press, Cambridge, MA.

Harris, M.S. and N. Umeda (1987). Difference limens for fundamental frequency contours in sentences. *Journal of the Acoustical Society of America* 81: 1139-1145.

't Hart, Johan (1981). Different sensitivity to pitch distance, particularly in speech. *Journal of the Acoustical Society of America* 69: 811-821.

———, René Collier, and Antonie Cohen (1990). *A perceptual study of intonation: An experimental-phonetic approach to speech melody.* Cambridge University Press, Cambridge, UK.

Haudricourt, André, G. (1954). De l'origine des tons en Vietnamien. *Journal Asiatique* 242: 68-82.

Hayes, Bruce (1979). The rhythmic structure of Persian verse. *Edebiyat* 4: 193-242.

——— (1989). Compensatory lengthening in moraic phonology. *Linguistics Inquiry* 20: 253-306.

——— (1995). *Metrical stress theory: Principles and case studies.* The University of Chicago Press, Chicago, IL.

——— (1999). Phonetically-driven phonology: The role of optimality theory and inductive grounding. In Michael Darnell, Edith Moravscik, Michael Noonan, Frederick Newmeyer, and Kathleen Wheatly (eds.), *Functionalism and formalism in linguistics, vol. I: General papers*: 243-285. John Benjamins, Amsterdam, The Netherlands.

——— and Donca Steriade (to appear). Phonetics in phonology: An introduction. In Bruce Hayes, Robert Kirchner, and Donca Steriade (eds.), *The phonetic basis of phonology.* Cambridge University Press, Cambridge, UK.

He, Jiashan (1983). *Gelaoyu jianzhi* (A grammatical sketch of the Gelao language). *Zhongguo shaoshu minzu yuyan jianzhi congshu* (A collection of grammatical sketches of the minority languages in China). Minzu Chubanshe (The Nationality Publishing House), Beijing.

He, Ningji (1985). Beijinghua erhe yuanyin ganzhizhong de shijian yinsu (The durational factors in Beijing Chinese diphthong perception). In Tao Lin and Lijia Wang (eds.), *Beijing yuyin shiyan lu* (A collection of phonetic studies on Beijing Chinese): 196-224. Beijing University Press, Beijing, China.

He, Wei (1979). Huojia fangyan de liandu biandiao (Tone sandhi in the Huojia dialect). *Fangyan* (Dialects) 1979.2: 122-136.

He, Weitang (1986). Guangdongsheng Zengcheng fangyan yinxi (The phonemic system of the Zecheng dialect of Guangdong Province). *Fangyan* (Dialects) 1986: 133-138.

——— (1987). Guangdongsheng Zengcheng fangyan de biandiao (Tone sandhi in the Zecheng dialect of Guangdong Province). *Fangyan* (Dialects) 1987: 44-48.

Heikkinen, Terttu (1986). Phonology of the !Xũ dialect spoken in Ovamboland and Western Kavango. *Southern African Journal of African Languages* 6.1: 18-28.

Heine, Bernd (1980). *The non-Bantu languages of Kenya.* Bernd Heine and Wilhem J.G. Möhlig (eds.), *Language and dialect atlas of Kenya,* Vol. II. Dietrich Reimer Verlag, Berlin.

Heine, Bernd (1982). *The Nubi language of Kibera—An Arabic Creole: Grammatical sketch and vocabulary.* Bernd Heine and Wilhem J.G. Möhlig (eds.), *Language and dialect atlas of Kenya,* Vol. III. Dietrich Reimer Verlag, Berlin.

Henderson, Eugénie J.A. (1959). The tones of the Tai dialect of Songkhla. *Bulletin of the Institute of History and Philology, Academia Sinica,* 30.1: 233-235.

Henry, F. (1948). Discrimination of the duration of a sound. *Journal of Experimental Psychology* 38: 734-743.

Hetzron, Robert (1960). *The verbal system of Southern Agaw.* University of California Press, Berkeley and Los Angeles, CA.

Hirano, Minoru, John Ohala, and William Vennard (1969). The function of laryngeal muscles in regulating fundamental frequency and intensity of phonation. *Journal of Speech and Hearing Research* 12: 616-628.

Hoffman, Carl (1963). *A grammar of the Margi language.* Oxford University Press, London, UK.

Hoijer, Harry (1974). *A Navajo lexicon.* University of California Press, Berkeley and Los Angeles, CA.

Hollenbach, Barbara (1977). Phonetic vs. phonemic correspondence in two Trique dialects. In William R. Merrifield (ed.), *Studies in Otomanguean phonology*: 35-67. *Summer Institute of Linguistics Publications in Linguistics,* Publication, No. 54.

Hombert, Jean-Marie (1975). *Towards a theory of tonogenesis: An empirical, physiologically and perceptually-based account of the development of tonal contrast in language.* Ph.D. dissertation, UC Berkeley.

——— (1976a). Noun classes and tone in Ngie. In Larry M. Hyman (ed.), *Studies in Bantu Tonology, Southern California Occasional Papers in Linguistics,* No. 3: 1-21.

——— (1976b). Perception of tones of bisyllabic nouns in Yoruba. *Studies in African Linguistics,* Supplement 6: 109-121.

———, John J. Ohala, and William G. Ewan (1979). Phonetic explanations for the development of tones. *Language* 55: 37-58.

Hongladarom, Krisadawan (1996). Rgyalthang Tibetan of Yunnan: A preliminary report. *Linguistics of the Tibeto-Burman Area* 19.2: 69-92.

Hooper [Bybee] Joan L. (1976). *An introduction to natural generative phonology.* Academic Press, New York, NY.

Horowitz, L.M., M.A. White and D.W. Atwood (1968). Word fragments as aids to recall: The organization of a word. *Journal of Experimental Psychology* 76: 219–226.

———, P.C. Chilian and K.P. Dunnigan (1969). Word fragments and their reintegrative powers. *Journal of Experimental Psychology* 80: 392–394.

Hou, Jingyi (1980). Pingyao fangyan de liandu biandiao (Tone sandhi in the Pingyao dialect). *Fangyan* (Dialects) 1980.1: 1-14.

——— (1982a). Pingyao fangyan sanzizu de liandu biandiao (Tone sandhi of reduplicative trisyllabic words in the Pingyao dialect). *Fangyan* (Dialects) 1982.1: 7-14.

——— (1982b). Pingyao fangyan guangyoungshi sanzizu de liandu biandiao (Tone sandhi of regular trisyllabic words in the Pingyao dialect). *Fangyan* (Dialects) 1982.2: 85-99.

——— (1983). Changzhi fangyan jilüe (A grammatical sketch of the Changzhi dialects). *Fangyan* (Dialects) 1983.4, 260-274.

——— (1985). *Changzhi fangyan zhi* (A record of the Changzhou dialect). Yuwen Chubanshe (The Philology Publishing House), Beijing.

House, A. and G. Fairbanks (1953). The influence of consonant environment upon the secondary acoustical characteristics of vowels. *Journal of the Acoustical Society of America* 25: 105-113.

House, David (1990). *Tonal perception in speech. Travaux de L'Institut de Linguistique de Lund* 24. Lund University Press, Lund, Sweden.

Howie, John M. (1970). *Acoustical studies of Mandarin vowels and tones*. Cambridge University Press, Cambridge, UK.

——— (1974). On the domain of tone in Mandarin—some acoustical evidence. *Phonetica* 30: 129-148.

Hu, Tan, Aitang Qu and Lianghe Lin (1982). Zangyu (Lasa hua) shengdiao shiyan. (Experiments on Lhasa Tibetan tones). *Yuyan Yanjiu* (Language Studies), 1982.1: 18-38.

Hualde, Jose Ignacio (1992). *Catalan*. Routledge, London, UK.

Hubbard, Kathleen Anne (1994). *Duration in moraic theory*. Ph.D. dissertation. UC Berkeley.

Hudak, John (1993). *William J. Gedney's 'The Saek language: Glossary, texts, and translations'. Michigan Papers on South and Southeast Asia*, No. 41. Center for South and Southeast Asian Studies, The University of Michigan.

Hudson, R.A. (1973). Syllables, moras and accents in Beja. *Journal of Linguistics* 9.1: 53-63.

Hulst, Harry van der and Jeroen van der Weijer (1995). Vowel harmony. In John A. Goldsmith (ed.), *Handbook of phonological theory*: 494–534. Blackwell Publishers, Oxford, UK.

Hyman, Larry M. (1973). The role of consonant types in natural tonal assimilation. In Larry M. Hyman (ed.), *Consonant types and tone, Southern California Occasional Papers in Linguistics* 1: 151-179.

Hyman, Larry M. (1979). Phonology and noun structure. In Larry M. Hyman (ed.), *Aghem grammatical structure*: 1-72. *Southern California Occasional Papers in Linguistics* 7. University of Southern California.

——— (1985). *A theory of phonological weight*. Foris Publications, Dordrecht, The Netherlands.

——— (1987). Prosodic domains in Kukuya. *Natural Language and Linguistic Theory* 5: 311-333.

——— and Ernst Rugwa Byarushengo (1984). A model of Haya tonology. In George N. Clements and John Goldsmith (eds.), *Autosegmental studies in Bantu tone*. Foris Publications, Dordrecht, The Netherlands.

——— and Francis X. Katamba (1990). Final vowel shortening in Luganda. *Studies in African Linguistics* 21.1: 1-59.

——— and Francis X. Katamba (1993). A new approach to tone in Luganda. *Language* 69.1: 34-67.

——— and Armindo Ngunga (1994). On the non-universality of tonal association 'conventions': Evidence from Ciyao. *Phonology* 11.1: 25-68.

——— and Russell G. Schuh (1974). Universals of tone rules: evidence from West Africa. *Linguistic Inquiry* 5: 81-115.

Innes, Gordon (1963). *The structure of sentences in Mende*. University of London, School of Oriental and African Studies, London, UK.

——— (1969). *A Mende-English dictionary*. Cambridge University Press, London, UK.

Issachenko, A.V. and H.-J. Schädlich (1970). *A model of standard German intonation*. Mouton, The Hague, the Netherlands.

James, Deborah (1981). *An autosegmental analysis of Siane*. Summer Institute of Linguistics, Norman, Okla.

Jamieson, Allan R. (1977). Chiquihuitlan Mazatec phonology. In William R. Merrifield (ed.), *Studies in Otomanguean phonology*: 93-105. *Summer Institute of Linguistics Publications in Linguistics,* Publication, No. 54.

Jassem, Wiktor (1959). The phonology of Polish stress. *Word* 15: 252-269.

Jensen, Paul J. and K.M.N. Menon (1972). Physical analysis of linguistic vowel duration. *Journal of the Acoustical Society of America* 52: 708-710.

Jernudd, Björn H. (1983). Phonetic notes on tone and quantity in the For language. In M. Lionel Bender (ed.), *Nilo-Saharan language studies*: 80-95. Michigan State University, East Lansing, MI.

Jha, Sunil Kumar (1985). Acoustic analysis of the Maithili diphthongs. *Journal of Phonetics* 13: 107-115.

Jiang, Yinti (1991). Shuozhoushi Shuochengqu fangyan de liandu biandiao (Tone Sandhi in the Shuochengqu dialect of the Shuozhou City). *Fangyan* (Dialects) 1991.4: 255-258.

Jiang-King, Ping (1996). *An optimality account of tone-vowel interaction in Northern Min*. Ph.D. dissertation, The University of British Columbia.

Jin, Peng (1983). *Zangyu jianzhi*. (A grammatical sketch of the Tibetan language). *Zhongguo shaoshu minzu yuyan jianzhi congshu* (A collection of grammatical sketches of the minority languages in China). Minzu Chubanshe (The Nationality Publishing House), Beijing.

Johnson, Lawrence (1976). Devoicing, tone and stress in Runyankore. In Larry M. Hyman (ed.), *Studies in Bantu Tonology, Southern California Occasional Papers in Linguistics,* No. 3: 207-216.

Jones, Daniel (1928). *The tones of Sechuana nouns*. International Institute of African Languages and Cultures Memorandum VI.

de Jong, Kenneth and Bushra Adnan Zawaydeh (1999). Stress, duration, and intonation in Arabic word-level prosody. *Journal of Phonetics* 27: 3-22.

Jordan, A.C. (1966). *A practical course in Xhosa*. Longmans Southern Africa (PTY) Ltd., South Africa.

Jun, Jongho (1995). *Perceptual and articulatory factors in place assimilation: An Optimality Theoretic approach*. Ph.D. dissertation, UCLA. Distributed as *UCLA Dissertations in Linguistics* #2.

Kager, René (1996). On affix allomorphy and syllable counting. In U. Kleinhenz (ed.), *Interfaces in phonology. Studia Grammatica* 41: 155-171 Akademie Verlag, Berlin, Germany.

Kakita, Yuki and Shizuo Hiki (1976). Investigation of laryngeal control in speech by use of thyrometer. *Journal of the Acoustical Society of America* 59: 669-674.

Kao, Diana L. (1971). *Structure of the syllable in Cantonese*. Mouton, The Hague, The Netherlands; Paris, France.

Kari, James (1976). *Navajo verb prefix phonology*. Garland Publishing Inc., New York, NY, USA; London, UK.

Karlgren, Bernhard (1926). *Études sur la phonologie chinoise. Archives d'Études Orientales* 15. Norstedt, Stockholm, Sweden.

Kaschube, Dorothea (1954). Examples of tone in Crow. *International Journal of American Linguistics* 20.1: 34-36.

——— (1967). *Structural elements of the language of the Crow Indians of Montana. University of Colorado Studies, Series in Anthropology*, No. 14. University of Colorado Press, Boulder, Colorado.

Kaun, Abigail R. (1995). *The typology of rounding harmony: An Optimality Theoretic approach*. Ph.D. dissertation, UCLA. Distributed as *UCLA Dissertations in Linguistics* #8.

Keating, Patricia A. (1985). Universal phonetics and the organization of grammars. In Victoria A. Fromkin (ed.), *Phonetic linguistics: Essays in honor of Peter Ladefoged*: 115-132. Academic Press, Orlando, FL.

——— (1988a). The phonology-phonetics interface. In F.J. Newmeyer (ed.), *The Cambridge survey, vol. 1: Linguistic theory*: 281-302. Cambridge University Press, Cambridge, UK.

——— (1988b). Underspecification in phonetics. *Phonology* 5: 275-292.

——— and Abigail Cohn (1988). Cross-language effects of vowels on consonant onsets. *Journal of the Acoustical Society of America* 84, supplement 1: S84.

Keller, Charles E. (1976). A grammatical sketch of Brao, a Mon-Khmer language. *Summer Institute of Linguistics Working Papers*, Vol. 20, Supplement 1. Grand Forks, North Dakota.

Kenstowicz, Michael (1972). Lithuanian phonology. *Studies in the Linguistics Sciences* 2.2: 1-85.

——— (1994). *Phonology in generative grammar*. Blackwell Publishers, Cambridge, MA, USA; Oxford, UK.

———, Emmanuel Nikiema and Meterwa Ourso (1988). Tonal polarity in two Gur languages. *Studies in the Linguistic Sciences* 18.1: 77-103.

Kim, Sung-A (1999). Tone spread decomposed. In Pius Tamanji, Masako Hirotani, and Nancy Hall (eds.), *Proceedings of NELS 29*, Vol. 2. GLSA Publications, Amherst, MA.

Kimenyi, Alexandre (1976). Tone anticipation in Kinyarwanda. In Larry M. Hyman (ed.), *Studies in Bantu tonology, Southern California Occasional Papers in Linguistics* 3: 167-181.

——— (1979). *Studies in Kinyarwanda and Bantu phonology*. Linguistic Research, Inc. Carbondale USA and Edmonton Canada.

Kirchner, Robert (1996). Synchronic chain shifts in Optimality Theory. *Linguistic Inquiry* 27: 341-350.

——— (1997). Contrastiveness and faithfulness. *Phonology* 14: 83-111.

——— (1998). *An effort-based approach to consonant lenition*. Ph.D. dissertation, UCLA.

Kisseberth, Charles (1970). On the functional unity of phonological rules. *Linguistic Inquiry* 1: 291-306.

Klatt, Dennis H. (1973a). Discrimination of fundamental frequency contours in synthetic speech: implications for models of pitch perception. *Journal of the Acoustical Society of America* 53: 8-16.

——— (1973b). Interaction between two factors that influence vowel duration. *Journal of the Acoustical Society of America* 54: 1102-1104.

——— (1975). Vowel lengthening is syntactically determined in connected discourse. *Journal of Phonetics* 3: 129-140.

——— (1976). Linguistic uses of segmental duration in english: Acoustic and perceptual evidence. *Journal of the Acoustical Society of America* 59: 1208-1221.

Kohler, Klaus J. (1990). Segmental reduction in connected speech in German: Phonological facts and phonetic explanations. In William J. Hardcastle and Alain Marchal (eds.), *Speech production and speech modelling*: 69-92. Kluwer Academic Publishers, Dordrecht, The Netherlands.

Krueger, John (1977). *Tuvan manual*. Indiana University Publications, Bloomington, IN.

Kuipers, Aert H. (1967). *The Squamish language*. Mouton, The Hague, The Netherlands.

La Velle, Carl R. (1974). An experimental study of Yoruba tone. *UCLA Working Papers in Phonetics* 27: 160-170.

Ladefoged, Peter (2001). *A course in phonetics*, 4th edition. Harcourt College Publishers, Fort Worth, TX.

Lanham, L.W. (1958). The tonemes of Xhosa. *African Studies* 17.2: 65-81.

——— (1963). The tonemes of Xhosa: A restatement. *Studies in Linguistics* 17.1: 35-58.

Laniran, Yetunde O. (1992). *Intonation in tone languages: The phonetic implementation of tones in Yorùbá*. Ph.D. dissertation. Cornell University.

Leben, William (1971). Suprasegmental and segmental representation of tone. *Studies in African Linguistics*, supplement 2: 183-200.

——— (1973). *Suprasegmental phonology*. Ph.D. dissertation, MIT.

——— (1978). The representation of tone. In Victoria A. Fromkin (ed.), *Tone: A linguistic survey*: 177-219. Academic Press, New York, NY.

Leer, Jeff (1985). Prosody in Alutiiq (The Koniag and Chugach dialects of Alaskan Yupik). In Michael Krauss (ed.), *Yupik Eskimo prosodic systems: Descriptive and comparative studies*: 77-133. Alaska Native Language Center, Fairbanks, AK.

Lehiste, Ilse (1964). *Acoustical characteristics of selected English consonants*. Indiana University Press, Bloomington, IN.

——— (1970). *Suprasegmentals*. MIT Press, Cambridge, MA.

——— (1972). Timing of utterances and linguistic boundaries. *Journal of the Acoustical Society of America* 51: 2108-2124.

——— and G.E. Peterson (1961). Transitions, glides, and diphthongs. *Journal of the Acoustical Society of America* 33: 268-277.

Leon, Frances and Morris Swadesh (1949). Two views of Otomi prosody. *International Journal of American Linguistics* 15.2: 100-105.

Leslau, Wolf (1958). Moč a, a tone language of the Kafa group in South-Western Ethiopia. *Africa* 28.2: 135-147.

Li, Fang-Kuei (1977). *A handbook of comparative Tai*. University Press of Hawaii, Honolulu, HI.

Li, Jinfang (1996). Bugan—A new Mon-Khmer language of Yunan Province, China. *Mon-Khmer Studies* 26: 135-159.

Li, Jinling (1997). *Hefeihua yindang* (The sound record of Hefeihua). Jing-Yi Hou (ed.), *Xiandai hanyu fangyan yinku (The sound archives of modern Chinese dialects)*. Shanghai Jiaoyu Chubanshe (Shanghai Education Publishing House), Shanghai.

Li, Lan (1997). *Guiyanghua yindang* (The sound record of Guiyang). Jing-Yi Hou (ed.), *Xiandai hanyu fangyan yinku* (The sound archives of modern Chinese dialects). Shanghai Jiaoyu Chubanshe (Shanghai Education Press), Shanghai, China.

Li, Rong (1979). Wenling fangyan de liandu biandiao (Tone sandhi in the Wenling dialect). *Fangyan* (Dialects) 1979.1: 1-29.

Li, Xinkui, Huiying Chen and Yun Mai (1995). *Guangzhouhua yindang* (The sound record of the Guangzhou). Jing-Yi Hou (ed.), *Xiandai hanyu fangyan yinku (The sound archives of modern Chinese dialects)*. Shanghai Jiaoyu Chubanshe (Shanghai Education Publishing House), Shanghai.

Liang, Min (1980). *Maonanyu jianzhi* (A grammatical sketch of the Maonan language). *Zhongguo shaoshu minzu yuyan jianzhi congshu* (A collection of grammatical sketches of the minority languages in China). Minzu Chubanshe (The Nationality Publishing House), Beijing.

Liang, Yuzhang and Aizhen Feng (1996). *Fuzhouhua yindang* (The sound record of Fuzhou). Jing-Yi Hou (ed.), *Xiandai hanyu fangyan yinku* (The sound archives of modern Chinese dialects). Shanghai Jiaoyu Chubanshe (Shanghai Education Press), Shanghai, China.

Liberman, Mark, J. Michael Schultz, Soonhyun Hong, Vincent Okeke (1993). The phonetic interpretation of tone in Igbo. *Phonetica* 50.3: 147-160.

Lieberman, Philip (1960). Some acoustic correlates of word stress in American English. *Journal of the Acoustical Society of America* 32: 451-454.

Lin, Tao (1983). Tantao Beijinghua qingyin xingzhi de chubu shiyan (Preliminary investigation of the properties of Light Tones in Beijing Chinese). *Yuyanxue Luncong* (Forum in Linguistics) 10.

Lindblom, Björn (1967). Vowel duration and a model of lip mandible coordination. *Speech Transmission Laboratory Quarterly Progress Status Report* 4: 1-29. Royal Institute of Technology, Stockholm, Sweden.

——— (1975). Experiments in sound structure. *Revue de Phonétique Appliquée* 51: 155-189. Université de l'Etat Mons, Belgique.

——— (1986). Phonetic universals in vowel systems. In John J. Ohala and Jeri J. Jaeger (eds.), *Experimental phonology*: 13-44. Academic Press, Orlando, FL.

———, Bertil Lyberg, and Karin Holmgren (1981). *Durational patterns of Swedish phonology: Do they reflect short-term motor memory processes?* Indiana University Linguistics Club, Bloomington, IN.

——— and Karin Rapp (1973). Some temporal regularities of spoken Swedish. *Papers from the Institute of Linguistics* (*PILUS*) 21. University of Stockholm, Sweden.

Lindqvist, Jan (1972). Laryngeal articulation studied on Swedish subjects. *Speech Transmission Laboratory Quarterly Progress and Status Report* 2-3: 10-27. Royal Institute of Technology, Stockholm, Sweden.

Liu, Danqing (1997). *Nanjinghua yindang* (The sound record of Nanjing). Jing-Yi Hou (ed.), *Xiandai hanyu fangyan yinku (The sound archives of modern Chinese dialects)*. Shanghai Jiaoyu Chubanshe (Shanghai Education Publishing House), Shanghai.

Liu, Xingce and Ping Xiang (1997). *Wuhanhua yindang* (The sound record of Wuhan). Jing-Yi Hou (ed.), *Xiandai hanyu fangyan yinku (The sound archives of modern Chinese dialects)*. Shanghai Jiaoyu Chubanshe (Shanghai Education Publishing House), Shanghai.

Long, Yaohong and Guoqiao Zheng (1998). *The Dong language in Guizhou Province, China*. Translated from Chinese by D. Norman Geary. *Summer Institute of Linguistics and the University of Texas at Arlington Publications in Linguistics*, Publication No. 126.

Lu, Jinyuan (1986). Lüsi fangyan jilüe (A grammatical sketch of the Lüsi dialects). *Fangyan* (Dialects) 1986.1: 52-70.

——— (1994). Lüsi fangyan liangzizu liandu biandiao (Tone sandhi of disyllabic words in the Lüsi dialect). *Fangyan* (Dialects) 1994.1: 46-55.

Lyberg, Bertil (1977). Some observations on the timing of Swedish utterances. *Journal of Phonetics* 5: 49-59.

Maddieson, Ian (1984). *Patterns of sounds*. Cambridge University Press, Cambridge, UK.

Magen, Harriet (1984). Vowel-to-vowel coarticulation in English and Japanese. *Journal of the Acoustical Society of America* 75, supplement 1: S41.

Maingard, L.F. (1957). Three Bushman languages. *African Studies* 16.1: 37-71.

——— (1958). Three Bushman languages, Part II: The third Bushman language. *African Studies* 17.2: 100-115.

Manley, Timothy M. (1972). *Outline of Sre structure. Oceanic Linguistics Special Publication*, No. 12. University of Hawaii Press, Honolulu.

Manuel, Sharon Y. (1990). The role of contrast in limiting vowel-to-vowel coarticulation in different languages. *Journal of the Acoustical Society of America* 88: 1286-1298.

Mao, Yuling (1997). *Kunminghua yindang* (The sound record of Kunming). Jing-Yi Hou (ed.), *Xiandai hanyu fangyan yinku (The sound archives of modern Chinese dialects)*. Shanghai Jiaoyu Chubanshe (Shanghai Education Publishing House), Shanghai.

Mao, Zongwu and Zuyao Zhou (1972). A brief description of the Yao language. In Herbert C. Purnell Jr. (ed.), *Miao and Yao linguistic studies—Selected articles in*

Chinese: 239-255. Translated by Yü-Hung Chang and Kwo-Ray Chu. *Linguistics Series V, Data Paper*, No. 88. Cornell University, Ithaca, New York.

———, Zhaoji Meng and Zongze Zheng (1982). *Yaozu yuyan jianzhi* (Grammatical sketches of the Yao languages). *Zhongguo shaoshu minzu yuyan jianzhi congshu* (A collection of grammatical sketches of the minority languages in China). Minzu Chubanshe (The Nationality Publishing House), Beijing.

Maran, La Raw (1971). *Burmese and Jingpho: A study of tonal linguistic processes. Occasional Papers of the Wolfenden Society on Tibeto-Burman Linguistics*, vol. IV. University of Illinois, Urbana, IL.

——— (1973). On becoming a tone language: a Tibeto-Burman model of tonogenesis. In Larry M. Hyman (ed.), *Consonant types and tone, Southern California Occasional Papers in Linguistics* 1: 97-114.

Marks, Donna Louise (1976). *Zapotec verb morphology: Categories and tonomechanics with special attention to Sierra Juarez Zapotec*. MA thesis, The University of Texas at Arlington.

Marslen-Wilson, William D. (1989). Access and integration. In William D. Marslen-Wilson (ed.), *Lexical representation and process*: 3-24. MIT Press, Cambridge, MA

——— and Alan Welsh (1978). Processing interactions and lexical access during word recognition in continuous speech. *Cognitive Psychology* 10: 29–63.

——— and Lorraine K. Tyler (1980). The temporal structure of spoken language understanding. *Cognition* 8: 1-71.

——— and Pienie Zwitserlood (1989). Accessing spoken words: The importance of word onsets. *Journal of Experimental Psychology: Human Perception and Performance* 15: 576-585.

Maspéro, H. (1912). Études sur la phonétique historique de la language annamite: les initiales. *Bulletin de l'Éxtrême Orient* 12: 114-116.

Matisoff, James A. (1973a). *The grammar of Lahu. University of California Publications in Linguistics* 75. University of California Press, Berkeley and Los Angeles, CA.

——— (1973b). Tonogenesis in Southeast Asia. In Larry M. Hyman (ed.), *Consonant types and tone, Southern California Occasional Papers in Linguistics* 1: 71-96.

Max, Ludo and Patrick Onghena (1999). Some issues in the statistical analysis of completely randomized and repeated measures designs for speech, language, and hearing research. *Journal of Speech, Language, and Hearing Research* 42: 261-270.

McAllister, Jan (1991). The processing of lexically stressed syllables in read and spontaneous speech. *Language and Speech* 34: 1-26.

McCarthy, John and Alan Prince (1986). *Prosodic morphology*. Ms., University of Massachusetts and Brandeis University.

——— and ——— (1993). Generalized alignment. *Yearbook of Morphology* 1993: 79-153.

——— and ——— (1995). Faithfulness and reduplicative identity. In Jill Beckman, Laura Walsh Dickey, and Susan Urbanczyk (eds.), *University of Massachusetts Occasional Papers in Linguistics 18: Papers in Optimality Theory*: 249–384. GLSA Publications, Amherst, MA.

McCawley, James D. (1968). *The phonological component of a grammar of Japanese*. Mouton, The Hague, The Netherlands.

——— (1970). A note on tone in Tiv conjunction. *Studies in African Linguistics* 1: 123-129.

McHugh, Brian (1990a). *Cyclicity in the phrasal phonology of Kivunjo Chaga*. Ph.D. dissertation, University of California, Los Angeles.

——— (1990b). The phrasal cycle in Kivunjo Chaga tonology. In Sharon Inkelas and Draga Zec (eds.), *The phonology-syntax connection*: 217-242. The University of Chicago Press.

Meeussen, A.E. (1970). Tone typologies for West African languages. *African Language Studies* 11: 166-271.

Meng, Qinghai (1991). Yangqu fangyan liangzizu de liandu biandiao (Tone sandhi of disyllabic words in the Yangqu dialect). *Fangyan* (Dialects) 1991.1: 50-55.

Meng, Qinghui (1997). *Shexianhua yindang* (The sound record of Shexian). Jing-Yi Hou (ed.), *Xiandai hanyu fangyan yinku (The sound archives of modern Chinese dialects)*. Shanghai Jiaoyu Chubanshe (Shanghai Education Publishing House), Shanghai.

Miao Language Team, Division of Minority Languages, Institute of Races, Chinese Academy of Sciences (1972). A brief description of the Miao language. In Herbert C. Purnell Jr. (ed.), *Miao and Yao linguistic studies—Selected articles in Chinese*: 1-25. Translated by Yü-Hung Chang and Kwo-Ray Chu. *Linguistics Series V, Data Paper*, No. 88. Cornell University, Ithaca, New York.

Miller, J.L. and A.M. Liberman (1979). Some effects of later-occurring information on the perception of stop consonant and semivowel. *Perception and Psychophysics* 25: 457-465.

——— and F. Grosjean (1981). How the components of speaking rate influence perception of phonetic segments. *Journal of Experimental Psychology: Human Perception and Performance* 1: 208-215.

Miller, Wick R.C. (1965). *Acoma grammar and texts*. University of California Press, Berkeley and Los Angeles, CA.

Miller-Ockhuizen, Amanda (1998). Towards a unified decompositional analysis of Khoisan lexical tone. In Mathias Schladt (ed.), *Language, identity, and conceptualization among the Khoisan*: 217-243. Rüdiger Köppe Verlag, Köln, Germany.

Mohrlang, Roger (1971). Vectors, prosodies, and Higi vowels. *Journal of African Languages* 10: 75-86.

Moore, Brian C. (1995). *An introduction to the psychology of hearing*. Academic Press, San Diego, CA.

Moore, Corinne B. (1995). *Speaker and rate normalization in the perception of lexical tone by Mandarin and English speakers*. Ph.D. dissertation, Cornell University.

——— and Allard Jongman (1997). Speaker normalization in the perception of Mandarin Chinese tones. *Journal of the Acoustical Society of America* 102: 1864-1877.

Morev, L.N., A.A. Moskalyov and Y.Y. Plam (1979). *The Lao language*. U.S.S.R Academy of Sciences, Institute of Oriental Studies.

Morse, Robert H. (1963). Phonology of Rawang. *Anthropological Linguistics* 5.5: 17-41.

Morton, John and Wiktor Jassem (1965). Acoustic correlates of stress. *Language and Speech* 8: 159-181.

Mtenje, Al D. (1993). Verb structure and tone in Ciyao. In Salikoko S. Mufwene and Lioba Moshi (eds.), *Topics in African linguistics*: 179-190. John Benjamins, Amsterdam, The Netherlands.

——— (1995). Tone shift, accent and domains in Bantu: The case of Chichewa. In Francis Katamba (ed.), *Bantu phonology and morphology. Lincom studies in African linguistics* 6: 1-27. Lincom Europa, München-Newcastle.

Mugele, Robert (1982). *Tone and ballistic syllable in Lalana Chinantec*. Ph.D. dissertation, University of Texas at Austin.

——— and Michael Rodewald (1991). Aspects of Bandi tonology. *Studies in African Linguistics* 22.2: 103-134.

Munro, Pamela (1996a). Cherokee papers from UCLA: An introduction. In Pamela Munro (ed.), *Cherokee papers from UCLA. UCLA Occasional Papers in Linguistics* 16: 3-7.

——— (1996b). The Cherokee laryngeal alternation rule. In Pamela Munro (ed.), *Cherokee papers from UCLA. UCLA Occasional Papers in Linguistics*, No. 16: 45-60.

Mutaka, Ngessimo M. (1994). *The lexical tonology of Kinande. Lincom studies in African linguistics* 1. Lincom Europa, München-Newcastle.

Myers, Scott (1998). Surface underspecification of tone in Chichewa. *Phonology* 15: 367-391.

Nabelek, I. and I.J. Hirsh (1969). On the discrimination of frequency transitions. *Journal of the Acoustical Society of America* 45: 1510-1519.

Nellis, Neil and Jane Goodner Nellis (1983). *Diccionario Zapoteco de Juarez*. Instituto Lingüistico de VeraNo.

Newman, Paul (1972). Syllable weight as a phonological variable. *Studies in African Linguistics* 3: 301-323.

——— (1974). *The Kanakuru language. West African Language Monographs* 9. University of Leeds, in association with the West African Linguistic Society.

——— (1986). Tone and affixation in Hausa. *Studies in African Linguistics* 17.3: 249-267.

——— (1990). Hausa and the Chadic languages. In Bernard Comrie (ed.), *The world's major languages*: 705-723. Oxford University Press, New York, NY, USA; Oxford, UK.

Nguyên, Dình-Hoà (1990). Vietnamese. In Bernard Comrie (ed.), *The world's major languages*: 777-796. Oxford University Press, New York, Oxford.

Nguyen, Dang Liem (1970). *Vietnamese pronunciation*. University of Hawaii Press, Honolulu.

Noonan, Nichael (1992). *A grammar of Lango. Mouton Grammar Library* 7. Mouton de Gruyter, Berlin, New York.

Odden, David (1983). Aspect of Didinga phonology and morphology. In M. Lionel Bender (ed.), *Nilo-Saharan language studies*: 148-176. Michigan State University.

——— (1986). On the role of the Obligatory Contour Principle in Phonological theory. *Language* 62: 353-383.

——— (1988). Floating tones and contour tones in Kenyang. *Studies in African Linguistics* 19.1: 1-34.

——— (1990). Tone in the Makonde dialects: Chimahuta. *Studies in African Linguistics* 21.2: 149-187.

——— (1990). Tone in the Makonde dialects: Chimaraba. *Studies in African Linguistics* 21.1: 61-105.

——— (1995). Tone: African languages. In John A. Goldsmith (ed.), *Handbook of theoretical phonology*: 444-475. Blackwell Publishers, Oxford, UK.

Ohala, John J. (1974). Phonetic explantion in phonology. In Anthony Bruck, Robert A. Fox, and Michael W. LaGaly (eds.), *Papers from the parasession on natural phonology*: 353-389. Chicago Linguistic Society, Chicago, IL.

——— (1975). Phonetic explantions for nasal sound patterns. In Charles A. Ferguson, Larry M. Hyman, and John J. Ohala (eds.), *Nasálfest: Papers from a Symposium on Nasals and Nasalization*: 49-66. Language Universals Project, Stanford University, CA.

——— (1978). Production of tone. In Victoria A. Fromkin (ed.), *Tone: A linguistic survey*: 5-39. Academic Press, New York, NY.

——— (1979). The contribution of acoustic phonetics to phonology. In Björn Lindblom and Sven Ohman (eds.), *Frontiers of speech communication research*: 355-363. Academic Press, London, UK.

——— (1983). The origin of sound patterns in vocal tract constraints. In Peter F. MacNeilage (ed.), *The production of speech*: 189-216. Spinger, New York.

——— (1990). The phonetics and phonology of aspects of assimilation. In John Kingston and Mary E. Beckman (eds.), *Papers in laboratory phonology I: Between the grammar and physics of speech*: 258-275. Cambridge University Press, Cambridge, UK.

——— and Haruko Kawasaki (1984). Prosodic phonology and phonetics. *Phonology Yearbook* 1: 113-127.

——— and William G. Ewan (1973). Speed of pitch change. *Journal of the Acoustical Society of America* 53: 345.

Okell, John (1969). *A reference grammar of Colloquial Burmese*. Oxford University Press, London, UK.

Okoth-Okombo, Duncan (1982). Duoluo morphophonemics in generative framework. Bernd Heine, Wilhem J.G. Möhlig and Franz Rottland (eds.), *Language and dialect atlas of Kenya, Supplement* 2. Dietrich Reimer Verlag, Berlin.

Okrand, Marc (1977). *Mutsun grammar*. Ph.D. dissertation, University of California, Berkeley.

Oller, D. Kimbrough (1973). The effect of position in utterance on speech segment duration in English. *Journal of the Acoustical Society of America* 54: 1235-1247.

Omondi, Lucia Ndong'a (1982). The major syntactic structures of Dholuo. Bernd Heine, Wilhem J.G. Möhlig and Franz Rottland (eds.), *Language and dialect atlas of Kenya, Supplement* 1. Dietrich Reimer Verlag, Berlin.

Ourso, Meterwa (1989). *Lama phonology and morphology*. Ph.D. dissertation, University of Illinois, Urbana Champaign.

Owens, Jonathan (1980). Observations on tone in the Booran dialect of Oromo (Galla). *African Language Studies* 17: 142-196.

Pace, Wanda Jane (1990). Comaltepec Chinantec verb inflection. In William R. Merrifield and Calvin R. Rensch (eds.), *Syllables, tone and verb paradigms. Studies in Chinantec languages* 4: 21-62. *Summer Institute of Linguistics and the University of Texas at Arlington Publications in Linguistics*, Publication No. 95.

Paster, Mary (1999). *Issues in the tonology of Gã*. Senior honors thesis, The Ohio State University.

Paulian, Christiane (1974). *Le Kukuya: Langue teke du Congo*. S.E.L.A.F., Paris.

Perkell, Joseph S. and Dennis H. Klatt (1986). *Invariance and variability in speech processes*. Lawrence Erlbaum Associates Publishers, Hillsdale, NJ.

Peterson, G. and Ilse Lehiste (1960). Duration of syllable nuclei in English. *Journal of the Acoustical Society of America* 32: 693-703.

Pickett, Velma B. (1967). Isthmus Zapotec. In Robert Wauchope (general ed.), Norman A. McQuown (volume ed.), *Handbook of Middle American Indians, Vol. 5: Linguistics*: 291-310. University of Texas Press, Austin.

Pike, Eunice V. (1986). Tone contrasts in Central Carrier (Athapaskan). *International Journal of American Linguistics* 52.4: 411-418.

Plomp, R. (1967). Pitch of complex tones. *Journal of the Acoustical Society of America* 41: 1526-1533.

Polak-Bynon, Louise (1975). *A Shi grammar—Structures and generative phonology of a Bantu language*. Annales de Musée Royal de l'Afrique Centrale. Tervuren.

Pollack, Irwin (1968). Detection of rate of change of auditory frequency. *Journal of Experimental Psychology* 77: 535-541.

Pols, Louis C. (1986). Variation and interaction in speech. In Joseph S. Perkell and Dennis H. Klatt (eds.), *Invariance and variability in speech processes*: 140-162. Lawrence Erlbaum Associates Publishers, Hillsdale, NJ.

Port, Robert F. (1979). The influence of tempo on stop closure duration as a cue for voicing and place. *Journal of Phonetics* 7: 45-56.

Potter, Brian (1997). *Wh/Indefinites and the structure of the clause in Western Apache*. Ph.D. dissertation, University of California, Los Angeles.

———, Matthew Gordon, John Dawson, W.J. de Reuse and Peter Ladefoged (2000). Phonetic structure of Western Apache. *UCLA Working Papers in Phonetics* 98: 10-38.

Pratt, Mary (1972). Tone in some Kikuyu verb forms. *Studies in African Linguistics* 3.3: 325-378.

Prieto, Pilar (1992). Vowel reduction in Western and Eastern Catalan and the representation of vowels. *Romance Languages Annual* 1991: 567–572.

Prince, Alan (2001). *Invariance under re-ranking*. Paper presented at *WCCFL* 20, USC.

——— and Paul Smolensky (1993). *Optimality Theory—constraint interaction in generative grammar*. Ms., Rutgers University, University of Colorado at Boulder.

Pulleyblank, Douglas (1986). *Tone in lexical phonology*. D. Reidel Publishing Company, Kluwer Academic Publishers Group, Dordrecht, The Netherlands.

Qian, Huiying (1997). *Tunxihua yindang* (The sound record of Tunxi). Jing-Yi Hou (ed.), *Xiandai hanyu fangyan yinku* (The sound archives of modern Chinese dialects). Shanghai Jiaoyu Chubanshe (Shanghai Education Publishing House), Shanghai, China.

Recasens, Daniel (1996). An articulatory-perceptual account of vocalization and elision of dark /l/ in the Romance languages. *Language and Speech* 39: 63-89.

———, Jordi Fontdevila, and Maria Dolors Pallarès (1995). Velarization degree and coarticulatory resistance for /l/ in Catalan and German. *Journal of Phonetics* 23: 37-52.

Rice, Keren D. (1989a). The phonology of Fort Nelson Slave stem tone: Syntactic implications. In Eung-Do Cook and Keren D. Rice (eds.), *Athapaskan linguistics: Current perspectives on a language family*: 229-264. Mouton de Gruyter, Berlin, Germany; New York, NY, USA.

——— (1989b). *A grammar of Slave (Dene)*. Mouton de Gruyter, Berlin, Germany; New York, NY, USA.

Rietveld, A.C.M. and C. Gussenhoven (1985). On the relation between pitch excursion size and prominence. *Journal of Phonetics* 13: 299-308.

Ritsma, Roelof J. (1967). Frequencies dominant in the perception of complex sounds. *Journal of the Acoustical Society of America* 42: 191-198.

Robbins, Frank (1961). Quiotepec Chinantec syllable patterning. *International Journal of American Linguistics* 27.3: 237-250.

Ross, Elliott D., Jerold A. Edmondson, G. Burton Seibert, and Jin-Lieh Chan (1992). Affective exploitation of tone in Taiwanese: an acoustical study of "tone latitude". *Journal of Phonetics* 20: 441-456.

Rossi, Mario (1971). Le seuil de glissando ou seuil de perception des variations tonales pour les sons de la parole. *Phonetica* 23: 1-33.

——— (1978). La perception des glissandos descendants dans les contours prosodiques (The perception of falling glissandos in prosodic contours). *Phonetica* 35: 11-40.

Rottland, Franz (1983). Southern Nilotic (with an outline of Datooga). In M. Lionel Bender (ed.), *Nilo-Saharan language studies*: 208-238. Michigan State University.

Rubach, Jerzy (1984). *Cyclic and lexical phonology: The structure of Polish*. Foris Publications, Dordrecht, The Netherlands; Cinnaminson, NJ, USA.

Ruhm, Howard B., Eugene O. Mencke, Braxton Milburn, William A. Cooper, Jr. and Darrell E. Rose (1966). Differential sensitivity to duration of acoustic stimuli. *Journal of Speech and Hearing Research* 9: 371-384.

Rupp, James E. (1990). The Lealao Chinantec syllable. In William R. Merrifield and Calvin R. Rensch (eds.), *Syllables, tone and verb paradigms. Studies in Chinantec languages* 4: 63-73. *Summer Institute of Linguistics and the University of Texas at Arlington Publications in Linguistics*, Publication No. 95.

Saeed, John I. (1982). Central Somali—A grammatical outline. *Afroasiatic Linguistics* 8.2.

——— (1993). *Somali reference grammar*, 2nd revised edition. Dunwoody Press, Kensington, MD.

Sanderson, George Meredith (1954). *A dictionary of the Yao language*. The Government Printer, Zomba, Nyasaland.

Sapir, Edward and Harry Hoijer (1967). *The phonology and morphology of the Navaho language*. University of California Press, Berkeley and Los Angeles, CA.

Schachter, Paul and Fe T. Otanes (1972). *Tagalog reference grammar*. University of California Press, Berkeley, Los Angeles, CA.

Schaub, Willi (1985). *Babungo. Croom Helm descriptive grammars series*. Croom Helm, London, Dover NH.

Schneeberg, Nan (1971). Sayanchi verb tonology. *Journal of African Languages* 10, Part 1: 87-100.

Schuh, Russell G. (1971). Verb forms and verb aspects in Ngizim. *Journal of African Languages* 10, part 1: 47-60.

——— (1981). A dictionary of Ngizim. University of California Press, Berkeley and Los Angeles, CA.

——— (1991). Bolanci genitives—with remarks on underlying contour tones and tone sequences. In F.A. Soyoye and L.O. Adewole (eds.), *Current perspectives in African linguistics—In honor of Professor Ayo Bamgbose. Ife African language and literature series* 3. Ile-Ife, Nigeria.

Sharp, A.E. (1954). A tonal analysis of the disyllabic noun in the Machame dialect of Chaga. *Bulletin of the School of Oriental and African Studies* 16: 157-169. University of London.

Shi, Qisheng (1997). *Shantouhua yindang* (The sound record of Shantou). Jing-Yi Hou (ed.), *Xiandai hanyu fangyan yinku (The sound archives of modern Chinese dialects)*. Shanghai Jiaoyu Chubanshe (Shanghai Education Publishing House), Shanghai.

Shields, J.L., A. McHugh, and J.G. Martin (1974). RT to phoneme targets as a function of rhythmic cues in continuous speech. *Journal of Experimental Psychology* 102: 250-255.

Shimuzu, Kiyoshi (1983). *The Zing dialect of Mumuye—A descriptive grammar*. Helmut Buske Verlag, Hamburg.

Shryock, Aaron (1993a). *Consonants and tones in Musey*. Ms., UCLA.

——— (1993b). A metrical analysis of stress in Cebuano. *Lingua* 91: 103-148.

——— (1996). The representation of stricture: Evidence from Musey. In Chai-Shune Hsu (ed.), *UCLA Working Papers in Phonology*: 162-182.

Simoes, Antonio R.M. (1996). Duration as an element of lexical stress in Spanish discourse: An acoustical study. *Hispanic Linguistics* 8: 352-368.

Sinclair, Donald E. and Kenneth L. Pike (1948). The tonemes of Mesquital Otomi. *International Journal of American Linguistics* 14.2: 91-98.

Small, Larry H. and Kevin D. Squibb (1989). Stressed vowel perception in word recognition. *Perceptual and Motor Skills* 68: 179-185.

Smith, Jean and Pam Weston (1974). Mianmin phonemes and tones. In Richard Loving (ed.), *Workpapers in Papua New Guinea Languages 7: Studies in Languages of the Ok Family*: 5-33. Summer Institute of Linguistics, Ukarumpa, Papua New Guinea.

Smolensky, Paul (1995). *On the internal structure of the constraint component of UG*. UCLA colloquium talk, April 7, 1995.

——— (1996). *The initial state and 'Richness of the Base' in Optimality Theory*. Rutgers Optimality Archive, ROA-154-1196.

Snoxall, R.A. (1967). *Luganda-English dictionary*. Oxford University Press, Clarendon Press, Oxford, UK.

Snyman, Jannie Winston (1970). *An introduction to the !Xũ! (!Kung) language. Communications from the School of African Studies, University of Cape Town*, no. 34. A.A. Balkema, Cape Town, South Africa.

——— (1975). *Žu|'hõasi Fonologie en Woordeboek. Communications from the School of African Studies, University of Cape Town*, no. 37. A.A. Balkema, Cape Town, South Africa.

Spears, Richard A. (1967). Tone in Mende. *Journal of African Languages* 6, Part 3: 231-244.

Sproat, Richard and Osamu Fujimura (1993). Allophonic variation in English /l/ and its implications for phonetic implementation. *Journal of Phonetics* 21: 291-311.

Stampe, David (1972). *How I spent my summer vacation*. Ph.D. dissertation, University of Chicago.

Stark, Sharon and Polly Machin (1977). Stress and tone in Tlacoyalco Popoloca. In William R. Merrifield (ed.), *Studies in Otomanguean phonology*: 69-92. *Summer Institute of Linguistics Publications in Linguistics*, Publication No. 54.

Steriade, Donca (1991). Moras and other slots. In D. Meyer and S. Tomioka (eds.), *Proceedings of the 1st Meeting of the Formal Linguistics Society of the Midwest*. University of Wisconsin, Madison.

——— (1995). *Neutralization and the expression of contrast*. Ms., UCLA.

——— (1999). Phonetics in phonology: The case of laryngeal neutralization. In Matthew K. Gordon (ed.), *UCLA Working Papers in Linguistics, Papers in Phonology* 3: 25-146.

——— (2000). Paradigm uniformity and the phonetics-phonology boundary. In Michael Broe and Janet Pierrehumbert (eds.), *Papers in laboratory phonology V: Language acquisition and the lexicon*: 313-334. Cambridge University Press, Cambridge, UK.

——— (2001a). Directional asymmetries in place assimilation: A perceptual account. In Elizabeth Hume and Keith Johnson (eds.), *The role of speech perception in phonology*. New York: Academic Press.

——— (2001b). The phonology of perceptibility effects: the P-map and its consequences for constraint organization. Ms., UCLA.

Stevens, Kenneth, Samual K. Keyser, and Haruko Kawasaki (1986). Toward a phonetic and phonological theory of redundant features. In Joseph Perkell and Dennis Klatt (eds.), *Invariance and variability in speech processes*: 426-449. Lawrence Erlbaum Associates Publishers, London, UK.

Stevens, S.S. and J. Volkman (1940). The relation of pitch to frequency: A revised scale. *American Journal of Psychology* 53: 329-353.

Stevick, Earl W. (1965). *Shona basic course*. Dept. of State, Washington DC.

——— (1969a). Pitch and duration in Ganda. *Journal of African Languages* 8, Part 1: 1-28.

——— (1969b). Tone in Bantu. *International Journal of American Linguistics* 35.4: 330-341.

Stieber, Zdzisław (1973). *A historical phonology of the Polish language*. Carl Winter Universitätsverlag, Heidelberg, Germany.

Story, Gillian (1989). A report on the nature of Carrier pitch phenomena: With special reference to the verb prefix tonomechanics. In Eung-Do Cook and Keren D. Rice (eds.), *Athapaskan linguistics: Current perspectives on a language family*: 99-144. Mouton de Gruyter, Berlin, Germany; New York, NY, USA.

Stott, L.H. (1935). Time-order errors in the discrimination of short tone durations. *Journal of Experimental Psychology* 18: 741-766.

Strangert, Eva (1985). *Swedish speech rhythm in a cross-language perspective. Acta Universitatis Umensis, Umeå Studies in the Humanities* 69. Almqvist and Wiksell International, Stockholm, Sweden.

Strecker, David (1990). Tai languages.In Bernard Comrie (ed.), *The world's major languages*: 747-775. Oxford University Press, New York, NY, USA; Oxford, UK.

Sundberg, Johan (1973). Data on maximum speed of pitch changes. *Speech Transmission Laboratory Quarterly Progress and Status Report* 4: 39-47. Royal Institute of Technology, Stockholm, Sweden.

——— (1979). Maximum speed of pitch changes in singers and untrained subjects. *Journal of Phonetics* 7: 71-79.

Suwilai, Premerirat (1996). Phonological characteristics of So (Thavung), a Vietic language of Thailand. *Mon-Khmer Studies* 26: 161-178.

Svantesson, Jan-Olof (1983). *Kammu phonology and morphology. Travaux de L'institute de Linguistique de Lund* XVIII. Liber Förlag, Lund, Sweden.

——— (1991). Hu—A language with unorthodox tonogenesis. In J.H.C.S. Davidson (ed.), *Austroasiatic languages: Essays in honour of H.L. Shorts*: 67-79. School of Oriental and African Studies, University of London.

Tauli, Valter (1973). *Standard Estonian grammar, part 1: Phonology, morphology, word-formation*. Almqvist & Wiksell, Uppsala.

Tesfaye, Ashenafi and Klaus Wedekind (1990). Characteristics of Omotic tone: Shinasha (Borna). *Studies in African Linguistics* 21.3: 347-368.

Teslar, Joseph Andrew and Jadwiga Teslar (1962). *A new Polish grammar*. The Polish Book Importing Co., Inc., New York, NY.

Thelwall, Robin (1983a). Twampa phonology. In M. Lionel Bender (ed.), *Nilo-Saharan language studies*: 323-335. Michigan State University, East Lansing, MI.

——— (1983b). Meidob Nubian: Phonology, grammatical notes and basic vocabulary. In M. Lionel Bender (ed.), *Nilo-Saharan language studies*: 97-113. Michigan State University, East Lansing, MI.

Thompson, E. David (1983). Kunama: Phonology and noun phrase. In M. Lionel Bender (ed.), *Nilo-Saharan language studies*: 281-322. Michigan State University, East Lansing, MI.

Thompson, Napier G.I. (1998). Tone sandhi between complex tones in a seven-tone southern Thai dialect. *Proceedings of ICSLP-'98*, Vol. 2: 53-56.

Traill, Anthony (1975). The tonal structure of !Xõ. In J.W. Snyman (ed.), *Bushman and Hottentot linguistic studies*: 11-48. University of South Africa, Pretoria.

——— (1985). *Phonetic and phonological studies of !Xóõ Bushman*. Helmut Buske Verlag, Hamburg, Germany.

——— (1994). *A !Xóõ dictionary*. Rüdiger Köppe Verlag, Köln.

Tranel, Bernard (1992-1994). Tone sandhi and vowel deletion in Margi. *Studies in African Linguistics* 23.3: 111-183.

Tresbarats, Chantal (1990). Tone in Abidji verb morphology. *Studies in African Linguistics* 21.1: 107-143.

Trihart, Lee (1976). Desyllabified noun class prefixes and depressor consonants in Chichewa. In Larry M. Hyman (ed.), *Studies in Bantu Tonology, Southern California Occasional Papers in Linguistics,* No. 3: 259-286.

Trubetzkoy, Nikolai S. (1939). *Grundzüge der Phonologie.* Güttingen: Vandenhoeck and Ruprecht. English translation by Christiane A.M. Baltaxe. University of California Press, Berkeley and Los Angeles, 1969.

Tucker, A.N. (1962). The syllable in Luganda: A prosodic account. *Journal of African Languages* 1: 122-166.

——— (1964). Kalenjin phonetics. In David Abercrombie, D.B. Fry, P.A.D. MacCarthy, N.C. Scott and J.L.M. Trim (eds.), *In honour of Daniel Jones*: 445-470. Longmans, Green & Co. Ltd.

——— and M.A. Bryan (1970). Tonal classification of nouns in Ngazija. *African language studies* 11: 351-182.

——— and J. Tompo Ole Mpaayei (1955). *A Maasai grammar with vocabulary.* Longmans, Green & Co. Ltd.

Visser, Hessel (1998). The phonological system of Naro. In Mathias Schladt (ed.), *Language, identity, and conceptualization among the Khoisan*: 117-136. Rüdiger Köppe Verlag, Köln.

Voegelin, Charles (1935). *Tübatulabal grammar. University of California Publications in American Archaeology and Ethnology,* Vol. 34, No. 2: 55-189. University of California Press, Berkeley, CA.

Voorhoeve, Jan (1971). Tonology of the Bamileke noun. *Journal of African Languages* 10, Part 2: 44-53.

Wall, Leon and William Morgan (1958). *Navajo-English dictionary.* Navajo Agency, Branch of Education, Window Rock, AZ.

Wang, Junhu (1997). *Xi'anhua yindang* (The sound record of Xi'an). Jing-Yi Hou (ed.), *Xiandai hanyu fangyan yinku (The sound archives of modern Chinese dialects).* Shanghai Jiaoyu Chubanshe (Shanghai Education Publishing House), Shanghai.

Wang, Ping (1988). Changzhou fangyan de liandu biandiao (Tone sandhi in the Changzhou dialect). *Fangyan* (Dialects) 1988.3: 177-194.

Wang, Sen and Xiaogang, Zhao (1997). *Lanzhouhua yindang* (The sound record of Lanzhou). Jing-Yi Hou (ed.), *Xiandai hanyu fangyan yinku (The sound archives of modern Chinese dialects).* Shanghai Jiaoyu Chubanshe (Shanghai Education Publishing House), Shanghai.

Wang, Xiaosong (1996). Prolegomenon to Rgyalthang Tibetan phonology. *Linguistics of the Tibeto-Burman Area* 19.2: 55-67.

Wang, Yunjia (1996). Qingsheng wenti yanjiu (The issue of Light Tones). *Shijie Hanyu Jiaoxue* (International Journal of Chinese Pedagogy) 1996.3.

Wang, Zhijie (1997). Ying-Han yinjie biyunwei de butong xingzhi (The difference in quality between nasal codas in English and Chinese). *Xindai Waiyu: Yuyanxue yu Yingyong Yuyanxue* (Foreign Languages Today: Linguistics and Applied Linguistics) 1997: 18-27.

Ward, Ida C. (1944). A phonetic introduction to Mende. In K.H. Crosby, *An introduction to the study of Mende*: 1-7. W. Heffer and Sons Ltd., Cambridge.

Watkins, Laurel J. (1984). *A grammar of Kiowa*. University of Nebraska Press, Lincoln and London.

Weidert, Alfons (1975). Componential analysis of Lushai phonology. *Amsterdam studies in the theory and history of linguistic science, Series IV—Current issues in linguistic theory*, Vol. 2. John Benjamins Publishing Company, Amsterdam.

——— (1977). *Tai-Khamti phonology and vocabulary*. Franz Steiner Verlag, Wiesbaden.

——— (1987). Phonation and tonology of stopped syllables. In Alfons Weidert (ed.), *Tibeto-Burman tonology: A comparative account. Amsterdam Studies in the Theory and History of Linguistic Science, Series IV—Current Issues in Linguistic Theory*, Vol. 54, 368-482. John Benjamins Publishing Company, Amsterdam, The Netherlands; Philadelphia, PA, USA.

Wen, Duanzheng (1985). *Xinzhou fangyan zhi* (A record of the Xinzhou dialect). Yuwen Chubanshe (The Philology Publishing House), Beijing.

——— and Guangming Zhang (1994). 'Xinzhou fangyan cidian' yinlün (Introduction to 'Dictionary of the Xinzhou dialect'). *Fangyan* (Dialects) 1994: 1-12.

Wheatley, Julian K. (1990). Burmese. In Bernard Comrie (ed.), *The world's major languages*: 834-854. Oxford University Press, New York, NY, USA; Oxford, UK.

Whiteley, W.H. (1966). *A study of Yao sentences*. Oxford University Press, Oxford, UK.

Wightman, Collin W., Stefanie Shattuck-Hufnagel, Mari Ostendorf, and Patti J. Price (1992). Segmental durations in the vicinity of prosodic phrase boundaries. *Journal of the Acoustical Society of America* 91: 1707-1717.

Williams, Edwin S. (1976). Underlying tone in Margi and Igbo. *Linguistic Inquiry* 7.3: 463-484.

Wilson, Colin (2000). *Targeted constraints: An approach to contextual neutralization in Optimality Theory*. Ph.D. dissertation, Johns Hopkins University.

Wiltshire, Caroline R. (1992). *Syllabification and rule application in harmonic phonology*. Ph.D. dissertation, University of Chicago.

Woo, Nancy (1969). *Prosody and Phonology*. Ph.D. dissertation. MIT.

Wright, Richard (1996). Tone and accent in Oklohoma Cherokee. In Pamela Munro (ed.), *Cherokee papers from UCLA. UCLA Occasional Papers in Linguistics* 16: 11-22

Wu, Zongji and Maocan Lin (1989). *Shiyan yuyinxue gaiyao* (Essentials of experimental phonetics). Gaodeng Jiaoyu Chubanshe (Higher Education Press), Beijing, China.

Xie, Liuwen (1992). Jiangxisheng yudu fangyan liangzizu liandu biaodiao (Tone sandhi of disyllabic words in the Yudu dialect of Jiangxi Province). *Fangyan* (Dialects) 1992.3: 222-227.

Xie, Zili (1982). Suzhou fangyan liangzizu de liandu biandiao (Tone sandhi of disyllabic words in the Suzhou dialect). *Fangyan* (Dialects) 1982.4: 245-263.

Xiong, Zhenghui (1979). Nanchang fangyan de shengdiao jiqi yanbian (The tones and their historical changes in the Nanchang dialect). *Fangyan* (Dialects) 1979.4: 275-283.

Xu, Lin, Yuzhang Mu and Xingzhi Gai (1986). *Lisuyu jianzhi* (A grammatical sketch of the Lisu language). *Zhongguo shaoshu minzu yuyan jianzhi congshu* (A collection of grammatical sketches of the minority languages in China). Minzu Chubanshe (The Nationality Publishing House), Beijing.

Xu, Yi (1994). Production and perception of coarticulated tones. *Journal of the Acoustical Society of America* 95: 2240-2253.

——— (1997). Contextual tonal variations in Mandarin. *Journal of Phonetics* 25: 61-83.

——— (1998). Consistency of tone-syllable alignment across different syllable structures and speaking rates. *Phonetica* 55: 179-203.

——— (1999). Effects of tone and focus on the formation and alignment of f_0 contours. *Journal of Phonetics* 27: 55-105.

Ye, Xiangling (1979). Suzhou fangyan de liandu biandiao (Tone sandhi in the Suzhou dialect). *Fangyan* (Dialects) 1979.1: 30-46.

Ye, Xiangling and Yuqing Sheng (1996). *Suzhouhua yindang* (The sound record of Suzhou). Jing-Yi Hou (ed.), *Xiandai hanyu fangyan yinku* (The sound archives of modern Chinese dialects). Shanghai Jiaoyu Chubanshe (Shanghai Education Press), Shanghai, China.

Yip, Moira (1989). Contour tones. *Phonology* 6: 149-174.

——— (1995). Tone in East Asian languages. In John A. Goldsmith (ed.), *Handbook of theoretical phonology*: 476-494. Blackwell Publishers, Oxford, UK.

——— (to appear). Feet, tonal reduction and speech rate at the word and phrase level in Chinese. In Rene Kager and Wim Zonneveld (eds.), *Phrasal phonology*. Foris Publications, Dordrecht, The Netherlands.

Yokwe, Eluzai Moga (1987). *The tonal grammar of Bari*. Ph.D. dissertation, University of Illinois, Urbana-Champaign. UMI Dissertation Information Service.

You, Rujie (1994). *Shanghaihua yindang* (The sound record of Shanghai). Jing-Yi Hou (ed.), *Xiandai hanyu fangyan yinku* (The sound archives of modern Chinese dialects). Shanghai Jiaoyu Chubanshe (Shanghai Education Press), Shanghai, China.

Young, Robert W. and William Morgan Sr. (1987). *The Navajo language: A grammar and colloquial dictionary*, revised edition. University of New Mexico Press. Albuquerque, NM.

——— and ——— (1992). *Analytical lexicon of Navajo*. University of New Mexico Press. Albuquerque, NM.

Young, Stevens (1991). *The prosodic structure of Lithuanian*. University Press of America, Lanham, NY.

Yue-Hashimoto, Anne O. (1987). Tone sandhi across Chinese dialects. In Chinese Language Society of Hong Kong (ed.), *Wang Li memorial volumes, English volume*: 445-474. Joint Publishing Co., Hong Kong.

Zec, Draga (1988). *Sonority constraints on prosodic structure*. Ph.D. dissertation, Stanford University.

Zee, Eric and Ian Maddieson (1979). Tones and tone sandhi in Shanghai: Phonetic evidence and phonological analysis. *UCLA Working Papers in Phonetics* 45: 93-129.

Zeng, Yumei (1997). *Xiangtanhua yindang* (The sound record of Xiangtan). Jing-Yi Hou (ed.), *Xiandai hanyu fangyan yinku (The sound archives of modern Chinese dialects)*. Shanghai Jiaoyu Chubanshe (Shanghai Education Publishing House), Shanghai.

Zhang, Chengcai (1997). *Xininghua yindang* (The sound record of Xining). Jing-Yi Hou (ed.), *Xiandai hanyu fangyan yinku (The sound archives of modern Chinese dialects)*. Shanghai Jiaoyu Chubanshe (Shanghai Education Publishing House), Shanghai.

Zhang, Hongnian (1985). Zhenjiang fangyan de liandu biandiao (Tone sandhi in the Zhenjiang dialect). *Fangyan* (Dialects) 1985.3: 191-204.

Zhang, Huiying (1979). Chongming fangyan de liandu biandiao (Tone sandhi in the Chongming dialect). *Fangyan* (Dialects) 1979.4: 284-302.

——— (1980). Hou, Jing-Yi. (1982a). Chongming fangyan sanzizu de liandu biandiao (Tone sandhi of trisyllabic words in the Chongming dialect). *Fangyan* (Dialects) 1980.1: 15-34.

Zhang, Jie (1998). Checked tones in Chinese dialects—Evidence for phonetically-driven phonology. In *Proceedings of CLS 34*, Vol. 1: 439-453.

——— (1999). Duration in the tonal phonology of Pingyao Chinese. In Matthew K. Gordon (ed.), *UCLA Working Papers in Linguistics, Papers in Phonology* 3: 147-206.

——— (2000). Non-contrastive features and categorical patterning in Chinese diminutive suffixation—MAX[F] or IDENT[F]? *Phonology* 17: 427-478.

——— (2001). *The contrast-specificity of positional prominence—evidence from diphthong distribution*. Paper presented at the 75th annual meeting of the LSA. Washington, DC.

Zhang, Shengyu (1979). Chaoyang fangyan de liandu biandiao (Tone sandhi in the Chaoyang dialect). *Fangyan* (Dialects) 1979.2: 93-121.

——— (1980). Chaoyang fangyan de liandu biandiao II (Tone sandhi in the Chaoyang dialect II). *Fangyan* (Dialects) 1980.2: 123-136.

Zhang, Zhenxing (1982a). Zhangping (Yongfu) fangyan tongyin zihui (Synonyms in the Zhangping(Yongfu) dialect). *Fangyan* (Dialects) 1982.3: 203-228.

——— (1982b). Zhangping (Yongfu) fangyan de danzidiao (The citation tones of the Zhangping (Yongfu) dialect). *Fangyan* (Dialects) 1982.4: 264-275.

——— (1983). Zhangping (Yongfu) fangyan de liandu biandiao (Tone sandhi in the Zhangping (Yongfu) dialect). *Fangyan* (Dialects) 1983.3: 175-196.

Zoll, Cheryl (1996). *Parsing below the segment in a constraint based framework*. Ph.D. dissertation, UC Berkeley.

——— (1997). Conflicting directionality. *Phonology* 14: 263-186.

——— (1998). *Positional asymmetries and licensing*. Rutgers Optimality Archive, ROA-282-0998.

Index

www.ingramcontent.com/pod-product-compliance
Lightning Source LLC
Chambersburg PA
CBHW071456110726
47908CB00003B/628

* 9 7 8 1 1 3 8 9 6 8 4 6 2 *